The Official Damn Small Linux® Book

NEGUS LIVE LINUX SERIES

The Official Damn Small Linux® Book

The Tiny Adaptable Linux® That Runs on Anything

Robert Shingledecker, John Andrews, Christopher Negus

PRENTICE HALL

An Imprint of Pearson Education

Upper Saddle River, NJ ■ Boston ■ Indianapolis ■ San Francisco

New York ■ Toronto ■ Montreal ■ London ■ Munich ■ Paris ■ Madrid

Cape Town ■ Sydney ■ Tokyo ■ Singapore ■ Mexico City

Many of the designations used by manufacturers and sellers to distinguish their products are claimed as trademarks. Where those designations appear in this book, and the publisher was aware of a trademark claim, the designations have been printed with initial capital letters or in all capitals.

The authors and publisher have taken care in the preparation of this book, but make no expressed or implied warranty of any kind and assume no responsibility for errors or omissions. No liability is assumed for incidental or consequential damages in connection with or arising out of the use of the information or programs contained herein.

The publisher offers excellent discounts on this book when ordered in quantity for bulk purchases or special sales, which may include electronic versions and/or custom covers and content particular to your business, training goals, marketing focus, and branding interests. For more information, please contact:

U.S. Corporate and Government Sales
(800) 382-3419
corpsales@pearsontechgroup.com

For sales outside the United States please contact:

International Sales
international@pearsoned.com

 This Book Is Safari Enabled

The Safari® Enabled icon on the cover of your favorite technology book means the book is available through Safari Bookshelf. When you buy this book, you get free access to the online edition for 45 days.

Safari Bookshelf is an electronic reference library that lets you easily search thousands of technical books, find code samples, download chapters, and access technical information whenever and wherever you need it.

To gain 45-day Safari Enabled access to this book:

- Go to http://www.prenhallprofessional.com/safarienabled
- Complete the brief registration form
- Enter the coupon code MZMJ-WP3L-2RXB-HYLV-GTMI

If you have difficulty registering on Safari Bookshelf or accessing the online edition, please e-mail customer-service@safaribooksonline.com.

Visit us on the Web: www.prenhallprofessional.com

Library of Congress Cataloging-in-Publication Data

Shingledecker, Robert.

  The official Damn Small Linux book : the tiny adaptable Linux that runs on anything / Robert Shingledecker, John Andrews, Christopher Negus.

    p. cm.

  ISBN 0-13-233869-6 (pbk. : alk. paper) 1. Linux. 2. Operating systems (Computers) I. Andrews, John, 1971- II. Negus, Chris, 1957- III. Title.

  QA76.76.063S555554 2007

  005.4'32—dc22

2007020589

ISBN-13: 978-0-13-233869-1
ISBN-10: 0-13-233869-6

Text printed in the United States on recycled paper at RR Donnelley in Crawfordsville, Indiana.
First printing August, 2007

Editor-in-Chief
Mark L. Taub

Acquisitions Editor
Debra Williams Cauley

Development Editor
Songlin Qiu

Managing Editor
Gina Kanouse

Project Editors
San Dee Phillips
Jovana San Nicolas-Shirley
Michael Thurston

Copy Editor
Kelli Brooks

Indexer
Erika Millen

Proofreader
Water Crest Publishing

Publishing Coordinator
Dan Uhrig

Multimedia Developer
Dan Scherf

Interior Designer
Jake McFarland

Cover Designer
Alan Clements

Composition
Jake McFarland
Nonie Ratcliff

John Andrews' dedication:
I would like to dedicate my parts of this book
to Jennifer, Marja, Kelsey, and Maddie, who had
to deal with a busy husband and daddy while
I took the time to write my chapters.

Robert Shingledecker's dedication:
In loving memory of my parents, Winston and Stella.

Christopher Negus' dedication:
As always, I dedicate my contribution to this book
to my wife, Sheree.

Contents

Acknowledgments

I would like to thank all the fine folks at Prentice Hall for giving me this opportunity. A special thanks to Chris Negus for shepherding me through the authoring process. Standing on the shoulders of giants such as Richard Stallman, Linus Torvalds, Klaus Knopper, and many others who have contributed and continue to contribute to Free Open Source Software, a big thank you. For without such, this project would not exist.

Thanks to John Andrews for founding and sharing his creation. Many thanks to the community of DSL users. Thanks for the suggestions, bug reports, sharing your knowledge with others, and the many application extensions known as the MyDSL repository. Thanks to community members, mikshaw, thehatsrule, cbagger01, and many others who over several years have continually helped make this project a success.

I would also like to express my thanks to Joe Rabinsy for reading my initial manuscripts and offering suggestions for improvements.

—Robert Shingledecker

I am very in debt to my wife, Jennifer Lew-Andrews, who has acted like an unpaid editor for everything I've written in this book. Robert Shingledecker is largely responsible for incorporating the advanced functionality into DSL that has made it so popular today.

The DSL community also needs to be acknowledged. Much of the reforms and improvements in DSL are direct results of the feedback and hacks posted in the DSL forums by our knowledgeable users. I'd like to thank Melodie and Antonina who do a lot behind the scenes to keep DSL afloat as we put time and money into the project. Finally, a big "thank you" to Chris Negus who worked very hard to make this book a reality.

—John Andrews

Special thanks to Debra Williams Cauley and Mark Taub of Prentice Hall for believing that a book about a small, free operating system could find a big audience. Thanks to Songlin Qiu, Jovana San Nicolas-Shirley, and San Dee Phillips for seeing the book through the production phases and Kelli Brooks for her thorough copy editing. Thanks to Joe Brockmeier and Bryan Helvey for their thoughtful technical editing.

Finally, I'd like to thank John Andrews and Robert Shingledecker for taking the time to share their insights into what I believe is the finest compact desktop operating system available today.

—Christopher Negus

About the Authors

Robert Shingledecker's IT career spans 35 years, beginning with hand-coding machine language programs targeted for Burroughs Corporation minicomputers. Later, he enjoyed using an assembler and then COBOL. Always having a passion for computers, he was an advocate for COMAL, and was an early hacker on MINIX and Coherent OS.

In regards to Linux projects, Robert led the first large-scale deployment of Linux in the city of Garden Grove, California, where in 1994 he deployed Samba on DG/UX systems. He also designed a massively scalable Linux/AOLserver/Sybase e-commerce system. Robert then became CTO of several Linux-based dot-com companies.

While building Linux-based, no install, live CD-ROM appliances, including firewalls, VPN, web, email, and database appliances, he became interested in Damn Small Linux. Soon, Robert joined John Andrews to help lead Damn Small Linux development.

Now retired, Robert spends his time writing code and working on Damn Small Linux. He also enjoys traveling.

John Andrews is the creator of Damn Small Linux (DSL). As owner of a bead and jewelry store in 1996, John learned HTML and Perl to develop his own website. It eventually broadened to running websites for others on Linux servers. His interest in Linux encouraged him to switch to a Linux desktop full time.

The appeal of fast and efficient applications led John to develop Damn Small Linux. After trying several mini-distributions, primarily for diagnostic and system recovery, John wanted to build a sub-50MB distribution that essentially had what he needed to accomplish a day's work; the result was the Damn Small Linux distribution. John's proficiencies include Perl, shell scripting, Lua, awk, *SQL, php, and some C programming languages.

Christopher Negus has been one of the world's leading writers of Linux books for nearly a decade. His *Red Hat Linux Bible* series has sold more than one-quarter million copies worldwide. Chris also authored or coauthored the books *Linux Bible* (2005 through 2007 editions), *Linux Toys, Linux Toys II,* and *Linux Troubleshooting Bible* for Wiley Publishing. For Prentice Hall, Chris is the editor of the *Negus Live Linux Series* and author of that series' flagship book, *Live Linux CDs*.

Before becoming a full-time author, Chris Negus worked on UNIX operating system development teams at AT&T Bell Labs, UNIX System Labs, and Novell in the 1980s and 1990s. In particular, Chris worked in the areas of UNIX system administration and networking.

When not working on computer books, Chris likes to spend time with his family: Sheree, Seth, and Caleb. Chris also enjoys playing soccer, singing opera (when nobody can hear him), and making things out of old computers.

Introduction

Damn Small Linux (DSL) started as an exercise by John Andrews to fit an entire desktop computer system into a compressed 50MB image. Within a few years, DSL grew to one of the most popular Linux systems in the world (in the Top Ten, by some accounts) without growing beyond that 50MB target.

In a world where desktop systems are bloated with eye candy and many rarely used features, you may wonder what makes this little operating-system-that-could so popular? Well, it could be that people don't want to throw away a usable computer because the latest Windows system won't run. It could be that people are tired of waiting for common computer operations to complete while who-knows-what goes on in the background. Or maybe it's just a love for simplicity and elegance.

DSL sets out to include all the basic features you need in a modern desktop computer system—and then makes those features functional, fast, and efficient. As a result, DSL can run well on hardware that is smaller, older, or less powerful than what most of today's desktop systems demand.

Some wonderful offshoots of DSL development are that you can do the following with DSL:

- **Take it anywhere.** It fits on a live CD, USB flash drive (also called a pen drive or a thumb drive), Zip drive, or a bootable business card CD that you can carry around with you.
- **Run it anywhere.** All you need is a standard PC (with a minimal processor, small amount of RAM, and no required disk space) that you can reboot. Or, you can run a special version of DSL that's set up to run from a Windows desktop. If you like, you can even do a traditional hard drive install of DSL.

- **Add software.** If you only need a couple more applications, a few clicks download, install, and save the applications you need.

- **Build projects.** To make a computer into a music server, tiny web server, or digital media frame, DSL doesn't fill up your hard disk or RAM with software you don't need so you have more room for the music, web content, or digital images you want (see Part IV, "Making Damn Small Linux Projects," for these and other projects).

- **Run securely.** By running DSL from a CD (or other read-only medium), you are assured that a secure operating system is only a reboot away. If you think that someone has compromised or intruded on your system, simply check that any data you save is not infected, reboot your DSL live CD, and you are running securely from a clean copy.

As the project grew, DSL also grew by adding an important developer. When Robert Shingledecker joined the Damn Small Linux development team, he implemented some of the key features of DSL previously mentioned. Robert's innovations brought about easy procedures for installing DSL to a USB flash drive and adding MyDSL extensions to a running DSL system.

Today, Damn Small Linux (`www.damnsmalllinux.org`) has a thriving community of supporters, active forums and mailing lists, and tons of interesting ways to use and customize it. This book provides you with an entry to all the possibilities of what Damn Small Linux can be for you.

As You Read This Book

To make the best use of the individual talents of the three authors of this book, we divided it up by chapters that play best to each of our strengths. As you read, you will notice that we often use the first person. Because the person describing a feature was often the person who developed the feature, first person seemed a good way to go.

If you find yourself wondering who "I" is in each chapter where it appears, we are providing that information here.

Robert Shingledecker wrote the following chapters:

- "Booting DSL" (Chapter 2)
- "Configuring and Saving DSL Settings" (Chapter 4)
- "Extending Applications with MyDSL" (Chapter 5)
- "Installing DSL in Alternate Ways" (Chapter 8)

- "Adding Applications and Creating Shareable Extensions" (Chapter 10)
- "Setting Up a Full Remastering Environment" (Chapter 11)

John Andrews wrote these chapters:

- "Using DSL Applications" (Chapter 3)
- "Running a Native Pen Drive Install" (Chapter 6)
- "Running DSL Embedded in Windows" (Chapter 7)
- "Performing a Traditional Hard Drive Install" (Chapter 9)
- "Running DSL on Alternate Hardware" (Chapter 12)
- "Making an Edna Music Server in DSL" (Chapter 13)

Christopher Negus contributed most of the introductory material and appendices, as well as the following chapters:

- "Overview of Damn Small Linux" (Chapter 1) and this introduction
- "Using Skype VoIP Service in DSL" (Chapter 14)
- "Running a Digital Media Frame in DSL" (Chapter 15)
- "Setting Up an XAMPP Web Server in DSL" (Chapter 16)

The bottom line is that most of the chapters Robert and John wrote tell you about features they developed for DSL. Chapters that Chris wrote help to introduce the features Robert and John describe and add a few fun and interesting projects to the mix.

AUDIENCE FOR THIS BOOK

If you want to use, customize, or contribute to one of the world's most popular compact Linux operating systems, Damn Small Linux, this book is for you.

You don't have to be a computer expert to use Damn Small Linux. Even as a beginner, this book can help you use DSL as a portable computer system that you carry with you or as a permanently installed Linux system.

If you are a computer expert, you can use this book to learn more advanced skills, such as remastering DSL to make your own, custom DSL live CD. You can also learn how to package your own MyDSL software extensions to contribute to the growing repository of software available to use with Damn Small Linux.

If you are just someone who likes to tinker with computers, this book can teach you how to build interesting projects using Damn Small Linux as their base. Because the basic DSL is so extraordinarily compact in size and efficient in its use, you can make use of a much wider range of PC hardware (such as older, low-powered computers) than you would need to build projects with other computer systems.

ORGANIZATION OF THIS BOOK

This book is designed to get you up and running quickly with Damn Small Linux. After you have had your hands on DSL and understand how it works, we move quickly to present you with the many ways you can use this versatile mini-operating system. You will learn a variety of permanent and portable ways of using DSL.

The book is divided into four major parts and two appendices:

- **Part I, "Using Damn Small Linux"**—In this part, you learn what DSL is and how to use it to do what you want. Chapter 1 provides an overview of the many uses and features of DSL. That chapter features a question-and-answer section where John Andrews and Robert Shingledecker describe DSL's design decisions and goals of the project. Chapter 2 provides tips for booting up DSL, including ways to start services and deal with hardware issues from the boot prompt.

  Chapter 3 provides descriptions of the applications (both graphical and command line) that come with DSL. Chapter 4 tells how to make DSL look and feel the way you like, and how to save all your personal settings and data for the next reboot. Chapter 5 shows how to get additional software, packaged as MyDSL extensions, to add the applications you want to your DSL configuration.

- **Part II, "DSL Beyond the Live CD"**—To help you do more than simply run DSL from a live CD, chapters in this section address how to run DSL in different ways and on different media. Chapter 6 addresses how to install DSL on a USB flash drive (pen drive) to have a totally portable and writeable live DSL.

  In Chapter 7, you learn how to run DSL *virtualized* so you can use it on a Windows desktop system. Chapter 8 describes alternate ways of installing DSL to a hard drive, including setups where a CD drive is not available (using floppies, Zip drives, or other media). Chapter 9 covers more traditional hard drive installs, where all DSL files are copied and booted from a hard drive.

- **Part III, "Creating Extensions and Remastering"**—In this part, we get into the more technical aspects of DSL. Chapter 10 explores how the MyDSL facility of DSL works to add applications to your DSL system, including ways of creating your own MyDSL extensions. Chapter 11 describes remastering procedures so you can build a custom version of DSL for yourself.
- **Part IV, "Making Damn Small Linux Projects"**—Ways of using DSL to build interesting projects are covered in this chapter. Chapter 12 describes cool different types of hardware that DSL will run on. In Chapter 13, you can learn how to make a music server in DSL using Edna Music Server software.

  Chapter 14 shows how to set up a DSL system to act as a Skype VoIP client for making audio calls over the Internet. In Chapter 15, you learn to build a digital media frame based on DSL. Chapter 16 tells how to set up a tiny, yet full-featured, web server using DSL and the XAMPP project.
- **Appendix A, "On the CD"**—This appendix provides details about the contents of the CD that comes with this book. The CD includes all the components you need to run the procedures and build the projects described throughout the book.
- **Appendix B, "Using MyDSL Extensions"**—This appendix offers descriptions of the free MyDSL extensions that you can download, install, and store to run with your DSL system.

WHAT YOU NEED TO USE THIS BOOK

You should use this book alongside the CD that is packaged with the book. Although you can certainly read the book without following along with the CD, descriptions and instructions the book provides are most helpful if you have your hands on DSL.

To use the CD that comes with this book, all you really need is a personal computer. The easiest way to use the CD is to boot the CD from your PC. If your PC doesn't have a CD drive, however, we include instructions for getting DSL to run on older machines that may include floppy drives or Zip drives for booting the system.

You may want to have alternative media available for storing your DSL data. In particular, a USB flash drive (also called a pen drive or thumb drive) can be particularly useful as a medium for storing your DSL settings, data, as well as DSL itself.

Some of the projects described in the last part of this book require extra hardware. Check Chapter 12 for some interesting PC hardware for running DSL. Speakers and microphones are useful for audio projects in Chapters 13 and 14. Making a digital media frame requires an old laptop computer, a frame, and a few other bits.

Part I

Using Damn Small Linux

## CHAPTER 1

Overview of Damn Small Linux

The Damn Small Linux mantra is *small is beautiful*.

Weighing in at about 50MB, Damn Small Linux (DSL) is a fully functional, mini-live CD desktop operating system. Despite its size, DSL can do just about everything you would expect from a modern desktop system, such as browse the web, send and receive email, write documents, manage files, play music, work with spread sheets, and manipulate images.

Many operating systems offering similar software features require a mountain of expensive computer hardware to run well and are burdened with slow, bloated applications. Damn Small Linux takes a different tack.

Unlike what you get with other computer systems, applications packaged with DSL are chosen for their size, speed, and efficient features. Even on low-powered hardware, applications in DSL are startlingly fast and surprisingly powerful. Despite its size, DSL runs faster and more efficiently than many desktop operating systems for the most important things you need a desktop operating system to do.

The book you are holding in your hand is *The Official Damn Small Linux Book*. We say official because the authors of this book include the two key developers of DSL: John Andrews, the creator of Damn Small Linux, and Robert Shingledecker, the lead developer for many of the technical innovations in DSL.

Although this book will step you through the components you can use in DSL, it will also take you much further. You will learn how to install and run DSL from different devices, save your data across reboots, and add applications to DSL to meet your needs. Later, the book will walk you through how to build projects with DSL, such as a music server, Internet telephone service, and portable web server.

MEASURING DAMN SMALL LINUX SUCCESS

Despite its small size, Damn Small Linux has consistently ranked among the most popular Linux distributions. According to rankings from various websites that monitor Linux sites, DSL has consistently been among the most active. According to Google, there are nearly 1,000,000 references to Damn Small Linux on the web. Yahoo indicates the existence of about 1,480,000 inbound links to the Damn Small Linux home page.

At Distrowatch (`www.distrowatch.com`) for the past three years, DSL has consistently ranked in the top ten Linux distributions for page hits, often ranking among well-known Linux systems such as Debian, Slackware, KNOPPIX, and Gentoo. According to Alexa (`www.alexa.com`), which monitors website popularity, in early 2007, the DSL website (`www.damnsmalllinux.org`) was around 33,350 in popularity on the web. That number made it more popular than home websites for Ubuntu, SuSE, Slackware, KNOPPIX, Mepis, Morphix, and other Linux distributions.

As for media coverage, dozens of articles and reviews have been written about Damn Small Linux. In May, 2004, DSL was highlighted on TechTV's *The Screen Savers* show. A DSL CD has been included with magazines such as *Linux Format*, *Linux User & Developer*, *Sys Admin*, *Linux Journal*, *PC Magazine*, *PC World*, *Computer Power User (CPU)*, and *Linux Pro*.

Although Damn Small Linux was not the first Linux live CD (in fact, it was originally based on the KNOPPIX live CD), there are many *firsts* to its credit. DSL was the first Linux live CD distribution to do the following:

- Offer backup and restore capabilities.
- Use download scripts to add software while it was running (in ramdisk).
- Employ extendable software modules that could be used from live CD or disk.
- Integrate USB install scripts.
- Run virtually on Windows desktops using a special embedded version of DSL that includes Qemu virtualization software.
- Offer low-RAM extensions designed to run on live CDs or USB drives.

DSL also included many *firsts* specifically associated with desktop-oriented live CDs. It was the first desktop-oriented live CD to fit on a bootable business card, offering the smallest footprint of any desktop operating system. It also was the first to use the Tiny X Kdrive server as the desktop's X display server. To implement many standard Linux utilities, DSL was the first to use the BusyBox space-saving utility.

Although the features just mentioned help gauge the success of DSL, the best way to measure DSL's value to you is to try it out for yourself.

UNDERSTANDING WHAT DAMN SMALL LINUX DOES BEST

When you boot up Damn Small Linux, the first thing you see is a boot screen. In most cases, you can press Enter and after a few moments, a desktop system appears. With a few clicks, you could be browsing the web, editing documents, playing music, or doing dozens of other activities. Figure 1-1 shows an example of a busy DSL desktop.

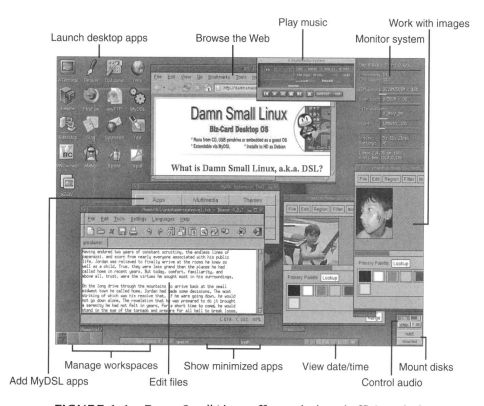

FIGURE 1-1   Damn Small Linux offers a sleek and efficient desktop interface.

The DSL desktop in Figure 1-1 shows some of the basic features of the DSL desktop, along with a few applications. You can launch applications (by a single left mouse click) from the icons shown in the upper-left corner of the screen. In the upper-right corner, view data about system resources (CPU, processes, file system, etc.). The docked.lua tool (lower-right corner) lets you adjust audio and mount disk partitions. The bottom panel displays the current date/time, minimized applications, and a tool for managing workspaces. Use the tool in the lower left to move applications among workspaces.

The applications shown running in Figure 1-1 include the Firefox web browser, XMMS music player, XPaint image editor, and Beaver text editor. In the upper-right corner is the excellent torsmo system monitor, for watching all your system resources (processor, RAM, swap, disk, and other resource usage). These and other applications that are available natively in DSL are described in detail in Chapter 3, "Using DSL Applications."

One administrative tool displayed in Figure 1-1 is the MyDSL Extension tool. You can use that tool to download and install applications that are prepackaged to run in DSL (see Chapter 5, "Extending Applications with MyDSL").

Although the applications shown in the DSL desktop in Figure 1-1 are packaged with the basic 50MB bootable image DSL, the value of Damn Small Linux doesn't end there. If DSL doesn't do exactly what you want it to do (and where you want to do it), the project helps you improve on what you can do with DSL in the following ways:

- **It's expandable**—Using the MyDSL feature and a connection to the Internet, tons of extra applications can be downloaded and installed on your running DSL system with just a couple of mouse clicks. Because DSL has its roots in other popular Linux distributions (in particular, Debian and KNOPPIX), software created for those distributions can often also just be dropped in and run in DSL. See Appendix B, "MyDSL Extensions."

- **It's portable**—Although the standard DSL is made to run on a medium as small as a 50MB bootable business card, it can be easily made to run from your hard disk, standard CD or DVD, USB pen drive, or other fixed and removable media. It can even run embedded from installed Linux or Microsoft Windows systems.

  Many people have put DSL on a USB pen drive, along with other applications and data (documents, music, images, and presentations). So instead of carrying a whole laptop with you, you can carry everything you need on a USB flashdrive or pen drive that's about the size of a stick of gum.

Keeping the basic DSL system small, fast, and efficient makes it both a neat tool in itself and a great foundation to build on. Here is a list of some of the best reasons for using DSL:

- **Old machines get new life**—DSL can run on computers with as little as 16MB of RAM and a 486DX processor. DSL developers offer versions of DSL that boot on older machines that need a smaller boot image (using Syslinux). As a result, the PC gathering dust in the closet can find new life as a simple desktop system, or by adding some extra software, a firewall, web server, or music player PC.

- **Fits in small places**—Damn Small Linux fits on a bootable business card CD. So carrying around DSL can take up as little space as a credit card in your wallet. DSL's small size also means that, in places where there is limited storage space (such as an old hard disk or handheld device), you can devote what space you have to holding your extra applications and personal files.

- **Runs fast!**—Because the DSL operating system and the applications that come with it are small, lightweight, and tuned for efficiency, they run fast, even on meager hardware. If you have at least 128MB of RAM, you can also use DSL's toram feature, which runs the entire DSL operating system from memory. Using toram, applications launch almost instantaneously and run faster than you would believe.

- **Runs efficiently**—By focusing on important desktop features, instead of every possible desktop feature, the DSL desktop makes it easy to get to the features you need. All your desktop applications and system tools are available with a right-click of your mouse from anywhere on the desktop. Desktop tools let you easily view your system processing, change workspaces, mount storage media, and adjust your audio volume.

- **Travels with you**—By their nature, live CD operating systems are made to be portable. Because of its excellent hardware support, DSL runs on most common PC hardware. So, if you are going somewhere that already has a PC you can use, you may not need to lug your laptop with you. You can simply carry DSL and any extra software or data you need in your pocket.

- **Versatility**—Using the tools that come with DSL itself, you can configure DSL to run in many different ways from different storage devices. Besides the default (a DSL boot image burned to a live CD), easy install procedures let you install and run DSL from a USB flash drive, hard disk, or other storage media.

There are also different ways in which you can configure to save and use DSL, your applications, and your data. For example, you can keep your data on a flash drive, whereas DSL itself is run from a live CD or hard disk. When a new version of DSL comes out, you simply boot that new version and combine it with your data. No messy upgrade or reinstall procedures are needed.

- **Security**—Running your operating system from a read-only media can reduce the ability of an intruder to take over (and effectively own) your computer. If you suspect your computer's security has been compromised, you can simply do a clean reboot of DSL. The operating system itself returns to its original state, so you only need to check the data you have saved for potential problems.

Because DSL was created primarily as a desktop system, there are also no network services running by default that an intruder could exploit. If you want to turn on or add new network services, you can add firewall software from MyDSL (see Chapter 16, "Setting Up an XAMPP Web Server in DSL") and configure a professional-quality firewall built on the standard Linux iptables facility.

- **Network and server features**—DSL automatically detects and configures most wired Ethernet cards, and includes tools for configuring many wireless cards. With an available DHCP server on the wire, DSL can often just boot up to an active Internet connection. Applications for using the Internet, web browsing, email, file transfer, instant messaging, and others are included in the basic DSL distribution.

  DSL also includes efficient versions of some network servers that you can enable, if you choose. From the DSL menu, select System, Daemon and choose a service to start. Start ssh to allow secure remote login (`ssh`), file copy (`scp`), or FTP service (`sftp`) to your machine. Or choose nfs-common to be able to share directories over the network. Choose Monkey web server to start a simple web server (HTTP) or FTPd to open your DSL system as an FTP server. Because it is Linux, there are also tons of other services you can add to DSL from open source projects.

- **Build projects**—By starting with a minimal operating system, it's easy to make a system that is configured to do a specialized task. For example, if you want a system tuned just to be a firewall, music player, telephony device, or some other specialized device, you can add only the software you need to an otherwise efficient system. The result can be a system that does just what you need, so all your additional space can be devoted to holding your data. Part IV of this book, "Making Damn Small Linux Projects," contains several interesting projects you can build, starting with DSL.

The uses and advantages of DSL just described are the ones we have found. After you start using DSL, you will probably find many uses on your own.

GETTING THE MOST OUT OF DAMN SMALL LINUX

Within a short time, you should be able to figure out how to boot from the DSL live CD and use the DSL desktop. However, this book is here to teach you how to adapt

DSL to do exactly what you want it to do. To that end, chapters in this book guide you through techniques for tuning DSL to suit your needs and adapting DSL to suit your computer equipment.

The following are some of the major topics covered in this book.

Booting DSL

With a PC and copy of Damn Small Linux (like the one on this book's CD), most people can reboot and be up and running DSL with no instruction. If some other piece of hardware isn't working, pressing F2 shows you boot options that can help overcome most simple problems.

When you boot DSL, there are other boot-options you can pass to DSL that help direct the boot process. Some of those options can make DSL work better for your particular hardware (such as video cards that can't be properly detected). Others let you run DSL in special ways (such as running DSL completely from RAM). Still others let you identify where bundles of data are located that you can pull into your DSL system (such as your backed-up desktop settings or saved applications).

Boot options you might need to get DSL working initially are included in Chapter 2, "Booting DSL." Some options for identifying where your personal settings are backed up to and restored from are covered in Chapter 4, "Configuring and Saving DSL Settings." Options for running DSL in different hardware environments are covered in Chapter 8, "Installing DSL in Alternate Ways."

Customizing the Desktop

Fluxbox is the window manager that is used by default with Damn Small Linux. Despite its compact size, there are many ways to tune Fluxbox to look and behave the way you like. A window manager defines how menus, mouse activities, keyboard navigation, backgrounds, and other features related to the look and feel of your graphical interface operate.

From the Fluxbox desktop, most DSL activities can be directed from a single desktop menu (right-click the desktop to see the DSL menu). Select Desktop, Fluxbox Configuration to see a listing of available desktop settings that you can change. Figure 1-2 shows examples of these menus.

Besides changing the look and feel of your desktop, you can use various desktop utilities to manage your workspaces, mount and unmount file systems, and manage tasks. Using various desktop tools and applications is described in Chapter 3.

FIGURE 1-2
Customize your
desktop settings
from the DSL
menu.

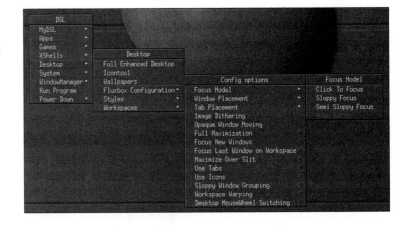

Adding Applications with MyDSL

Although not everyone needs every available piece of software to run with their live CD, nearly everyone needs at least a few software packages beyond those chosen for DSL. Using the MyDSL facility that was designed for DSL, you can add prepackaged software to your live system, save those packages to restore later, and include them (or not) the next time you reboot DSL.

Chapter 5 includes descriptions of the MyDSL facility. Descriptions of MyDSL center on the MyDSL Extension tool, shown in Figure 1-3.

FIGURE 1-3 Customize
your desktop settings from
the DSL menu.

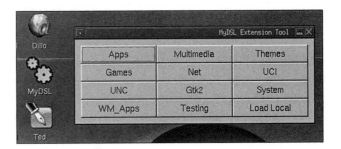

Saving and Restoring Settings and Data

For any live CD to be useful over time, you need to be able to save your data files, your system settings, and any additional applications you use regularly, across reboots. DSL offers a lot of flexibility in how you save your personal files across reboots.

The DSL backup and restore features let you choose exactly what files and directories of data you want to back up and where you want that data to be stored. If you save that data in a specific way, DSL automatically finds and restores that data on your next reboot. The data can be on a disk partition, USB flash drive, or CD, depending on how you chose to store it.

Chapter 4 contains procedures for backing up and restoring your data.

Running DSL on Older PCs

One thing that DSL does better than most operating systems (certainly most new, commercial systems) is let you reuse older computer equipment. DSL works on computers with as little as 16MB of RAM and a 486DX processor (see Chapter 2 for details). In fact, because of its size and efficiency, DSL actually runs well on many machines that some people would just throw away.

To facilitate some of these older machines, DSL developers created special procedures that take into account the weaknesses of some older hardware. For example, you may be dealing with a machine that either can't boot from a CD drive or has no CD drive at all. So, you may need to install DSL to hard disk, and then boot it from a floppy or a boot loader on the hard disk. These techniques are described in Chapter 8.

Building Projects with DSL

The small size and efficient processing of DSL doesn't just make it a neat desktop system. Those attributes also make DSL a great platform for building useful projects. For example, by adding just a few software packages, you can transform that old computer into a useful web server, music server, or Internet telephony machine.

In the Part IV of this book (Chapters 12 through 16), you can find descriptions of projects you can build using DSL as the foundation. Because the operating system and few extra packages don't take up a lot of room, limited disk space can be used to store the music, web content, or other data needed to go with your software project.

Making Your Own DSL Software

There is no MyDSL package available for the software you want. Likewise, you may find it more efficient to put together the software you want on a remastered DSL image than to simply add packages after the fact. This book describes how to handle both of those cases.

In Chapter 11, "Setting up a Full Remastering Environment," there are descriptions of how you can take the software you want and create a shareable MyDSL extension for it. In Chapter 12, "Running DSL on Alternate Hardware," you can learn how to remaster your own DSL image to include any applications or data you like (without having to merge extra applications and data at boot time).

WHAT IS DAMN SMALL LINUX?

Before heading on any further, we need to define exactly what Damn Small Linux is. Damn Small Linux is an operating system, designed to run from live media (such as a bootable business card-size CD) that, at its heart, is controlled by a Linux kernel. It is based on another Linux live CD called KNOPPIX, which, in turn, was created from a Linux distribution called Debian.

Now, we need to sort all that out.

Understanding Operating Systems

An operating system is computer software that manages the interactions between the computer hardware and the applications you run to use that hardware. In the proprietary personal computing world, you are probably most familiar with Microsoft Windows and Mac OS/X operating systems. In the free and open source software (FOSS) world, most operating systems trace their roots back to UNIX.

Damn Small Linux is one of many FOSS operating systems that carries the Linux name because it includes the Linux software that is referred to as the kernel. The Linux kernel is the most critical part of the operating system because it provides the most basic system services: process management, device driver framework, file system support, and other critical system features. As new hardware, file system types, and other components are connected to a Linux system, they can be added to the kernel in what are called *loadable kernel modules*.

Linus Torvalds created the Linux kernel and continues to lead Linux kernel development today. This software is available from the Linux Kernel Archives (http://kernel.org). Most Linux distributions add a set of basic system utilities from the Free Software Foundation GNU project (www.gnu.org), which include many clones of commands that were originally available on UNIX systems.

Although the latest available kernel is the 2.6 kernel, DSL has chosen to stay with the 2.4 kernel tree. This is primarily because the 2.6 kernel is considerably larger. As security holes are found, however, backports of fixes from the 2.6 kernel are included with the 2.4 kernel used by DSL. Backports for improvements can be added in the same. way.

Likewise, instead of including the GNU utilities in the basic DSL, many Linux utilities are implemented through a single, compact utility called BusyBox. (Because BusyBox is not completely compliant with the GNU utilities some people expect, a MyDSL package called gnu-utils is available to bring those important utilities into DSL.)

Although the kernel, a command interpreter (called the shell), and a few utilities are really all you need to have an operating system, most Linux systems include other components as well. For example, the X Window system provides the graphical framework for using most Linux systems, including DSL. A window manager (such as Fluxbox in DSL) implements menus, icons, and other graphical desktop elements.

Understanding Live CDs

Most computer operating systems are installed permanently on a hard disk. A live CD, on the other hand, is typically created so that you can safely ignore any software installed on a computer's hard disk and so you can run entirely from the operating system contained on the CD. This has some advantages and some disadvantages.

Live CDs have the advantage of letting you put together a known set of software and be sure that you can return to that software the next time you reboot. This makes a live CD a great medium for demonstrations, portable desktops, or rescue media. You can take a whole computer system with you in your pocket that you can run from most PCs (provided you are allowed to reboot the PC).

The downsides of live CDs include some of the same features that are their attributes. For example, with any system that you use over time, you want to save some data and applications. By default, live CDs are run from the read-only CD-ROM medium. So, you can't just save files the same way you would if you were running your system from hard disk.

Damn Small Linux has overcome many of the challenges of using a desktop system that was designed to run from a live CD. Some features that were already mentioned (and will be described further later in the book) let you save files and applications so they are available the next time you boot DSL. There are also ways in which you can install DSL to hard disk, so it will behave like most installed operating systems.

 NOTE

Although the term live CD is commonly used to describe a computer system image that is typically booted and run from a read-only medium, the same type of image can be run from other media as well. As you will see from descriptions in this book, a *live CD* can also run from a DVD, USB flash drive, or ZIP drive. Likewise, a live CD can be booted from a floppy disk, and then continued from CD, hard disk, or other medium.

Based on Debian and KNOPPIX

Because a Linux kernel alone doesn't let you do that much with a computer, most Linux distributions draw on the vast landscape of free and open source software. Debian GNU/Linux is one of the most popular free operating systems available today. KNOPPIX is a live CD Linux distribution that was created from Debian software. Technology from both of those projects is incorporated into DSL.

The Debian distribution (http://debian.org) has literally thousands of software packages that have been compiled to run on Debian. Debian packages are stored in .deb format and can be downloaded and installed from the Internet using tools such as apt-get and dpkg. Many Debian applications can be downloaded and installed to DSL using apt-get (available from the dsl-dpkg MyDSL package).

KNOPPIX (www.knopper.net/knoppix/index-en.html) was the first popular desktop-oriented live CD. It included a highly regarded facility for detecting and configuring hardware (a must for live CDs). Using compression techniques, it was able to fit the equivalent of about 1.5G of software within a standard 700MB CD image. Many specialized utilities were included in KNOPPIX to configure some of the trickier hardware components, such as wireless cards, printers, and modems.

Damn Small Linux creator John Andrews began with some of the technology just described. Then he began whittling it down and tuning it up.

ANSWERS FROM THE DSL DEVELOPERS

In case you didn't notice from the cover, this book combines the experiences of three writers. John Andrews created Damn Small Linux. Robert Shingledecker has developed many of the critical technical innovations of DSL. Christopher Negus has authored many Linux books, such as the *Red Hat Linux Bible*, *Linux Toys*, and *Live Linux CDs*.

So in this section, you get to find out first-hand how and why DSL came about. Chris asks John and Robert some hard-hitting questions about why they have developed DSL, what are its greatest attributes, and where it is going.

John, what encouraged you to create DSL?

John: It was a reaction to the trend of ever increasing size of applications and the typical Linux desktop environment. I wanted to see if it were possible to build a functional desktop environment that could be compressed into 50MBs.

One of my original draws to Linux was the fast and light applications that were available in the late 90s. By the time I was working on DSL, many of the applications I loved seemed to slow down to a crawl on my computer.

In essence, the typical Linux desktop was pushing me to a hardware upgrade the same way Microsoft and Mac operating systems tend to do. I hoped (and still do hope) that there would be a resurgence of efficiency in the Linux community where people treat code bloat like the cancer it is.

DSL is also a testament to function over form. We avoid over indulging in eye candy. Some core applications that are in DSL have better functionality than their later incarnations that are larger in size. To the developers of DSL, it is not about the latest or the best looking; it is about functionality and stability.

I was searching for a light portable environment that I could take with me on a business card CD. At the time, the best sub 50MB distribution was LNX-BBC, but its orientation is much more toward being a rescue disk. I thought it would be possible to work within the same limited space but instead build a distribution that focused on having a functional desktop. Being an efficiency fan, I modeled DSL after my desktop and used most of the same lightweight applications.

Robert, what encouraged you to join DSL development?

Robert: I have been involved with Linux CD-ROMS since the early 1990s. I created install-type CDs to automate the specialized setup of servers and desktops while I was working at the City of Garden Grove, California. Later, I worked for a Linux startup and created live Linux CD server appliances. We created firewalls, mail servers, VPN, LAMP-style systems, several database servers, MySQL, Postgres, and even some prototype commercial ones like Raining Data's D3.

These live CDs were automated to provide whatever services the customer desired. During this development, I had created my own live desktop. Occasionally, I would check Distrowatch.com to see if anyone else was doing the desktop approach. I always felt that there are far more desktops than servers. Demo Linux and later KNOPPIX were far too slow to be practical for everyday use at that time. When I found John's Damn Small Linux, I liked what I saw and began to explore ways to expand its capabilities.

What were the first goals of Damn Small Linux and have they changed?

John: The first goal of DSL was to have a functional and efficient Linux desktop distribution that was under 50MB, small enough to fit on a business card-size CD. Over the years, business card CDs became a lot less relevant as affordable USB pen drives have started coming into the market. Yet, we have maintained the 50MB upper limit, which has forced us to think in unconventional ways and innovate instead of just adding applications.

The goal of maximum functionality in a tiny package has been a constant. What has changed are the applications and the growth of the extension technology.

Robert: I certainly have not had a roadmap. Things just progressed in an evolutionary way: from adding a flexible backup/restore system to needing a write-enabled /opt directory to add more programs. Later, we created self-contained compressed mountable applications, originally called .ci extensions, later named UCI. My goal was to honor John's original goal of keeping the distribution at or under 50MB.

Many would remaster DSL only to add or change an application. So, my thoughts were focused on how to allow easy yet flexible additional applications to be added to DSL. These additional applications I called MyDSL extensions. Originally, they were tarballs and UCI. They would either load into the RAM disk under /opt or mount under /opt. Some of the user community really wanted to use Debian on the live DSL CD. This led to a script to make much of the filesystem write-enabled, which led to the .dsl extension type. This is basically a tarball, but the unique extension type would trigger the script to set up all the symlinks needed.

Recently, I added the capability to use mountable compressed overlay images. These new overlay mounts do not need to be self-contained, yet they have the same advantage in low system resource use as the UCI. I try to keep DSL updated with newer technology, while at the same time, keeping the distribution under 50MB and also acknowledging and fully supporting the smaller, older, less capable hardware.

We are constantly looking for the best of breed, *small is beautiful* applications and utilities—for example, Lua. We heavily use Lua and Lua Fltk and create many of our own GUIs. We are not only a small distro; we run well on small resources.

What draws people to DSL?

John: DSL bucks the trend of ever-increasing bloat and the ever-increasing demands on hardware. People who use DSL are not into eye candy for eye candy's sake. They want their computer to work and be reliable. The fact that DSL runs from an ISO image and is inherently durable also makes it appealing, DSL is very hard to break and easy to fix. Of course, there is the modularity and portability aspects, too.

If you want an application, you can just grab it. If you want to take your desktop on the road, it is very easy to do via USB pen drive, or live CD and remote backups. DSL's small but functional base also makes a great platform to build on for custom applications. DSL is a Linux desktop without the 500 pounds of Styrofoam padding.

Robert: DSL is a small distribution and one that runs very well on very small resources. It is extremely flexible in offering many choices of configuration and expandability. After you read the chapters that follow, you will begin to realize the potential.

The DSL project welcomes the user community. The MyDSL extensions only represent the framework. The actual extensions are requested, discussed, and created by the community of DSL users. This active community shares in the ownership of these seamless extensions.

What is the most interesting hardware known to running DSL?

Robert: What comes to my mind is the original ThinkNic Internet Appliance, which is a CD-based machine with a 4MB ramdisk (to save configuration), a Winmodem, and an Ethernet port. We fully support this "first of breed" Linux appliance.

John: For me, the most interesting hardware to run DSL has not been applied yet—there are so many possibilities. I personally work on a homemade laptop based on a eBox III thin client and a cheap 8-inch LCD monitor. I'd like to be able to hook it up to a small solar panel. It will have to run an IDE flash Disk On Module (dom); it will be passively cooled and 100% silent.

Why is DSL good for hobbyists?

John: Oh, there is just so much you could do with DSL. It is small, it requires very little RAM, it can run on ancient hardware, and it can run without a hard drive. DSL can run in RAM with as little as 128MB. It could run with as little as 16MB of RAM with a conventional hard drive install. With DSL, you can take junk and make it into workable hardware.

DSL is also easy to modify, and upgrade. We have an extension system that allows DSL to morph in any direction a developer could want without the need to do a custom remastering. We make heavy use of scripting languages. So if you want to get into the meat of what makes DSL DSL, all you have to do is dig around.

Robert: The fun of tinkering with that old hardware you found in the closet. Now you have a neat small web server, a picture frame, or a car MP3 player. Your creativity is set free to explore and share with a community of DSL users. You can create and share MyDSL extensions or learn to code with Bash, Perl, C, Lua, Lua/Fltk. It's all in there.

DSL includes lots of hardware support. So, you can build a web surfing appliance for Grandma. Or perhaps buy or obtain old "throw-away" laptops. We support many of them. Or even buy an embedded device and use DSL as the embedded OS. We are like Tinkertoys for Linux: a Linux construction kit. It's all about having fun!

What are the challenges to someone who comes to DSL from MS Windows?

John: In the modern MS desktop, you are prevented from looking under the hood. In DSL, there is no hood at all—you are free to dig as deep as you want to. There are no restrictions, and you will want to learn a little about the way DSL works to get the most out of it.

Robert: All the decisions are NOT forced on you. If tinker toys or a construction kit are not fun for you, the basic desktop is still fully functional when you start out. However, with so many choices and options available for extending DSL, it can be overwhelming to a new user. But they will soon want to explore.

Even the community of DSL users does not agree on a single installation or run-time environment for DSL. We often have "Tastes Great! Less Filling!" types of forum debates.

Also, DSL is Linux, and therefore we respect the UNIX file permissions. Some users are used to running everything as the superuser. We do not. Some expect every new device to be instantly supported, which is not possible given our con-straints of size and development. Usually, answers and solutions can be had within the resources of the community.

What future plans do you have for DSL?

John: Tough calls lay in our future. The truth is, very few in the Linux applications development community sees the future of Linux the same way we do. This puts us in a bind. Many of the lean projects are getting abandoned and replaced with other projects that have an enormous amount of package dependency.

Our old friend GTK1.2 is being left behind by most currently developed proj-ects. Other light graphical tool kits are slow in development or even stalled for years at a time. There are a few nuggets of hope out there, and I will never give up on the pursuit of a tiny and functional desktop. I hope that projects like DSL encourage developers of lean applications to continue their work.

In the shorter run, you will likely see a smaller and a larger DSL cousin, as well as more framework for those who want to build custom applications based on the DSL infrastructure.

Robert: I would like to see more modularization of DSL. Offer even more choices to the community. Our process is not formal. It is evolutionary based on our own interests and those expressed by the community of DSL users. And it must be fun and interesting for me and John too!

THE DAMN SMALL LINUX COMMUNITY

Damn Small Linux has a thriving, active community of contributors and users. Although Robert and John direct the activities of the central 50MB DSL distribu-tion, the framework for MyDSL extensions offer the opportunity for anyone to extend the functionality of DSL for themselves and others. To grow the knowledge base of DSL, there are several communications venues available. And, of course, financial contributions are welcome for helping the project grow.

Communications opportunities for the DSL project include forums, a wiki, and a place to blog about DSL. Here's where you can find out more about those opportunities:

- **DSL forums** (`www.damnsmalllinux.org/cgi-bin/forums/ikonboard.cgi`)— In the forums, you can find information on more than 30 topics relating to DSL. Popular topics include hard drive installs, DSL ideas and suggestions, and networking issues.

- **DSL wiki** (`www.damnsmalllinux.org/wiki`)—The DSL wiki brings together a lot of information related to the DSL project. From the wiki, you can find answers to frequently asked questions, learn about installation and boot options, and read about common issues that DSL users encounter.

- **DSL IRC** (`irc://irc.freenote.net/damnsmalllinux`)—Participate in real-time, online chats with other DSL users.

- **DSL blog** (`www.damnsmalllinux.org/talk`)—At the DSL blog, you can feel free to present your musings and personal experiences that relate to Damn Small Linux.

Because DSL is freely distributed, development is funded through contributions and through purchases from the DSL store. Contributing to DSL in one of these ways can do a lot to further development of Damn Small Linux. Here are suggestions for contributing:

- **DSL donations** (`www.damnsmalllinux.org/donate.html`)—If you enjoy DSL and can afford to contribute, monthly subscriptions of $1, $2, $5, and $10 contributions can be made from this page. You can also make one-time donations via PayPal or credit card.

- **DSL store** (`www.damnsmalllinux.org/store`)—At the DSL store, you can purchase a variety of mini-ITX computer supplies. This is also the place to buy a DSL CD or DSL on a bootable USB pen drive (currently, 1GB models are offered). One of the great features of the bootable USB drive is that it includes the QEMU version of DSL that can be booted and run on a Windows desktop.

Before I became associated with John and Robert to write this book, I purchased a DSL USB pen drive from the DSL store. I still use that drive today to show people DSL. I can plug the USB drive into a running Windows system, select one file from that drive, and in a few moments give a demonstration of Damn Small Linux within a window on the Windows desktop.

ON THE CD

DSL itself only takes up about 50MB of space on your boot media. However, with several different versions of DSL (for booting from different media) and some available MyDSL software extensions, you can experience DSL in different ways. For those reasons, we have included a standard-size CD with this book (about 700MB) that we have filled with a whole lot of software you can use with DSL.

The CD that comes with this book boots up to the latest version of Damn Small Linux. By default (press Enter), you will get exactly what you would were you to download the standard 50MB DSL image from the Internet. With our specially remastered CD, however, you get a whole lot more.

- **Official Damn Small Linux (dsl-3.3.iso)**—This is the standard DSL that you would normally burn to CD and boot live.
- **Official DSL for older machines (dsl-3.3-syslinux.iso)**—If you have a PC that requires a floppy boot image on the CD to boot up, you can use this ISO image. This image (contained in the /images directory) features the Syslinux boot loader, which includes a small 1.4MB boot image. To use this ISO, you need to burn it to a separate CD.
- **Virtual DSL for Windows with QEMU (dsl-3.3-embedded.zip)**—This archive is unzipped on the live CD so that you can run DSL virtually within a window on your Windows desktop.
- **Virtual DSL scripts for VMware (dsl-3.3-vmx.zip)**—Using the scripts included in this zip file, you can run DSL virtually from a variety of environments using VMware.
- **Special DSL projects**—Chapters 13 through 16 describe how to create special software and hardware projects with Damn Small Linux. You can directly boot up to versions of DSL that include the software packages needed to complete those projects. These projects include:
  - —**DSL Edna music server:** Manage, play, and serve your music collection from DSL using Edna music server software (see Chapter 13, "Making an Edna Music Server in DSL").
  - —**DSL Skype VoIP service:** Make Internet telephone calls using Skype IP telephony service (see Chapter 14, "Using Skype VoIP Service in DSL").
  - —**DSL digital picture frame:** Play slide shows of any collection of digital images from DSL as a standalone digital picture frame (see Chapter 15, "Running a Digital Picture Frame in DSL").

—**DSL web server:** Include XAMPP software with DSL to create an instant web server to share your web content over the Internet (see Chapter 16).

- **DSL boot images**—Some older hardware that has no bootable CD drive (or no CD drive at all) may need a floppy boot image to be able to boot DSL. Several different boot images are included in the /images directory of the CD.

- **Chapter 10 and Chapter 11 scripts**—Scripts that are described in Chapter 10, "Adding Applications and Creating Shareable Extensions," and Chapter 11 in this book are contained in the /chapter10 and /chapter11 directories, respectively, on the CD. The scripts will help you make your own MyDSL extensions and remaster your own DSL live CD.

- **MyDSL packages**—There are several extra software packages that are very popular with DSL users. By including some of these packages, available as software extensions with the MyDSL facility, on the CD, we can save you the trouble of downloading them over the Internet. In the /mydsl directory in the top-level directory of the CD, you can find packages for installing standard GNU utilities (gnu-utils package), ALSA sound drivers and utilities (alsa-sound package), and the OpenOffice.org office applications (openoffice package).

You can use the software contained on the CD if you don't have an Internet connection. As time goes by, however, you should check the Damn Small Linux website for the availability of later versions of the software included on the CD.

SUMMARY

Damn Small Linux is the premiere business card-size Linux desktop live CD available today. Within its 50MB footprint, DSL contains nearly every type of application you would expect to find in a modern desktop operating system. Although DSL is designed to run from a read-only CD medium, you can add data, software extensions, and system settings that can be backed up separately and used again the next time you reboot.

This chapter is an introduction to the features that make DSL both a useful and fun operating system for computer enthusiasts. It presents some of the ways in which you can boot, install, reuse, and enhance DSL that are described in greater depth in later chapters of the book. It also discusses ways in which you can learn more about the DSL community and contribute to its success.

## CHAPTER 2

Booting DSL

Whether you are using a bootable business card purchased from DamnSmallLinux.org (and thank you for the support), the CD that comes with this book, or a Damn Small Linux (DSL) image you downloaded and burned, DSL is made to boot up easily on nearly any PC. In most cases, after you insert the medium, reboot, and press Enter, the DSL desktop (see Figure 2-1) appears in a few moments.

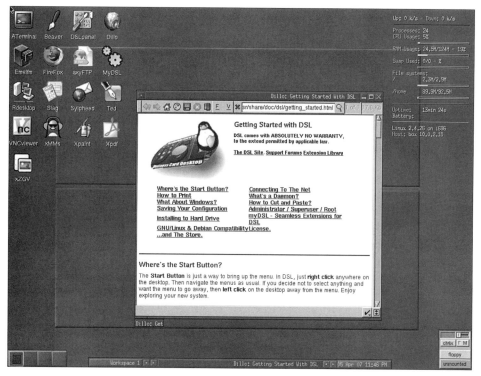

FIGURE 2-1   The DSL desktop appears automatically when you boot DSL.

Great! At this point you may think "I am done and on to the next chapter." But if DSL fails to boot right off or if there's something extra you want out of the boot process, don't worry. There are plenty of ways you can improve your experience with DSL that start right from the boot prompt. Understanding how DSL boots is a good way to begin.

UNDERSTANDING HOW DSL BOOTS

DSL's booting capabilities are inherited from KNOPPIX's hardware autodetection. KNOPPIX has set the standard in being able to autoconfigure a wide variety of hardware and set the bar for live CD-based systems.

DSL has chosen a bootup default of Xvesa (a generic X Window System server), 1024×768 (screen resolution), PS/2 mouse, and no DMA (direct media access, which makes disks faster when the hardware supports it). Your system may not support these default settings.

Because it is derived from KNOPPIX, DSL has many boot time options to allow support for many other systems configurations. So, whether you want to fix a broken boot process or simply boot DSL in different ways, using the boot options described in this chapter, you can do the following:

- Change video settings.
- Disable selected hardware devices.
- Change the desktop window manager or other desktop settings.
- Choose to run DSL entirely from RAM.
- Set passwords for root and dsl users.
- Change the supported language (from the default English).
- Start system services to allow such things as remote login, Web, printing, file sharing, system logging, and other services.
- Include (or not include) backed up files or MyDSL applications from different storage devices.

These items describe how to change the way DSL boots up on your computer. The next section describes the computer hardware you need for DSL to work.

HARDWARE REQUIREMENTS

With the power of the average PC growing exponentially in the past few years, you might be able to grab an older PC from your closet or from a used computer store for just a few dollars. Because DSL was created to run fast on older processors and in low RAM environments, DSL will run on many PCs that won't run Windows Vista or even some Enterprise-level Linux systems.

Let's start by reviewing the hardware that is required to successfully boot DSL. The recommended hardware is as follows:

- 486DX (recommended Pentium I) 32MB RAM
- IDE bootable CD drive or 3.5" floppy drive plus nonbootable CD drive
- SVGA VESA compatible graphics card
- Monitor capable of 800×600 pixel resolution
- Serial mouse, PS/2 mouse, or USB mouse

Although the hardware just mentioned is the minimal requirement to boot DSL from a CD, if you only have a floppy drive, the actual minimum requirement is the following:

- 486DX 16MB RAM
- 500MB hard drive
- 3.5" floppy drive
- SVGA VESA compatible graphics card
- Serial mouse

Because the minimum hardware (486DX) typically has a floppy drive and not a CD drive, hard disk space is needed to contain DSL. This minimum hardware configuration and its installation of DSL are discussed in Chapter 8, "Installing DSL in Alternate Ways." The focus of this chapter is booting from or with a CD and with at least the recommended hardware configuration.

NOTE

The latest Damn Small Linux will boot on newer Intel-based Mac computers. However, not all hardware components (such as network cards) are supported. It is theoretically possible that you could install DSL to hard disk on one of these machines using Apple Bootcamp (www.apple.com/macosx/bootcamp). But that configuration is not officially supported by DSL.

SOFTWARE REQUIREMENTS–DSL VERSIONS

Damn Small Linux is available in several different versions. The version you use depends on the environment in which you are running DSL. The four versions DSL offers include:

- **A SYSLINUX version**—Used for older PCs that require the boot medium to be no larger than a floppy image (even if that image is on a CD). For more information on the SYSLINUX boot loader, refer to the SYSLINUX FAQ (http://syslinux.zytor.com/faq.php).

- **An ISOLINUX version**—Used most often for booting live CDs, because it needs no special floppy emulation disk. For more information on the ISOLINUX boot loader, refer to the ISOLINUX FAQ (http://syslinux.zytor.com/iso.php).

- **A Qemu Virtual Machine version**—Sets up Qemu to run DSL virtually within a running Linux system.

- **A VMware Virtual Machine version**—Sets up VMware to run DSL virtually within a running Windows system.

The first two versions concern booting from the CD, which is the topic of this chapter. The other two versions are discussed in Chapter 7, "Running DSL Embedded in Windows." Why are there two versions for CD? Because DSL targets older and smaller hardware, many such systems could only boot from a CD if there existed an actual emulated boot floppy. This emulated boot floppy was restricted to the size of a real floppy. Later machines were made without such a restriction.

So, the first rule is this: If your machine cannot begin the boot process, or if your machine is an older variety, use the SYSLINUX version.

The SYSLINUX version of DSL emulates a single floppy at boot time. There are fewer drivers in the SYSLINUX version because they must all fit within a single floppy-sized file. The reason Knoppix and the other derivatives went with ISOLINUX is that there is no single floppy size limitation. The ISOLINUX version has many more drivers to support booting from newer computers.

GETTING DAMN SMALL LINUX

There are several versions of Damn Small Linux included on the CD that comes with this book. You can read about what those versions are and how to use them by referring to Appendix A, "On the CD." However, if you don't have the CD handy or if a later version of DSL is available, you might consider downloading a copy of DSL to make your own bootable CD.

Downloading Damn Small Linux

If you are new to the concept of live CDs, it is possible that you don't know how to download an ISO and make a bootable CDROM. The first step is to find a local DSL download mirror. You can always check the latest list of available download sites by checking the Damn Small Linux website download section at:

```
http://www.damnsmalllinux.org/download.html
```

Using the Ibiblio site as an example, navigate to the site's current directory:

```
ftp://ibiblio.org/pub/Linux/distributions/damnsmalllinux/current
```

Based on the previous discussion, select which version you want to download. The ISOLINUX version of DSL, which is what you want in most cases, is named `dsl-?.?.iso`, where the ?.? is replaced by the DSL version number.

There are many ways to create a bootable CD and many operating systems to perform this task. You want to use a CD writing program with a burn image or write to disk option.

Many Linux systems have the k3b utility and cdrecord command to burn CDs. For Windows users, Nero and Roxio are popular commercial programs. Also available for Windows are freeware CD Burner XP Pro (`www.cdburnerxp.se`) and Infra Recorder (`http://infrarecorder.sourceforge.net`) applications.

Getting to the Boot Prompt

Try booting up the DSL live CD. If neither the SYSLINUX nor ISOLINUX versions get you to the boot screen, here are a few things you can try:

- Make sure that your CD burn didn't fail. If you downloaded and burned your own CD, it is best to burn at a very low rate. I suggest slowing down the burn process to a speed of 4. Yes, even if you have a new 52X burner.

- Some computers have difficulty booting from a CD-RW CD. It is best to use a CD-R CD.

- If you have a different live CD (such as KNOPPIX), try booting from that live CD to see if your problem is specific to DSL.

- Your computer's BIOS may not be set to boot from CD. Immediately after the boot process starts, go to your computer's BIOS settings (press F2, Del, or some other key, as instructed, to enter your BIOS). Check that the boot order includes booting from CD and make sure that the CD will boot before the hard disk in your boot order.

If your computer does not boot from CD, you can try creating a boot floppy. Download the DSL standard boot floppy image, `bootfloppy.img`. You might want to check for a local download mirror to reduce your download time. Check the Damn Small Linux website download section: `www.damnsmalllinux.org/download.html`.

Next, locate the file to download. For example,

```
ftp://ibiblio.org/pub/Linux/distributions/damnsmalllinux/current/
bootfloppy.img
```

Write this image to a known good floppy disk. Don't use old floppies because they will likely cause grief when read errors occur. Use typical tools to create the boot floppy. Usually this means rawwrite for Windows or dd for Unix/Linux type systems.

For example, if your Unix/Linux system's first floppy device was located at `/dev/fd0`, with `bootfloppy.img` located in your current directory, you could use the following dd command to write that image to an inserted floppy:

```
# dd if=bootfloppy.img of=/dev/fd0 bs=16k
```

Depending on the version of rawwrite you are using, the process of writing the bootfloppy.img file to a floppy from a DOS prompt (with the boot image locate at the root of C: and rawwrite in the C:\windows\command directory) should be similar to the following:

```
C:\> cd \windows\command
C:\windows\command> rawwrite
Enter disk image source file name: C:\bootfloppy.img
Enter target diskette drive: A:
Please insert a formatted diskette into drive
A: and press –ENTER– : <Enter>
```

The rawwrite program for Windows can be found at this site:

```
http://www.chrysocome.net/rawwrite
```

After you create the floppy disk, be sure to change your computer's BIOS so that the floppy is the first device to boot from. Place the newly created floppy into the drive and turn on or reboot your system. If you have used a good floppy and had no read errors, you are presented with the DSL boot screen.

Hopefully, you have arrived at the DSL boot screen (see Figure 2-2). If you arrived here because you need the boot floppy or needed to download and create the SYSLINUX version, just press Enter at the DSL boot prompt.

After you can see the DSL boot screen, there are many options you can enter at the boot prompt to steer the direction of the boot process. The following sections describe the DSL boot process and how you can modify it.

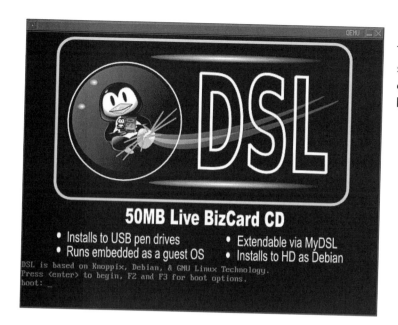

FIGURE 2-2
The DSL boot screen lets you add options to the boot process.

UNDERSTANDING BOOT STAGES OF DSL

There are three stages to boot DSL. The first stage is to get to the boot prompt. The boot prompt allows entry of additional boot options. The second stage is the auto-configuration and environment initialization of DSL. This stage processes the boot time options and sets up the runtime environment of DSL. The third stage is sometimes required (and sometimes requested) to perform additional setup not available via autoconfiguration—for example, serial, two-button, or USB mouse, non-US keyboards, or nondefault 1024×768 screen resolution.

If your computer can boot your DSL CD, you should see the boot screen similar to the one shown in Figure 2-2.

Let's dig deeper into the boot process of DSL.

 NOTE

This chapter covers the booting process only as it relates to the normal task of booting from a live CD. A more advanced and detailed discussion is presented in Chapter 11, "Setting Up a Full Remastering Environment."

The First Boot Stage: Choosing Boot Options

The boot prompt lets you customize the DSL startup process. For example, you can specify at the boot to load entirely into RAM, where your backup files are located, or even where additional applications are stored. To reach the boot prompt, you use the CD, the floppy disk, or a USB pen drive. The value of understanding this stage is so you can understand the boot options that can be used to change how DSL boots.

> ## NOTE
>
> USB pen drive specifics are discussed in Chapter 6, "Running a Native Pen Drive Install."

Getting to the Boot Prompt

To get to the boot prompt, follow these steps:

1. Start with the computer either on or off:

   - **Starting with the computer on**—If the computer is already on, insert the DSL CD. If you happen to be running Windows and the CD drive is set to autorun mode, information about DSL appears. Restart the computer so that it boots from the DSL CD.

   - **Starting with the computer off**—If the computer is off, turn it on and immediately insert the DSL CD. On some computers, pressing the Pause/Break key immediately after turning power on pauses the startup, giving you more time to insert the CD. Press the Pause/Break key again to resume startup. Some computers have a key sequence to enter into a boot menu; see your computer's documentation. You might also want to press the key sequence to enter BIOS setup to give you time to insert the DSL CD.

2. **The boot screen appears**—Most newer computers automatically check for a bootable CD in the first CD drive. The DSL boot prompt should then appear, with the DSL boot splash screen (see Figure 2-2). If your computer can't display the black and white DSL logo, you get a blue background with only the three text lines and a boot prompt.

3. **Booting DSL**—At the boot prompt, press Enter to boot DSL accepting all the defaults. If you do nothing for 60 seconds, DSL boots automatically.

Did you get the DSL desktop screen as shown in Figure 2-1? If not, then the next step is to try some boot options that are described in the following sections.

Help at the Boot Prompt

When the DSL boot screen is displayed, you should be familiar with the boot prompt in the lower-left corner. This is where you can either press Enter, wait a few seconds, or Press F2 or F3 for the help screens.

The help screen is a summary of the boot prompt options. Pressing F2 or any other key cancels the timer so DSL does not automatically boot; this way, you have plenty of time to peruse all of the displayed options.

Figure 2-3 shows the screen that appears by pressing F2 at the boot prompt.

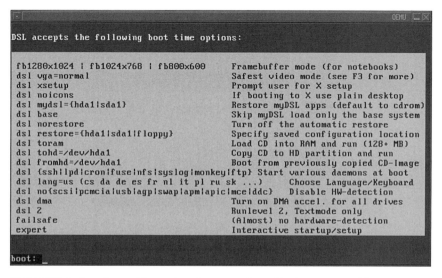

FIGURE 2-3   Press F2 to view boot options for language, video, restoring settings, and other features.

Figure 2-4 shows the screen that appears by pressing F3 at the boot prompt.

As you can see from the boot options screen, there are a lot of options that you can try. However, most of these options are there to overcome rare special problems or offer enhanced ways of using DSL (such as running totally from RAM). The fact is that for most users, DSL will just boot up without additional options, so they can stop reading after the opening paragraph of this chapter.

There are some machines that require additional boot options. Usually, difficult machines have problems related to VGA capabilities, power management, and PNP BIOS that special boot options can help overcome. Other boot options can be used to turn on special features (such as adding passwords or starting services). Some of those options are discussed in other chapters and briefly discussed in the "Advanced Boot Options" section later in this chapter.

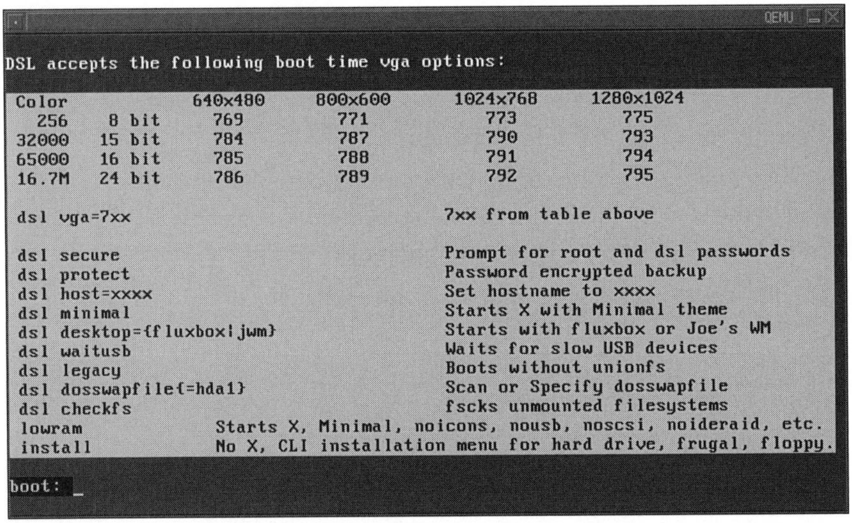

```
                                                                    QEMU
DSL accepts the following boot time vga options:

Color            640x480    800x600    1024x768    1280x1024
   256    8 bit    769        771        773         775
 32000   15 bit    784        787        790         793
 65000   16 bit    785        788        791         794
 16.7M   24 bit    786        789        792         795

dsl vga=7xx                             7xx from table above

dsl secure                              Prompt for root and dsl passwords
dsl protect                             Password encrypted backup
dsl host=xxxx                           Set hostname to xxxx
dsl minimal                             Starts X with Minimal theme
dsl desktop={fluxbox:jwm}               Starts with fluxbox or Joe's WM
dsl waitusb                             Waits for slow USB devices
dsl legacy                              Boots without unionfs
dsl dosswapfile{=hda1}                  Scan or Specify dosswapfile
dsl checkfs                             fscks unmounted filesystems
lowram                 Starts X, Minimal, noicons, nousb, noscsi, noideraid, etc.
install                No X, CLI installation menu for hard drive, frugal, floppy.

boot: _
```

FIGURE 2-4 Press F3 to view boot options for setting passwords, choosing a desktop, or setting other boot time features.

Trying Different Boot Options

Let's roll up our sleeves, try some common boot options, and discuss some common solutions. At the boot prompt, let's try a few basic options.

- **Video boot options**—By default, DSL boots into a high resolution, vga=791 mode. This might be too high a resolution for your computer's video. Using the boot option vga=normal might help.

  boot: **dsl vga=normal**

Many older laptop/notebook computers require framebuffer video instead of the Xvesa. So, you might want to try:

  boot: **fb800x600**

Note that I did not use the word dsl as the first option. Depending on your notebook computer, it might be fb1024x786. If you get an error about no fbdev, using framebuffer likely will not help.

Notice the vga resolution table on the F3 screen (see Figure 2-4). Any one of these values can be selected with the vga= option.

As I noted, it can be a combination of options that is required. Try this common selection of options:

  boot: **dsl vga=normal noapic noacpi pnpbios=off acpi=off noapm**

Success? Great. Now, you should try again, only this time backing off each of the preceding options, one at a time, until you have the exact set of options required to boot. We call this fine-tuning the options for your particular machine. On the other hand, you may still be facing issues and not yet able to boot into DSL.

- **failsafe boot option**—A powerful preset combination of options is called `failsafe`. Try this:

    boot: **failsafe**

If `failsafe` works for you, how can you fine-tune your options? You can always see your boot options from the command line or in X windows. From a command line or a shell window, type **showbootoptions**; or from the DSL desktop, select DSLpanel, System Stats, Boot Tab. Then, you may try booting by eliminating each of the displayed boot options of `failsafe`. You want to do this, because some of these options prevent sound and other features that you will later want to use and enjoy.

- **lowram boot option**—For machines with 64MB of RAM or less, you might want to consider another preset combination of options. `lowram` is used like `failsafe` and is optimized for low RAM systems. Again, you may want to use `showbootcodes` or the System Stats Boot tab to see the preset options and then begin the fine-tuning for your specific needs.

- **toram boot option**—For machines that are rich in RAM, you might want to try the `toram` boot option. Adding this option to your list of other options loads DSL entirely into RAM. This provides a superfast system, as no further access to the CD is required. You should not attempt this until you first establish your machine's required boot options and have at least 128MB RAM.

The Second Boot Stage: Autoconfiguration

DSL's second stage is autoconfiguration and environment initialization. This stage begins as soon as the Enter key is pressed at the first stage boot prompt. All of our entered boot options are processed to determine which parts of autoconfiguration are attempted. Normally, this process runs without intervention. Figure 2-5 shows a typical autoconfiguration in process.

Upon successful completion, this stage typically ends by initializing the X Window System. The X Window System is used to host the graphical DSL desktop. Of course, the use of the boot time option of 2 (`dsl 2`) prevents X from starting and terminates the boot process at a shell prompt for the root user.

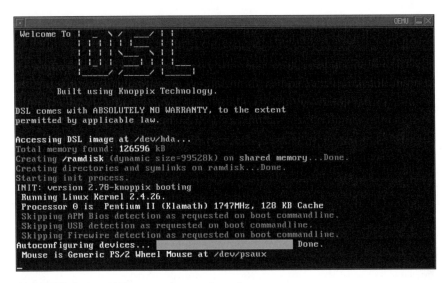

FIGURE 2-5 DSL second stage booting.

Hopefully, you have achieved success. Some may have the DSL desktop displayed and ready for exploration. Some are happy to arrive at the system prompt of runlevel 2. But for others, the third stage of booting is required.

NOTE

As previously stated, the third stage of booting DSL may be desired for those that have a serial, two-button, or USB mouse, a foreign language keyboard, and so on. You may use the boot time option of xsetup to force DSL to enter the third stage of booting.

For those who still have not been able to go further, you might have very esoteric hardware, perhaps too new or too old to be supported. However, help and hope are still available with the power of the Internet and the Damn Small Linux forums (see www.damnsmalllinux.org/cgi-bin/forums/ikonboard.cgi).

Many users have passed through the forums and the collective knowledge is immense. Try posting a request for help providing as much detail about your system as possible. Who knows? Maybe someone else has the same system as you and has a readily available answer. And remember that no question is too dumb to ask. We all had to start somewhere.

The Third Boot Stage: Setting Up X

This stage is sometimes required. It can be the result of specifying a video boot option. It can also be called for when using the `xsetup` boot option. But normally, users never see the third stage booting of DSL.

The first screen (see Figure 2-6) allows selection of the type of X server to use. Typically, if you have selected an fb800×600 or similar framebuffer boot option, the choice is clear.

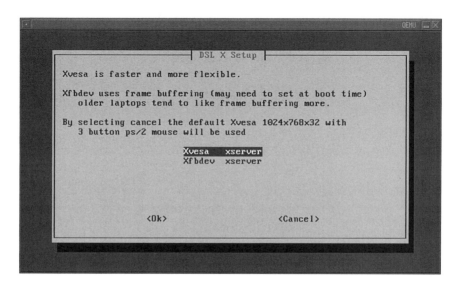

FIGURE 2-6   The first DSL X setup screen.

Even though this screen is displayed, you still have the option to bail out and use the DSL defaults. To do so, just press Tab to Cancel and press Enter. If OK is selected, the following series of additional setup screens are presented. Figure 2-7 prompts if a USB mouse will be used.

Figure 2-8 is for the serial mouse and non-wheel ps2 mouse selection. The PS/2 port is the round, green port that's on the back of most PCs. Serial ports are rectangular and are typically labeled as COM1, COM2, and so on.

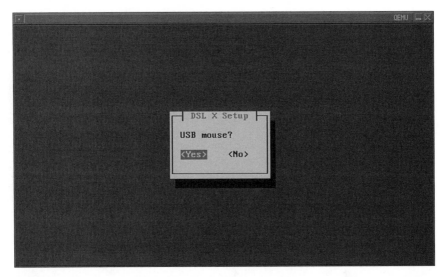

FIGURE 2-7   The DSL X setup mouse selection.

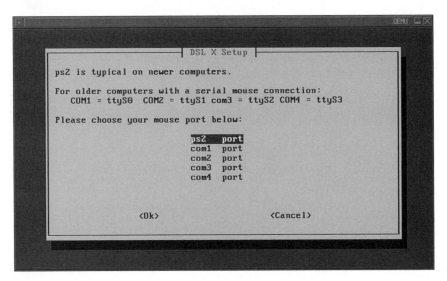

FIGURE 2-8   DSL alternate mouse options.

Figure 2-9 is critical for those users that have a two-button mouse. By pressing both buttons at the same time, you emulate the "third" button. Many applications use or require a three-button mouse.

The screen resolution screen in Figure 2-10 appears because Xvesa was selected back on the initial X setup screen (refer to Figure 2-6).

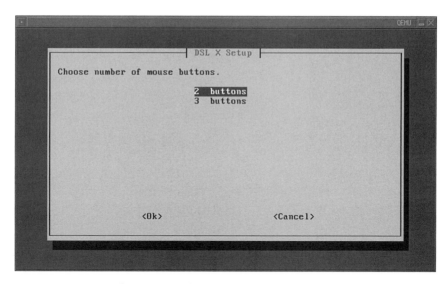

FIGURE 2-9   Select two or three mouse buttons.

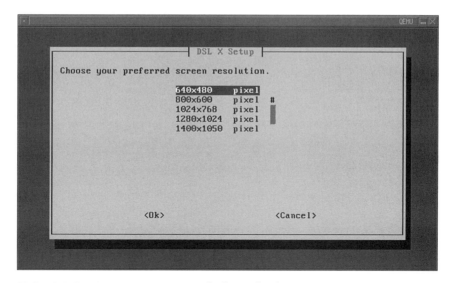

FIGURE 2-10   DSL screen resolution selection.

Color depth selection, as shown in Figure 2-11, is also an Xvesa-based selection. The higher number of bits represents more available colors but also might cause the desktop to perform more slowly. If you chose Xfbdev as your X server, this screen does not appear.

The final X setup screen presents a keyboard selection (see Figure 2-12).

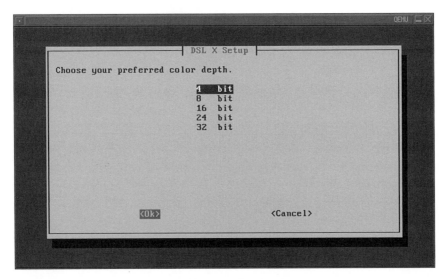

FIGURE 2-11 DSL screen color depth selection.

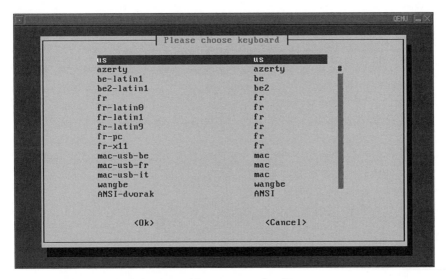

FIGURE 2-12 DSL keyboard language selection.

NOTE

Not all programs in DSL support all languages. The programs selected for DSL, as described in Chapter 3, "Using DSL Applications," were based on small size and functionality and not international language support.

Upon selecting the desired keyboard, DSL attempts to start the X Window System. If all goes well, you shortly arrive at your final destination, the DSL desktop (refer to Figure 2-1). If you find that the screen is unreadable or the colors are horribly off, you can continue your quest to find the appropriate boot codes for your particular hardware. You can press Ctrl+Alt+Backspace to exit X; at the system prompt, type **xsetup.sh** and select another set of options for this, the third stage DSL booting.

After you have arrived at the DSL desktop, you want to save your configurations for X, resolution, mouse, and keyboard. The full details of configuration backup and restore are covered in Chapter 4, "Configuring and Saving DSL Settings."

ADVANCED BOOT OPTIONS

To boot DSL and be able to assign passwords to the super-user root and user DSL, add the `secure` boot option. This option is a must if you also plan to start daemons—that is, services available for local or network use. You are prompted during the boot sequence to enter your chosen passwords. For example, to start the NFS (Network File System) and SSH (Secure Shell) services, you can type the following options at the boot prompt:

```
boot: dsl nfs ssh secure
```

Using the `host` boot option allows you to set the hostname of your machine. This is very useful when providing other network services or if you happen to run many DSL boxes.

Add `dma` to your boot option list if you have newer hardware. This direct memory access method speeds up access to your CD drive, as well as to your hard drives. (Most PCs built in the past ten years support DMA.)

Running in Background Services Daemons of DSL

DSL provides several local and network services. These services run unattended in the background. Most distributions start many background processes. DSL does not. In fact, this is another reason why DSL is not just a small distribution but runs so well on very small resource machines. Knowing this, you must use a boot code to start up each of the services that DSL provides.

Services you can start from the DSL boot prompt include printing service (`lpd`), remote login service (`ssh`), scheduled command execution (`cron`), system logging (`syslog`), Web service (`monkey`), file transfer service (`ftp`), and file system in user space (`fuse`).

SUMMARY

Successful booting of DSL can be as easy as inserting the CD and pressing Enter. For the majority of users, this is their experience. Given that there are always exceptions to the rule, this chapter has tried to step you through all three stages of booting DSL. At each stage, you saw common examples based on actual feedback from many users who have come to the Damn Small Linux forums with their questions and particulars of their hardware. Hopefully, sharing these stages has made booting DSL a pleasant experience.

## CHAPTER 3

Using DSL Applications

Damn Small Linux is designed to be a fully functional desktop in a very small package. The native applications in DSL are chosen for their blend of compact size, speed of use, and functionality.

The DSL developers and user community has spent more than three years refining our choice of applications in DSL, and we believe in the quality of our overall package. There have been several changes over the last few years as we worked out the best combination of features to fit into our small package.

THE LOGIC BEHIND OUR CHOICES

The three dominant issues in choosing applications for DSL have been reliability, library dependency, and usability. In this process, we changed media players, spreadsheet application, browsers, word processors, calculators, text editors, and the widget language on which we base our desktop GUIs.

GTK+ is a toolkit for creating graphical user interfaces. GTK+ was originally developed for the Gimp image editing program. An experienced Linux user may notice that there are no GTK2 applications in DSL and may wonder why. Many of our applications are actually based on the older GTK1.2 toolkit. The two reasons are that GTK1.2 applications tend to be:

- **Smaller**. They take up less space and have fewer dependencies.
- **Faster**. Speed is very important in the DSL computing philosophy.

Before we get started, it is important to note that this chapter focuses on the applications within DSL, not applications available via the MyDSL extension system. (See Chapter 5, "Extending Applications with MyDSL," for descriptions of MyDSL extensions.)

THE FLUXBOX WINDOW MANAGER

Initially, Fluxbox seems very minimalist: there is no Start button, and people are often found scratching their heads wondering where the menu is. However, you will soon discover that what can appear to be confusing at first is actually a blessing.

Before screaming, "This Damn Small Linux stuff is too confusing—I am going to go back to Windows," grab your mouse and press your right-click button. You see that? Bam! There is your menu. Notice how fast it loaded? Without any hesitation, it just pops up in a flash. This is the Fluxbox menu.

To navigate the Fluxbox menu, just scroll the mouse over it vertically. As the mouse moves, you will see submenus pop up, and as you navigate your mouse over the submenus, sometimes additional menus open as well. The application that is selected becomes highlighted as the mouse scrolls over it. To select a menu, press the left mouse button once and the single click opens the application. That is how the menu operates.

You will soon appreciate the Fluxbox menu's speed and efficiency. Unlike traditional taskbar navigation, you do not have to move your mouse pointer all the way down to your screen's lower-left corner and click the little button to get the menu to display. The mouse is always just one click away from displaying your menu.

Fluxbox offers a lot more than just the ease of menu navigation. With a little investigation, you will discover that the seemingly simple environment actually makes it possible to work on your computer faster.

Navigating Virtual Desktops

Another great aspect of Fluxbox is that it supports virtual work environments—in DSL there are four virtual desktops by default. There are a few ways to navigate between virtual workspaces. If you have a wheel-equipped mouse, the easiest way to move from one workspace to another is to just spin the wheel up or down.

At first, you may not notice that your virtual workspace is changing. If there are no applications currently open, the only change is the Workspace number located on the narrow taskbar at the bottom of your screen. In addition, the squares on the Pager (that little rectangular thing in the lower-left corner) also shift to indicate a change.

The Pager is actually very handy, and we will return to it in a bit. For users without a wheel mouse, you can switch from one work environment to another by clicking the little arrow buttons on the left side of the task bar at the bottom of the screen (see Figure 3-1).

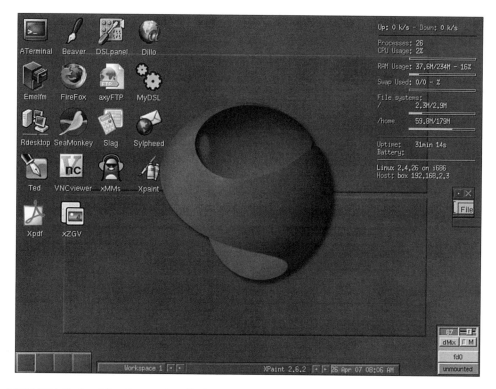

FIGURE 3-1   The Damn Small Linux Desktop.

If you have not yet opened an application, you should at this time. Let's try opening the Aterm window. Locate the icon with Aterm in the upper-left corner of your screen; click it once. An Aterm *terminal emulator* appears, ready to use a *shell* command interpreter. Although a terminal emulator is comparable to a DOS window in Microsoft operating systems, it is arguably more powerful.

Your open window looks like a transparent rectangle and has ds1@box:~$ in the upper-left corner. As you can see, Aterm is ready to receive instructions. However, we are not going to give it any for the moment! We are opening this *term* window (*term* is short for terminal emulator) to demonstrate an additional way to jump to another workspace. This one may be useful if you want to push an application to a workspace that is less crowded.

At the top of the Aterm terminal, you should notice a bar that reads Bash—on one end is a dot (.) and on the other an underscore, a square, and a big X. For now, ignore that and instead put your mouse arrow near where it says "Bash."

There are a couple of options to move this Aterm window to a different workspace. One way is to right-click the bar. Doing so opens up a menu with several entries. For now, look at the first one, which reads "Send To." Bring the mouse arrow to it; the Save To menu item becomes highlighted, and a Workspace 1 submenu opens. If you select one of these options, the Aterm window moves to another workspace.

Alternatively, you could press your left mouse button down in the same bar and instead of a drop-down menu, you get a multidirectional symbol, which indicates that you are now free to move this Aterm window anywhere you like. This includes dragging it to a different virtual workspace by moving the Aterm window to the left or right of the screen. Give it a try! It may seem very foreign to you if you are not accustomed to virtual workspaces. They are extremely useful when you are multitasking, and eventually you may come to depend on them.

The Fluxbox Pager

As mentioned earlier, the application in the lower-left corner is a Pager; more specifically, it is called Fluxter, a lightweight pager made just to work with Fluxbox. Fluxter is configurable by editing the /home/dsl/.fluxbox/fluxter.bb file to your liking. The default settings offer a good mix of functionality without crowding the workspace. Fluxter intelligently monitors which theme Fluxbox is using and alters its look to match the theme.

How to Use Fluxter

Fluxter is very simple to use. To figure out how it works, open up a few applications. As they materialize on the desktop, notice that they have corresponding shapes in the pager. See Figure 3-2. Now, take your mouse and left-click one of the shapes, hold down on the mouse button, and move the shape around. The application that corresponds to the shape in Fluxter is moved in the desktop. If you drag the shape to another cube in Fluxter, the corresponding application moves to the virtual workspace it represents.

FIGURE 3-2   Fluxter: square shades represent applications.

Fluxter can also be used to switch virtual desktops. To do so, simply click the middle mouse button on the virtual desktop you want to go to.

NOTE

It is possible to simulate a middle button click by pressing the left and right buttons together on a two-button mouse. However, please note that you must configure your X setup (/usr/sbin/xsetup.sh) so that it thinks you have a two-button mouse, not a three-button mouse, by default. To change the default setting, run the xsetup.sh script. After running the X setup script, three button emulation will be activated when you restart the X server.

More Fluxbox Functionality

At the top of each application window, you should see four buttons. On the left side, you can see a button with just a dot (.); pressing that button causes the application to stick to the screen, meaning it will be present in all virtual workspaces. You can see the application suddenly appear in all the cubes in the Fluxter pager. Observe that the dot increases in size when pressed. Depressing the button causes the application to have normal virtual desktop function again.

The buttons on the right side are probably much more familiar. The one with the underscore bar iconifies, which means it pulls the application off the desktop space and into the taskbar. You can click it in the taskbar to restore the application. The middle one on the right with the box-shaped icon maximizes and contracts an application. Finally, the big X button closes the application.

Double-clicking with the left mouse button on the top window dressing causes an application to pull up into the titlebar. Fluxbox calls this function *shade*.

Resizing applications is really simple: just bring the mouse arrow to either of the bottom corners of an application, then press and hold the left mouse button down. You should notice that the mouse arrow gets replaced by a right angle graphic. While holding the mouse button down, move your mouse and you can see that the application is changing shape. Unclick the mouse and the application holds the new shape.

Grouping Applications with Tabs

One of the features that sets Fluxbox apart from other window managers is the ability to group windowed applications. This powerful adaptation makes a working environment very space efficient and extremely work efficient. Because of this capacity, Fluxbox is a joy to use, even in tight resolutions such as 800×600.

Figure 3-3 shows an example of a multitab window with a terminal currently being displayed. (Bash indicates the shell that is running within that terminal.)

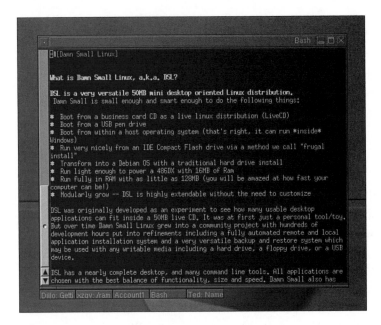

FIGURE 3-3 Fluxbox lets you use tabs to keep multiple windows within a single window frame.

To use tabs, you need a three-button mouse, or a two-button mouse with three-button emulation. You will notice that all windowed applications have a small tab at the lower left of the windows trim.

For your first attempt at using tabs, let's launch two applications. For this demonstration, we will use applications that have a light contrast: Aterm and Dillo. Click the ATerminal icon (upper-left icon) and the Dillo icon (upper-right icon) to open each. Now, take your mouse arrow and hover it over the Aterm tab (it says Bash). Click and hold your middle mouse button.

Now, while holding the middle mouse button down, move your mouse so that it is in the center of Dillo in the second window. You should see a small rectangle move with the mouse. Drag that rectangle to the middle of Dillo and unclick the middle mouse button. You now see Aterm taking on the shape and location of Dillo. Dillo and Aterm are sharing the same space and windowing.

Do you notice that in the lower left of the windowing decor, there are now two tabs? You can change which application is displayed by left-clicking its corresponding tab. If you are using a wheel mouse, you can bring the mouse arrow to the top window dressing and spin the wheel up and down to rotate through the applications. The active application will show in bold font.

When you resize one tabbed application, all the applications resize with it. Also, there is no limit to how many. I am sure it is obvious how this grouping of applications can be very handy if you are trying to work on a project that utilizes many tools simultaneously.

I use the tabs constantly, particularly if I am going to use a small or poor resolution monitor. Instead of having several applications open in small windows, I often stack the applications together and maximize them so that they are in full screen mode. I found it much more efficient to work with applications this way, particularly when I have a wheel mouse.

It is possible to move grouped applications to other virtual desktops the same way I described moving single applications earlier. In addition, you can specify to which virtual workspace you would like to send the applications group by clicking the top border area of the windowing. After the menu drops down, mouse over Send Group To. At this point, you can select which virtual workspace you want by clicking one of the selections.

Mounting Drives and Controlling Volume

Look for the application in the lower-right corner, a volume and drive mounting application that we descriptively call Docked.lua. You will see that the application is basically split into two sections:

- **Volume Control**—The top section is a volume control. Its function is simple: you move the dial with your mouse to adjust the volume. The button with the big M is mute—press it and the sound stops. Press it again or adjust the volume and the sound comes back on. There is also a button labeled dMix. Click it and a more advanced sound mixer launches.

- **Drive Control**—On the lower half of the application, you will see a gray bar with lettering like *hda1*, *sda1*, *cdrom*, or some other variation. These are drives that have been found to be mountable by DSL.

  The lower button gives you the status of the drive. It reads *mounted*, *unmounted*, or *irregular*, with the corresponding colors of green, red, and blue. To cycle through the drives, click the top button. When you see the drive that you would like to mount or unmount, click the lower button. Then, the application either does as you wish or shows an error explaining why the mounted status could not be changed.

Figure 3-4 shows an example of the Docked.lua tool.

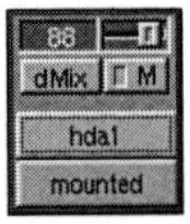

FIGURE 3-4 Change audio settings and mount and unmount drives for the Docked.lua tool.

Drive names in DSL have a logical order; you just have to learn how the labeling works:

- hda is the first IDE drive (primary master).
- hdb is the second IDE drive (primary slave).
- sda is the first SCSI or USB drive.
- sdb is the second SCSI or USB drive.

For the partitions, the convention is to add a number to the end of the drive. Here are few examples:

- hda1 is the first partition on the first IDE drive.
- hdb5 is the fifth partition on the second IDE drive.
- sda2 is the second partition on the first SCSI or USB device.

Often, hda1 corresponds to the C drive in Microsoft Windows. hdb1 could be your D drive in Microsoft Windows, but the labeling convention in Microsoft Windows is a bit of a mystery.

USING THE JWM WINDOW MANAGER

Damn Small Linux also comes equipped with another window manager, called JWM—actually, the version of JWM in Damn Small Linux is cut down a bit and has some of the features stripped out. JWM looks more familiar to people who are coming from a Microsoft Windows environment. JWM has a task bar and a Start button. If you find the wide-open world of Fluxbox too overwhelming, try JWM. It is also worth noting that JWM is very resource efficient, so if you have a very low power computer, you may want to give JWM a try. To try JWM, click on "Switch to JWM" on "WindowManager" sub-menu on the Fluxbox menu.

Using DSL Applications

In this section, I divide applications into two classifications—GUI and terminal-based. Terminal applications may be used within a windowing environment in a terminal emulator, such as Aterm, or could be used without X if you happen to be in text mode. So, if you are ever on a computer that cannot run Fluxbox and you are forced to work in command mode, you can take solace in the fact that DSL does not leave you hanging.

Okay, let's start looking at the applications.

X-Based Applications

In this first section, we are outlying the X-based applications found in Damn Small Linux. Here, you can find some applications that are commonplace among most Linux distributions, and some that you may be trying out for the first time in Damn Small Linux.

Aterm—The AfterStep Terminal Emulator

Aterm is our terminal emulator of choice for its compact size and ability to customize. Despite its small size, Aterm is full-featured. It is capable of pseudo-transparency without being a resource hog. Aterm is capable of tinting, font color alterations, as well as shade settings. Another eye-candy trick is that the contents of the terminal will fade when off focus.

 TIP

If you want to adjust the font size, try Shift+KeyPad_Add and Shift+Keyad_ Subtract. If you want a large font that is easy to read, start Aterm from the command line by typing `aterm -fn 10x20`.

For more information on Aterm, refer to the Aterm home page (`http:// www.afterstep.org/aterm.php`).

The Ace of Penguins

Ace of Penguins is a suite of solitary games including FreeCell, Golf, Mastermind, Merlin, Minesweeper, Pegged, Solitaire, Taipedit, Taipei, and Thornq. I have played these games way too much. I advise staying away if you want to remain productive.

AxY FTP a GUI FTP Client for X

Authored by Alexander Yukhimets, the version of AxY FTP we are running in DSL is a GTK1.2 port. AxY FTP should have a very familiar interface for many, because it relies on the classic two-panel design made popular in the 1990's, ws_ftp (a Microsoft Windows program). AxY FTP has a convenient session manager panel that can save your accounts and passwords. It also supports recursive downloads, recursive uploads, and passive and nonpassive data transfers.

Beaver—Our GUI Text Editor

Beaver was originally developed by Damien Terrier. Its name is actually an acronym for *Beaver is an Early AdVanced EditoR*, which plays on the UNIX joke of having a self-recursive name. In DSL, it is simply the most feature-rich editor available in its size range. It packs features that browsers more than double its size lack.

Beaver is very easy; it has multiple tabs and the ability to do search and replace over multiple buffers. Coders find the optional color highlighting easy on the eyes. Casual desktop users are familiar with the typical key bindings for cut and paste.

Another critical feature that Beaver has is the capability to undo and redo operations. For coders, Beaver's capability to turn on and off word-wrap is a must. Some of the lesser-known features of Beaver include its capability to convert text documents in and out of DOS format. This is handy if you are sharing a file between platforms. Beaver is also capable of converting text case to uppercase, lowercase, or proper case (the first letter of every word is capitalized). The version of Beaver in DSL is 0.2.7 and has been updated with bug fixes.

For more information on Beaver, you can visit the project's website at the following address: http://www.nongnu.org/beaver.

Calcoo—An RPN and Algebraic Calculator

This GTK1.2-based calculator is full-featured, yet only 108Kbytes. Get more information on Calcoo from its project site at http://calcoo.sourceforge.net.

Dillo—A Very Light Web Browser

Dillo is an alternative lightweight browser designed by Jorge A. Arellano Cid for embedded or otherwise constraint systems. Such a browser is a natural for DSL.

The development of Dillo has been very methodical over the years and the project's authors are very careful to write clean and concise code. This means that Dillo has a very solid base, yet it lacks features of a fully functional, modern browser.

Despite Dillo's limited features, the version we have in DSL is highly modified with several patches that greatly enhance its capabilities. Our version of Dillo can do the following:

- Negotiate SSL pages and password authentication
- Render frames and Iframes
- Text search
- Perform GUI configuration
- Support referer data
- Perform user-agent configuration
- Perform gzip compression
- Perform meta-refresh

Users of Dillo will be amazed at how fast it loads and how quickly pages render.

For more information on Dillo, refer to the Dillo project site at www.dillo.org. Refer here for details on Dillo internationalization: http://teki.jpn.ph/pc/software/index-e.shtml.

EmelFM—A Highly Configurable Two-Panel File Manager

EmelFM has a simple-to-use interface; bookmark and history lists; multiaction selection for each file type, filename, size, and date filters; a very handy built-in command line; user-defined menu; loadable plug-ins; and configurable toolbar.

In DSL, we integrate EmelFM into our desktop for the convenience of the user. For example, in the Fluxbox menu, we have both user- and root-level options. We also built in a MyDSL button for extension management and have emelFM use native DSL applications as the default whenever applicable.

Basically, we configure EmelFM so that it works in our lightweight environment; thus, it will call Aterm instead of Xterm, as well as our Wordview Lua program (written by Robert Shingledecker) to view Microsoft doc files. Figure 3-5 shows an example of an EmelFM window.

For details on emelFM, visit its project site at http://emelfm.sourceforge.net/.

Firefox—The Open Source Web Browser from the Mozilla Foundation

Firefox is a very robust and capable browser. It is by far the largest application in Damn Small Linux, yet we do make provisions to get the size down, including building against GTK1.2 and having our version use system fonts.

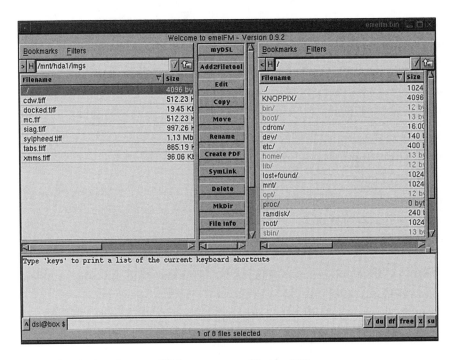

FIGURE 3-5   Use emelFM to manage files in DSL.

Firefox is very capable; it has a full Javascript interpretation engine, renders SSI, does FTP, authentication, animated GIFs, tabbed browsing, is Java ready, and can do just about anything else you would need from a browser.

See the Firefox home page (www.mozilla.com/en-US/firefox) for further information.

gPhone—A VoIP Application

gPhone, or Gnome-a-Phone, is an IP-to-IP Internet telephone that uses librtp for audio compression. Although gPhone isn't designed to make calls to public telephones (as the Skype service described in Chapter 14, "Using Skype VoIP Service in DSL," can), it does include nominal support for RTP/RTCP. This enables gPhone to allow you to talk to other Internet telephone services that support those protocols.

For more information on gPhone, visit http://gphone.sourceforge.net.

gRun—A GTK-Based Run Dialog

The gRun run dialog is a simple application written for GTK1.2 that allows you to launch applications without the need for the Aterm window or selecting a menu.

gRun also stores a list of recent usage, so you may select from a drop-down menu to save typing time.

Access via 'Run Program' on root menu.

GtkFind—A File Finder Program

The GtkFind program provides a great front-end to the command-line `find` program. It has lots of options and takes the guesswork out of the command line for those who are uninitiated.

Access via /Applications->Tools->Find from root menu.

Gvu—A PostScript Viewer

Gvu, the PostScript Viewer, is part of the Siag office suite. It is easy-to-use and intuitive. A PostScript (PS) file is a file that is formatted for printing by the ghostscript interpreter. Applications such as Firefox have the capability to save these files for later digital viewing instead of sending them off to the printer. Gvu can magnify sections of the PS document, which makes it very handy for difficult reading.

Refer to this site for information on Gvu: `http://siag.nu/applets/gvu.html`.

Ted—An Easy Rich Text Processor

Ted is an easy-to-use word processor that saves documents in Rich Text Format (RTF). RTF is a standardized, cross-platform markup, readable by many word processing programs, including Open Office, Gnumeric, and Microsoft Word. One little-known feature of Ted is that it can also save documents in HTML and the underlying code is surprisingly clean. The author of Ted (Mark de Does) was kind enough to fix a compatibility issue it had with Fluxbox for us.

For more information on Ted, refer to the following: `http://www.nllgg.nl/Ted/`.

Siag (Scheme in a Grid)—A Spreadsheet Program

When compared to contemporary spreadsheet applications, Siag is truly a compact program, yet it is very robust. In addition to its native .siag format, Siag can also read Comma Separated Values (CSV), plain text, Lotus 1-2-3, Scheme Code, Open Office Calc, and some Microsoft Excel documents.

Siag has hundreds of functions, many of which are Excel compatible. Siag also uses Scheme, which means that custom functions can be written for Siag if you have a particularly challenging task.

For extensive documentation on Siag, refer to the documentation on the Siag development site at `http://siag.nu/online-docs/siag/siag.html`. Figure 3-6 shows an example of the Siag application.

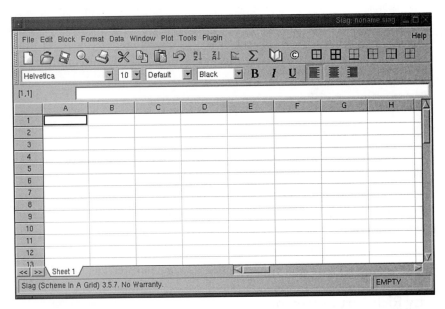

FIGURE 3-6 Despite its compact size, Siag can work with many different spreadsheet formats.

Sylpheed—Lightweight and User-Friendly Email Client

Sylpheed is a great email client. It is fast and very capable, yet very easy-to-use with a very clean interface. Sylpheed is compatible with both POP3 and IMAP mail protocols and can do SMTP authentication. Sylpheed offers multiple account capabilities and threaded viewing options.

Figure 3-7 shows an example of the Sylpheed window. Refer here for Sylpheed documentation:

`http://sylpheeddoc.sourceforge.net/en/manual/manual.html`

VNC Viewer—A Client for the VNC Remote Desktop Protocol

VNC stands for Virtual Network Computing. VNC is a very capable remote desktop application. With VNC, you can remotely manage a desktop for UNIX/Linux, Mac, and Windows platforms.

Refer to the RealVNC site (`www.realvnc.com`) for VNC documentation:

`http://www.realvnc.com/`

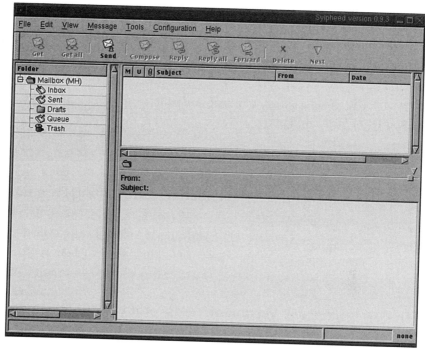

FIGURE 3-7   Sylpheed is a lightweight, but powerful, email client.

Rdesktop—A Remote Desktop Protocol Client

Rdesktop is a client for the Windows Terminal Server. Rdesktop communicates via Remote Desktop Protocol (RDP). The original author is Matthew Chapman, who had to do a lot of reverse engineering and reference obscure documentation to get it to work.

Refer to the Rdesktop home page for further information: `www.rdesktop.org`.

Xpdf—A PDF Viewer That Runs Under X

Xpdf is a viewer for the Portable Document Format, or PDF. It is designed to be small and efficient. Refer to `www.foolabs.com/xpdf` for further information.

XMMS—The X Multimedia System

XMMS is a media player for Linux. Anyone who has used Winamp should be at home with the XMMS interface. In fact, the two applications can share skins. The version of XMMS in DSL is capable of playing Audio Streams, MP3s, Ogg Vorbis, CD Music/Audio, wave files, and MPEG video files.

Please note that the preceding mentions file types! The version of XMMS in DSL is capable of playing not just music files but also MPEG video and music CDs, which makes it a robust media player.

The XMMS home page is www.xmms.org. Figure 3-8 shows an example of the XMMS player.

FIGURE 3-8 Play a variety of music and other audio files in the XMMS player.

Xpaint —A Simple Image Manipulation and Painting Program

Xpaint has some advanced features and can manipulate multiple images at the same time. Although Xpaint is not as advanced as The Gimp, it does work well for simple image editing. For instance, we used it to take snapshots of our DSL release.

The Xpaint home page is http://sf-xpaint.sourceforge.net/.

xTris —A Multiplayer Version of Tetris for the X Window System

Xtris is a single- or multi-player version of the classic Tetris game. It is a true server/client application so one can connect to remote hosts and compete with other players via a local LAN or the Internet. If no other player is available, you can play one bot or several of them to increase the difficulty.

Refer to the following page for more information on the xTris game:

http://www.ibiblio.org/pub/X11/contrib/games/xtris.README

ZXGV—A Thumbnail-Based Image Viewer

ZXGV is a fast and functional image viewer. It can rotate and resize images for viewing. One nice feature is that it can zoom images to fit the window

The ZXGV home page is http://rus.members.beeb.net/xzgv.html.

Xzoom Screen Magnification Application

This is a nice application for people who are visually impaired or just need to take a closer look at something on the desktop. For further information, refer to the Xzoom man page at http://huygens.ca.infn.it/cgi-bin/man/man2html?xzoom+1.

Terminal-Based Applications

Damn Small Linux also has many terminal-based programs. Many new Linux users are intimidated by text-based applications, but many find that some things are just easier to do in a terminal window. If you are new to Linux, do yourself a favor and give these applications a try. You may just realize that their simplicity is enjoyable.

ftp—A Basic Terminal-Based FTP Program

The `ftp` utility is really very easy to use. Many of the navigation and observation commands are the same as regular term functions. For instance, type **ls** to get a list of files available in a directory or **pwd** to get your current working environment. If you get stuck, just type **help** for a list of commands. And if you need to find out what a command is, just type help *command* (replacing *command* with the command name you are interested in).

index—Personal Database Management System

Index is a minimal database management system. The author intended Index to be used by those who want to maintain databases of their own personal information. Index is easy to set up and use. Start it by simply typing the index command.

By default, Index begins with four empty databases available. There is a business phone database (bphone), a database for saving your CD collection (cdlist), a database of CDs that you want (cdwantlist), and a personal phone database (pphone).

Type the name of the database you want to use. You can then use Index to add entries (a), find entries in the database (f), and read the database one entry at a time (r). When you are done, type **s** to save modifications, **q** to save and exit, or **x** to exit.

CDW CD Burning Application

CDW is a more friendly way to use cdrecord and mkisofs with its ncurses-based GUI. Although it easy to use after you are familiar with the commands, a user of CDW should reference the README to learn all the key functions. To start CDW, type the cdw command.

Figure 3-9 shows an example of the CDW screen. We have the main README page available at `http://damnsmalllinux.org/docs/cdw_README.txt`.

Microcom Serial Terminal Emulator

Microcom is a Minicom-like serial emulator with scripting support. Microcom is really tiny (14k) because it was written to fit into floppy-based Linux distributions. You can start Microcom by typing the microcom command. Find more information about Microcom from its home page:

`http://microcom.port5.com`

FIGURE 3-9 Copy and burn CDs using the CDW screen.

Midnight Commander File Manager

Midnight Commander (or mc for short) is a very powerful and popular text-mode file manager. Because mc can be used both locally and remotely, it is a favorite among Linux enthusiasts. Old DOS hacks who remember Norton Commander will find MC very comfortable with its two-panel layout.

Figure 3-10 shows an example of the Midnight Commander screen. Refer here for the Midnight Commander information page: www.ibiblio.org/mc.

FIGURE 3-10 Manage files in text mode with Midnight Commander.

Naim—A Console AIM, ICQ, IRC, and Lily CMC Client

Naim is a user-friendly term-based instant messaging and IRC client. You can start it from the desktop (select Apps, Net, AIM/IRC/ICQ, AIM) or from the command line (type the naim command). We have the IRC command in our Fluxbox menu that lets you plug right in to the DSL IRC channel. So, select Apps, Net, AIM/IRC/ICQ, nIRC #DamnSmallLinux if you have a quick question.

For a quick start of Naim, check out http://naim.n.ml.org/quickstart.

Nano—A Simple Terminal-Based Text Editor

Nano is a GNU clone of the well-known Pico editor, though with some improvements that make it more friendly for coding. Improvements include regular expression search-and-replace and auto-indent. Like Pico, Nano is exceptionally easy to use.

Nano's home page is located at www.nano-editor.org.

Netrik—A Minimal Text Browser

According to the authors, "Netrik is the ANTRIK Internet Viewer/Browser/Explorer/Navigator/whatever." Netrik is critical for our net-man and web-dictionary applications. We needed something that could render HTML, yet be small enough to not push out other applications. Netrik proved to be perfect for the job. What amazes us at DSL is that Netrik is *only* 79.3Kbytes in size.

Visit the Netrik home page at http://netrik.sourceforge.net/.

smbclient—A Command-Line Client to Windows File Sharing

smbclient allows you to connect to a Microsoft Windows share network with FTP-like interactions.

For information on smbclient, refer to its man page at:

http://samba.org/samba/docs/man/manpages-3/smbclient.1.html

SQLite—A Small, Self-Contained SQL Relational Database Management System

SQLite is small, stable, embeddable, and fast. SQL comes with a standalone command-line program that can be incorporated into Bash or Perl scripts in DSL. We also have Lua bindings for SQLite via murgaLua.

We have a personal information manager written in Perl, which relies on SQLite for the back-end database management.

Refer to the SQLite home page for more information: www.sqlite.org.

Vi(m)—An Advanced Terminal-Based Text Editor

Many people claim that using Vim is the most efficient way of editing documents. True, the advanced features of Vim take time to master, but after you commit them to memory, so much editing power is at your fingertips, you need not take your fingers off the keyboard.

The basic commands for Vim are really not that complicated. To see a good list of the basic commands, reference this URL: http://www.selectorweb.com/vi.html.

Lua Applications

The developers of DSL are big fans of the programming language Lua (`http://lua.org`). We are currently using a build of Lua that has bindings to the Fast Light Tool Kit (FLTK), SQLite bindings, and networking capabilities.

This build of Lua was developed by John Murga and is aptly named murgaLua after the author. We take advantage of the GUI bindings to develop many tools, desktop utilities, and front ends for command-line applications, such as the DSL Control Panel and the MyDSL Manager.

Figure 3-11 shows a sample of tools that rely on murgaLua. Information about murgaLua may be found here: `www.murga.org/devPages/murgaLua/index.html`.

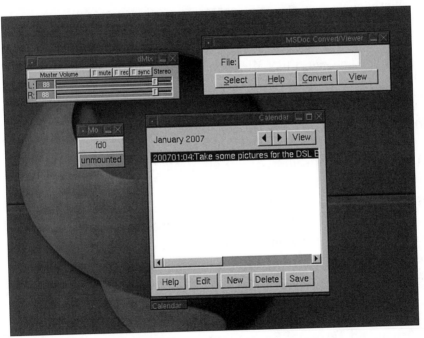

FIGURE 3-11 DSL tools relying on murgaLua include dMix, MSDoc, Calendar, and Mount.lua.

Here is a short list of some of the tools found in DSL that rely on murgaLua.

MS Word Viewer

This is a front end for the command line antiword Microsoft word viewer. With this application, you can select the .doc to view and pick whether you want to view the document as a PDF or PostScript.

Calendar

This clever program, built on murgaLua and PScal, can keep you organized. Calendar does a very nice job of formatting schedules, which get displayed in an easy-to-read calendar format.

dMix

dMix is a GUI front end for the sound volume control umix. dMix is very simple to use and allows one to control the left and right side volume controls independently or sync them up for quick volume control.

Mount.lua

This is a click to mount and unmount storage devices (floppy, CD-ROM, and disk partitions) in this GUI tool.

Docked

The docked tool is used with Fluxbox, which incorporates much of the utility of dMix and Mount.lua.

Daemon Applications

A daemon is a program that runs in the background waiting to be used upon request. Often daemons are perform specific functions like remote connections, or printing.

Damn Small Linux is equipped with four daemons to help interact with the outside world. They are Open Secure Shell, NFS, BetaFTP, and the Monkey Web Server. Please note that all these daemon services are off by default and you need to enable them. Services may be controlled via the DSL control panel or the Fluxbox menu in the System, Daemons submenu. Also note that you have to set up a user password to remotely log in to a Damn Small Linux computer via either Secure Shell or FTP protocol.

Open Secure Shell

Although it is standard on most distributions, many are surprised to learn that Damn Small Linux is equipped with an OpenSSH secure shell daemon. This makes it possible to securely access a remote computer running Damn Small Linux by logging in as user `dsl` or `root`. Using scp (a command-line utility to remotely transfer files between computers), it is also possible to securely transfer files into or out of Damn Small Linux remotely. Damn Small Linux has both the server and the client tools to do remote shelling and SCPing files around. Also, Damn Small Linux is equipped with a very handy utility, which allows one to remotely mount a file system via SSHD; the utility is called SSHFS, and we are big fans of it!

For information on OpenSSH, visit the manual page at `www.openssh.com/manual.html`.

For more information on the SSH Filesystem, visit `http://fuse.sourceforge.net/sshfs.html`.

BetaFTPD

BetaFTPD is an incredibly small (27K) single-threaded FTP server. Its small size made it a natural for Damn Small Linux, and its author, Steinar H. Gunderson, believes that being single threaded makes it more secure while also being easy on RAM. Yet, mainly include BetaFTP easy cross-platform file sharing when one does not have access to an SCP client.

For more information on BetaFTPD, go to `http://betaftpd.sourceforge.net/`.

Network File System

As the name implies, network file system (NFS) is a system that allows one to share files across a network by remotely mounting disk partitions. It is similar in concept to the Windows file sharing system. Damn Small Linux has NFS-Common, which provides a tool set that allows you to use the NFS protocol.

Developer's note: In many ways, using SSHFS with Secure Shell can be used as an alternative to NFS. Many find it easier to use and more secure.

You can find an NFS howto page at `http://nfs.sourceforge.net/nfs-howto/ar01s02.html`.

Monkey Web Server

Monkey Web Server is a simple and small web server, yet it is easy to configure and supports server side scripting. We include a get started page for Monkey as the default home page for localhost. To see it, just access the control panel and click the Monkey Web button, then point your web browser to `http://localhost`. The server files are located at `/opt/monkey/` if you want to customize your setup.

The Monkey Web Server website can be found at `http://monkeyd.sourceforge.net/`.

SUMMARY

There you have it: an overview of our primary window manager, basic desktop functionalities, and the core of our applications. There is still more to learn about DSL, but hopefully this chapter is enough to get you exploring. One thing to keep in mind: You cannot break DSL when running from a CD. So, don't be afraid to explore, have fun, and get some dirt under your nails.

## CHAPTER 4

Configuring and Saving DSL Settings

One of the biggest challenges in creating Damn Small Linux (DSL) was to make an integrated desktop. The usual integrated desktop environments like KDE or GNOME are just too large. Even Xfce and others were not the smallest available. John Andrews originally chose the window manager of Fluxbox and an icon program called XtDesk. Later, I created GUI configuration programs to give a feel for some integration. Whether you like a Windows-style double-click or single-click icons, it is now easy to set up.

DSL's small size is also the result of John's carefully selected applications. But many of these applications have many different user interfaces. John and I continue to improve the GUI interface programs. The purpose is to provide a common, consistent user interface.

DSL also continues to support CLI or command-line interface programs. Therefore, an extra challenge in creating these new GUI programs was to continue to support the CLI versions. Not every conceivable configuration will be covered here. Many programs' setups can be found at their respective home sites. Of course, all the custom applications and GUI interfaces created by John and me will be thoroughly covered.

This chapter will cover most of the basic aspects of configuring DSL. Topics covered will be the backup and restore, desktop, connecting to the Net, printing, and web backup. Let's begin with the backup and restore procedure. No use in configuring anything if it cannot be contained in the backup and restored upon the next system boot.

Backing Up and Restoring Your Configuration

DSL being primarily a live CD, or emulation thereof, means that the base system is read only. So how do you save your settings? Mastering DSL's backup and restore method is essential to enjoying DSL without using a traditional hard drive install.

The following section describes how to back up your DSL settings, files, and applications to a single archive file on a local medium (such as a floppy disk, pen drive, or hard disk). If you would like to back up (and later restore) your archive to an FTP server on the network, refer to the "Saving Your Settings on the Web" section later in this chapter.

Backup and Restore—The Basics

Looking at the desktop, notice the DSLpanel icon. It is the most used icon to configure DSL. By clicking this icon, you are presented with the control panel shown in Figure 4-1.

FIGURE 4-1 Configure backups and other DSL features from the DSL control panel.

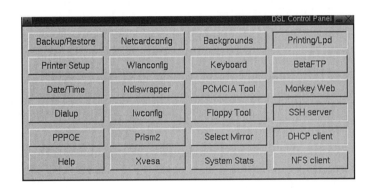

Click the Backup/Restore button. Using the Fluxbox menu, choose System, then Backup/Restore. The Filetool pop-up window, shown in Figure 4-2, prompts you for the name of the device (representing a hard disk, USB flash drive, or other writeable medium) where you want the backup to be stored.

FIGURE 4-2 Choose the device that will hold the backup configuration.

When this dialog is first displayed, the Device input area is blank. Therefore, there is no location to place your backup data and you would lose all of your settings. You must enter a valid device. In DSL terms or Linux terms, this usually means, in order of popularity, the following options:

- A pen drive (or other USB flash drive) is usually **sda1** or **sda2**, where the number corresponds to the partition number.
- For the floppy drive, enter **floppy** or **fd0**.
- For an IDE hard drive, the first drive would be **hda1**, **hda2**, and so on.
- For the second hard drive, use **hdb1**, **hdb2**, and so on.

NOTE

Pen drives appear as SCSI drives in Linux. If you have a SCSI or serial ATA hard drive installed on your computer, it may appear as sda1 and your pen drive may appear as sdb1. If you see multiple partitions beginning with sd in the mounting tool on the desktop, try opening each drive to make sure you have the correct one before proceeding.

The home directory is automatically included in the backup, as well as some areas of /opt. The full details of this will be discussed later. For now, click the Backup button and you start the automatic backup/restore procedure of DSL.

I suggest you become familiar with the basics of backup and restore. Start by making a small change to your system and then reboot. This will help ensure that you understand how the backup process works, before you risk losing hours of configuration.

Upon reboot, as long as the device is physically present—that is, the pen drive is plugged in—DSL automatically scans for your backup file. If the backup file is found, the contents of that backup file are restored without the need to further specify any device.

Selecting Files and Directories to Back Up with .filetool.lst

After setting up your new system, you want to save all of your settings. There is a file called .filetool.lst. It is a simple text file of files and directories listed one per line using a full path that the user wants to save/restore. Type **ls -l /home/dsl** to see the .filetool.lst file, because simply typing ls will not show files that begin with a dot (.).

Use any of the DSL editors to change/update the .filetool.lst file. For example, select Beaver, and then type in .filetool.lst to open that file for editing.

The default contents of the `.filetool.1st` file cause the entire home/ds1 directory to be backed up. However, you can choose to selectively back up only certain files.

 NOTE

It is very important to note that the entry /home/ds1/.filetool.1st must *not* be removed from the `.filetool.1st` as this provides for persistence for the `.filetool.1st`.

The default `.filetool.1st` file in DSL 3.3 looks like this:

```
opt/ppp
opt/bootlocal.sh
opt/powerdown.sh
opt/.dslrc
opt/.mydsl_dir
home/ds1/
```

Excluding Files and Directories from the Backup

Exclude files from the backup with the file /home/ds1/.xfiletool.1st. Adding entries to this file excludes them from the backup. Cache and other files are in the default `.xfiletool.1st`:

```
/home/ds1/.xfiletool.1st
```

This file lists exceptions to files in `.filetool.1st`, which means if you have a directory listed in `.filetool.1st`, you can use `.xfiletool.1st` to prevent certain files or subdirectories within that directory from being added to your backup.

This file works by using pattern matching rather than full file pathnames. In this way, you can exclude multiple files with the same name that may be found in separate directories. If you want to exclude a specific file, you can still use the full path to the file. The default file in DSL 3.3 looks like this:

```
Cache
XUL.mfasl
home/ds1/mnt
home/ds1/.jwmrc
home/ds1/.opera/cache4
home/ds1/.opera/images
home/ds1/.fluxbox/mydsl.menu
```

Notice that Cache is listed without a path, which means all files named Cache within directories listed in `.filetool.1st` are excluded from the backup. You can also use wildcards to extend the exclusion. For example, if it lists Cache*, all files whose names begin with Cache are excluded.

Restoring Your Setting

Your backup of selected files and directories is automatically searched for and restored during the boot process. No user interaction is required. DSL searches your storage media for your backup archive based on the order of detected drives that are added to the /etc/fstab file. It checks each disk partition until it finds a backup.tar.gz file in the root directory of one of those devices.

You can override this feature by specifying the device that holds your backup file:

boot: **dsl restore=hda2**

Specifying the restore device actually speeds up the boot process as attached and available physical devices do not have to be searched. However, not specifying the restore boot option means a hands-free automatic boot.

NOTE

If you decide at some point that you don't want to use your backed-up settings, add the norestore option to the DSL boot command. If you want to permanently remove the settings, delete the backup.tar.gz file from the root directory of the device on which it is stored.

The restore option, together with a .xinitrc file, provides the user with much more control of his preferred environment. See the "Configuring the Desktop" section for further information on using the .xinitrc file and other features to choose which settings and applications start up when the desktop is launched.

Now that we have covered backup and restore, let's continue with the desktop configuration options.

CONFIGURING THE DESKTOP

With your backup procedure in place, configuring your desktop to your preferences is a good next step. Start by choosing a desktop interface, then set up icons, backgrounds, and wallpaper in a way that pleases you.

Selecting Your Desktop

Fluxbox is the default window manager used by Damn Small Linux. DSL also lets you switch to the Joe's Window Manager (JWM), if you prefer. JWM offers a desktop interface that is somewhat similar to the Microsoft Windows desktop interface. The version of JWM in DSL is a heavily modified and stripped-down version of the original JWM.

You can change window managers by displaying the desktop menu (right-clicking the desktop) and selecting WindowManager, Switch to JWM. You can switch back to Fluxbox from the desktop menu by selecting Exit, Switch to Fluxbox. (Before switching window managers, keep in mind that this action will restart the X Window system and close any applications you have open.)

You can add applications to open when your desktop launches by editing configuration files in the dsl home directory (/home/dsl). For example, by editing the .xinitrc, you can start up your favorite X programs. You can start non-X programs by editing the .bash_profile and then adding it to your .filetool.lst.

If you need to load additional modules and system-specific required files, you can do so by editing the /opt/bootlocal.sh file and then adding it to your filetool.lst.

Managing Icons

Most distributions have the luxury of using prebuilt integrated desktop systems, or even icon management systems, such as Rox (http://rox.sourceforge.net). In keeping with DSL's "smaller is better" theme, XtDesk icon program was used. The challenge was that, although XtDesk icons were very functional, there were no GUI configuration tools. I created a small Lua/Fltk GUI together with making a few modifications to the XtDesk code to create DSL's own unique icon management tool.

First, let's discuss the standard XtDesk editing capabilities. When you right-click an icon, a small pop-up appears. Sometimes, the pop-up contains alternate or related programs to start and the bottom section of the pop-up is labeled Properties. Clicking Properties brings up a screen similar to the one shown in Figure 4-3.

You can move the box cursor and edit any of the icon properties. The MenuCommand1 option is the alternate right-click way to launch the program. The Status option is custom to DSL and should be used for base application. The additional applications called MyDSL extensions should not use the Status field. Usually, this screen is used to manually change X and Y coordinates, change the caption, and so on.

FIGURE 4-3   Edit icon properties to change how an application behaves.

For more icon management, DSL has its own Icon Tool. From the main menu, select Desktop, then select Icontool (in JWM, select Setup, Desktop, Icontool); you are presented with the DSL Icon tool shown in Figure 4-4.

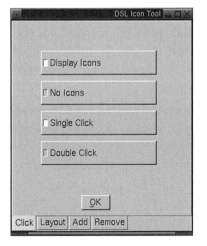

FIGURE 4-4   Choose to display icons (or not) and single- or double-click.

The first panel of the DSL Icon Tool is obvious. Here is where you choose to display icons on the desktop or not. Click the button of your choice and then the OK button. If you choose to have icons, the second set of buttons is enabled and allows you to choose single- or double-click to enable the associated action of the icon.

Indicating the Icon Layout

When the Layout tab is selected (see Figure 4-5), you have the choice to use screen X and Y coordinates or automatic layout. If you want to use X and Y coordinates, it makes sense that you also select Double Click from the Click tab. Using Double Click means the first click selects the icon; therefore, you can drag and drop the icon into the position that you want.

FIGURE 4-5 From the Layout tab, indicate how icons are arranged on the screen.

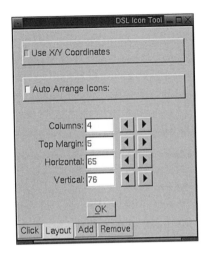

The default settings for DSL are Single Click and Auto Arrange Icons layout. This works well, especially when used with the MyDSL system. Using the MyDSL system and automatic layout makes for a nice system. Otherwise, you find yourself constantly adjusting icons.

The automatic layout provides much control of your desktop icons, from top margin, number of columns, to vertical and horizontal spread. Of course, as with any configuration change, the backup restore makes your changes persistent across reboots.

Adding New Desktop Icons

The Add panel of the Icon tool allows for easy addition of a desktop icon (see Figure 4-6). DSL comes with some built-in generic icons. All icons for the XtDesk icon system are stored in /home/dsl/.xtdesktop. There, you can add more icons from your own collection.

To begin using the Add tab, select an icon from the list. Then, simply fill out the form. Give your icon a label. Specify X and Y coordinates only if you are using the manual layout method. Finally, enter the full path to your application's executable.

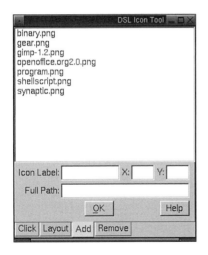

FIGURE 4-6   From the Add tab, you can add more icons to your DSL desktop.

Removing Icons

The final panel of the Icon tool allows for the removal of the standard base DSL's applications (see Figure 4-7).

FIGURE 4-7   Indicate which icons you would like removed from the DSL desktop.

Sometimes, you find a built-in application that you never use. Or, maybe you like a tidy desktop. By selecting from the preceding list, you may remove that application's desktop icon.

NOTE

You are not actually deleting the application when you select to remove it from the desktop. DSL as a live CD or emulation thereof means that the base system is a compressed read-only file. This procedure is really only hiding the chosen icon. In fact, if you look into the directory of icons /home/dsl/.xtdesktop, you see the .hide filename extension being used. To actually remove a base application requires a full remastering. This advanced topic will be discussed in Chapter 11, "Setting Up a Full Remastering Environment."

Selecting Backgrounds and Wallpapers

With DSL having two default window managers, changing background images or even selecting a color means having a custom program. You can access this program from the desktop icon control panel by using the Backgrounds button; or from the main menu, select Desktop and then click Wallpapers to see the DSL Background Selector tool (see Figure 4-8).

FIGURE 4-8 Change the desktop background with the Wallpaper/Background tool.

The Wallpaper/Background tool allows the selection of a new background image. You can select from the list presented or add your own collection of favorites. The image can be scaled to fit your screen resolution or centered as an emblem. By clicking OK, you can see the selected item on the screen. At this point, it is not installed. This allows you to try out different images to see what you like. After you have settled on a choice, click the Install button.

By pressing the Help button, you can see where these images are stored. The suggested method to add more images is to store them in /home/dsl/.fluxbox/backgrounds.

The DSL Background Selector tool also allows for color selection. Pressing the Color button presents you with a color chooser, like the one shown in Figure 4-9.

FIGURE 4-9   Choose colors to use for your DSL background.

Here, you can select from just about any color possible, or any shade thereof, or even type in known RGB codes.

NOTE

As shown in Figure 4-9, the selected blue color is the default background used by the JWM window manager in DSL. If you have selected a background image and want to restore the original background color, use these settings.

Any choice you make with the DSL Background Selector tool persists with the standard backup restore procedures.

Setting Date and Time

To set your system's date and time, from the DSL Control Panel, select Date/Time. From the main desktop menu, select System and then Set Date Time. If you happen to be using the JWM desktop, you can click the time displayed in the lower-right corner of the task bar. After you have selected the custom date application Figure 4-10 will be displayed.

Using the arrows, adjust the displayed values to the correct date and time. Press the OK button. A small pop-up window is displayed asking you to restart the window manager so that the displayed time can be updated on the desktop. This step is only needed if you are using the standard Fluxbox desktop. To restart Fluxbox, from the main system menu, select Window Manager and then Restart. This date application also writes to the system hardware clock so that the correct date and time should persist, even after reboots.

FIGURE 4-10 Set the current time and date from the Date tool window.

Identifying Screen Resolution

DSL uses a very minimal X Window system called TinyX KDrive. It supports both Xvesa 2.0 standard as well as framebuffer. The default boot for DSL is to use Xvesa. As most users use Xvesa, I have created a custom application to select available screen resolutions based on querying Xvesa.

From the DSL control panel, select Xvesa; or from the system menu, select System and then Xvesa. Based on your particular hardware and its compliance with the Xvesa 2.0 standards, a custom application is displayed, as shown in Figure 4-11, only if Xvesa is running.

FIGURE 4-11 Change screen resolution when the Xvesa display server is in use.

The button you see depends on your hardware. Clicking a button followed by OK causes the system to switch resolutions. Your choice of resolution is retained in the normal backup and restore procedure. Be warned that once you click OK, the desktop restarts and any open windows will be closed. So be sure to save your work before you click OK.

CONNECTING TO THE NET

To connect to the Internet or other network, DSL includes configuration tools for configuring modems, wired Ethernet, and wireless Ethernet connections. If your computer has a physical wired Ethernet connection capable of accessing the Internet, it may come up automatically, without your having to do any configuration. If manual configuration is needed, refer to the following sections.

Configuring a Modem

DSL supports dialup modems that are hardware based. Most all external modems are hardware based. There is a class of modems that are not fully functional hardware devices. This class of modem is called WinModems. WinModems have their firmware created specifically to run on Microsoft Windows. So, to Linux these devices don't behave like standard modems.

As you might expect, most Linux distributions have limited support for WinModems. In fact, some WinModems are proprietary. DSL supports the most popular of the WinModems, the Lucent Technologies Ltmodem.

From the DSL Control Panel icon, click Dialup; or from the main menu, click System, Net Setup, and finally Dial-up PPP. A PPP Dial pop-up window appears, as shown in Figure 4-12.

FIGURE 4-12 Select a provider name when you configure a PPP dial-up connection.

To begin the setup for a dial-up PPP connection, click the Config button. The setup goes through many screens. The first one is the pppconfig main menu, shown in Figure 4-13.

The main screen allows creating, changing, and deleting individual ISP provider information. Let's step through the creation of a provider connection. Tab down to OK and press Enter.

The next screen prompts you for a unique name for this connection record. You should use simple, one-word identifiers. For example, your employer's connection information could be called work, or theoffice. Notice that the name must not contain spaces. After you have entered the name, tab down to OK and press the Enter key.

FIGURE 4-13 Begin setting up a PPP connection.

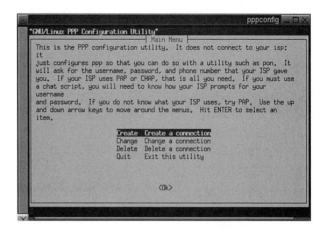

The next screen, shown in Figure 4-14, is very important. It determines how your ISP provides nameserver information. The nameservers provide access to sites on the Internet by name. Without a correctly working nameserver, it will appear that your access is down.

FIGURE 4-14 Choose a dynamic or static DNS service.

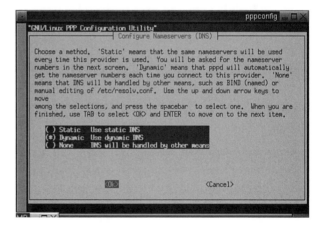

The next step is to specify the handshaking method to verify authentication. Usually, PAP is used and should be highlighted, as shown in Figure 4-15.

The next step presents you with the username screen. In this screen, you should replace the sample text with the login name that your provider has assigned to your account. Most times, this is a single word. Sometimes, it contains the ISP name, such as username@ispname. You should use exactly what your ISP has given to you. Then, you should Tab to OK to continue.

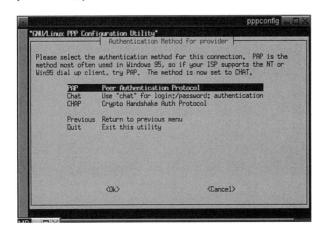

FIGURE 4-15 Most ISPs use PAP to authenticate a dial-up connection to the Internet.

You are then presented with your password screen. Enter the password that was provided by your ISP. You must enter it exactly as provided. Then Tab to OK to continue.

The modem speed screen is displayed; it is normal to leave this screen with the default value. Press Tab until OK is selected and press Enter to continue.

The modem method of dialing screen appears. You should use the default Tone unless you happen to still use Pulse dialing. Tab to OK and press Enter.

Next, enter the number to dial to access your ISP. Do not include dashes or spaces. Enter as all numbers. Tab to OK and press Enter to continue.

The next screen prompts you to search for your modem. Tab to Yes and press Enter to continue. Usually, you have to specify your modem device. This is true if you happen to be using a WinModem. The only WinModem that DSL supports is the Lucent WinModem.

If you are presented with the screen shown in Figure 4-16, use the help text to convert COM ports to DSL required device names. In Figure 4-16, I have entered the DSL device for COM2. Now, if you happen to have the Lucent Winmodem, you type in **/dev/ttyS14**. After you have entered the device name, Tab to OK and press Enter to continue.

The screen shown in Figure 4-17 displays a recap of all your specific data. It is very important to notice that you must select Finished, then Tab to OK and press Enter.

FIGURE 4-16 Enter the Linux device name that represents the COM port connected to your modem.

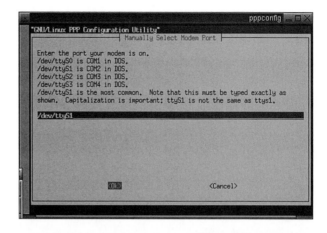

FIGURE 4-17 If your PPP dial-up settings look correct, select OK to save those settings.

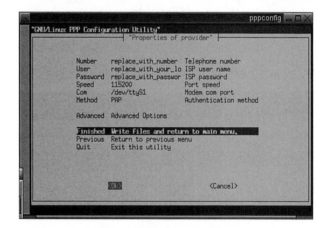

NOTE

All of your setup information is in your backup and restore. You do not need to edit or prepare any other files. Use the simple backup and restore procedure already discussed.

Upon completion of your modem setup, you are returned to the dialup dialog box. Simply enter the provided name and click the Dial button. Another window opens and displays all the messages while the communication link is being established. You do not need to concern yourself with the details of these messages. However, if an error occurs, you need to know what that may be for further assistance either from your ISP or the DSL forums. Near the end of the messages log, there is a display of the actual IP number that you have been assigned for this dialup session. When you see an IP number, the communication link is established and you may begin to use the Internet applications included with DSL.

Ethernet Configuration

Wired and wireless Ethernet connections are supported in DSL. If you cannot automatically connect to a network, the following sections help you to configure an Ethernet connection manually.

Wired Options

Because DSL boots with an automatic DHCP request, often nothing is required to have immediate network access. For those users who have more demanding needs, DSL offers the Netcardconfig program. To access this program, from the DSL Control Panel, select Netcardconfig; or from the system menu, select System, Net Setup, Netcardconfig.

Step through the questions as they are presented. If you are connected to a device or LAN with an available DHCP server, you can select Yes and probably be connected to the Internet. If you can't detect the DHCP server or need to configure your addresses manually, select No. Then you will be expected to enter a static IP address, netmask, broadcast address, default gateway, and DNS nameservers. If you don't know what that information is, contact your Internet Service Provider for assistance.

Wireless

Wireless network access is something that cannot be initially automatically set up because of the requirement of a network access point and encryption key. You should always boot your system with the nodhcp boot option. Having DSL try to connect to a DHCP server could block you from manually setting up your wireless connection, so nodhcp prevents that from happening.

All DSL wireless setup attempts are automatically detected upon a normal shutdown. You are prompted to save your wireless setup. Each custom GUI creates a script of your wireless setup information. These scripts can be found in the /opt directory.

Many older wireless cards work with the Iwconfig, Prism2 config, or Wlanconfig tools. For later wireless cards, however, for which open source drivers are not yet available, you may need to use Ndiswrapper, which lets you provide a wireless card's Windows driver to get the card to work in Linux.

Some wireless PCMCIA cards can hang your system when you boot up on some older hardware. I suggest you look here for a list of wireless cards that have been verified to work in DSL:

`http:/www.damnsmalllinux.org/wiki/index.php/Verified_Wireless_Cards`

Native Wireless Configuration Tools

DSL provides several simple GUI tools to aid in wireless setup with only the most common required fields. If you have more demanding needs, the Wlanconfig program prompts for almost every conceivable option.

You may choose to select Wlanconfig from the DSL control panel or from the system menu by selecting System, Net Setup, Wlanconfig. However, most users need only the simple GUI tools shown in Figure 4-18.

FIGURE 4-18 Configure a wireless connection using a simple graphical iwconfig tool.

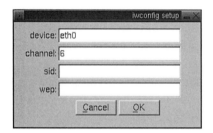

- The sid field is the name of the wireless access point. This can be left blank to use the closest or strongest signal. Otherwise, enter the name of the access point.
- The wep field is the encryption key. If none is used, leave it blank. Otherwise, you must enter the key as colon separated pairs—for example, 12:34:56:78:FF. This key should be a hexadecimal representation of the encryption key entered when the wireless router was configured.

Press OK when you are ready to attempt a connection. A small pop-up displays the results of your connection attempt, as shown in Figure 4-19.

FIGURE 4-19 Add information to identify your wireless access point and encryption key.

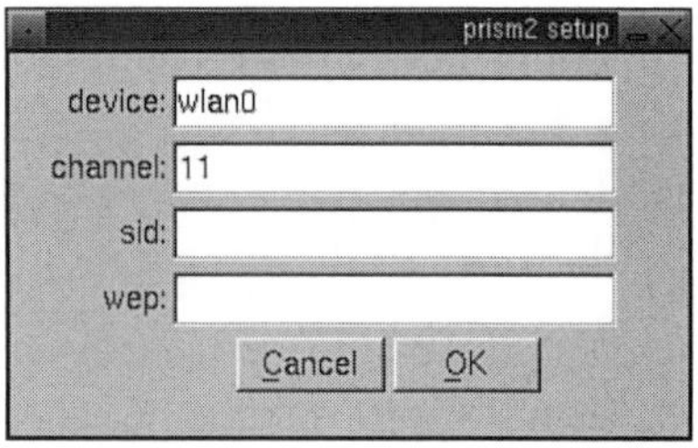

Other Wireless Card Using Ndiswrapper

If you find that your wireless card is not natively supported by drivers contained in DSL, the catch-all wireless solution is Ndiswrapper. Ndiswrapper uses the same drivers that Microsoft Windows uses. The drivers may be obtained from the software CD that was included when you bought your wireless card. The drivers may also be obtained from the vendor's support website.

A very good source for selecting which Windows driver to use is the Ndiswrapper website itself:

`http://ndiswrapper.sourceforge.net/mediawiki/index.php/List`

To open the ndiswrapper setup window, select the Ndiswrapper button from the DSL Control Panel. The ndiswrapper setup window appears as shown in Figure 4-20.

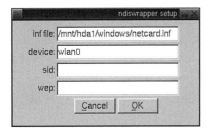

FIGURE 4-20   For wireless cards supported by Ndiswrapper, identify the card's .inf file.

Using Ndiswrapper usually means having two files: an `.inf` file together with a `.sys` file. Often, when DSL is used on a machine that also runs Windows, you can simply mount the drive that contains Windows and specify the full windows path to the `.inf` file. Note that you use the forward slash and not the backward slash, as shown in Figure 4-20.

- The `sid` field is the name of the wireless access point. This can be left blank to use the closest or strongest signal. Otherwise, enter the name of the access point.
- The `wep` field is the encryption key. If none is used, leave it blank. Otherwise, you must enter the key as colon separated pairs—for example, 12:34:56:78:FF. This key should be a hexadecimal representation of the encryption key entered when the wireless router was configured.

Press the OK button when you are ready to attempt a connection. A small pop-up displays the results of your connection attempt.

It is worth noting here that sometimes it is desirable to manually enter the Ndiswrapper commands and test the results of each step. To do so, you must open a Superuser terminal window. From the Aterm icon, right-click to select Aterm as Super User to open this terminal window. Following are the manual steps:

```
# ndiswrapper -i NET8180.INF
# ndiswrapper -l
# modprobe ndiswrapper
# iwconfig
```

Those are the minimal manual commands to see if the Ndiswrapper and two Windows drivers can access your card. If the result of the iwconfig command displays a wlan0, you know that you may proceed to configure the card with the GUI.

PRINTING USING APSFILTER

The built-in printing system in DSL is Apsfilter. This printing subsystem was chosen because it was one of the smallest printing services available.

To begin, you must first set up the printer: using the DSL control panel, select Printer Setup or from the main menu, select System, Printing/lpd, Configure Printer.

The first screen to appear is the license screen. Accept the license by entering y and pressing Enter. You are then presented with a series of screens, one regarding email of the creator of the Apsfilter system and other information screens. You can either accept the offer of email address or you can press Enter to read the information screens. When you see the permission screen for /usr/share/apsfiler, enter y and press Enter. Because you are running from a live CD, or emulation thereof, these permissions have been preset for you. Next, the Add Another Printer or Overwrite the Existing Entries screens appear. If this is the first time to add a printer, enter a and press Enter.

Figure 4-21 shows the screen where you begin the actual setup for your printer. Usually, only the first three steps are needed.

Printer Driver Selection

For this example, I am going to set up my HP4050TN PostScript printer. The first step is to enter 1 and press the Enter key. The Printer Driver Selection screen appears, as shown in Figure 4-22.

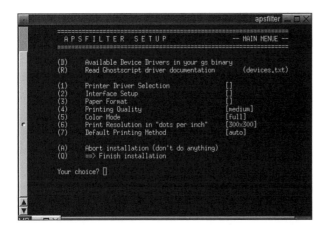

FIGURE 4-21 Use Apsfilter to configure your printers in DSL.

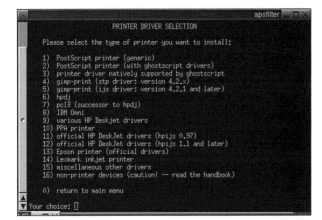

FIGURE 4-22 Select which driver to use for your printer.

For my PostScript printer, I will enter **1**. You should choose an option that is appropriate for your printer. Many users seem to have good results with option 4 gimp-print. You can try several different options depending on your printer, or possibly set your printer to use a standard emulation.

In my example, I enter a **1** and press the Enter key. If you have chosen a different option, you will likely see a navigation screen. This screen displays options available while searching for your printer driver. Again, if you are unable to find your specific printer driver, chances are your printer might provide an emulation mode of a supported printer. After you have selected a printer driver, the main setup screen appears. You are now ready for the selection of the interface. Enter **2** and press Enter. The Interface Setup screen appears.

Printer Interface Setup

The Interface Setup screen, shown in Figure 4-23, is fairly obvious given its choices. In this example, I will use network printing using a JetDirect network card in my HP4050TN. In my case, I input **3** and press the Enter key.

FIGURE 4-23 Choose the interface or device to which the printer is connected to your system.

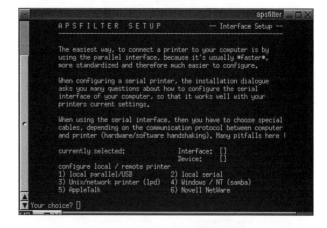

After you have selected a printer from over the network, as a JetDirect printer is, a network setup screen appears, as shown in Figure 4-24.

FIGURE 4-24 Identify the name and IP address of the remote printer.

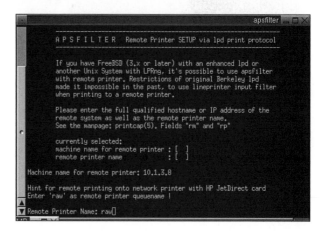

To use a JetDirect or other UNIX network printer, first enter the internal IP number assigned to your printer. In Figure 4-24, you can see I have entered the address of 10.1.3.8, my JetDirect card's IP number. Because I am using a JetDirect card, my remote printer name is raw. If you are using other interface selections, other screens appear for you to select the printer port and are usually much easier to set up than a network printer.

For example, let's assume that you do not have a network printer and instead you chose a local parallel/USB printer, option 1 on the interface setup screen. In that case, instead of a network screen, you see a device selection screen. Because DSL is Linux-based, you select from the Linux options. Typically, printers are connected directly to LPT1 port. So, for a parallel connected printer, you enter a full path to the Linux device on LPT1, which is **/dev/lp0**; or, if your printer is connected via the first USB port, you enter **/dev/usb/lp0**.

After you have selected your printer device, you again return to the main setup screen. Notice on the main setup screen, as options are selected, they appear on this screen. You are now ready to select the paper format for your printer. Select option 3 from the main setup screen.

Paper Format

Obviously, paper format selection is one of the easier selections to make (see Figure 4-25). Select your paper size and press Enter.

FIGURE 4-25 Choose the paper size used for your printer.

The main setup screen again appears with your selections shown.

Printing a Test Page

You have now selected the three necessary options in order to print. But first, you need to test your selections. To try out your selections, input **T** to print a test page, as shown in Figure 4-26.

The Test Page screen prompts again for the letter T and a follow-up y. Enter those values and press Enter. A screen appears showing commands sent to your printer. You should not concern yourself with these details. If the test page prints successfully, press Enter to return to the main menu setup screen.

FIGURE 4-26 Print a test page to make sure the printer is working properly.

If your test page did not print anything, you may need to go back to the main menu (see Figure 4-27) and check your printer interface to make sure the full path is exactly as shown on the screen example and that there are no typing errors. If your printer tried to print but failed to produce a useful result, you must go back to step 1 from the main menu and try a different printer driver. You do not need to reenter all three steps. Only change a single item and try the test page again. If you have trouble finding a printer driver, check to see if your printer has an emulation mode, where the printer itself can be set to appear as a different, usually more generic printer that is supported by Apsfilter.

After a successful test page is produced, you are ready to install your printer specifications. From the main menu, enter **I** as your choice.

You are prompted to enter a name for your printer, as shown in Figure 4-28. The default is lp. If you have several printers, you might want to enter something else.

Be aware that no spaces are allowed in the printer name; you may instead use an underscore. For example, I could name my printer HP_4050_TN. Upon entering a name, another screen is displayed showing the results of the setup. Press Enter to continue.

The name that you entered for your printer is used to identify which printer an application will print to. After this step is finished, you have completed the setup. At this point, the main menu screen again appears and you might want to continue to set up another printer or enter **Q** to quit. Upon selecting the quit option, you are again presented with several information screens. Simply press Enter until the application exits and you are returned to the DSL control panel.

From the DSL control panel, you should select Printing/lpd to start the printing queue. Alternatively, you can use the main menu and select System, Printing/lpd, Start.

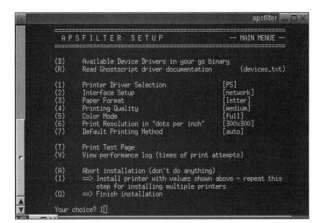

FIGURE 4-27   Check that your printer settings are correct.

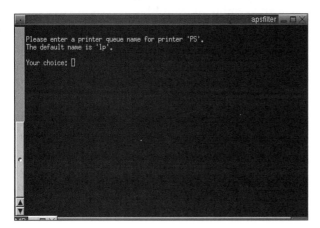

FIGURE 4-28   Enter a name for your printer or use the default lp name.

You are now almost ready to begin printing from any of the DSL applications. Remember when you had to name your printer? How can you specify the printer to each application? The easiest way is to use an *environment variable*. You can open terminal window and type **export PRINTER=the_name_we_gave_our_printer**. Doing this eliminates having to specify the printer name in each invocation of printing from each application. You have set up the system default printer.

Now that you have your printer set up and working, how do you back up the printer specifications? Upon a normal shutdown, the system detects that a printer setup was attempted. You are prompted to save your printer setup. If you confirm, the saving is automatic. Upon reboot, the only necessary step is to start the printing daemon from the DSL control panel.

SAVING YOUR SETTINGS ON THE WEB

DSL has always had the goal of being a nomadic desktop operating system. You have seen the backup and restore procedure. You have seen the configuration of many custom tools. But sometimes, these tools and their settings are specific-to-specific hardware. Some of your saved configurations apply everywhere. Perhaps you would like to save these generic machine agnostic settings to the web, so you can restore them from anywhere that you have web access.

We refer to the procedure for saving generic DSL settings so you can restore them later over the web as a *Webdata backup*. To use the Webdata backup feature, you must have a preexisting and fully functional FTP account.

Begin setting up for your own Webdata backup by looking at the `.webdata.lst` file (`/home/dsl/.webdata.lst`). It is just a sample of what files to back up to the ftp site. The `.webdata.lst` file is very similar to `.filetool.lst`. Just use your choice of text editor to add or remove lines from this file. All items specified in this file are included in the web backup. It is up to you. Just be aware of not including machine-specific data.

The following shows the contents of the default `.webdata.lst` file:

```
home/dsl/.webdata.lst
home/dsl/Mail
home/dsl/.sylpheed
home/dsl/.mozilla
home/dsl/.vimrc
```

After backing up the file `.webdata.lst` itself, the file notes other items from `/home/dsl` to back up. The `Mail` folder is the default location where your mail client (Sylpheed) will save your mail and the `.sylpheed` directory is where it saves its settings. In the `.mozilla` directory, your web bookmarks, history and other web browsing settings are stored. The `.vimrc` file is the configuration file that holds settings related to the `vi` text editor. You will want to add files and directories to the `.webdata.lst` list that contain the settings and data for the applications you use on a regular basis.

As already noted, files that you are less interested in saving are those that are related to a specific machine, since this type of backup is meant to be shared by different machines as you travel to different locations. So, for example, the `home/dsl/.xserverrc` file is specific to your particular display and video card, so it might not work on a different machine. Better to have that sort of information detected and set at boot time.

Once you have your `.webdata.1st` file set up as you would like, use the following procedure to perform the Webdata backup:

1. From the main menu, select System, Webdata Backup/Restore. The window shown in Figure 4-29 appears.

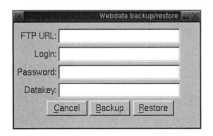

FIGURE 4-29   Choose a location on the web for backing up your data.

2. In the Webdata Backup/Restore window, enter the following information:

   - **FTP URL**—Enter the host address (hostname or IP address) of your ISP's FTP server.

   - **Login**—Enter your ftp login name needed to get read/write access to this FTP server.

   - **Password**—Enter your ftp password for the user login.

   - **Datakey**—Enter a password to be used to access the encrypted data. Type any password you like, but be sure to remember it. You will need it later to restore your backup.

3. Select Backup. The program displays the ftp connection messages. If everything works properly, a `data.des` file will be copied to the home directory for the user account you used to access the FTP server. If something fails, look at the terminal window that opened. It should indicate if you typed the wrong host name, user name, or address, or if the server is otherwise not available.

4. To restore the data, simply run this GUI program again and select Restore. With the data backed up to a public FTP server, you should be able to access your data the next time you boot DSL from any machine that has an Internet connection.

   Be sure that you know your encrypted password; otherwise, no one is going to be able to help you. Of course, the upside to that is that no intruder who gains access to the FTP server will be able to access your backed-up data without knowing that password.

The `.netrc` file is automatically created in `/home/dsl` when running the webdata script and then is destroyed upon completion. This is for security reasons and also not to interfere with the use of the ftp GUI program that you may need for other servers or uses.

I don't think it would make sense to back up the entire home/ds1 as the purpose is to allow you to move from machine to machine and have access to the data that would be machine independent. The main point is to have your data available from anywhere that you can connect to the web.

But as always, you have the flexibility to do whatever you want or need to do.

SUMMARY

Having the tools to set up your Damn Small Linux desktop the way you want is important to making DSL a fun system to work with. Being able to save the files and settings you accumulate as you use Damn Small Linux is critical to making DSL more valuable from one reboot to the next.

DSL offers tremendous flexibility in choosing which files and directories to backup, as well as where you want those backups to go.

Once you know how to do a basic backup, this chapter describes ways in which you might want to configure and customize your desktop. Configurations include different ways of setting up network connections, using dial-up, wireless or wired LANs. It also includes procedures for configuring a printer. Customizations include ways of setting your background, arranging icons, and choosing screen resolutions.

To make your Damn Small Linux system more mobile, this chapter describes how to backup your data to an FTP server on the web. Later, you can restore your data (such as web bookmarks, mail folders, and editor settings) from any computer from which you can boot DSL and gain access to the web.

## CHAPTER 5

Extending Applications with MyDSL

This chapter covers the what, why, and when of the process of adding applications to Damn Small Linux (DSL) live CDs. We call this process the *MyDSL system*. The additional applications are called *extensions*.

These extensions can be added to your system in many ways. I'll describe how to use the MyDSL system from the simplest GUI, which steps you through the process, to the usual downloading via a web browser, and finally how to download and install from the command line.

After you have an extension, you most likely want to save it for future use. I will discuss how these extensions should be saved and the use of a persistent store. Discussions include how to automate a hands-free boot with all your favorite application extensions loaded and ready to use, as well as the tradeoff of hands-free and boot time speed. The last section of this chapter contains a discussion of some common setup and usage errors.

INTRODUCING MyDSL

To expand beyond the software that comes on the standard 50MB DSL live CD, we created the MyDSL system. MyDSL has become one of the most successful features of DSL. You can use the MyDSL system to add software extensions to your running DSL system, save extensions for later use, and even create your own extensions.

Overcoming Shortcomings of Hard Drive Installations

If you have participated in Damn Small Linux forums in the past (http:// damnsmalllinux.org/cgi-bin/forums/ikinboard.cgi), you may remember the *advantage* posts from the forums. These posts discussed how live CD users were always at a disadvantage when it comes to selection of applications. The typical live CD contains the selection of applications that the distribution maintainers, such as John and I, have selected. Their choices may not be your choices.

At the time, it was not possible to add applications to live CD systems. Therefore, most live CD offerings were huge with as many applications that could be packed onto a CD. Users wanting to install additional software knew hard drive installs were the way to go. Besides, that was the way it was always done: Get a CD and install it to your hard drive. After a system is installed, the Debian Apt system is an excellent tool for adding applications.

How is it be possible for a 50MB distribution to compete? During these early days, DSL had many who copied DSL and remastered it, only to offer a few more applications and add a few more MB. Some of the remasters would wholesale copy every new feature that was created for DSL. My thoughts turned to wanting to offer something different. I wanted something that could compete with the slightly larger remasters.

I did not want to be just bigger. I did not want to abandon our users on smaller hardware, or the 50MB limit. But I also wanted to offer *the advantage* to live CD users that it seemed only hard drive installed users had. My solution was to be able to easily add software without the complex remastering process. To allow users to easily create any sized ISO they wanted. This would allow DSL to compete with the slightly larger distributions. DSL would become variable sized.

The Birth of MyDSL

With the accumulated experience of the previous milestones, I set out to create the MyDSL system. I had to keep in mind the less capable hardware that DSL had built its reputation on. I began by leveraging John's breakthrough techniques of download scripts, along with my writeable /opt for shared apps. As proof of concept, I adapted and packaged the OpenOffice.org office suite as the first MyDSL application under the name openoffice.

I created openoffice as a simple gzipped tarball and dropped it into /opt. I then created boot time options to load the software from that package back into /opt. That way, the package didn't have to be included in the base DSL system. It also meant the package wouldn't have to be included in the backup/restore process, which would have been a huge burden to bear every time DSL shut down. I then added a separate software package (oo-user.tar.gz) to hold the icon and menu items specifically for DSL as a live CD and for the default user ds1. This was going to work!

I tried adapting other applications to include in the MyDSL system. Some apps would need a small wrapper script to force the library and bin paths to be under /opt. Still more features were needed to make other apps work. I had seen a DSL user's script that made more of the file system writeable to make the Opera browser work in DSL. I emailed him and asked his permission to use some of his script. Opera was never included in DSL because it is ad sponsored. I broke off the parts that I wanted and modified them to what I had in my mind.

Using the features I just described, I could offer a tiered approach to boot time loaded modules. At about the same time, I became fascinated with mountable applications. I formatted these applications as compressed images (adding a .ci to those files). I quickly changed openoffice to openoffice.ci. This would really help in reducing systems resources as the application was mounted, so it could be used from that mount point, instead of being copied into memory. Later, I combined the ci file and its associated user file into a single file (with a .uci suffix).

Finally, I put together six example modules. Today, they are called *extensions*. I also made a small simple script to quickly and easily create a custom mydsl.iso and burn it to CD. That script and other remastering are covered in Chapter 11, "Setting Up a Full Remastering Environment."

Being able to combine a DSL live CD with multiple extensions overcomes some deficiencies that live CD users face that might otherwise push them toward hard drive installs. DSL emerges as a very flexible, any-sized distribution with MyDSL.

Loading Extensions Dynamically

After the release of sample MyDSL extensions and the mkmydsl custom CD maker, the most requested feature was to load the extensions without requiring the user to make a CD.

John and I were a little hesitant at first. We were concerned because of bandwidth. If users became lazy, they would just download the extensions every time. So, I made a boot time option to specify a persistent store for the extensions. This was to be specified by mydsl=hdxx, where hdxx would be replaced by the name of the hard disk partition on which the extensions would be stored (such as hda1 for the first partition of the first IDE hard disk).

I added the code for dynamic loading. A GUI front end to the MyDSL system was created. Today, DSL even offers more extension type thanks to unionfs, another mountable extension type. Unionfs is a special file system type that allows users to add or change files anywhere in the file system, instead of just the /opt and /home/ds1 directories. With unionfs, changes to the DSL file system are stored in a special directory (usually in RAM) named /ramdisk that is overlayed on the entire file system.

Exploring the MyDSL Software Bazaar

The MyDSL system has become a huge success. MyDSL offers four extension types. Two of them are mountable. Because the MyDSL extensions are mounted, instead of being loaded into RAM, even users with low-memory systems can enjoy the advantage of using these extensions.

The process of creating MyDSL extensions was made public so that the community of DSL users could join in the fun and feeling of ownership by sharing the software packages they create. In fact, this was also a design goal. John and I would stay focused on the core DSL, only creating and providing infrastructure that the community would need.

Many members of the DSL user community have contributed many software titles as MyDSL extensions. These applications are usually repackaged from Debian packages, but can also be compiled from sources. Details of this building process are covered in Chapter 10, "Adding Applications and Creating Shareable Extensions."

For the user of the MyDSL system, it is an easy graphical click-and-load method of installation. In fact, most find it easier to add software using MyDSL than many other package management systems.

Although hard drive installed users may use the features of MyDSL, there is no uninstall feature. Having no uninstall feature isn't a problem when you run DSL from a live CD because you can remove the extension from the pen drive or hard disk where the extension is stored. The next time you reboot, the extension will be gone. For a hard drive install, there is no easy way to remove extensions after they're installed.

 NOTE

Hard-drive-installed systems should continue to use the full Debian package management system for adding and deleting software. MyDSL was designed for live CD and emulations thereof.

From this point, all of my discussion is from the point of view of running a live CD or emulation to work with the MyDSL system. I will start with the most automatic and therefore recommended way. Because the MyDSL extensions are hosted on various mirrors on the Internet, you must have a working Internet connection.

Using Desktop Icon for Easy Point-and-Click Access

On the standard DSL desktop, you will see the MyDSL icon. That icon is your entry point to adding software that is packaged for the MyDSL system.

Using the Desktop Icon

Click the MyDSL desktop icon to access the graphical user interface of the MyDSL system. Figure 5-1 shows an example of that icon.

 FIGURE 5-1   The MyDSL desktop icon.

Occasionally, you may see the Extension tool with a blank screen, rather than displaying available extensions. The cause of this could be that you are not connected to the Internet. If you have a working Internet connection, it is most likely that the configured MyDSL download mirror cannot be accessed. If this is the case, you can access the DSL panel to select a different mirror server to use. See the "Changing Download Repository Mirror" section discussed in this chapter.

Displaying the Extension Tool

If DSL can connect to a working repository, the MyDSL Extension tool displays all the software categories available from the online repository. Categories include the testing area, as well as a browser for loading extensions stored on a local disk. Figure 5-2 shows an example of the MyDSL Extension tool.

MyDSL Extension Tool		
Apps	Multimedia	Themes
Games	Net	UCI
UNC	Gtk2	System
WM_Apps	Testing	Load Local

FIGURE 5-2   Display available software categories from the Extension tool window.

The following is a list of categories that appear in the MyDSL Extension tool window:

- **Apps**—General category of applications.
- **Multimedia**—Applications for audio and video playback and editing.
- **Themes**—Packages to help customize the look and feel of your desktop.
- **Games**—Yes, you can play games on Linux…
- **Net**—Anything related to networking and the web.

- **UCI**—General category of self-contained mountable applications.
- **UNC**—General category of Unionfs mountable applications.
- **Gtk2**—Applications that require the Gtk2 runtime.
- **System**—Tools and utilities for managing, tweaking, and monitoring your system.
- **WM_Apps**—Alternative window managers and tools specific to window managers.
- **Testing**—General category of newly created extensions (use caution).
- **Load Local**—Opens a typical file browser to extensions saved on your drives.

> **NOTE**
>
> The testing area includes newly submitted packages from the DSL user community. These packages should be considered experimental and need testing and feedback before they are moved into the regular area. Use with extreme caution.

In addition to these 12 categories for extension classification, there are four extension types:

- `tar.gz` is the simplest type. It must install to the only native writeable area for DSL. This means it must unpack to /opt and therefore must be self-contained.
- `.dsl` is also based on the use of the `tar` command. However, this extension type causes much of the file system to become writeable.

> **NOTE**
>
> In earlier DSL versions (legacy boot), only /home, /opt, and /tmp directories were writeable. Most of the remaining file system was mounted read-only. Because the .dsl extension types are simply extracted to the root of the file system, much more of the file system potentially has to be writeable for those installs to work. Therefore, installing a .dsl extension causes a check that the system script `mkwriteable` has been run to make the whole file system writeable.

- .uci type extensions are compressed loop images that are self-contained and mount under the /opt directory. All tar.gz extensions can easily be made into a uci type.

- .unc represents our latest extension type. Extensions of this type can only be used on later versions of DSL that support the unionfs file system. These extensions are compressed cloops that mounts into the base file system.

Don't worry about fully understanding these extension types. Only know that both UCI and UNC are the preferred types. Both of these are mounted and therefore use considerably less system resources than the other two. Because these extension types are mounted, you can return your system to a pristine state by simply unmounting the extensions or rebooting. This is true no matter which type of the many installation types DSL offers is being used. You can save even more /ramdisk space by storing your UCI and UNC extensions on your hard disk or pen drive.

The tar.gz and .dsl should really only be used if no other version of the extension is currently available and your system has the resources to support them. Because the tar.gz and .dsl types copy all files from the extension file to separate locations in the file system, a low memory system can quickly run out of space in /ramdisk, as well as run out of inodes (one is consumed for each file and directory).

Now, let us continue with the normal procedure to use and enjoy the MyDSL system.

Choosing and Getting Extensions

When you click one of the extension categories, an extension browser opens and displays a list of all available MyDSL packages in that category. For example, click the UCI category to see the list of UCI extensions shown in Figure 5-3.

FIGURE 5-3   The Extension browser panel lists available software extensions.

Clicking one of these packages displays its info file providing information about the extension. This includes the name and web address of the program's creator, a brief description of the program, and any additional info that might be needed to run the program. To follow along with our example, click xmahjongg.uci.info. An info page for the Xmahjongg software extension appears, as shown in Figure 5-4.

FIGURE 5-4
MyDSL extension info panel.

It is very important to always look in the Comments section to see if there are any prerequisite software packages that need to be installed prior to this one. In this case, there are no other packages required.

At this point, you could click the Cancel button and continue to browse the UCI repository. But to continue with this example, let's proceed to download. Click the Download button to start the download and installation process.

Application Download Dialog Box

Next, a dialog box is displayed, requesting the directory where the application will be downloaded. This directory must exist on your system and the user dsl must have write privileges. It is usually desirable to use the default /tmp directory to save the extension (see Figure 5-5).

The file will be downloaded into this directory and will be verified for integrity, using the md5 checksum file. Should another message box be displayed, indicating a bad download has occurred, you will need to try again.

Click the Download button to proceed.

FIGURE 5-5 Choose the directory where the extension will be downloaded.

Viewing Application Download Status

A progress bar displays showing the status of the download (see Figure 5-6). The progress bar disappears when it reaches 100 percent.

FIGURE 5-6   Watch the application download status as the download progresses.

Downloading with the Extension tool also means the program will be automatically installed. This is the preferred way to install extensions, as you are not merely downloading them for later use. When the extension is successfully downloaded, the Extension tool installs and sets up the chosen application, menu, and usually a desktop icon. The Extension tool also checksums the downloaded extension to ensure a good download. If the download is corrupt, a pop-up message informs you so you may try again.

Launching Newly Installed Application

With the extension downloaded and installed, go back to the desktop and bring up the system menu. Not all, but most applications will have a menu item listed under the MyDSL section of them. Some system applications do not need a menu to start, such as the collection of GNU utilities. Figure 5-7 shows our new game listed under the MyDSL section of the menu.

FIGURE 5-7   After installing Xmahjongg, a new entry appears on the MyDSL menu.

Select the Xmajhongg menu item to start the application. Also note that many of the MyDSL extensions automatically provide a desktop icon. Figure 5-8 shows the Xmahjongg desktop icon.

FIGURE 5-8   The Xmahjongg icon is added to your desktop to start the application.

When an extension provides a desktop icon, simply click to launch the application. Also remember to right-click the icon to see if other application options are available. Figure 5-9 shows a successful start of the Xmahjongg application.

Accessing Locally Stored Extensions with the MyDSL Extension Tool

MyDSL extensions that are stored on a local hard disk or pen drive can also be installed with the Extension tool. The Load Local button opens a file browser with which you can locate and install an extension from any mounted disk. Figure 5-10 shows this Load Local MyDSL Extension window.

FIGURE 5-9
Successful launch
of the Xmahjongg
application.

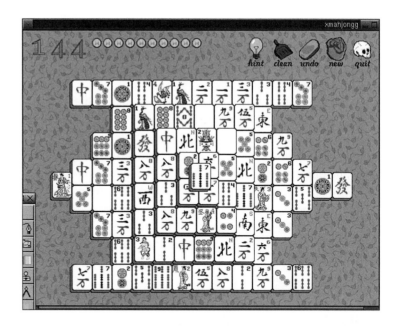

FIGURE 5-10 Find and
choose extensions from local
disks to install in DSL.

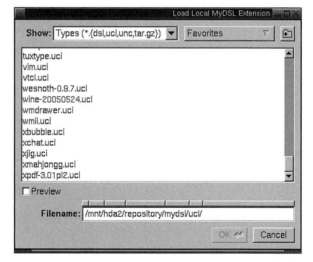

Use of the file browser is just like any typical file browser. Of course, any physical devices must be mounted before any files can be displayed. In the preceding figure, I show that drive hda2 is mounted on the /mnt directory and I have navigated to the same UCI collection. It is just that this is now accessing my local drives. In this case, use of the local extension browser does not need access to the Internet.

CHANGING DOWNLOAD REPOSITORY MIRROR

Damn Small Linux is hosted at many sites on the Internet. The main one is Ibiblio (`http://distro.ibiblio.org`). Ibiblio is the default. Ibiblio is also mirrored (which is transparent to the user). Still, at times, accessing Ibiblio can become slow.

Other Internet sites have agreed to also host the DSL repositories. Many of the mirrors may be closer to you. In fact, some may just be faster for you to access. For these reasons, we make it possible to change the default download site. To change the default download site, select the DSL panel icon from the desktop and click Select Mirror. A small dialog appears, as shown in Figure 5-11.

FIGURE 5-11   The Mirror select dialog shows the mirror being used to get DSL extensions.

Here, you see the default Ibiblio site and default protocol. At this point, you can click the Select button to see a current list of mirror sites, as shown in Figure 5-12.

FIGURE 5-12   Mirror selection.

You can scroll through this list and select any mirror. Both mirror name and protocol are shown via their full URL. When you have selected one, it populates the Mirror Select dialog and you can click OK to proceed. Doing so saves your new choice. It is remembered via normal backup and restore procedures.

The Mirror Select dialog is not limited to just the current available mirror sites. In fact, you can type in any site and protocol that you want. The purpose of this is that you may want to host your own private repository on a local server. Perhaps this is a private collection for a home network. This may also be a company intranet, school, or training center.

Accessing DSL Extensions via a Web Browser

Besides using the MyDSL panel, you can also view and access DSL extensions directly from your Web browser.

Getting Extensions from the Official DSL Website

The MyDSL application extensions can be found in the repositories that are linked on the DSL main project page:

`http://www.damnsmalllinux.org`

Scroll down until you see the Download link. Click that link to be taken to the Download page, as shown in Figure 5-13.

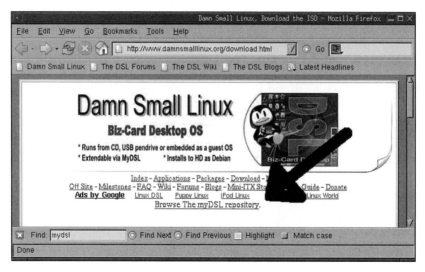

FIGURE 5-13 Get to myDSL repositories from the DSL download page.

Click the Browse the myDSL Repository link. This takes you to the extension area. You can also quickly access the extension area by adding a desktop icon that includes a link to this site.

Getting Extensions via DSL's Help Screen

Web access to the repositories can also be achieved by clicking the Dillo desktop icon. The usual Getting Started help screen appears. An active link to the repositories (Extension Library) is available within that page. Figure 5-14 displays the web interface to an extension repository using the Dillo browser.

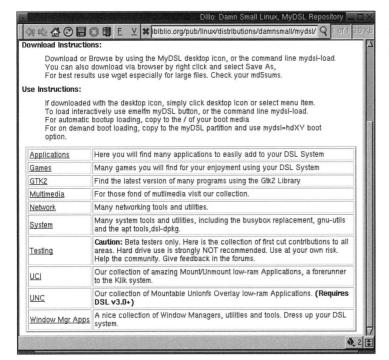

FIGURE 5-14
Web interface for
online repositories.

When using a web browser to access the repositories, getting and installing extensions is not as automatic. The preferred way is to use the MyDSL desktop icon as discussed earlier, as that method automates the whole process. (Just one click to download and verify the extension, instead of searching around on the Web site, then checking and installing it manually.) The following procedure describes how to get MyDSL extensions via your web browser.

1. With the extension repository displayed in your browser, select the UCI link. The UCI extensions are displayed. The columns at the top are Date, Lv, Description, Version, Size, Application, Info, and md5sum. The Lv column is color-coded by extension type. Green or Blue for the mountable types of uci and unc. Yellow is used for tar.gz. Red for .dsl. These colors are meant to provide a quick visual of the system resources and modifications that will be done to your system.

   Green and blue are the safest and preferred types. Clicking the Date heading sorts the extensions by Date. Clicking the Application heading sorts by name. The columns that are critical for a successful download and running of the extension are Info, Application, and md5um.

2. Scroll down the UCI page to find the extension you want, such as the xmahjongg extension shown on the lower-right corner of Figure 5-15.

FIGURE 5-15

Web extension
selection screen.

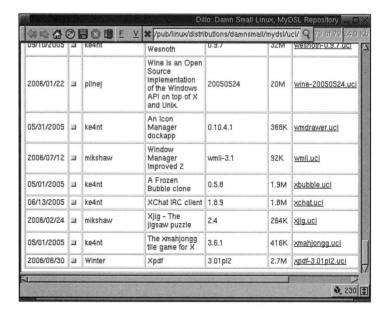

3. Click the info link in the Info column to see the extension's info page, as described in the automated process. This step is critical. You should always read the info file. Use the back arrow to return to the available extensions.

4. Right-click the extension name link in the Application column (third column from the right), then select the Save Link As item in the browser's submenu.

 NOTE

We do not recommend downloading MyDSL extensions to your home directory. MyDSL extensions are large and static. The fact that DSL is used primarily as a live CD, or emulation thereof, implies that a backup/restore is required for saving personal settings. Having large static—that is, non-changing—items in your backup only slow down your system. Or worse, they cause your backup to fail as it may become too large for the chosen backup device. It is best to have a persistent store for collection of MyDSL extensions.

So far, this is all fairly standard for downloading files via a browser. However, there are pitfalls to be aware of. Don't forget to read those info files. Many times an extension requires additional extensions or may have special instructions. Many questions arise from failure to perform the extra step to read the extensions' info file.

5. Right-click the md5sum link corresponding to your selection. After it has downloaded both the extension and the corresponding `md5.txt` to the same directory, you must manually verify that you indeed have a valid download. To do this, use the command

```
$ md5sum -c extension_name.ext.md5.txt
```

The `extension_name.ext` is replaced by the name of the extension you downloaded. You should see OK as the result. If not, you must redownload until the extension can be validated by its checksums.

All of these extra and manual steps can be avoided by using our automated GUI download system.

SAVING YOUR EXTENSIONS

Because DSL was created as a nomadic guest operating system, no drives or devices are automatically mounted. In fact, the default user dsl does not have administrator privileges to have write access to physical devices. The default for using the MyDSL system is to download the extensions to `/tmp`, which resides on the RAM disk (`/ramdisk`).

After downloading and trying the extension, you most likely want to keep it. Recall that MyDSL extensions were built with the live CD user in mind. Therefore, upon a reboot or shutdown, the extensions are gone.

Having a persistent store for your favorite extensions means you must mount a drive and copy the extensions to that location. There are many ways to accomplish this task:

- **File manager**—Using one of the file managers to save files is discussed in Chapter 3, "Using DSL Applications." For this task, you have to select the root version of the appropriate file manager.

- **Save during shutdown**—I did provide a sort of safety net upon shutdown. If you have any extensions still residing on the RAM disk-based `/tmp` directory, a dialog prompts you to save them. If you select OK, the system file manager emelfm opens with root privileges to allow you to save your extensions.

Remember that you can use the mounting tool in the lower-right corner of the DSL desktop to mount the partition from your hard disk or pen drive where you want to install the extension.

Boot Time Automatic Extension Loading

Because you save your extensions in their packaged form to a persistent store, you must specify how they are to be loaded upon your next boot.

MyDSL extensions install automatically during the boot process, either by placing them in a location which is searched by default or by placing them in a directory of your choice and using the boot time option mydsl=*location*, where *location* can be the Linux device name. For example, mydsl=hda1 or mydsl=sda1 represents the first partition on your first IDE hard disk or SCSI hard disk (or pen drive), respectively. The location can even include a full path to the directory (such as mydsl=hda1/mydsl).

First, let's discuss the default locations for DSL. By using a default, you do not need a boot time option and therefore can have a hands-free boot up.

- **On the boot disc**—The first default location is the top level of your DSL installation. This top level, whether it be a mkmyDSL CD (discussed in Chapter 11) or on an emulation type install (discussed in Chapter 8, "Installing DSL in Alternate Ways"), is to place your extensions where the /KNOPPIX and /boot directories are located.

- **On attached storage devices**—The second default location is in a directory named mydsl in the top level of each available attached device.

Using either of these two default specifications means you do not need to use a boot option. The system scans each available drive device looking for a mydsl directory.

> **NOTE**
>
> Specifying the device name can have faster boot times. You don't get the hands-free boot, but it also means that the system does not have to scan drives looking for a mydsl directory.

In DSL version 1.2, I introduced the capability to specify a directory of your choice for mydsl extensions. This can be useful if you have multiple sets of applications and want to choose which set to load for any given session.

For example, you can put your extensions in a directory called /mnt/hda2/games and use the boot option mydsl=hda2/games. You can even have multiple setups. Have another collection of extensions in a directory called /mnt/hda2/office. Then, at boot time, decide to play games or work. This type of flexibility helps save resources on low RAM machines. Remember, everything we do with DSL we keep in mind the older, smaller machines. We want everyone to enjoy DSL.

If you have multiple extension repositories, you can only indicate one at boot time (indicating more than one will cause only the last one entered at the boot prompt to be loaded). After DSL boots, you can add extensions from other directories using the Load Local option from the MyDSL tool.

Another design goal was to make an *optional* menu of rarely used extensions. You can create a directory called optional in a subdirectory of the mydsl directory. Extensions that are stored under this directory are not automatically loaded, but instead are listed in a separate menu section in the MyDSL desktop menu under the category Install Optional Extensions. This gives you quick access to installing these extensions at any time during your session.

Optional Command-Line Extension Access

Besides offering nice and simple GUI tools or the usual web access, I also was sure to allow the use of command-line tools. These tools can be used in your own custom scripts to further automate access to the MyDSL repositories. These tools could also be used to set up and install in a command-line-only environment. You may choose to run DSL without the X windows system. Of course, you must be careful to read the extension's info file to see that it can run without X.

These tools also allow the user who is comfortable with the CLI to quickly access the repositories. Let's begin by exploring the command-line tools that make up the MyDSL system.

Remote Access via the Command Line

The first such tool is the mydsl-wget command. This is a tool that uses the wget command to download a specific myDSL extension from your favorite DSL mirror.

```
Usage: mydsl-wget full-extension-name repository
```

Full-extension-name is the filename of the MyDSL extension and its extension type—for example, xmahjongg.uci. The repository corresponds to the repositories that I have been discussing. Listings of these repositories are displayed in Figure 5-2 from the Extension tool and in the links as shown in Figure 5-14. If you want to save the file to a specific existing and writeable local directory, you should specify the directory as part of filename, as in the following example:

```
$ mydsl-wget /mnt/hda2/mydsl/xmahjongg.uci uci
```

Otherwise, the file is downloaded to the current directory. Recall the danger of storing extensions in your home directory.

Local Access with the Command Line

The second tool is the `mydsl-load` command. Running `mydsl-load xmahjongg.uci` loads the named extension (in this example, `xmahjongg.uci`). You may also use a full path name to manually load extensions this way. This command is rarely used except in conjunction with the above `mydsl-wget`. It could be used in a scripted way, but with all the boot time load options, it is usually not needed.

SETUP AND USAGE ERRORS

As I stated early on, the community of DSL users creates the collection of MyDSL extensions. The extensions are not an official part of DSL. Only the infrastructure to support for MyDSL is official. Having said that, the community of users is also responsible for the updates and corrections of any problems associated with the extensions.

Sometimes, your system may be impacted when using an extension. If you have just downloaded the extension, a reboot will eliminate it. If the extension is already in a persistent store and part of your automatic loading, you need to remove it.

There are situations when the infrastructure does not seem to be working correctly. Typically, I have found the following to be common situations:

- **Nothing happens or a blank screen**—Check that you have a working Internet connection. Also check that you can access the chosen download mirror.
- **Please mount media containing optional dir and try again**—This message usually occurs when running DSL in `toram` mode. When running in `toram` mode, the media is unmounted for removal. If there was an optional directory on such media, the submenu for their installation expects the media to be mounted for access to the stored extensions. This message may also appear when manually downloaded extensions are corrupt, or when system memory may not be sufficient to support all the loaded extensions.
- **Non DSL User error message**—This appears when extensions are trying to be loaded by anyone except the default DSL user. As I have said many times, the extensions are designed for live CD and therefore the single default DSL user. The exception to this is the command-line-only installation as previously discussed.

Summary

To fully experience DSL, you want to be able to "extend" your application choices. In this chapter, I have covered the history of the design decisions that made this possible. I take you step-by-step using the various install modes of these application extensions. I share with you not only how to install them, but also how to save them, where and why to save them, and the impacts when they are not used correctly.

Part II

DSL Beyond the Live CD

## CHAPTER 6

Running a Native Pen Drive Install

There are two basic setups for a USB install: USB-ZIP and USB-HDD. Depending on your computer's BIOS settings, one install may work better than the other. Unfortunately, there does not yet seem to be a standard for USB boot. However, it looks like eventually USB-HDD will become the standard. Many systems will boot one setup but reject another. If you have an older computer (i.e., before 2001), odds are that the BIOS is incapable of booting via USB at all. In addition, many systems are just inconsistent. For instance, some computers require that you turn off quick boot in the BIOS, whereas others require USB keyboard emulation to be turned on; other systems will only boot from the USB ports in the rear of the computer. There is also the problem of pen drive incompatibility. Some newer computers that support the USB 2.0 standard will not work with older pen drives that work with the USB 1.1 standard, and older computers that only support the USB 1.1 standard are incompatible with 2.0 USB pens. As you can see, booting from USB can be tricky! If you find that it is impossible for your system and hardware to support native USB booting, you still have the option of using a boot floppy, which we'll talk about later in this chapter.

It should be noted that in this discussion, all technical references are done from within the Damn Small Linux operating system. That is, we are assuming you are running Damn Small Linux when you are determining the device location for formatting or running our install scripts—not all Linux systems register devices in the same way.

USB BOOT TYPES—BACKGROUND ON THE TWO TYPES OF USB LAYOUTS

This section has an overview of USP pen drive preinstallation formatting, the process for both types of USB installations, and some history as to why it is necessary to provide both types of installations. There are also some types on how to install DSL on a pen drive and run while using an older computer without a USB-compatible BIOS system.

USB-ZIP

This is the format that was used with the Iomega external Zip drives. When we set up a USB pen drive to boot via USB-ZIP, we are emulating the layout of the old Iomega drives; in effect, we are fooling the BIOS into thinking it's booting an old Zip drive. We do this by splitting the USB pen into two partitions and keeping the size of the first partition small. The geometry for the partition needs to have 64 heads and 32 sectors. If you do not know what that means, don't worry about it—our install script does the math automatically.

USB-HDD

In contrast, our USB-HDD format uses a single fat partition. This is a simpler setup that is more compatible with other operating systems that only recognize the first partition on a pen drive.

The method you chose is dictated by what your hardware supports. If you are making a bootable pen drive for portable use, go for USB-HDD as its hardware compatibility is greater than USB-ZIP. Additionally, if your pen is doing double duty as a portable storage device, your Windows operating system will be able to see the full size of your storage device.

Determining the Physical Address of Your USB Drive

When running from Damn Small Linux, most USB drives on most systems will be labeled as sd(*something*), as in sda, sdb, sdc, and so on. If you have more than one pen drive in your system, the first drive will be labeled sda and the second drive will be labeled sdb. The first partition on the first pen drive will be called sda1, the third partition on the second pen drive will be called sdb3, and so on. This will hold true 99% of the time, but to avoid the confusion, just keep one USB device in your computer while running the install script.

TIP

When preparing to install Damn Small Linux into a pen drive, boot from the CD with the pen already plugged in. This way, the device will be autodetected in the boot process and will be recognized in dmesg and /etc/fstab, as well as the mountapp, which relies on the data from it.

Both the USB-ZIP and USB-HDD install scripts have the option of listing available USB storage devices. If you are uncertain of your pen drive's logical location, invoke this option in the script for piece of mind. If you accidentally format the wrong drive, all the data on that drive may be lost.

If you are going to run cfdisk ahead of time, you need to know your device *before* you run the install script. To do that, you need to look at the output from dmesg.

Practical Prep for a USB Install

Before you do anything, you need to know how your system displays your USB pen to Damn Small Linux.

I have done a lot of USB installs and one thing that I always do is run cfdisk on the device ahead of time. Sometimes, this step is not needed, but I have found that setting up a fresh partition table seems to make the failure rate go down and speed up the booting process. I've read that if a user messes with the indigenous partition of a pen drive, he may damage the device and make it unusable; however, I have never had this happen to me with all the pens I have formatted for the DSL store. Some pens' native partitions are really mixed up to the point where cfdisk is not capable of reading them. When that happens, I start cfdisk with the flag -z, meaning start with a zero partition table. Using cfdisk, I create a single table that is marked as FAT16—this ensures that the pen is partitioned properly and that the USB install scripts can do their job.

For further reading on cfdisk, visit:

```
http://www.linux.org/docs/ldp/howto/IBM7248-HOWTO/cfdisk.html
```

I would like to take a moment to talk to you about the work that went into both the USB-ZIP and USB-HDD scripts. Robert put a lot of work into field testing these scripts before they went into the Damn Small Linux ISO. Also, everything you need to get Damn Small Linux running from a pen drive is included in our little 50MB base distribution. So, there is no need to be connected to the Internet and download additional files. Fortunately for Damn Small Linux users, the multistep process has been condensed into answering a few questions.

Boot: Install

There are two ways to run the scripts outlined in this chapter: one way is via a terminal window from within the DSL desktop and the other is via a shell script written specifically to be run as a boot option for installation purposes. The examples in this chapter were completed in a term window from the desktop so that I may show you screen images; however, running the boot install option has some advantages.

The following are the benefits:

- It is faster. By not booting to a full desktop, the startup time is diminished.
- It uses less RAM—again, no desktop overhead.
- If you need to make a boot floppy, there is no need to manually download anything—the script takes care of that.

To access the installation script, type **install** at the boot prompt.

After the boot process, the screen promptly displays the install application. The display look much like what you see in Figure 6-1.

FIGURE 6-1 The install script simplifies USB installations.

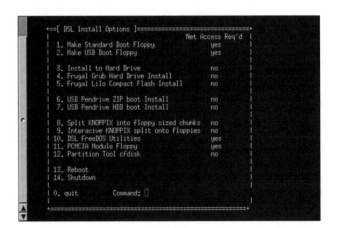

USB-HDD

Before you get started on the USB-HDD install, make sure your pen drive is ready to go by creating a single FAT16 partition using cfdisk as outlined in the preceding section. After that is established, select the USB-HDD script by navigating to Apps -> Tools -> Install to USB Pen Drive and clicking For USB-HDD Pen Drive; or if you are running the boot install script, type **7** and then press Enter/Return. You will be greeted by the USB-HDD install script with a quick synopsis of what is needed to complete a USB-HDD install.

You should now see a terminal window with a dialog that looks a lot like that shown in Figure 6-2.

FIGURE 6-2 The USB-HDD installation script opening dialog.

Let's run through the various parts of the dialog as it is displayed.

1. Your BIOS must support USB-HDD booting.

As mentioned in the beginning of this chapter, you need to determine if your system's BIOS supports USB-HDD booting. Many systems do not, but more and more newer computers do support this method of booting.

2. A single FAT partition will be made.

This is the big difference between a USB-HDD and a USB-ZIP install. The partition table is simple for USB-HDD, with no need to set up an arbitrary partition table to trick the BIOS into thinking it is booting a Zip drive.

3. Do not have your pendrive mounted.

Please don't! You may potentially damage your pendrive if you run this script while mounted.

Next there is a warning that Damn Small Linux is not responsible for any hardware damage or data loss—you are proceeding fully responsible for your actions, knowing that if anything is damaged, the developers of DSL cannot take responsibility. If you are uncomfortable with being responsible for your own actions running this script, then just go ahead and close the window!

Still there? Cool! Let's keep going....

The very next line reads:

`Display your USB storage device information log?`

Type **y** and press Enter. You should see a nicely formatted readout with the pen drive's physical location highlighted in green, as displayed in Figure 6-3.

FIGURE 6-3   The pen drive location is highlighted in green.

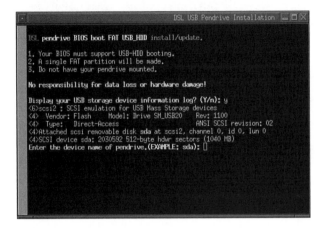

You already should have a good idea of how your pen drive is seen in Damn Small Linux because you took the time to find the device earlier before you ran cfdisk—the preliminary step I recommended in the beginning of the chapter. Hopefully, this printout confirms your previous information.

If all the indicators are coinciding and it looks like your pen drive is actually being recognized as a device you expected, go ahead and enter the device name (in the figure, the device is recognized as sda, so in this example, you would type in **sda** and press Enter). Please note that there is no default answer to the questions and that you will need to supply the script with the information.

The next dialog asks if this is an upgrade—meaning that you are *reinstalling* Damn Small Linux on your pen drive—whereas an install means that you are installing Damn Small Linux onto your pen drive for the very first time. If you are upgrading, type **u** and press Enter. If this is a new installation, type **i** and then press Enter.

Next, the script asks if you are installing DSL from a [LiveCD], a [F]ile (meaning an iso you downloaded), or from the [W]eb (meaning that the script will download the latest iso for you automatically). If you choose the LiveCD option, you do not need an Internet connection nor do you need to download any extra files.

Next you will be presented with a question about drive location, as shown in Figure 6-4.

FIGURE 6-4 Choose the location of the DSL image.

At this point, you are given the opportunity to add boot options like `toram`, `ssh`, or `vga=normal`. There are many boot options to explore; take some time to study them if you have special needs for your bootable pen drive as it runs Damn Small Linux. Our defaults are sensible, so if you do not want to take the time to dig into options now, just run with what we have—it will work on most computers. Type in your boot options (if you have any) and press Enter. (To explore the boot options available and how to use them, consult Chapter 2, "Booting DSL.")

Next, you are asked to choose language options: for German, type **de**; for Spanish, type **es**; and so on. Leave this option blank if you want English. After selecting your option, press Enter.

The script now asks if you are ready to proceed. If yes, type **y** and press Enter. It then asks you one more time if you *really* want to proceed with the warning that you are about to destroy all the data on the selected device. This is your last chance to exit the script before serious things happen; if you have any concerns, now is your very last chance to exit the script.

The script is now prepared to format your pen drive. This is the point where all the data on your drive will be erased and is your last chance to back out, as shown in Figure 6-5.

Next, the script formats the single partition on your pen drive, applies Syslinux to the pen drive partition, and then sets up the system image in that partition. If all goes smoothly, you will read "USB installation has completed" in green and all you have to do is press Enter to exit the script.

FIGURE 6-5 The point of no return—double-check your setting before going further.

At the end of the process, the installation script should look close to what is shown in Figure 6-6. After the installation is complete, you are free to close the term window.

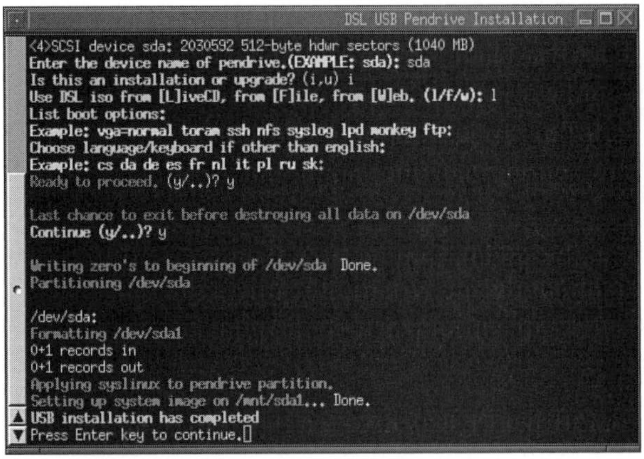

FIGURE 6-6 This is what the script should look like when everything has been completed.

USB-ZIP Installation

After running cfdisk to format your pen drive, it is time to run the install script. To access the script, open the Fluxbox menu and navigate to Apps -> Tools -> Install to USB Pen Drive and click For USB-ZIP Pen Drive. This opens up a term window with a dialog, or if you are running from the install boot option, type 6, and then press Enter. Be sure to read the text because it has important instructions and warnings.

After the script is launched, you will be presented with an introductory dialog, as shown in Figure 6-7.

FIGURE 6-7 The USB-ZIP install script opening dialog.

Let's review the opening dialog.

1. Your pendrive must be at least 64MB in size.

   That is the minimum; of course, today manufacturers are not even making pen drives that small. It seems like the price of pen drives and all flash devices are rapidly dropping as the sizes are ever expanding. At the time of this writing 1Gig pen drives were available for $20. But don't worry about the excess space—you can use all that space in the second partition for extensions or other media.

2. Your pendrive will be formatted into two partitions.

3. One small one for USB_ZIP boot compatibility, and used to hold DSL.

   Numbers 2 and 3 refer to setting up the geometry for the computer's BIOS to recognize the pen device as a USB-ZIP bootable drive in which the partition needs to have 64 heads and 32 sectors as the operational space for the first partition.

4. The remaining partition will be used for backup & extensions.

   The second partition is automatically used for back up of your home directory and any other files or directories that you deem necessary and add to your filetool.lst. In addition, it is the default home for your MyDSL extensions while booting off of your pen.

Take heed of the warning and make sure you don't have the pen drive mounted. If you do, exit the install script, unmount your pen drive, and then relaunch the install script.

If everything looks okay, you are ready to begin the install process. Type **y** to get started.

In the next dialog in the USB-ZIP install script, you are asked if you would like to see USB storage device information. Unless you are completely certain of the device location, you should type **y** and verify the location. The script greps information from dmesg, probes it for SCSI emulation, and displays the information in a way that is easy to read. If all looks good, the device will be highlighted in green.

With your pen drive's physical location verified, the script now asks you if this is a new install or an upgrade. If this is a new pen drive install, type **i**; and if it is an upgrade (meaning you already have Damn Small Linux working on this pen drive and you want to reinstall or upgrade the version of Damn Small Linux you are using), type **u**.

Before the script proceeds, it needs to know if you are installing DSL for the first time or are upgrading. The dialog is shown in Figure 6-8.

FIGURE 6-8 After the pen drive location is displayed, you are asked if you want to upgrade or install.

In the very next step, you are asked what the target device is. Look at the data from the dmesg probe that the script completed two steps ago, and type in the device location. Be sure to input the device proper and not the full path—for example, for /dev/sda, just put sda.

Next, you are asked: Use DSL iso from [L]iveCD, from [F]ile, from [W]eb. The most straightforward and fastest install is to choose LiveCD. Because you are running from the CD in this tutorial, there is no need to download any additional files. The File or Web options could be invoked if you want to download the latest version of Damn Small Linux and install it to your USB drive without having to take the additional step of burning another CD. If you do want to use the latest ISO while installing from an older version of DSL, you can download it ahead of time and use the File option, or let the script download it for you by selecting the Web option.

Next, you are asked if you want any special boot options, such as toram, ftp, or vga=normal. DSL has a lot of boot options that may be useful or may help boot on specific hardware; however, the developers do choose sensible defaults so our standard boot configuration will work for most users. (Consult Chapter 2 where Robert outlines in detail the boot options available.)

Customization of the boot-up process is possible by adding variable when prompted, as shown in Figure 6-9.

FIGURE 6-9   Special boot options may be entered at this point.

In the very next question, you are given the option of selecting another language for support other than English. English is Damn Small Linux's default language, but there is some support for other languages as well. Booting from a live CD with the language option of your choice *before* you select an option in the USB boot install is a good idea. This way, you confirm that everything is working to your liking with the selected language. Enter your language choice when prompted, as shown in Figure 6-10, and leave blank if your choice is 'English'.

FIGURE 6-10   Enter your choice of language.

The next prompt, as shown in Figure 6-11 (the one in *red*), displays the device that is about to be formatted and written to—this is the point of no return. If you type **y**, the script continues with the install process; and if you type in anything else besides y and press Enter, the script just exits. Double check to make sure the physical device is being displayed correctly, and if you are confident that it looks good, proceed by typing **y** and pressing Enter.

FIGURE 6-11 Your last chance to exit the script before it begins the installation process.

From this point on, the script does its magic. First, it sets up the partition geometry, and then it formats both the boot and the storage partitions. Next, the script sets up the boot loader, boot image, and the system image in the first partition. Finally, the script is finished, and there should be nothing left to do except press a key to exit the program. Your USB pen drive should be ready to boot. At the conclusion of the script, the dialog will look like Figure 6-12.

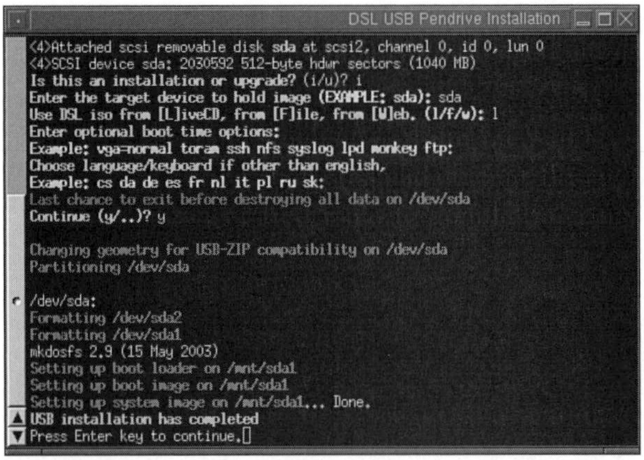

FIGURE 6-12 If all goes well, your script should conclude with a similar dialog.

What to Do When Your Computer's BIOS Does Not Support USB Booting

What if you want to use your pen on a computer that does not support USB booting? You have two options:

- Boot from a floppy with our specially created bootfloppy-usb.img.
- Boot from a CD with a special boot parameter that tells Syslinux to access the system image at the device location where the pen resides.

Creating a Boot Floppy for the USB Pen Drive

The first thing you need to do is download the usb boot floppy image. You can find the image at any of the download sites. One place to find it is at:

```
ftp://ibiblio.org/pub/Linux/distributions/damnsmall/current/
bootfloppy-usb.img
```

If you are running Damn Small Linux (or virtually any other Linux distribution), you can download the latest USB boot floppy image by opening up a term window and typing the following:

```
wget ftp://ibiblio.org/pub/Linux/distributions/damnsmall/current/
bootfloppy-usb.img
```

After using `wget` to download the USB boot floppy image, you can format the floppy disk by issuing this command into the term window:

```
dd if=bootfloppy-usb.img of=/dev/fd0
```

Armed with your newly bootable floppy drive, you can boot your USB pen drive even if the computer you are using has a BIOS that does not support USB booting.

Using a LiveCD to Boot a Pen Drive

The 50MB hockey ring CDs are smaller and travel better than floppy disks. It may be easier for many people to use a bootable USB pen drive and then use a mini CD as an alternative boot media in place of a floppy drive.

You can mimic much of the behavior of USB booting with a boot CD and a pen drive when you are using a computer without the capability to boot from a USB device naturally. We will review a few options you can use at the boot prompt to take advantage of your pen drive.

To use your MyDSL extensions from your pen drive, type the following:

```
dsl mydsl=sda1
```

To use your backup/restore files from your pen drive, type the following:

```
dsl restore=sda1
```

To access the image on your pen drive, type the following:

```
dsl fromhd=/dev/sda1
```

If your CD and pen drive both have the same version of DSL on them, there is no real need to issue the command `fromhd=/dev/sda1`; however, you may want to do this if the version of DSL on your CD is older than your pen drive. By using the `fromhd` command, you do not have to burn a new CD every time there is a new release of DSL.

You also can combine all commands to access the pen drive in virtually the same way as a native boot from the pen drive by using all three commands at the boot prompt:

```
dsl fromhd=sda1 mydsl=sda1 restore=sda1
```

There are lots of hybrid possibilities when a user is traveling with DSL. It is possible to mix and match; for instance, you can choose to use your backup/restore from your pen drive and access your MyDSL extensions from your hard drive, or even pull down an encrypted restore file from an FTP server. To read further on these powerful and useful options, consult Chapter 5, "Extending Applications with MyDSL," for MyDSL extensions and Chapter 4, "Configuring and Saving DSL Settings," for backup and restore options.

After Install: Setting Default Backup/Restore and MyDSL Partitions

Before V3.3 of DSL, the default backup/restore partition and MyDSL location in the syslinux.cfg were hard coded and referenced by the install scripts while booting. Over time, it has become clear that different systems register a USB storage device differently. There are even occasions when a system "sees" the device in one location during the installation process, and then later sees it as a different device while in the booting process. So, steps have been taken to make both types of pen drive installations device independent. The boot process probes available devices for the backup file and mydsl directory. The backup/restore process is now transparent to the end user; however, you need to select your device for initial mydsl extensions once before automatic boot time detection auto saving works.

To verify where your pen drive is located, open up a root term window and type the following:

`fdisk -l`

Here is what a 1Gig pen drive looks like on a typical system after being formatted for a USB-HDD system:

```
Disk /dev/sda: 1039 MB, 1039663104 bytes
32 heads, 62 sectors/track, 1023 cylinders
Units = cylinders of 1984 * 512 = 1015808 bytes

   Device Boot     Start       End     Blocks   Id  System
/dev/sda1    *              1      1023     1014785    6  FAT16
```

This is what the fdisk's printout looks like for a 1Gig pen drive formatted for a USB-ZIP installation on a typical system:

```
Disk /dev/sda: 1039 MB, 1039663104 bytes
64 heads, 32 sectors/track, 991 cylinders
Units = cylinders of 2048 * 512 = 1048576 bytes

   Device Boot    Start       End    Blocks    Id  System
/dev/sda1    *             1        50      51184    6  FAT16
/dev/sda2             51       991     963584    b  Win95 FAT32
```

Saving Extension on a USB-HDD Installation

To have your MyDSL extensions saved and automatically used upon boot the next time, you need to save them in your pen drive's `mydsl/` directory. If you are booting your pen drive in toram mode, it is necessary to mount your pen drive first; this can be done by using the mount.app tool or by entering the mount command as super user in a terminal emulator. If your pen drive is seen as sda, you would type **mount /mnt/sda1**. If you are not booting in toram mode, your pen drive is mounted at cdrom/. So, if you are booting the pen drive in toram mode, you typically want to save your extensions at `/mnt/sda1/mydsl/`, and if you are not booting in toram mode, save your extensions at `/cdrom/mydsl/`.

Saving Extensions on a USB-ZIP Installation

To automatically load the MyDSL extensions stored on your pen drive at boot time, they need to be previously saved at the `mydsl/` directory on the pen drive's second partition, typically recognized as sda2. You can preselect the `mydsl` directory by running the MyDSL app and typing in the path to the directory on your pen drive before downloading. The typical path would be /mnt/sda2/mydsl/.

A Note on DSL-embedded.zip

We offer a bundled package of DSL with Qemu; the details of this setup will be discussed in Chapter 7, "Running DSL Embedded in Windows." However, we wanted to include a quick note about what some users are doing to make their DSL-embedded.zip equipped pen drives also BIOS bootable from within the MS Windows platform. The results are inconsistent, but if you want to try, you need to first download the win32 executable version of Syslinux.

You can download the Windows version of Syslinux from:

http://www.kernel.org/pub/linux/utils/boot/syslinux/

Copy syslinux.exe to the root of your C drive.

Open a DOS prompt and type the following:

syslinux.exe h:

Windows recognizes your pen drive to be h:. If it is a different letter, use that one.

The version of Syslinux used in DSL does not work with very large pen drives. It does function with drives that are 1Gig and smaller. If you have an extra large drive, you may download a later version of Syslinux, which is compatible with drives exceeding 1Gig.

You can find the latest version at

http://www.kernel.org/pub/linux/utils/boot/syslinux/

Developments in the Wiki

Finally, it is worth noting that there are some interesting alternative install methods being developed by our user base. If you are interested in exploring the latest hacks, refer to our wiki page:

http://damnsmalllinux.org/wiki/index.php/Installing_to_a_USB_Flash_Drive

SUMMARY

We outlined the steps required to install DSL-Embedded on a USB pen drive, ways of modifying the default setup including the use of MyDSL extensions and custom boot options. We also reviewed how to use your pen drive on systems without a compatible BIOS.

We hope you find Damn Small Linux a valuable travel companion. It is much easier to carry around a pen drive than a laptop. So, next time you are on the road, try carrying your desktop in your pocket instead of in your briefcase.

## CHAPTER 7

Running DSL Embedded in Windows

Damn Small Linux is fast and light. This has not only made DSL a popular choice for older hardware, but has managed to make it a favorite for running in a virtual environment.

Running an operating system in a virtual environment has significant overhead. This is because the user has to run the native (or top-level operating system) as well as the emulation layer before engaging the embedded system; thus, we have multiple layers of resource allocation in running an operating system in a virtual environment.

Logically, the lighter and smaller the operating system that is used when running in a virtual environment, the less of a resource hog it will be. This is why Damn Small Linux lends itself so well to this environment.

In this chapter, we are going to examine the ins and outs of running Damn Small Linux in Qemu and VMPlayer. There are other emulation programs available, but these two are currently popular because of their low cost ($0), ease of use, and performance.

RUNNING DSL IN QEMU

Qemu is a very capable machine emulator. It is capable of emulating different computer architectures. For instance, you can run an operating system designed for an ARM processor on a common PC. Compared to other emulation software, Qemu achieves good performance do to what its developers call *dynamic translation*.

The technical details of dynamic translation are beyond the scope of this overview. However, it is essentially a technique that allows guest code to be executed in the native operating system even if the host operating system runs on a different CPU architecture.

The way we will be using Qemu is relatively trivial in comparison to running an operating system on an exotic processor. We will be running an operating system (Damn Small Linux) designed for an x86 processor in a host operating system (Microsoft Windows) also designed for an x86 processor. Yet, in this setting, the possibilities are great. Using Qemu, one has the full power of DSL available on any PC, including network tools and all the command-line goodness on which the technically literate depend. Figure 7-1 shows an example of DSL running on a Windows XP host.

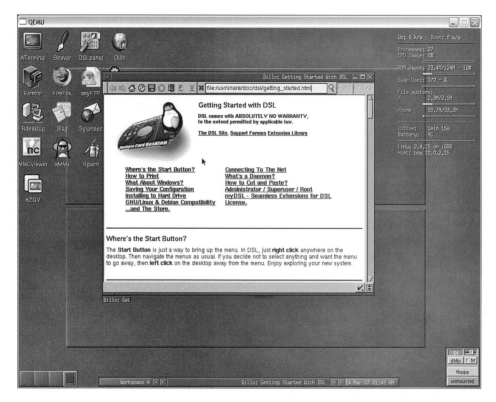

FIGURE 7-1 Damn Small Linux can run in Qemu on a Windows XP host system.

Another popular use for DSL+Qemu is to work in relative privacy on a computer that may not be the most secure. Although not as secure as running DSL on the BIOS level (i.e., from a LiveCD or booting from a pen drive), this setup does add that extra layer of obfuscation that at least keeps the technically challenged out of your business.

I often find myself using DSL+Qemu when I am stuck on a Microsoft Windows computer for a day and I start to miss my GNU/Linux tools. Instead of going through the hassle of downloading Cygwin (a collection of free tools to simulate a Unix enviornment), I just download the `dsl-embedded.zip` file, and everything I need is ready to use—it is quick and self-contained. After use, I can just delete my extracted files and move on without any cleanup fuss or the legacy of unwanted files being left behind on the host computer.

The first step is to download `dsl-embedded.zip` from one of the DSL download sites. After this is saved, you can uncompress the zip file to your hard drive or USB pen drive, or put the files on a CD, depending on your needs. DSL-Embedded may be run from anywhere that your native OS has access.

Using DSL-Embedded

Qemu is open source. This is very good for us because it enables us to bundle Qemu together with Damn Small Linux in a package that is ready to roll—something that is very fortunate for the new user who may find the documentation and the command-line arguments a bit tricky. We put together *bat* scripts that do all that for you.

We provide several options for running DSL Embedded. Depending on your needs, system capabilities, your user rights on the Windows system, and the permanence of your setup, your choices vary. We will outline the various options available and what they provide to the end user.

Setting Up a Generic Virtual DSL with dsl-base.bat

If you want to boot DSL Embedded without worrying about access to the native hard drive or creating a virtual hard drive, just run the following from Windows to get started:

```
dsl-base.bat
```

This is a very generic setup without any hardware-specific parameters.

If you are on someone else's computer without using your own portable drive (such as a pen drive), this is probably the bat file you want to run; it does not create and access a virtual drive or probe for and access any backup files or MyDSL extensions.

You should have access to the native Windows network access—so reaching out to the rest of the world via the Internet should be straightforward. You should also have sound, but realize that your audio performance may not be ideal with the added overhead of running DSL in a virtual environment. Note: to ungrab the Qemu window, press Ctrl-Alt to free up your mouse from the DSL-Embedded desktop.

Setting Up and Using a Virtual Hard Drive

If you can have write access to the computer, or if you are setting up a pen drive with DSL-Embedded, you probably want to create a virtual hard drive for DSL to use while running with Qemu. After this is set up, it will be the simplest way to have access to your backup files and extensions while running DSL-Embedded.

Most people who are interested in creating a virtual hard drive are running DSL-Embedded from a pen drive. The rest of this section will use the pen drive as a physical reference point for consistency, yet some may want to have this setup sit on the regular hard drive on their personal computer. The steps are the same as what follows; just substitute any reference to a pendrive with your own local path.

To create a Qemu virtual hard drive, you have to use the `qemu-img.exe` program included in the `dsl-embedded.zip` file. After it is unpacked, the program sits in the Qemu directory or *folder* as recognized by MS Windows. The following procedure describes how to create a virtual hard drive for DSL:

1. Open a DOS window and navigate to the `qemu` folder inside your pen drive. In MS DOS, the navigation command is `CD`. If your pen drive is recognized by Microsoft Windows as drive E, you would type the following:

   CD E:\qemu

2. Use the `qemu-img.exe` program to create a virtual hard drive. This hard drive will have a physical presence on your pen drive; you will see it there as `harddisk`. (This virtual hard drive will be used later when selecting the `dsl-vhd.bat` file to boot `dsl-embedded`.)

   After navigating to your Qemu folder, you need to use `qemu-img.exe` to create your virtual hard drive. The size you choose is limited by the space available on your pen drive, and it is up to you to choose what is best for your needs.

NOTE

Keep in mind that this hard drive is *virtual* in the sense that it is not a real drive (instead, it is a file on your pen drive). The virtual hard drive is actually *real* in that it takes up real space on your pen drive that you cannot use to store your non-DSL related files.

The command to use with `qemu-img.exe` is

   E:\qemu> **qemu-img.exe create hard disk *SIZE***

where SIZE is the actual size you want the virtual hard drive to be. For a 64MB virtual hard drive, type

   E:\qemu> **qemu-img.exe create harddisk 64M**

For a 500MB virtual hard drive, type

```
E:\qemu> qemu-img.exe create harddisk 500M
```

If, for some odd reason, you cannot navigate to the qemu directory on your pen drive, you may use a full-length path in your command:

```
C:\> E:\qemu\qemu-img.exe create E:\qemu\harddisk 64M
```

It is important to remember that the virtual hard drive needs to actually be named harddisk as this is how it is referenced in the dsl-vhd.bat file. After creating your harddisk image, go ahead and close your DOS window.

3. Run the following command, which boots DSL at level two (command-line prompt), to perform a few steps that will format your virtual hard drive (so DSL-Embedded will start to use it for file restoration):

```
E:\qemu> 1st-boot.bat
```

You are likely to see some errors during the boot phase because the virtual hard drive is not yet formatted correctly.

4. After the boot process is finished, format the virtual hard drive as the Linux native ext2 file system. At the Linux shell command prompt, type

```
# mke2fs /dev/hdb

mke2fs warning:
Warning: /dev/hdb is entire device, not just one partition!
Proceed anyway? (y/n) y
```

You will receive a warning because you are telling mke2fs to format the entire virtual drive instead of just a single partition.

5. Type y and press Enter.

After mke2fs runs, you mount the drive and make a copy of the cloop module to the access point. Damn Small Linux automatically probes to look for modules.

6. Mount the new virtual drive:

```
# mount /mnt/hdb
```

7. Create the mydsl and mydsl/modules directories:

```
# mkdir /mnt/hdb/mydsl
# mkdir /mnt/hdb/mydsl/modules
```

8. Copy over the `cloop` module:

```
# cp /KNOPPIX/lib/modules/2.4.26/kernel/drivers/block/cloop.o \
        /mnt/hdb/mydsl/modules/
```

9. Shut off DSL by typing this command:

```
# shutdown -h now
```

Your own drive now is ready to start using `dsl-vhd.bat`! When running `dsl-vhd.bat`, backup and restoration should automatically use `/mnt/hdb`, and your mydsl extensions will be accessed at `/mnt/hdb/mydsl/`.

> **NOTE**
>
> When you first do a normal `dsl-vhd.bat`, the X setup script runs and asks for your preferred resolution settings. If you just want to go with the defaults, press Tab to highlight the Cancel button and then press Enter to exit the script.

If you want to save your extensions, mount `/mnt/hdb` and download your extensions to `/mnt/hdb/mydsl`.

The mount tool in the lower-right side of your screen will not recognize your virtual hard drive. To mount it, open a term window and type the following:

```
# sudo mount /mnt/hdb
```

Accessing Native Files from Within the Virtual Environment

A new feature of Qemu is the ability to access your native files while booting in a virtual machine. The `pendrive.bat` file is designed to work in a pen drive that is used for both native BIOS booting and a virtual environment via Qemu.

Qemu allows read access to your files, so you can load your defaults and have access to your extensions and personal documents. However, normally, you cannot save them from the virtual environment.

Using the SMBClient, however, we can get write access via Windows network sharing access.

Here are the steps as found in the `readme` file in the `dsl-embedded.zip` archive:

1. In Windows, "share" your pen drive.

2. In Windows, note your machine's IP number. To do this, open a DOS window (command prompt) and type **ipconfig**.

3. Start DSL using the `pendrive.bat`.

4. From DSL running in Qemu, add files and change settings in your home directory.

5. From DSL, download any extensions you need into the `/cdrom/mydsl` directory.

6. From DSL, click DSLpanel, click Backup/Restore, and click Backup.

7. From the DSL menu, select Apps->Net->SMBclient and enter your specifics to connect (Domain, Machine, Share, Name, and Password). Then, type the following from the SMB prompt:

```
smb:\> lcd /cdrom
smb:\> put backup.tar.gz
smb:\> lcd mydsl
smb:\> cd mydsl
smb:\> put just_downloaded_extension
```

   (Repeat for all newly downloaded extensions)

```
smb:\> quit
```

8. Shut down DSL.

Using Your DSL-Embedded Equipped Pen Drive for Native BIOS Booting

This subject is covered in Chapter 6, "Running a Native Pen Drive Install," but I want to mention that you have to apply Syslinux to the drive before the BIOS will recognize the pen drive as being bootable. There is a version of Syslinux that is usable from within Windows, but we are getting feedback that sometimes it doesn't quite work with users' systems. You can always set up Syslinux by booting Damn Small Linux from the LiveCD provided with this book.

Be sure to read the `readme.txt` found in the `dsl-embedded.zip` file. There are tips in there that may be useful if you run into difficulties.

Increasing Qemu's Performance with KQemu

So, you think having an embedded Linux system at your disposal is pretty cool, but you wish the speed was a little faster? The Qemu developers have a fix for you.

KQemu is a Qemu accelerator, and it works nicely. During my experiments, I have reduced the virtual bootup time in half. This is a great development that makes running DSL-Embedded that much more enjoyable.

With the default configurations in DSL-Embedded bat files (1st-boot.bat, dsl-base.bat, dsl-vhd.bat, and pendrive.bat), we have Qemu run without KQemu enabled. You have to modify the .bat file of your choice configuration to enable KQemu acceleration.

Look for the following option on the qemu.exe command line:

```
-no-kqemu
```

Replace it with

```
-kernel-kqemu
```

You need to download the Microsoft Windows build of KQEMU at

```
http://www.h7.dion.ne.jp/~qemu-win/
```

At the time of this writing, version Kqemu-1.3.0pre11-install.exe was available. After downloading and installing KQEMU, you need to run the following:

```
net start kqemu
```

Either type it into the run command or open a command prompt and type the command in there. Figure 7-2 shows an example of KQemu being enabled from the Run utility:

FIGURE 7-2   Enter net start kqemu into the Run utility.

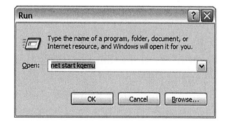

That should be all you need to do to enjoy your accelerated performance. Now go ahead and launch DSL-Embedded in your usual way.

RUNNING DSL IN VMPLAYER—VMWARE'S FREE VIRTUAL MACHINE

VMPlayer is VMWare's free virtual machine. It is a free download, but not freely distributable. Parts of the technology behind VMPlayer are open source and are apparently licensed under the GPL. We will explore using Damn Small Linux with the VMPlayer virtual machine from within the Microsoft Windows environment.

Figure 7-3 shows an example of Damn Small Linux running in VMPlayer in Windows XP.

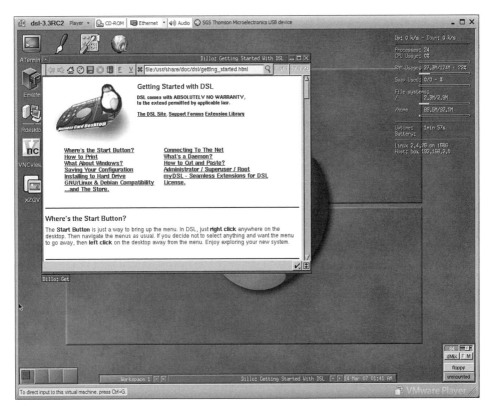

FIGURE 7-3 Damn Small Linux running in VMPlayer on a Windows XP host system.

Comparing VMPlayer to Qemu

In many ways, Qemu and VMPlayer performance benchmarks are comparable. Some studies have put Qemu with the KQEMU accelerator ahead in performance. In my limited testing, VMPlayer boots faster and seems to struggle less with resources during general use. It could be that our default settings in Qemu are limiting the system; we will have to do further testing to figure out the discrepancy.

VMPlayer is much larger than Qemu (25MB versus less than 2MB), and it needs to be installed on the host operating system. So, there is not a way to run VMPlayer from a low impact pen drive like QEMU. If you are in a situation where you are using a Windows computer and you want a way to get back into running

Linux embedded, this may be a great way to achieve your goal. A large download VMPlayer is easy to install and use.

Running VMPlayer with Damn Small Linux

Your first step is to download the latest version of VMPlayer. At the time of this writing, VMWare had posted 1.0.3 as the latest version.

The following is the URL for downloading VMPlayer:

```
http://www.vmware.com/download/player/
```

VMware says that VMPlayer needs a processor of least 400MHz, a minimum of 128MB of RAM, and 150MB of free space for installation.

The installation process is straightforward: just download and run the auto-installer. There are a few "extras" that you may or may not want installed, but they are easy to deselect. After you download and install VMPlayer, you are ready to run any *virtual appliance* listed at the VMWare site, including several operating systems.

There is an extensive list of virtual appliances at

```
http://www.vmware.com/vmtn/appliances/directory/
```

We provide DSL prepackaged to run with VMPlayer. You can download it from

```
http://distro.ibiblio.org/pub/linux/distributions/damnsmall/current/
```

Please note that for running DSL with VMPlayer, you want to choose the download that ends with vmx.zip. Thus, the file will look like dsl-[*version number*]-vmx.zip. After downloading the zip file, all you need to do is unzip the file and save the contents locally. (You may want to make a vmplayer folder and save the content to your desktop for easy access.)

The contents of our bundled file are just two files: the DSL ISO image and a configuration file labeled dsl.vmx. If you have already installed VMPlayer, your system will already recognize dsl.vmx as a VMPlayer configuration file. All you should need to do at this point is double-click the dsl.vmx icon.

After VMPlayer is running, you should notice some service buttons at the top of the VMPlayer screen. These buttons allow you to toggle on and off services available on the host computer, such as Ethernet access, audio, CD drive access, and access to USB devices.

While running DSL in VMPlayer, you should have access to the Internet and audio if these services are normally working in your computer. VMPlayer is simple to use with DSL and can be very handy.

SUMMARY

There are a lot of options when it comes to running DSL embedded, whether it is from a pen drive or used from a local file. If you've grown to rely on Linux and the powerful command-line tools it offers, DSL-Embedded may make your time in an otherwise constricted PC an enjoyable experience.

## CHAPTER 8

Installing DSL in Alternate Ways

Running Damn Small Linux (DSL) from a live CD works fine in many cases. But there are also good reasons for running DSL from hard disk. Some older PCs can't boot from a CD drive or may have no CD drive at all. There can also be speed and convenience reasons for running DSL from your hard drive. Some procedures described in this chapter let you install DSL on your hard drive without erasing the Windows or Linux systems that may be already installed.

Chapter 2, "Booting DSL," describes how to run DSL from a bootable CD or a DSL CD and DSL boot floppy. This chapter discusses:

- Popular alternate DSL installation methods
- How to get DSL to boot without a CD-ROM drive
- Methods to preview and install DSL without repartitioning your current Windows-based computer or changing the master boot record

OVERVIEW

The fact that DSL supports many older laptops, while many of those laptops have no CD drive, can be a challenge. The challenge is that you need a way to boot Damn Small Linux when booting from CD is not an option. Many older computers have only a floppy drive and hard drive. Some PCs may have a PCMCIA port. Some computers have a Zip drive attached. Some computers may have USB ports, but only those that support an old USB 1.1 specification.

Some systems have a CD drive, but that drive may be too slow. If the machine has a slow CD drive, you just may want to have the speed advantage of running DSL from the hard drive. In this chapter, I will discuss how to install on these limited systems using the devices just described.

DSL has been designed to provide many options for additional applications and customizations that were once only available to a traditional hard drive installation. As a result, you can also enjoy DSL "installed" on a hard drive without the traditional installation method. Basically, this involves:

- Setup of the DSL files from the CD-ROM onto a hard drive
- Running from the compressed KNOPPIX image

The huge advantage of this alternate methodology, running from the compressed image, is always starting with a pristine base system. It becomes an unbreakable system. Because if you do something to mess up the software, simply reboot to return to a clean system.

This chapter also covers the more challenging installations for DSL.

Let's start by defining these alternate installation methods:

- **Poorman's—The Easiest Way to Run DSL**

  This is where the compressed image of DSL is stored on persistent media. This is by far the easiest setup, as only one file, KNOPPIX, is needed. This includes partition types of Linux, DOS, Win9X, WinME, and in a more limited fashion Windows XP/NTFS. By definition, this installation type requires a boot floppy. The boot floppy is the DSL standard boot floppy. If additional boot options are required, they are typed at the boot prompt.

- **Frugal—The Most Popular Way to Run DSL**

  A Frugal install is a Poorman's installation *sans floppy* diskette and without the need to type boot options. (Sans floppy means you need additional DSL files on the target partition.) This is typically set up on traditional Linux and Linux Swap type partitions. But it too, like Poorman's, can be set up on DOS or Win9X. This is possible by using several boot loaders—for example, Lilo, Grub, Linld, and LoadLin.

NOTE

Windows versions later than ME no longer allow MSDOS mode operations. Therefore, you always need a boot floppy for either Poorman's or Frugal. However, these newer versions of Windows have the capability to run DSL virtually with either Qemu or VmWare (see Chapter 7, "Running DSL Embedded in Windows").

Installation methods described in this chapter assume you have Windows, just DOS, or even no operating system installed at all. The installation methods discussed here also apply to standard *white box* computers as well. But typically, such computers have CD-ROM drives or one can be easily added.

Also, be very aware that all the boot time options that were discussed in Chapter 2 apply here. This chapter's focus is the alternate installation types and how to set up the necessary DSL files even without a CD-ROM so that you can start the boot and therefore installation process of DSL.

After a successful alternate method is working, it is easy to move to the more advanced methods. After the Poorman's method is working, it is easy to then set up a frugal DSL install, or frugal hybrid, or even the traditional hard installation.

STARTING A DSL INSTALLATION

The first method for installing DSL to your hard drive assumes that your computer can boot from the DSL CD. If that's the case, boot the DSL CD and type the following boot option:

boot: **install**

This boot option brings up an installation menu as shown in Figure 8-1.

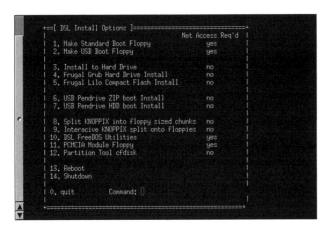

FIGURE 8-1   The DSL installation menu appears when using the install boot option.

This allows quick and easy access to the various installation methods. Pen drive installation is discussed in Chapter 6, "Running a Native Pen Drive Install," and traditional hard drive installation can be found in Chapter 9, "Performing a Traditional Hard Drive Install." Note that Poorman's is missing from this menu. This is because it is not needed if you can boot from CD.

FRUGAL—THE MOST POPULAR WAY TO INSTALL DSL

The DSL boot option of `install` provides easy access to a Frugal installation for those users who can boot from CD. The frugal installation available from this menu is for Linux file systems only. You must have a prepared Linux partition to use the Frugal installation options from this menu.

Notice that DSL offers two versions of Frugal installations. Menu option 4 uses the popular GRUB boot loader (`www.gnu.org/software/grub`) in the master boot record. Menu option 5 offers LILO boot loader (`http://freshmeat.net/projects/lilo`) installed into a partition on the computer's hard disk. A boot loader is a program that is installed on the boot medium (hard disk, live CD, or other bootable medium) and used to identify the operating system to boot and provide an opportunity to add boot options. Early Linux systems used the LILO boot loader, while more recent Linux systems most often use GRUB.

Let's begin by stepping through the Frugal installation process and finish up by discussing how to change boot options after an installation.

NOTE

You must have prepared your Linux and Linux swap partitions before you begin either Frugal installation scripts. DSL provides two tools to perform this task. Both `fdisk` and `cfdisk` are available. The procedure in the section that follows describes how to partition your disk with cfdisk.

Partitioning with Cfdisk

If your disk is already set up with Linux and Linux swap partitions, you may skip this step. I am going to briefly discuss a very simple setup using `cfdisk` to partition the entire disk for use with DSL. To begin, select option 12 from the DSL Install Options screen (see Figure 8-1). You are prompted to enter the target drive. The default is `hda`. Recall that in Linux the first hard drive device is a, the second drive is b, and so on. This brings up the Cfdisk Partition tool as shown in Figure 8-2.

To navigate this program, use the up and down arrows to select a partition or *free space*. Use the Tab key to choose an action displayed at the bottom of the screen.

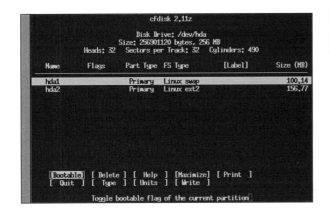

FIGURE 8-2 The cfdisk partitioning screen appears when option 12 is selected.

To set up the *entire* disk for DSL, if you have existing partitions to delete, select each one and choose Delete. To create the minimum partitions needed for DSL, perform the following steps. First, you create a 100MB Linux swap partition.

1. Highlight the area marked Free Space.
2. Highlight New and press Enter.
3. Choose Primary and press Enter.
4. Type 100 (to have a 100MB swap area) and press Enter.
5. Choose Beginning to create the partition at the beginning of the free space, and press Enter.
6. With the new partition highlighted above, highlight Type below and press Enter.
7. To assign the file system type of Linux swap to the file system, type 82 and press Enter. The 100MB Linux swap partition should appear in the top part of the screen.

Next, you create a Linux partition using the remaining disk space, as described in the following procedure:

1. Highlight the area marked Free Space.
2. Highlight New and press Enter.
3. Choose Primary and press Enter. You should see the Size line appear, displaying the amount of disk space remaining.
4. Press Enter to use all of the remaining disk space in the new partition, or type a number (and press Enter) to use a smaller amount of disk space. The partition will be automatically assigned to a Linux file system type (83).

> **NOTE**
>
> If you are planning to do a Frugal Lilo installation, you should also mark the Primary Linux partition as Bootable. Frugal Grub type installations use the the master boot record and so no such mark is necessary. You may wish to fully read the next two sections to better understand the differences before you commit your cfdisk setup. Of course, it is always easy to start cfdisk again soley for the purpose of marking a partition as bootable.

5. If you are sure you are ready to erase everything on your hard disk, choose Write and press Enter.

6. After the warning, if you still think it is a good idea, type yes and press Enter.

7. Choose Quit and press Enter to exit from Cfdisk.

Upon return of the DSL Install Options screen, select option 0 (Quit). This takes you to the system prompt where you can format the swap partition using the following command:

```
# mkswap /dev/hda1
```

Of course, the mkswap command needs to be adjusted if you did not choose the first hard drive for the swap partition. Because you have changed the partition table, you must reboot to continue with your installation options. Don't forget to boot as follows:

```
boot: install
```

You may need to add some boot options to the install command. For example, type install nopcmcia if you don't think that your computer hardware's PCMCIA interface is being properly detected and configured.

Frugal Grub Hard Drive Install

If you want easy access to later change boot options, or if you have a typical preexisting Windows installation, you should choose the Grub installation. This installation script provides an easy installation for most systems. If you have multiple drives, it is incumbent upon you to make the final edit required by your system for Grub.

1. Select menu option 4 from the DSL Install Options screen to begin the installation (refer to Figure 8-1). If you have not prepared your Linux partition(s), the script terminates with the following:

```
Sorry system has not detected a linux partition.
You may need to just reboot, so the system can re-read
the partition table, or create your partition(s) with cfdisk
and then reboot."
```

If the partition(s) is properly detected, you see the following disclaimer and are prompted to enter the target Linux partition:

```
DSL Compressed Image Install/Upgrade.

No responsibility for data loss or hardware damage!

A linux partition large enough to hold the image file
must be created prior to installation.

Enter the target partition to hold image (EXAMPLE: hda2):
```

2. Type the device name of the target partition. For example, if you are using the first IDE hard drive on your computer (hda), with the first partition (hda1) assigned to swap and the second partition (hda2) assigned as a Linux file system, you could type **hd2** and press Enter.

Next, you are prompted for the source of the DSL software you are installing, as follows:

```
Install from:
   [L]iveCD or Frugal Install
   [P]endrive
   Local [I]so File
   Fetching latest iso from [W]eb
   From Poormans via [B]ootfloppy
Choose (l/p/i/w/b):
```

3. If you have booted from the CD-ROM, the choice is obviously L for the live CD-ROM.

NOTE

Notice that Frugal Grub can be installed while running DSL from a pen drive, from a downloaded ISO file, either Isolinux or Syslinux version, or even from a Poorman's via the DSL boot floppy. I will talk more about Poorman's later in the "Poorman's—An Easy Way to Try DSL" section later in this chapter.

The following prompt appears, asking whether to format the target partition:

```
For INSTALL answer y to format, for UPGRADE answer n.
Format the target partition (y/..)? y

Last chance to exit before destroying all data on

Formatting target partition.
Setting up system image on target partition.
Setting up grub
```

4. When doing an installation, you want to format (y). Later, when you want to upgrade to a new version of DSL, you would not format the partition (n).

NOTE

Upgrading a Frugal installation is as easy as running the installation script again. Because Frugal implies running from the untouched compressed image, all of your extensions and backup of configurations are unaffected during an upgrade. Only three system files are copied to the target media.

The last prompt of the Frugal Grub installation is to accommodate existing Windows installations. Because Frugal Grub installs into the master boot record, you must notify the script to add an entry for Windows. This includes all versions of Windows through Windows XP.

NOTE

Later, in the "Poorman's—An Easy Way to Try DSL" section, I will discuss the Poorman's installation, which allows DSL to be installed within an existing Windows partition.

```
Do you have Windows installed on the first partition (y/..)?
Grub Installation Completed.
```

5. Type **y** if you have Windows installed on your first partition and you want to be able to choose to boot Windows or DSL from the Grub boot prompt. Type **n** if there is no Windows partition.

NOTE

Although we have not formally tested dual booting Windows Vista and DSL, there are some Windows Vista "features" that make dual booting with Linux difficult.

One issue is that Windows Vista erases the master boot record (which in our case is Grub or Lilo) when Windows Vista is installed. So you should install Windows Vista before installing Linux to not lose the Grub boot loader. The second issue is that Windows Vista uses a different version of NTFS that cannot be resized using tools in Linux or older Windows resizing tools. If you can overcome those issues, dual-booting with DSL and Windows Vista should be possible.

The Poorman's installation is now complete. However, if your hard disk has some configuration other than those just described (either all DSL or DSL plus a single Windows system on the first partition), you probably need to edit your Grub configuration file by hand.

"How do I edit the boot options in a Frugal Grub installation?" is one of the most frequently asked questions after installation.

All Frugal type installations emulate running from a CD-ROM; to the running system, this means that the system is mounted at /cdrom. Therefore, as superuser root, you may edit Grub's configuration file /cdrom/boot/grub/menu.1st. However, if you have booted your system with the toram boot option, you do not find this file until you mount the partition first. For example, let's say you install to hda2 and boot with toram; as superuser, mount /mnt/hda2, if necessary, and then edit /mnt/hda2/boot/grub/menu.1st.

Frugal Lilo CompactFlash Install

Why does this option refer to CompactFlash? I chose to name this option with CompactFlash for two reasons:

- For most users, the Lilo boot loader is more difficult to edit.
- Usually, the use of CompactFlash means one is building an appliance and therefore does not want easy access or even a boot menu option to appear.

Frugal Lilo also differs from Frugal Grub in that it does not install into the master boot record (MBR). It installs the boot loader into the target partition. You need to mark the partition as the active partition.

With Frugal Lilo, you don't need to worry about other operating systems being installed, or who will own the MBR. Frugal Lilo does have more prompts to eliminate or reduce the need to be editing the Lilo configuration file for you after installation changes.

NOTE

Before installing Frugal Lilo, it is best to have booted from the DSL CD-ROM and have learned the additional boot options that may be required or desired for your particular machine or purpose.

Use the following steps to do a CompactFlash Lilo install:

1. Select menu option 5 from the DSL Install Options screen (refer to Figure 8-1). You see the following disclaimer and prompt for the target partition:

   ```
   DSL Compressed Image Install/Upgrade.

   No responsibility for data loss or hardware damage!

   A linux partition large enough to hold the image file
   must be created prior to installation.

   This version uses Lilo Boot Loader in the specified partition.
   You must therefore make that partition the active/boot one.

   For Grub Boot Loader version, use frugal_grub.sh

   Enter the target partition to hold DSL image & Lilo (EXAMPLE:
   hda1):
   ```

   Again, if you do not have a Linux partition, the script exits with an error.

2. Type the device name of the target partition. For example, if you are using the first IDE hard drive on your computer (hda), with the first partition (hda1) assigned to swap and the second partition (hda2) assigned as a Linux file system, you could type hd2 and press Enter.

   As with Frugal Grub, you are prompted with the source location, as follows:

   ```
   Install from:
     [L]iveCD or Frugal Install
     [P]endrive
     Local [I]so File
     Fetching latest iso from [W]eb160
     From Poormans via [B]ootfloppy
   Choose (l/p/i/w/b):
   ```

3. If you have booted from the CD-ROM, the choice is L for the live CD-ROM.

> ## NOTE
>
> Like Frugal Grub, Frugal Lilo can be installed while running DSL from a pen drive, from a downloaded ISO file, either Isolinux or Syslinux version, or even from a Poorman's via the DSL boot floppy. Poorman's will be discussed in the "Poorman's—An Easy Way to Try DSL" section later in this chapter.

Because I have found that editing the Lilo configuration is not easy for new users, Frugal Lilo prompts with many of the boot options a user would need to use.

```
List boot options,
Example: toram ssh nfs syslog lpd monkey ftp:

Choose language/keyboard if other than english,
Example: cs da de es fr nl it pl ru sk:

Do you wish to specify a default restore partition (y/..)?

Enter the partition to be used for backup/restore.(EXAMPLE:
hda3):

Use default Xvesa settings, }Xvesa (y/..)?

Do you wish to specify a different partition for myDSL (y/..)?
Enter the partition to be used for myDSL applications.(EXAMPLE:
hda3):
```

4. Answer the questions as they are presented. If you don't know the answer to these prompts, you can leave them blank. Later, you will have to edit Lilo's configuration file for necessary changes.

The last prompt of the Frugal Lilo installation asks whether to format the target partition, as follows:

```
For INSTALL answer y to format, for UPGRADE answer n.
Format the target partition (y/..)?

Last chance to exit before destroying all data on target
partition.

Formatting target partition"
```

Setting up system image on target partition.

Setting up lilo

Installation complete.

5. When doing an installation, type **y** to format the partitions. Later, when you want to upgrade to a new version of DSL, you do not format the partition (n).

NOTE

Upgrading a Frugal installation is as easy as running the installation script again. Because Frugal implies running from the untouched compressed image, all of your extensions and backup of configurations are unaffected during an upgrade. Only three system files are copied to the target media.

After installation is done, you may find you need to edit the Lilo configuration file, lilo.conf. Editing lilo.conf requires not only finding and then editing this file, but also reinstalling Lilo. Let's begin with a standard installation, open a shell as superuser (root), and perform the following:

```
# beaver /cdrom/boot/lilo.conf
# ln -sf /cdrom/boot /
# lilo -C /cdrom/boot/lilo.conf
```

The beaver command is just the editor we chose to edit the lilo.conf file. The ln command does a soft link of the /cdrom/boot directory to the root of your file system. The lilo command uses the information from the lilo.conf file to add the updated boot loader information into the master boot record.

If your system was booted with the toram boot option, the procedure is slightly different. If necessary, you need to mount the partition where DSL was installed. Let's assume that you installed DSL in partition hda2; the procedure required becomes

```
# mount /mnt/hda2
# beaver /mnt/hda2/boot/lilo.conf
# ln -sf /mnt/hda2/boot/ /
# lilo -C /mnt/hda2/boot/lilo.conf
```

This completes my discussion of the native Frugal installation scripts that are provided within the DSL CD-ROM distribution. Both types, Grub and Lilo, have their advantages, and their use is entirely up to you.

Both installation scripts provide an easy but typical DSL installation. If your requirements are very complex, having many operating systems installed and having pre-existing boot loaders, it is incumbent upon you to edit the appropriate boot loader.

POORMAN'S—AN EASY WAY TO TRY DSL

If the PC on which you want to run DSL has a floppy drive, a Poorman's install is a good way to configure DSL. By creating a boot floppy and installing DSL to an existing disk partition (Linux or Windows partitions), you can boot DSL from many older machines without erasing any software already installed on the machine and without changing the master boot record.

Recall the DSL Install Options screen shown in Figure 8-1. With a Poorman's install, many times, you may need to use a more capable machine to boot the DSL CD-ROM and prepare boot floppies or even a floppy only installation set. The following procedures describe how to get the floppy images you need and do a Poorman's install to existing Linux or Windows partitions.

Prepare Boot Floppies

As previously defined, a Poorman's install is needed if your target computer either can't boot from its CD drive or has only a floppy drive. In either case, you need to create a DSL boot floppy. I have also prepared a DSL FreeDOS utilities diskette, containing a collection of DOS programs to assist in the installation and setup process.

Using a more capable DSL booted machine that has a CD drive and floppy drive, creating these floppies is easy and automatic from the DSL Install Options menu. However, you can manually download and create the floppies as needed.

To download these floppies, you should check for a local download mirror. DSL's mirror collection is available at `http://www.damnsmalllinux.org/download. html`.

1. Locate the files to download using a web browser or ftp client. For example:

   `ftp://ibiblio.org/pub/Linux/distributions/damnsmalllinux/current/ bootfloppy.img`

   and

   `ftp://ibiblio.org/pub/Linux/distributions/damnsmalllinux/current/ bootfloppy-utils.img`

2. After these diskette image files are downloaded, use typical tools to write to floppy diskette. For Windows, this usually means rawwrite. The rawwrite program for Windows can be found here:

http://www.chrysocome.net/rawwrite

After you have written the diskette image to a floppy disk, remove the disk so that you can use it to install DSL on the target machine. (Later, when instructed to boot from either of these two floppies, be sure that you have changed your system's BIOS setting so that the floppy is the first boot device.)

DSL Installed on Windows 9x or DOS Partition

Let's say you have a Windows 9x or DOS system with modem or Internet access and you want to try DSL. You do not want to disturb your Windows installation. You especially do not want to have to repartition your hard drive. To install DSL without affecting your current system, follow these steps:

 NOTE

Internet access is required for this section. Methods for system without Internet access will be discussed in the next section of this chapter.

1. Boot the machine on which you want to install DSL into Windows or DOS.

2. Download the embedded version of DSL to C:\. We are not going to attempt to run virtualization as discussed in Chapter 7. The embedded version is provided as a Zip file and therefore is very easy access for DOS and Windows system to unzip.

The embedded version, which I will call the Zip file version of DSL, can be found here:

ftp://ibiblio.org/pub/Linux/distributions/damnsmalllinux/current/
dsl-embedded.zip

3. If you have an unzip program on your Windows system, unzip this Zip file into a working directory—for example, c:\work.

If you do not have unzip, you can reboot your computer using the DSL Utilities boot floppy and you will find unzip and other utility programs that we will be using.

I will now focus on using the DSL FreeDOS Utilities diskette. Doing so allows a common base on which to proceed. If you already have unzip and are familiar, I am sure it will still be easy to follow along.

NOTE

If you have Windows XP, the FreeDOS boot floppy utilities will not work. With XP, you already have unzip; therefore, it is not needed.

Boot from the utilities diskette and then perform the following:

```
A:\> C:
C:\> unzip dsl-33~1.zip KNOPPIX/KNOPPIX
```

NOTE

The DSL Zip file name is munged because of the DOS 8.3 filename limit. With FreeDOS, you can type just a few characters and press the Tab key and the munged filename will be auto completed. If using Windows, you will probably be able to see and use the full Zip filename.

4. Replace the DSL Utilities diskette with the DSL boot floppy and reboot your system using the DSL boot floppy.

5. At the DSL boot prompt, type the following:

   ```
   boot: dsl 2 legacy frugal
   ```

   While booting from the DSL boot floppy, if errors appear or the system hangs, you likely need to use additional boot options. DSL boot options are discussed in Chapter 2.

6. When you see the system prompt #, enter the following:

   ```
   # mkdosswapfile
   ```

Reboot again and you have arrived at a Poorman's installation of DSL.

Congratulations! You are now running a DSL Poorman's installation within a Windows or DOS formatted partition.

DSL Installed on an Existing Linux Partition

The Poorman's method is also available within an existing traditional Linux installation. You may have another Linux distribution and want to try the Poorman's installation method. The steps are really the same as earlier:

1. Download the embedded version of DSL (the Zip file).

2. Unzip to extract only the KNOPPIX/KNOPPIX file as a level one directory on a Linux partition.

3. Boot your system from the DSL boot floppy.

During boot, your partitions are scanned for the KNOPPIX/KNOPPIX file and begin to boot DSL. Again, you may need to specify additional boot parameters just as you would do by booting from the DSL CD-ROM.

FRUGAL DSL INSTALL ON WINDOWS 9X OR DOS

Recall from the earlier definition of Frugal: A Frugal install is a Poorman's installation sans floppy diskette and without having to type additional boot options. The procedures discussed next apply to DOS, Windows 95, and Windows 98. Only systems that can boot to DOS native mode are supported. Windows ME can be patched to boot DOS native, but that is beyond the scope of this discussion. If you have Windows XP, you may want to use virtualization as discussed in Chapter 7.

Before you try these procedures, you should successfully perform the Poorman's installation in the preceding section. In fact, if you have found that you are in need of additional boot parameters, you should have them written down. The goal here is to have no floppy and not have to type additional boot parameters upon each boot.

Booting DSL from Native DOS Mode Using LinLd

The linld boot loader is a tiny DOS COM file. With linld, you can type all the boot information on the DOS command line similar to the DSL boot prompt, or you can use a simple DOS text file to store the boot options.

For more information on LinLd, see the announcement at

```
http://www.lwn.net/Articles/102210/
```

Let's continue on from our Poorman's method. You need to have Poorman's setup (in other words, you should have the C:\KNOPPIX\KNOPPIX file in place and the Zip file still resident on C:\ as well). Then, boot from the DSL FreeDOS Utilities diskette and perform the following:

```
A:\> C:
C:\> unzip dsl-33~1.zip linux24
C:\> unzip dsl-33~1.zip minirt24.gz
```

Recall the FreeDOS Tab key shortcut to typing filenames. If you are using Windows and are already familiar with unzip, all you do is unzip two more DSL system files to C:\.

Before you copy over the DOS boot files to the C:\ drive, let's test your setup. If you did not need any additional boot options, from the booted FreeDOS A: prompt, type

```
A:\> bootdsl
```

If you need additional boot parameters, you should add them to the file linld.cl. You can use the DOS type command to see the contents of this file. The DOS diskette also has the vi editor to edit this file to add or change boot options as needed.

After you have tested booting from the bootdsl batch file, you now are ready to copy over the DOS files needed to boot DSL via native DOS mode. While still booted from the DSL FreeDOS Utilities diskette, perform the following:

```
A:\> copy a:\bin\linld.com c:\
A:\> copy a:\linld.cl c:\
A:\> copy a:\bootdsl.bat c:\
```

Now, reboot your DOS or Windows computer to native DOS mode. With Windows 9x, it usually means holding down the F8 key. After you have booted to native DOS, typing **bootdsl** at the DOS boot prompt starts DSL.

Congratulations! You now have a Frugal DOS install using linld DOS boot loader of DSL. Next, you should select a backup device (see Chapter 4, "Configuring and Saving DSL Settings"); to start using MyDSL extensions, see Chapter 5, "Extending Applications with MyDSL."

Booting DSL from Native DOS Mode Using LoadLin

Another popular native DOS mode Linux boot loader is loadlin.exe, version 1.6c by Hans Lermen. This is a DOS EXE instead of a COM program. For more information, visit its website at

```
http://elserv.ffm.fgan.de/~lermen/
```

This DOS boot loader uses a simple DOS text file to store the boot options. So, just as with linld.com, continue from your existing Poorman's installation. You already have the KNOPPIX file located at C:\KNOPPIX\KNOPPIX and the downloaded DSL Zip file is located on C:\ as well. You have been able to boot from the DSL boot floppy and know your additional boot options, if any were required.

Let's boot from the DSL FreeDOS Utilities diskette and, if you have not already, extract the other two DSL system files:

```
A:\> C:
C:\> unzip dsl-33~1.zip linux24
C:\> unzip dsl-33~1.zip minirt24.gz
```

Before you set up any `loadlin` DOS files on the C drive, you should test by trying to boot DSL via `loadlin`:

```
A:\> loadlin @options.txt
```

If additional boot options are needed, you should add them to the `options.txt` file and reboot until you are satisfied that `loadlin` will work. Next, copy over the `loadlin` DOS files to your C: drive:

```
C:\> copy a:\bin\loadlin.exe c:\
C:\> copy a:\options.txt c:\
```

Reboot for DOS or Windows computer to native DOS mode. Windows 98 usually requires holding down the F8 key. After you have booted to the DOS prompt, type `loadlin @options.txt` to boot DSL.

Congratulations! You have a Frugal DOS Loadlin installation of DSL. Next, you should select a backup device (see Chapter 4 for information on backing up your data); to start using MyDSL extensions, see Chapter 5.

POORMAN'S REVISITED

Why revisit this topic? For some, the real challenge might be how to get the KNOPPIX/KNOPPIX file on their systems hard drive. After all, without that key file, you cannot use either method. The following are several ways you can go about getting the KNOPPIX/KNOPPIX file on your hard drive.

Use an Alternate Machine

You can actually remove the hard drive of the target computer and temporarily install it into another computer that does have a bootable CD-ROM, or net access. Install DSL. Because DSL uses KNOPPIX's hardware detection, replacing the hard drive back into the target computer, upon boot, detects the new environment. You may need to adjust boot options particular to this machine. Removing a hard drive, especially from laptops, may not be an easy or desired task. Read on for other methods to overcome this task.

Poorman's DSL from PCMCIA

Many laptops have PCMCIA slots. Some may have a PCMCIA hard drive. Also, there are PCMCIA CompactFlash adapters available. With such an easily removable device, you can insert this PCMCIA into a more capable computer (bootable CD-ROM or net access) and copy the KNOPPIX/KNOPPIX onto the memory of the PCMCIA.

To boot from PCMCIA on the target computer, you need to prepare a second DSL boot floppy. The PCMCIA Module Floppy, menu option 11 from the DSL Install Options as shown in Figure 8-1, creates this floppy. So again, use the more capable computer to create this diskette, or download directly and use rawwrite to create it.

Returning to the target computer, insert the PCMCIA card and boot with the DSL boot floppy with the following:

```
boot: dsl frompcmcia
```

During the booting process, you are prompted to insert the PCMCIA modules floppy. As usual, you may find that you need additional boot options. See Chapter 2 for examples of boot options you might need to get your computer hardware to boot DSL.

Poorman's DSL from USB Drive

What is this? USB was discussed in Chapter 6 and your machine cannot boot from USB. But you see, using a more capable machine to create the pen drive, as discussed in Chapter 6, you can boot DSL Poorman's using the DSL standard boot floppy like this:

```
boot: dsl fromusb
```

Poorman's DSL from a Zip Drive

Some of you may still have an Iomega zip drive. Because this is a removable device also, you can copy the KNOPPIX/KNOPPIX file onto a zip drive. Then, using the DSL standard boot floppy, boot with

```
boot: dsl fromzip
```

Installing from a Stack of Floppy Diskettes

If you have a really old PC, you may have no PCMCIA access, no USB port, and certainly no zip drive. Well then, you must have a floppy drive!

As I mentioned earlier, sometime you need a more capable machine to produce what is needed for the less able machine. We will call the more capable machine the source machine and the other the target machine.

Your source machine needs to be able to boot the DSL CD-ROM, either the Syslinux or Isolinux version, and must also have a floppy drive. You also need a stack of approximately 35 floppies. Make sure these are good—they should have no bad sectors and be in new or new-like condition. You also need the DSL FreeDos Utilities floppy mentioned at the beginning of this chapter.

At the boot prompt of the source machine, enter `install`. This displays the now familiar DSL installation menu as shown in Figure 8-1.

You have two choices. Depending on the actual size of the DSL release, menu option 8 creates approximately 34 data files. These data files will be named chunk01, chunk02, ... chunk34. Be sure that you have enough space to store an additional 50MB. Using this all-at-once option allows you to copy to floppies at your leisure. These files are not floppy image files like the boot floppies, but instead are data files.

When the process is complete, you will find all of the chunk files. Later, when you have time, you can return to the source computer and manually copy each chunk file to a corresponding floppy disk. Because these are data and not image files, you must first mount the floppy, perform the copy, then unmount the floppy using the `umount` command.

Alternatively, you may prefer menu option 9. This option creates a chunk and interactively prompts you to insert a blank floppy. This option loops through all chunk files sequentially. Your only interaction is to insert and remove floppies as prompted. This option eliminates all the manual commands needed with option 8. With this option, you need to set aside a good deal of time, but you save much typing.

You may find that you use both options. You may need to recreate a single floppy, and with option 8, you can selectively choose which chunk to copy.

After all the floppies have been created, you might want to take a break. Really, this is a time-consuming endeavor.

To restore all the chunk files on the target machine, boot the target machine with the DSL FreeDOS utilities diskette. Change to the C drive and make the KNOPPIX directory and enter the copy command as shown:

```
A:> c:
C:\> mkdir knoppix
C:\> cd knoppix
C:\KNOPPIX> copy b:\chunk*
```

Remove the utilities diskette from the drive and insert the first chunk diskette in the floppy drive. Press the Enter key when ready.

Wait for the copy to complete. You see a progress message as the copy is progressing. When the diskette is quiescent, remove the chunk diskette and insert the next one into the drive.

You can use the up arrow key to repeat the copy command copy b:\chunk*, then press the Enter key to proceed with the copy.

Repeat this process for all diskettes, which should be between 34 and 35 floppies.

NOTE

While the copy process is running, you might see a message that says: "Error reading from drive B:..." If that happens, press **a** for abort. Write down this chunk number.

Return to the source machine and do the following:

1. Format this "bad read" diskette.

2. Mount the newly formatted diskette.

3. Try to copy the chunk (cp chunkxy /mnt/auto/floppy).

4. Type sync to sync anything data cache to permanent storage.

5. Unmount the floppy disk (umount /mnt/auto/floppy).

Back on the target machine, reinsert this floppy, press the Up arrow to recall the copy command, and press Enter. If this diskette still fails, repeat with another new floppy.

After copying all "chunk" diskettes, return to the A: drive prompt. Replace the utilities diskette. This should stop the prompt for any B: drive. Next, move to the C:\knoppix folder:

```
A:\> C:
C:\> cd knoppix
C:\KNOPPIX> cat chunk* > knoppix
C:\KNOPPIX> del chunk*
C:\KNOPPIX> a:
A:\>
```

Now that you have C:\KNOPPIX\KNOPPIX, you can remove the utilities diskette and insert the DSL boot diskette. Reboot your computer. At the boot prompt, type the following:

boot: **dsl 2 legacy frugal**

The next step is to make a swap file. When you see the system prompt #, enter the following:

mkdosswapfile

Reboot again and you have arrived at a Poorman's installation of DSL.

You may need additional boot parameters (see Chapter 2 for more detail of boot options that are specific to the booting process).

After you have a successful installation of DSL, you might want to eliminate the need for the boot floppy. See the section "DSL Installed on Windows 9x or DOS Partition."

No Operating System Network Install via Tomsrtbt

A stack of floppies doesn't sound like much fun? Well, still one more option to explore. This option is not as easy as the others, as some manual configuration is required. This option is also a Linux-based option. Your target computer needs to be able to boot from a 1722k, 3.5-inch floppy. Let's start by reviewing the hardware requirement.

Hardware Requirements for Network Install

The hardware needed to do a DSL network install is the same hardware stated in Chapter 2, with the following exceptions:

- No CD-ROM drive is required.
- A floppy drive capable of booting a 1722k floppy is needed.
- A PCMCIA and a supported PCMCIA network card supported by tomsrtbt is needed.

NOTE

tomsrtbt is a single floppy Linux distribution. For more information, see http://www.toms.net/rb/. The tomsrtbt distribution offers among the best PCMCIA network support of all single floppy distributions.

Example systems that were used during development included the following specifications:

- 32MB memory
- 1.44 floppy drive
- 128MB HD
- 800×600 screen
- Linksys PCMCIA network card model PCMLM56 (also works with Xircom RealPort2 Model R2E-100)

Starting the Network Install

I have written a tiny ash shell script called frugal_lite.sh. It provides the traditional Poorman's install and boot floppy creation via the Net:

1. Download and create the tomsrtbt disk. (Go to http://www.toms.net/rb/.)

2. With your PCMCIA card inserted, try booting tomsrtbt and see if the network card is seen.

   After booting up tomsrtbt, be sure to *remove* the diskette.

3. Run the /sbin/ifconfig command. If you see your IP address, you can skip the next step.

4. If you see 1.1.1.1 when you type ifconfig, you must manually input your IP address, as in the following two lines:

   ```
   # ifconfig eth0 192.168.0.14 netmask 255.255.255.0
   # route add default gw 192.168.0.1
   ```

   Then, add your nameserver like this:

   ```
   # echo "nameserver xx.xx.xx.xx" >> /etc/resolv.conf
   ```

Next, test your network setup by pinging a known Internet site.

You must have established Internet access to continue.

5. Next grab the `frugal_lite.sh` from the `/images` directory on the CD or by running a command like this:

```
# wget http://ibiblio.org/pub/Linux/distributions/damnsmall/current/fru
gal_lite.sh
```

Using `fdisk`, create two Linux partitions, each large enough to hold DSL. I used 64MB to be safe. You could make them smaller.

Format the partitions by using the following commands:

```
# mke2fs /dev/hda1
# mke2fs /dev/hda2
```

6. Next, place a *good* (no bad sectors) floppy into the floppy drive.

 NOTE

The hard drive partitions are *not* mounted. The floppy is *not* mounted.

7. Run the `frugal_lite.sh` as follows:

```
# sh ./frugal_lite.sh
```

8. Follow the prompts. Upon completion, the system reboots off the DSL boot floppy and starts loading DSL.

Typically, older laptops (800×600) cannot display the default resolution of DSL (1024×768). The following boot method is needed:

```
boot: dsl vga=normal
```

Many other VGA options are available and may be needed by your hardware. Pressing F2 or F3 at the initial boot prompt displays all such choices. Many older laptops also use framebuffer as the display device. In this case, the following boot method is needed:

```
boot: fb800x600
```

9. After you get your system running from boot floppy (Poorman's), you can install again into the other partition using DSL's `frugal_grub.sh` or `frugal_lilo.sh`, giving you much more control of your system. Use the (L)ive CD install option, as the Poorman's is a virtual live CD.

10. If the other partition is large enough, do a regular `dsl-hdinstall` (see Chapter 9 for details) to that partition.

If you do this, reinstall into the other partition either frugal or full install. Next, you can get rid of the Poorman's install on that partition by using the fdisk utility. Using fdisk, change the partition type to type 82 (swap) and then format it for swap by using the mkswap /dev/hdaX command. For example, if it were the first partition on the first IDE hard drive, you would enter /dev/hda1 as the device entered.

SUMMARY

DSL can be booted, installed, and run similarly to running from the CD-ROM. Running from an installed compressed image has the advantage of speed over the CD-ROM, is an unbreakable pristine bootable system, frees the CD-ROM for other uses, and shares the MyDSL application extension system.

Installing DSL this way also allows DSL to be used on old laptops that may not even have a CD-ROM drive. Only a floppy drive, PCMCIA CF, USB port, or a network card supported by tomsrtbt is required. DSL can be easily previewed on Windows platforms without committing a partition and can be as simple as needing only a single file.

## CHAPTER 9

Performing a Traditional Hard Drive Install

This chapter covers various methods of a conventional hard drive installation (as opposed to a Frugal installation, which is covered in Chapter 8, "Installing DSL in Alternate Ways"). In this chapter, we will discuss when it is practical to do a conventional installation of Damn Small Linux (DSL), walk through hard drive preparation, how to use the DSL hard drive installation script, and finally, show some pointers on setting up a PC for multiboot.

CONVENTIONAL HARD DRIVE INSTALL VERSUS FRUGAL INSTALL

Most of the development in DSL has been dedicated toward a compact and modular operating system with a tiny but usable base of 50MB and easily integrated extensions to build out functionality as needed. This system has been adapted to work from within a CD, a pen drive, and conventional hard drive, or an IDE Compact Flash drive.

This method is so versatile because it essentially looks at these units (the core OS and the extensions) as solid images that are interlinked together. This means that DSL is run as a very durable compressed image, which is more difficult to damage than a conventional hard drive install. The Frugal system is also well-suited for nonconventional media, such as compact flash, due to its operation with a small ramdisk. A conventional hard drive install of Linux does many writes to disk, which eventually destroys compact flash.

So, why would someone want to do a conventional hard drive install using Damn Small Linux, if Frugal has so much going for it? Well, a user in our forum posted the same question and the results were interesting. Most users who do a conventional install do not know about the Frugal method. In addition, some say that there are applications they would like to have that aren't provided in the repository, and others say that they are using DSL on a low RAM system.

Even with knowledge of the Frugal method, the second and third explanations are still reasonable. If you know what you are doing and you want to run your particular applications from within a very compact system, DSL may be a very good fit. On the other hand, if you have a limited resource system, DSL may work well as a low-fat operating system (e.g., for hardware that was originally built for Windows 95 or Windows 98).

There was a group of Linux enthusiasts who installed Damn Small Linux on a pair of 486 computers with 16MB of RAM. They actually found the performance of this particular installation with DSL somewhat useful. Personally, I think that this is scraping the bottom of the usability scale, unless you are planning on spending most of your time in text mode.

However, there are many examples of people running DSL on machines that have only 32MB of RAM. I feel that a conventional hard drive install makes more sense than a Frugal installation for any conventional computer that has 64MB of RAM or less.

In this example, you are using the computer only as a DSL machine; thus, I am not going to outline the many facets of creating a multiboot system. If you follow this process, you end up with a computer that only boots DSL when you are finished. If you are interested in setting up a multiboot machine, there are lots of how-tos on the Internet to reference. Setting up a single boot computer with DSL is a much simpler process, and you do not need any outside utility to accomplish this.

A good how-to on multibooting can be found at:

`http://www.geocities.com/epark/linux/grub-w2k-HOWTO.html`

A traditional hard drive install of Damn Small Linux is not that difficult to do. However, before you start, there are some things you should know about software compatibility and hardware requirements.

Some Debian Compatibility

Damn Small Linux is not Debian! Damn Small Linux is built with KNOPPIX technology that is based on Debian technology. However, we have done a lot of customization to achieve such a small package.

This means that you are bound to run into some issues if you want to use Damn Small Linux as a means to install a Debian system. For example, many of the core libraries are based on *old stable*, which is no longer being supported by Debian. So, if you want to go from DSL to a full-fledge Debian system, you need to do a lot of updating.

Another thing to keep in mind is that DSL uses a special light build for our Xserver, called Kdrive, which we compiled and is not compatible with the Debian system. Eventually, apt-get tries to override the setup with a fuller Xfree86 configuration.

If you desire to go for a cutting-edge *Unstable* Debian edition, do not start with DSL. There are other options out there. Even using KNOPPIX gets you there with much less fuss.

Because much of the base Debian structure has been stripped out of DSL, we recommend that you do not try to upgrade to a more recent version using DSL. That being said, many old stable Debian applications can be installed in DSL without much hassle. If you are running older hardware, you will find the software provided in Debian old stable much more suited for your machine than the later software. Thus, it is probably in your best interest to stay with what is most easily compatible with DSL.

Hardware Requirements

Your hard drive should have at least 200MB of space. If you are planning on doing an install on a low RAM system, you need to allocate space for a *swap* partition that is used to supplement RAM.

A general rule of thumb is to provide double the size of your RAM for your swap. So, if you have 128MB of RAM, you should provide 256MB for your swap partition. If your system is on the lower end and has 64MB of RAM or less, you may want to increase the swap to three times the RAM size. This helps when you run larger applications such as Firefox.

On the other hand, if you have abundant RAM—for example, over 1Gig—you may not need a swap space at all. I have successfully used a system with 256MB of RAM without a swap partition, but I do have to be careful with my RAM allocation.

Remember: Do not do a conventional hard drive install if your computer has an IDE Flash drive. Instead, perform a Frugal install.

PRE-INSTALLATION PREPARATION

Before you get started with the installation process, you need to partition the hard drive and set up the swap file. For the purpose of this walkthrough, we are assuming that you are going to install DSL via a DSL live CD. Please note that the installation process will destroy all data on the hard drive, so be sure to archive any important files someplace other than the computer you are about to format.

Partitioning with Cfdisk

You need to set up a Linux partition and a swap partition. You will be using the cfdisk command as your partition editor. Cfdisk was selected for this example because it is relatively intuitive to use. Cfdisk can be used to examine your computer's current partition table, as well as delete and add new partitions.

In DSL, your primary IDE hard drive should be recognized as /dev/hda. In order to have writable access to the hard drive, you need to have a terminal open with root user privileges; this can be done by opening up a root Terminal window, or by typing **sudo su** if you are in text mode.

To launch Cfdisk, type

```
# cfdisk /dev/hda
```

In my example, I am altering a computer that previously had MS Windows 98 on it. Figure 9-1 shows the cfdisk interface.

FIGURE 9-1 Cfdisk displaying data for a hard drive partitioned for Windows 98 (note, it looks much the same way as Windows 95 would look to cfdisk).

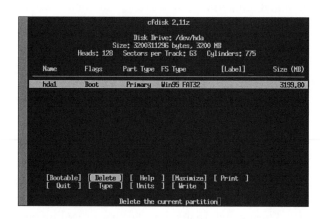

The figure shows the hard drive as it was originally set up for a MS Windows 98 install.

There is a lot of useful information in the top section of the image:

- **Disk Drive**: The disk drive you are viewing/editing, shown here as /dev/hda.
- **Size**: The size of the drive, which is about 3200MB in this case.
- **Heads/Sectors per Track/Cylinders**: The geometry of the drive shows the number of heads, sectors per track, and cylinders on the hard drive.

You will want to reference the size of the drive as you set up your partitions. You will be splitting the drive into a Linux partition, which will house DSL and a smaller Linux swap partition, which Linux uses similar to the way that MS Windows uses a swap file.

You are going to put the boot partition first in this example. However, you need to reserve a space for the swap partition, so you are going subtract out the size of the swap partition from the total size of the drive. The demonstration computer has 256MB of RAM, and you want to give this computer a swap partition, which is double that size.

You need to do some math:

```
3,200MB     Total Drive Space
- 512MB     The desired swap partition size
-------
2,688MB     The size of the boot partition
```

Now you have your number: 2688MB for your boot partition. Before you make it, you need to delete the existing table.

Cfdisk is pretty simple to use; to move the focus around, you simply use the arrow keys on your keyboard. The first step is to navigate to the Delete tab and press Enter. This removes the existing partition. If you have more than one preexisting partition, remove them all.

After you have nothing remaining but free space, navigate to the New button and press Enter. Next, it asks if this should be a Primary or Logical partition; select Primary and press Enter.

The next dialog asks for size. At this point, enter the amount you figured out for the boot partition (in our earlier example, it was 2688), then press Enter again. Cfdisk then asks if you want the partition to be at the beginning or end of the drive. For simplicity, choose the beginning. Now, you want to flag the partition Boot, so navigate to the Bootable button and press Enter. You also need to be sure that the partition is assigned the right file system type. To do that, navigate to the Type button, press Enter, and then select #83. That designates this partition as a Linux partition.

The second partition is used for swap. The first step in creating the new partition is to press the down arrow on your keyboard to highlight the remaining free space on the drive. Next, use the right arrow key to navigate to the New button. Choose Primary again, and then press Enter.

Because the math was already completed for your first partition, the size of this one should coincide with what you wanted for your swap file—you should be able to just press Enter to set the size. Do not mark this partition bootable! Navigate to the Type button and select #82, which is Linux swap. Figure 9-2 shows an example of the cfdisk interface, containing the partitioning just described.

FIGURE 9-2 An example of a hard drive partitioned for Linux.

This is the same hard drive now with both the Linux boot and Linux swap partition mapped out.

Now, you should have all the space assigned on your hard drive. The numbers are probably slightly off from what you selected, but not by much—maybe a few MBs. This is due to the physical limitations of the hard drive's internal geometry.

Next, navigate to the Write button and press Enter. You are prompted to type either **yes** or **no**. If everything looks good, type **yes** and press **q** to exit the program.

Creating the Swap File

This is a good time to format the swap partition. It is a simple process; in a terminal with root privileges, type **mkswap** and then the partition you assigned to be the swap partition in Cfdisk.

So, if the swap partition is assigned to hda2, you would type:

```
# mkswap /dev/hda2
```

Figure 9-3 shows an example of the output from the mkswap command after formatting the /dev/hda2 partition.

```
[/home/dsl]# mkswap /dev/hda2
Setting up swapspace version 1, size = 511963136 bytes
```

FIGURE 9-3 The mkswap command sets up a Linux swap area.

THE HARD DRIVE INSTALL SCRIPT

There are quite a few options when doing a conventional hard drive install of Damn Small Linux. You can install DSL without a boot loader, or you can choose to install either Grub or Lilo. Unless you are installing DSL on a computer from which you want to boot multiple operating systems, you probably want to have the script set up the boot loader for you.

You can install DSL in *single user mode*, which brings you right into a desktop at boot. Or, you could opt for a multiuser setup, which requires you to log in before you can access the desktop or command line. You also have the option of installing DSL with ext3, a journal file system, or the older ext2 file system.

For our demonstration, we are going to select Lilo because it is simple (gives less booting options) and this is an old computer that will only be booting DSL. In addition, we are going to install DSL to be set up for multiple users because it is slightly more secure with the additional requirement of logging in before the user is granted access to the system.

If you are not sure what choices to make, try a few different installation configurations to see what fits your needs and feels the most comfortable. For this example, I also chose to go with ext2, the nonjournalized file system, because it has a faster write and read access and uses less disk space. Others may find that the increase in reliability is worth the performance hit of the ext3 file system.

If your system is underpowered (or if you are in a hurry), you may want to do an installation from the DSL CD in "installation mode." Type **install** at the boot prompt:

    boot: **install**

This boots you into the following DSL Install Options:

```
+==[ DSL Install Options ]===================================+
|                                      Net Access Req'd  |
|   1. Make Standard Boot Floppy            yes          |
|   2. Make USB Boot Floppy                 yes          |
|                                                        |
|   3. Install to Hard Drive                no           |
|   4. Frugal Grub Hard Drive Install       no           |
|   5. Frugal Lilo Compact Flash Install    no           |
|                                                        |
|   6. USB Pendrive ZIP boot Install        no           |
|   7. USB Pendrive HDD boot Install        no           |
|                                                        |
|   8. Split KNOPPIX into floppy sized chunks   no       |
```

```
|  9. Interactive KNOPPIX split onto floppies    no        |
| 10. DSL FreeDOS Utilities                       yes       |
|                                                           |
| 11. PCMCIA Module Floppy                        yes       |
|                                                           |
| 12. Reboot                                                |
| 13. Shutdown                                              |
|                       Command:                            |
|  0. quit                                                  |
|                                                           |
```

To launch the hard drive installation script, type the number **3** as follows:

Command: **3**

The dsl-hdinstall script starts, as shown in Figure 9-4.

FIGURE 9-4 Opening dialog of the hard drive install script

You are asked what partition you want DSL to be installed on. In this example, we prepped /dev/hda1 to receive DSL, so you would type **hda1** at the prompt.

Next, you are asked if you want to run DSL with multiuser logins or have it boot directly into the desktop as user DSL. If you want to be prompted for a username and password before accessing your computer, type **y** and press Enter (otherwise, just press Enter).

The next question asks if you want ext3 (the journalized file system) or to stay with the default ext2 filesystem. If you want ext3, type **y** and press Enter; if you want to stick with the lighter ext2 filesystem, just press the Enter key.

As shown in Figure 9-5, you have a final chance to quit before erasing your hard disk partition and starting the installation.

After you type **y** and press the Enter key, the script begins to format the partition and install the files required to run DSL. This process may take a few minutes.

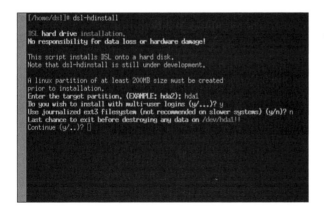

FIGURE 9-5   You have one last chance to opt out.

After the files have been copied over, the script asks if you want to install a boot loader. If your computer is going to be dedicated to DSL without having multiboot options (which is what most of you should be doing if you are using this chapter as a guide), you definitely need to type **y** for this option.

Here, you are given a choice between Grub and Lilo. Both have their merits; in general, most people agree that Grub is more versatile, whereas Lilo is simple to use if you just want to set it up and forget about it. Figure 9-6 shows the results of selecting Lilo.

```
The installation process is finished.
The next step is the boot loader.
Proceed to install a boot loader? (y/...): y
/dev/root on / type ext2 (rw)
/dev/scd0 on /cdrom type iso9660 (ro)
/dev/cloop on /KNOPPIX type iso9660 (ro)
/ramdisk on /ramdisk type tmpfs (rw,size=199688k,size=197433k)
/proc/bus/usb on /proc/bus/usb type usbdevfs (rw,devmode=0666)
unionfs on /KNOPPIX/bin type unionfs (rw,dirs=/ramdisk/bin=rw:/bin=ro)
unionfs on /dev type unionfs (rw,dirs=/ramdisk/dev=rw:/dev=ro)
unionfs on /etc type unionfs (rw,dirs=/ramdisk/etc=rw:/etc=rw)
unionfs on /KNOPPIX/lib type unionfs (rw,dirs=/ramdisk/lib=rw:/lib=ro)
unionfs on /KNOPPIX/sbin type unionfs (rw,dirs=/ramdisk/sbin=rw:/sbin=ro)
unionfs on /KNOPPIX/usr type unionfs (rw,dirs=/ramdisk/usr=rw:/usr=ro)
unionfs on /ramdisk/var type unionfs (rw,dirs=/ramdisk/var=rw)
/dev/hda1 on /mnt/hd type ext2 (rw)
Use [G]rub MBR or [L]ilo Active Partition? (g/l): l
Setting up boot loader (LILO) into the active partition..
Warning: '/proc/partitions' does not exist, disk scan bypassed
Added Linux *
Skipping /vmlinuz.old
The boot installation process is finished.
You must reboot to continue the final stage of the hard drive install.
Reboot now? (y/...): y
```

FIGURE 9-6   After the boot loader selection, you are prompted to reboot to finish the installation.

After the script is completed, it is necessary to reboot the system to finish the process. When the system is rebooted, you are asked to choose your root and user DSL passwords. That is the last step—now you have a conventionally installed Damn Small Linux on your computer.

> ### FURTHER READING FOR THOSE INTERESTED IN MULTIBOOTING
>
> Those interested in multiboot systems may want to look at the Gparted LiveCD, which features the Gparted software. With this live CD, you will have the ability to resive, move, or destroy exsisting partitions.
>
> Gparted LiveCD URL is: `http://gparted.sourceforge.net/`
>
> For those who are interested in dual booting with grub, there is a good howto at tldp.org: `http://tldp.org/HOWTO/Linux+Win9x+Grub-HOWTO/index.html`
>
> For those who are interested in multibooting with Lilo, there is another howto at tldp.org as well: `http://tldp.org/HOWTO/Multiboot-with-LILO.html`

ENABLING APT-GET WITH DPKG-RESTORE

We provide a script that simplifies the process of enabling `apt-get` on your computer. Assuming your computer has Internet access, all you need to do is open up a Terminal window and type the following as root:

```
# dpkg-restore
```

This restores the missing `apt` utilities and populates your computer's `apt-cache` with applications compatible with Debian Woody. We are pulling the application list from Debian's archive. Remember that many applications inevitably overwrite the DSL framework, and you eventually end up with either a broken desktop or a classic version of Debian (if you download applications that overwrite your libraries). So, be careful and know what you want to do with your system.

SUMMARY

We walked though the basic steps of installing Damn Small Linux conventionally on a hard drive, including hard drive preparation, and the installation process. As noted before, a conventional hard drive may not be the best choice for many; however there are special circumstances that make DSL a good fit for some computers, including limited RAM size.

If you venture into a conventional hard drive installation of DSL, congratulations! I am sure that you have an interesting story as to why you elected to complete such an adventurous process. However, if it keeps an ancient computer out of a landfill, more power to you!

Part III

Creating Extensions and Remastering

## CHAPTER 10

Adding Applications and Creating Shareable Extensions

Damn Small Linux can be easily extended to run many more applications than provided by the base 50MB system using the MyDSL extension system, as we saw in Chapter 5, "Extending Applications with MyDSL." In this chapter, we will discuss several ways to make your own MyDSL extensions.

There are many ways to approach the creation of an extension—whether it starts by modifying an existing package, be it a tarball, a Debian package, or compiling from sources. We will learn how to make all four types of MyDSL extensions: from the .tar.gz to .dsl, .uci, and .unc.

OVERVIEW

All UNIX-based systems add applications to the file system as a collection of files and directories. Typically, the method used is TAR (tape archive) or CPIO (copy input output). Later package management systems would combine installation scripts specific to their distributions. Some would add a database of installed applications and dependencies required.

Different package management systems typically have different software package formats, use different commands for managing their packages, and change the package name extensions to something unique for their distribution. For example, .deb was used for Debian packages and .rpm was used for Red Hat Linux packages. Tools such as dpkg and apt-get are commonly used to install and manage Debian packages, while rpm and yum commands are most often used with packaging derived from Red Hat Linux (such as Fedora, Red Hat Enterprise Linux, and others).

DSL's extensions are not much different than the very simplified description that I have just given. But why have them? Why not stay with the Debian package management system? Debian is already available for DSL.

As was discussed in Chapter 5, the MyDSL extensions offered much of the same benefits of the traditional hard drive installation to a person using the live CD-ROM or the compressed DSL file system image installed to hard disk. Besides, running directly from the DSL live CD-ROM means that very little of the file system is write-enabled. The live CD-ROM and compressed type installs are running (reading from) a compressed read-only file system.

Despite the fact that loading a .dsl type extension would cause much of the file system to become write-enabled, this file system is still on the RAM disk. If we were to rely on Debian, or other package management systems, laying down all of the files, directories, and a database for package management would quickly exceed the capacity of the ramdisk.

Additionally, trying to maintain a database of installed applications with their dependencies in RAM disk does not make any sense. Neither does it make any sense to use a persistent storage device to maintain this database of applications that are loaded into the RAM disk.

Creating MyDSL Extensions

I created the MyDSL extensions as a way of adding applications that makes sense for the way Damn Small Linux works. I called them extensions, and not packages, because the MyDSL facility does not offer any application removal. Because the extensions are loaded or mounted on ramdisk, simply reboot. The application extension is gone.

But wait; does that mean that you must download the extension every time you want to use it? No. DSL, like the other distributions, offers an extension loader, based on the extension name's extension. The extension loader can properly load and install copies of extensions stored on various persistent media.

Therefore, a MyDSL extension is a collection of related files, executables, and libraries that need to be added to DSL in order to provide the application. Just as almost every package in UNIX-like systems are variations of the tar archive, so too are MyDSL .tar.gz and .dsl extensions. The .uci and .unc extensions, on the other hand, are compressed images of a collection of related directories and files needed to provide the application.

Because the primary focus of DSL is to be a nomadic live CD-ROM or to run as a compressed installed image means that the only write-enabled area is on the ramdisk. That being the case, every bit of space saved means more room for other applications. Therefore, no matter what source the packaged application starts with, certain areas are immediately targets to be cut. Also, realize that .uci and .unc style extensions are far more efficient when it comes to using RAM.

NOTE

Because MyDSL extensions are designed for the live CD-ROM and compressed installations, and no package database is maintained, users of traditional hard installations should not use MyDSL extensions. They should use the Debian package management system. Using MyDSL extensions on a traditional hard installation is like force loading a foreign package, in that it is not readily available for removal.

NOTE

The reverse is not true. You can use Debian packaging tools to load an application onto the ramdisk of DSL. Descriptions of how to add Debian packaging tools to DSL are contained in the "UNC Extension Type" section later in this chapter.

Understanding MyDSL Extensions

Let's begin by defining the four extension types of MyDSL:

tar.gz: A tar archive collection of files that loads entirely into the base write-enabled areas defined on the ramdisk—that primarily being /opt, /tmp, and /home/dsl. With such limited write-enabled areas, most .tar.gz extensions are self-contained.

uci: A compressed image of a self-contained application that mounts under /opt. Usually contains a user.tar.gz, a subextension that defines a menu, and an icon for the application. Most .tar.gz extensions can be converted into this more RAM-efficient method.

dsl: A tar archive collection of files that loads into ramdisk anchored from /. The first invocation of this extension type causes most of the file system to become write-enabled.

unc: A compressed image of files and directories anchored from /. The system mounts this extension type under /opt and then adds each base directory to the system via unionfs file systems. Base directories that by default are already write-enabled are not added to the union space. This extension type usually contains a user.tar.gz, a subextension that defines a menu, and an icon for this application.

Notice that the `.tar.gz` and the `.uci` extension-types are both installed under /opt. In fact, it is usually easy to convert from `.tar.gz` to `.uci`. Similarly, both `.dsl` and `.unc` extensions are installed under /. It is also easy to convert from `.dsl` to `.unc`. Later, I will discuss the DSL tools to help in building and converting extensions.

In the rest of this chapter, I will demonstrate how to create the four MyDSL extension types. I will use the common application of Zile. Zile is an Emacs-like command-line editor.

COMMON ELEMENTS TO ALL MYDSL EXTENSIONS

Let's begin by discussing the common elements to all DSL extensions: the menu and icon. Being a live CD-ROM, and therefore not inherently a multiuser system, means the extensions are built for the default user `dsl`. Because you use a minimal window manager (as provided with Fluxbox) and a customized icon manager (called xtdesk), you need to provide your own menu and icon for each extension you create. Menus and icons are optional, but most users expect at least a menu item to be included.

NOTE

If the application is console based and commonly requires command-line options, a menu item is not very useful. The menu item is not required.

NOTE

Loading a Debian application using the standard Debian procedures does not provide a menu item or icon. Much of the Debian menu and icon supporting infrastructure was cut to reduce the size of DSL.

All other aspects of an extension—the actual files, directories, libraries, and paths—are common to any Linux distribution given the existing kernel, modules, and libraries.

The Menu Element

The menu for a MyDSL extension is actually a fragment of the Fluxbox standard. This menu fragment is a simple text file and is created under the directory /tmp/mydsl.menu. It must be the same name as the base extension name and must be unique. For example, for the `zile.dsl` extension, the menu item would be `/tmp/mydsl.menu/zile`. To ensure uniqueness, use version numbers as part of the name for both the extension name and the matching menu item name. No special characters or spaces are allowed in either. Typically, you would use DSL's beaver to create this file:

```
$ beaver /tmp/mydsl.menu/zile
```

Using the standard structure of the Fluxbox menu files, here are the contents of the Zile extension menu item:

```
[exec] (Zile) {aterm -e /usr/bin/zile}
```

 NOTE

Because Zile is a console application, it needs a hosting terminal window. DSL uses Aterm for such terminal windows. Therefore, notice that the preceding command path includes aterm -e as a prefix to the normal command path. If Zile was an X-based application, such prefix would not be necessary.

The Icon Element

The icon element consists of two files. The first file must be in an image format readable by DSL's icon manager, a modified version of xtdesk. Image formats png, gif, jpg, and xpm are supported. The icon's image file is located in the /home/dsl/.xtdesktop directory.

 NOTE

DSL offers several generic icons available for your extensions. These include binary.png, gear.png, and shellscript.png. To use one of these generics, just copy them using your extension's name as the basename. See Chapter 4, "Configuring and Saving DSL Settings," for details.

The second required file is the lnk and it is also located in /home/dsl/.xtdesktop directory. Typically, you would use your favorite text editor, such as DSL's beaver, to create this file:

```
$ beaver /home/dsl/.xtdesktop/zile.lnk
```

The lnk file is a simple text file with the .lnk extension, such as zile.lnk. The format of the file is as follows:

```
table Icon
Type: Program
Caption: zile
Command: aterm -e /usr/bin/zile
Icon: /home/dsl/.xtdesktop/zile.jpg
X: 420
Y: 384
end
```

The caption entry is what the icon manager will display under the icon image. By convention, all MyDSL extensions should use lowercase letters for this Caption field entry. DSL's base application uses uppercase letters. With this convention, all base applications will consistently display before any add-on MyDSL extensions when icon auto-layout is used. Auto-layout is the default for DSL.

Also notice that because Zile is a console-based application, the Command entry also has the prefix aterm -e.

The X and Y coordinates can be any number within the minimal screen resolution that DSL supports (640×480). Usually, these coordinates are ignored, as icon auto-layout is the default with DSL. The Icon tool and icon layout were discussed in Chapter 4.

NOTE

DSL base application icons use an additional Status: anchor field. MyDSL extensions should never use anchor status.

CREATING DSL AND UNC EXTENSIONS

Because DSL is based on Debian Woody, it is not very difficult to create extensions from the Woody repository. Because the Debian Woody repository is huge, let's start by taking a close look at creating a zile.dsl extension from the Debian Woody repository.

The DSL Extension Type

DSL extensions are loaded on the root file system on the ramdisk. This extension type, although easy to create, consumes a lot of RAM. It is also capable of overwriting core system files and libraries, as well as possibly changing permissions.

Because members of the DSL community create MyDSL extensions, care must be exercised in their use. System performance may be impacted. Often, ramdisk memory will be overrun and the system will hang. As a user, you must exercise care when loading everything into the ramdisk. Of course, a reboot is all that is needed to "delete" the offending extension. Or, if persistent storage was used, simply delete the offending extension from the storage device.

For the same reasons, we do not recommend using Debian package manager for live CD-ROM or other frugal type installs, as it too would overwhelm available RAM. Yet, we can still deploy the Debian package management system to aid in the creation of well-tested and known working packages.

It is not too difficult to create a .dsl extension from an existing Debian package. It used to be much manual work, using tar commands and removing and trimming files to conserve space. Now we have tools to aid in their creation.

Step 1: Setup DSL for Extension Building

Whenever you are building a dsl type extension, you should eliminate all possible accidental dependencies. That is, your extension should work on any base install of DSL. Therefore, to ensure this common pristine environment, you should always boot DSL as follows:

```
boot: dsl base norestore legacy
```

The options base and norestore starts DSL with a pristine environment. The legacy boot option is for compatibility for the lowest common use of DSL. Other boot options that are required by your hardware still need to be added. See Chapter 2, "Booting DSL," for details.

Step 2: Restore Debian Package Management System

From the main menu, select Apps -> Tools -> Enable Apt. A root shell window opens and an attempt is made to connect to the DSL repositories to restore all the files, and binaries needed to use dpkg and apt commands for our Debian Woody based system. Alternatively, you can manually open a root shell and enter the command dpkg-restore. A progress bar is displayed as the necessary environment is downloaded and installed. This is actually a MyDSL extension called dsl-dpkg.dsl that resides in the MyDSL system repository.

 NOTE

If you use the manual command dpkg-restore, you must as root also perform an apt-get update.

NOTE

You will want to save the ds1-dpkg.ds1 extension so you can create more extensions the next time you reboot DSL. Use the standard methods as described in Chapter 4. Later, when you need this system extension, you can use the MyDSL desktop icon Load Local and not have to keep downloading this extension.

Step 3: Install and Test Desired Package

Now, open a regular shell (ds1 user) to enter the further commands:

$ **sudo apt-get install zile**

Because DSL does not normally use Debian packages, there are no updates to the system menu. So, you must know the command to start the newly installed package. So, for this example, type **zile** from the shell prompt.

NOTE

In case you are not familiar with Zile/Emacs, you may find yourself stuck and unable to exit this program. If that is the case, you can simply press **Ctrl-x Ctrl-c** to exit.

The whereis command is very useful in determining the full path to the zile command. You will need this full path later in your configuration.

Thoroughly test the application. You will then be ready to repackage the application and all of its dependencies into a ds1 type extension.

Step 4: Create the Extension

From the open shell, enter the following :

$ **deb2ds1**

Enter the full name for your DSL extension.
Example: rox.ds1 **zile.ds1**

Enter the MyDSL menu name for your program.
Example: Rox Filer **Zile Emacs**
Is this an X application: (y/..) **n**

Enter the full path to the executable.
Example: /usr/bin/rox **/usr/bin/zile**

Step 5: Save Your Extension

Because you have already installed Zile via the Debian apt-get command, before you can really test your newly built extension, you must reboot. Recall that you booted with base and norestore options. So, use care to mount a persistent store and copy your zile.dsl.

Step 6: Test Your New zile.dsl

After copying your new extension, reboot DSL with the base and norestore options. Using the MyDSL tool, Load Local option, navigate to your saved extension and load it. Because you have not yet made an icon, use the System menu, MyDSL, Zile Emacs to launch the application.

Step 7: Add an Icon (Optional)

Although adding an icon is optional, it gives me the chance to discuss how to open an existing dsl extension. You will want to do this if you need to add, change, or edit any file(s) in your extension.

But first, let's create the icon file. Using the text editor beaver, create the icon as described earlier in "The Icon Element" section. The icon for Zile in /home/dsl/.xtdesktop/zile.lnk is identified as follows:

```
table Icon
Type: Program
Caption: Zile
Command: aterm -e /usr/bin/zile
Icon:   /home/dsl/.xtdesktop/program.png
X: 420
Y: 384
end
```

Next, copy zile.dsl to /home/dsl and then open it with the following commands:

```
# mkdir /home/dsl/work
# cd work
# tar -zxvf ../zile.dsl | tee > /tmp/zile.lst
```

Using the text editor, beaver, add the following line to /tmp/zile.lst:

home/dsl/.xtdesktop/zile.lnk

 NOTE

If you are also using a new image file for this extension, you would add that line to the file list as well.

To ensure that your permissions are correct on the additional files, you should use the following:

```
$ sudo chown -R 0.0 /tmp
$ sudo chown -R 1001.50 /home/dsl/.xtdesktop
```

Now, repackage the extension with the following command:

```
$ cd /home/dsl/work
$ tar -T /tmp/zile.lst -czvf ../zile.dsl
```

Step 8: Save Your Extension

If the extension creation was successful, copy your zile.dsl to any persistent store that you have used for other MyDSL extensions (typically, a mydsl directory).

Now, you have your final .dsl extension with both menu and icon elements. If you want to share this with the DSL community, skip forward to the "Sharing Your Extension with the World" section later in this chapter.

The UNC Extension Type

UNC Extensions are mountable using the unionfs file system. The main advantage of using this method is the very low RAM use. If only unc and uci extensions are used, you would use very little RAM. Compressed mounts save RAM, as only the runtime is loaded into memory very similar to the RAM usage of a traditional hard drive. Unionfs, as implemented in DSL, makes the same area of the file system write-enabled, as does the dsl extension type.

It is trivial to create a unc extension from an existing dsl extension. The base DSL system contains a tool to convert any dsl into a unc. Open a root xterm and run the script:

```
$ dsl2unc.sh zile.dsl
```

It is preferred to make the unc extension this way as much of the work is automated.

However, if you want to manually make a unc from an existing Debian package, read on. It is also not difficult to create. Let's take another look at the same Debian Zile example.

Step 1: Set Up DSL for Extension Building

As previously stated, when you are building an extension, you should eliminate all possible accidental dependencies. That is, your extension should work on any base install of DSL. Therefore, to ensure this common pristine environment, you should always boot DSL as follows:

boot: **dsl base norestore**

The options base and norestore start DSL with a pristine environment. Other boot options that are required by your hardware would still need to be added.

Step 2: Restore Debian Package Management System

If you have saved your Debian extension, dsl-dpkg.dsl, load this extension followed by the apt-get update. Otherwise, from the main menu, select Apps, Tools, Enable Apt. The Debian environment is downloaded again and its environment is set up.

Step 3: Install and Test Desired Package

Now, you must open a root shell to enter the further commands:

apt-get install zile

From a shell, for this example, type **zile**. Thoroughly test the application. You then are ready to repackage the application and all of its dependencies into a unc type extension.

Step 4: Reboot

Yes, that is correct. You want to ensure the state of the machine. By rebooting, you lose this installed application and any other extra packages that you may have used. This step is really only needed to "start from a zero-base state."

Step 5: Restore Debian Package Management System

As in step 2, you need some base Debian package management tools. However, you do not actually install the Zile application.

Step 6: Create the UNC

Open a root shell and enter the following commands:

```
# apt-get clean
# apt-get -d -y install zile
# mkdir /tmp/zile
# for F in `ls -1 /var/cache/apt/archives/*.deb`; do
# dpkg -x "$F" /tmp/zile
# cd /tmp
# mkisofs -R -hide-rr-moved -cache-inodes -pad zile/ \
    | create_compressed_fs - 65536 > /tmp/zile.unc
```

Step 7: Test Your New zile.unc

As normal user ds1, use the standard MyDSL system to load the extension. Because you have not yet made a menu or icon item, open a shell window and issue the command zile.

Step 8: Insert Common Extension Elements

Using this manual method to create a .unc extension means you must make the menu and icon elements as was discussed earlier in the "Common Elements to All MyDSL Extensions" section.

For a .unc type extension, the menu and icon elements are stored in a user.tar.gz file. It is really an additional MyDSL extension included within the unc. When the unc is mounted, the system looks inside the mount for a user.tar.gz ("user.tar.gz" is the literal filename) and then performs a mydsl-load on that .tar.gz. This makes for an easy single file download and load. The user.tar.gz file is optional, and generally includes a desktop icon, menu item, and any personal configs that your application requires but does not create. This file must be built the same way as any .tar.gz extension, including full paths and proper file ownerships/permissions.

Using DSL's text editor beaver, create the following in /tmp/mydsl.menu/zile:

```
[exec] (Zile) {aterm -e /usr/bin/zile}
```

To create the icon file, use the text editor beaver to create the icon as described earlier in "The Icon Element" section. Our icon for Zile in /home/ds1/.xtdesktop/ zile.lnk looks like this:

```
table Icon
Type: Program
Caption: Zile
Command: aterm -e /usr/bin/zile
Icon:   /home/ds1/.xtdesktop/program.png
X: 420
Y: 384
end
```

Next, you create the mini-extension of the user files. In this case, use the beaver text editor and create /tmp/user.1st. The contents of the /tmp/user.1st file is a list of the user files. Among those files are the zile menu (zile) and icon (zile.lnk) files.

```
home/ds1/.xtdesktop/zile.lnk
tmp/mydsl.menu/zile
```

NOTE

If you are also using a new image file for this extension, you would add that line to the file list as well.

To ensure that your permissions are correct on the new files, you should use the following:

```
$ sudo chown -R 0.0 /tmp
$ sudo chown -R 1001.50 /home/dsl/.xtdesktop
```

Next, package the user files with the following command:

```
$ tar -T /tmp/user.lst -czvf /tmp/user.tar.gz
```

Now, you are ready to open the .unc extension to add the user.tar.gz and then repackage the extension with the following command:

```
$ mydsl-load zile.unc
$ mkdir /home/dsl/zile
$ tar -C /opt/zile -cf - . | tar -C /home/dsl/zile -xf -
$ cp /tmp/user.tar.gz /home/dsl/zile
$ mkisofs -R -hide-rr-moved -cache-inodes -pad zile/ \
       | create_compressed_fs - 65536 > zile.unc
```

Step 9: Save Your Extension

If the extension creation was successful, copy your zile.unc to any persistent store that you have used for other MyDSL extensions.

CREATING TAR.GZ AND UCI EXTENSIONS

As previously defined, the tar.gz extension type in DSL is not the Linux typical tar.gz. Traditional UNIX systems install programs by running an install script or package manager, such as apt, as root. This process scatters files and directories all over the file system. In DSL, this extension type must be installed into /opt and typically must be self-contained or depend on the base libraries within DSL.

In the past, many applications for Linux were distribution independent and were distributed this way. For example, OpenOffice and Firefox were originally offered as simple tar.gz files. Lately, it has become very difficult to find applications that are truly distribution independent. The goal of such is very worthy.

In fact, the tar.gz as defined and used in DSL is much closer to the relocatable application concept first used by the RISC OS and later adopted by Apple's MAC OSX as application directories.

Having self-contained applications means simple installation and removal. No package manager needed. No dependencies to manage. Because all the files in DSL `tar.gz` extensions are contained in one directory structure, compressing those extensions into a `uci` type becomes trivial. Alas, these self-contained applications are either not popular or not available on Linux-based systems.

You are left with compiling from source. With the use of compiler `make` options, by compiling from source you can force the application to be relocated into the native write-enabled area of DSL, `/opt`.

Compiling from Source to Create a TAR.GZ Extension

Although it is beyond the scope of this single chapter to cover all aspects of compiling Linux source files, the purpose is to illustrate the concepts that would apply to DSL. I will again use the now familiar application of Zile.

Let's review why we might choose to go with a `.tar.gz` extension rather than the previously discussed `.dsl` extension. The primary reason is the issue of memory usage. Using only the natively write-enabled areas of DSL means the `.tar.gz` extension type does not need to force other areas of the file system to be write-enabled. As previously mentioned, writing files over existing system files can cause system instability.

By definition, the `.tar.gz` extension has write access to `/opt`, `/tmp`, and `/home` (`/etc` is possible, but not recommended due to lack of RAM space).

On the other hand, there are not many readily available self-contained applications. Sometimes, you can take a large binary executable, with its unique required libraries, and force it as a `.tar.gz` by using wrapper startup script. This script can force its library search path elsewhere by using the `LD_LIBRARY_PATH` environment variable. Although this is possible, it is not recommended because its nonstandard setup is usually not general enough for more than a specific use.

For these reasons, we recommend compiling from source. I will now describe how to build Zile from an existing live CD-ROM of DSL:

1. Boot DSL with the now familiar `base norestore legacy` options. You do this to ensure no accidental dependencies are introduced and that the extension will work all versions, installations, and runtime options of DSL.

2. Download the following extensions via the MyDSL system from the system area of the DSL repositories:

   ```
   gnu-utils.dsl
   gccl-with-libs.dsl
   dsl-dpkg.dsl
   ```

3. As user root, type the following:

   ```
   # apt-get update
   # apt-get install texinfo
   ```

4. Download Zile Is Lossy Emacs from the Sourceforge.net site (http://sourceforge.net/projects/zile). The version used at the time of this writing is zile-2.2.29.tar.gz.

5. Unpack the source file tar -zxvf zile-2.2.29.tar.gz.

6. Change directory to zile-2.2.29/.

7. Always read the included README file. If you are going to publish this as a public MyDSL extension, it is very important to know the license for this software. Only GPL and similar licensed work may be shared with the DSL community.

8. You should issue the command ./configure –help. Look at the resulting text for information on using the prefix option to relocate the software being built.

9. To configure Zile to be self contained under /opt, issue the command:

   ```
   # ./configure -prefix=/opt/zile -exec-prefix=/opt/zile
   ```

10. If no errors occur, proceed to creating your self-contained Zile application:

    ```
    # make
    # mkdir /opt/zile
    # make install
    ```

11. If you change the directory to /opt/zile, you should see the following directories: /opt/zile/bin and /opt/zile/share.

12. The goal is to be able to run the zile command from the command prompt. So, create a link from the Zile zile binary to a directory in your path using only the natively write-enabled areas:

    ```
    # ln -s /opt/zile/bin/zile /opt/bin/
    ```

13. Create the menu item as discussed earlier in the section, "The Menu Element." Because zile is a console-based program and its path is now /opt/bin/zile, your menu item /tmp/mydsl.menu/zile looks like this:

    ```
    [exec] (Zile) {aterm -e /opt/bin/zile}
    ```

14. Create the icon as described earlier in the section, "The Icon Element." Your icon for running the `zile` command in `/home/dsl/.desktop/zile.lnk` looks like this:

```
table Icon
Type: Program
Caption: Zile
Command: aterm -e /opt/bin/zile
Icon:   /home/dsl/.xtdesktop/program.png
X: 420
Y: 384
end
```

NOTE

I am using one of the generic icons available in DSL. Other generic icons are `binary.png`, `gear.png`, and `shellscript.png`. You can change the icon later by right-clicking the displayed icon. See Chapter 4 for details.

15. Create a file list for your new application. This prunes out directories and allows you to add the menu and icon. Create the file list for the entire Zile application by typing the following

```
# cd /
# find opt/zile -not -type d > /tmp/zile.list
```

16. Add link, menu, and icon lines to this file list using a text editor:

```
# beaver /tmp/zile.list
```

Here is what the `zile.1st` file looked like before adding your DSL-specific files:

```
opt/zile/bin/zile
opt/zile/share/zile/dotzile.sample
opt/zile/share/zile/TUTORIAL
opt/zile/share/zile/HELP
opt/zile/share/zile/FAQ
opt/zile/share/zile/AUTODOC
opt/zile/share/man/man1/zile.1
opt/zile/share/info/zile.info
```

Here is how `zile.1st` appeared after adding DSL-specific files:

```
opt/zile/bin/zile
opt/zile/share/zile/dotzile.sample
opt/zile/share/zile/TUTORIAL
```

```
opt/zile/share/zile/HELP
opt/zile/share/zile/FAQ
opt/zile/share/zile/AUTODOC
opt/zile/share/man/man1/zile.1
opt/zile/share/info/zile.info
opt/bin/zile
home/dsl/.xtdesktop/zile.lnk
tmp/mydsl.menu/zile
```

NOTE

In the spirit of keeping everything small, and because the tar.gz extension type stills resides on the ramdisk, you may want to also remove the lines with man pages, docs, and faq. Anything that is documentation can be removed without affecting the runtime.

17. Because you have been creating files, menus, and icons as root, you should take this step to correct any permission problems that you may have introduced. Run the following commands to correct permissions:

```
# chown -R 0.0 /{opt/,tmp/}
# chown -R 1001.50 /home/dsl/
# chown 1001.50 /tmp/mydsl.menu/zile
```

18. Create the tar.gz by using the following:

```
# tar -C / -T /tmp/zile.list -czvf /tmp/zile.tar.gz
```

19. You are now ready to test the new extension. Be sure to copy the extension to a persistent storage device. You certainly do not want to lose all your work!

20. Boot DSL again with the base, norestore, and legacy options. Manually load your new Zile extension. Works? Great! Congratulations! You have built a tar.gz MyDSL extension.

The UCI Extension Revealed

The hardest part of creating uci extensions has nothing to do with compressing them. The hardest part, as you have just seen, is to make a self-contained application under /opt.

The uci being a read-only compressed image means that it has the limitation of being read-only. That is why there is a user.tar.gz just like you saw with the unc type. Those parts that require write ability can be "linked" into a write-enabled directory. The user.tar.gz file is really an additional MyDSL extension included within the `uci`. When the `uci` is mounted, the system looks inside the mount for a user.tar.gz ("user.tar.gz" is the literal filename) and then performs a `mydsl-load` on that `tar.gz`.

This makes for an easy, single file download and load. The user.tar.gz file is optional, and generally includes a desktop icon, menu item, and any personal configuration files that need to be present. This file must be built in the same way as any .tar.gz extension, including full paths and proper file ownerships and permissions.

Sometimes, you are required to make a shell wrapper to start the application, because being self-contained implies that the application's libraries are also stored locally with the application. This usually implies requiring a LD_LIBRARY_PATH and sometimes a PATH change, thus the shell wrapper. Anyway, make the application. Test it as a .tar.gz. After the application is working, do the following to make a .uci:

1. Check that the application is installed and runs properly from the /opt/zile directory.

2. As root user, type the following to create a list of user files:

   # `tar -ztf zile.tar.gz home/ tmp/ opt/bin > /tmp/user.list`

3. Use that list to create the user.tar.gz file:

   # `tar -C / -T /tmp/user.list -czvf /opt/zile/user.tar.gz`

4. Change to the /opt directory and create the .uci file as follows:

   # `cd /opt`
   # `mkisofs -R -hide-rr-moved -cache-inodes -pad zile/ \`
      `| create_compressed_fs - 65536 > /tmp/zile.uci`

NOTE

The thing to notice is in step 2. You are creating a list of the user files that need write access, so you extract a list consisting of home, tmp, and any link files that I previously discussed. Here, it is just the link for the executable to be found in the standard PATH opt/bin.

To change/update a .uci file (for example, using zile.uci), do the following:

1. Mount the uci as normal (in this case, /opt/zile).

2. Create a work directory:

   # `mkdir /home/dsl/work`

3. Copy the contents of /opt/zile to the work directory:

```
# cd /home/dsl/work
# cp -a /opt/zile
```

4. Make a user directory and change to it:

```
# cd zile
# mkdir user
# cd user
```

5. Create a user.list file from the contents of the user.tar.gz file:

```
# tar -zxvf ../user.tar.gz | tee /tmp/user.list
```

6. Edit the actual files as needed.

7. Edit the /tmp/user.list file to reflect any added or removed files.

8. Package up the files again, using the edited user.list file:

```
# tar -T /tmp/user.list -czvf ../user.tar.gz
```

9. Remove the temporary user directory you created and return to the work directory:

```
# cd ..
# rm -rf user/
# cd ..
```

10. Run the mkisofs command, run it through the create_compressed_fs command to compress the resulting ISO image, and create the updated uci file (called zile.uci). Options to mkisofs command allow Rock Ridge extensions for Linux file naming (-R), cause each hard linked file to only appear once on the CD-ROM image (-cache-inodes), and pads the image by 150 sectors (-pad):

```
# mkisofs -R -hide-rr-moved -cache-inodes -pad zile/ \
    | create_compressed_fs - 65536 > ../zile.uci
```

11. Remove the work directory:

```
# cd ..
# rm -rf work
```

As the result of this procedure, you should have a new zile.uci MyDSL package in your /home/dsl directory.

SHARING YOUR EXTENSION WITH THE WORLD

After your extension is working and you have thoroughly tested it, you will likely want to share your creation. DSL provides many repositories for user-contributed extensions. All extensions to be shared must be GNU Public License (GPL) or similar license.

There are a couple of additional files needed to participate in the community repositories. The first is an information file. Users will want to browse a summary that describes your extension. This summary is available both via the website of repositories and is also part of the displayed screens when a user selects the MyDSL download browser tool.

The Info File for All to Read

The `.info` file is a simple text file and is an additional suffix to the extension name. For example, the `zile.dsl` information file is `zile.dsl.info`. Using a text editor such as beaver, create the following file:

```
Title:          zile.dsl
Description:    Zile is an Emacs like text editor
Version:        2.2.29
Author:         http://www.my_program.org/
Original-site:  http://www.my_program.org/
Copying-policy: GPL
------------------------------------------------------
Extension by:   <your email address>
Comments:       This is an Emacs like text editor.
                It is a console-based application.
                It can be run from CLI or X hosted by an aterm.
                It requires the xxxx.dsl and the yyyy.dsl to function.
                This was repackaged from the my_program_42.0-0_i386.deb
                found at ftp.us.debian.org woody.
                Includes icon and menu.
Change-log:     2006/08/24 - First Version
Current:        2007/02/12 - Upgraded and Revised for xxxx-new.dsl
```

The preceding is just an example. In the Comments section, you should include where you got the program. List any other MyDSL extensions that may be required by your extension.

Checksum File for Quality Assurance

The second file required is a checksum file. This file is mandatory and is part of an automated process when users use the MyDSL download tool. This file ensures that the user has received a good download.

Many things can happen when users are downloading files. Part of the automated download process verifies the checksum and notifies the user if the checksum is different. Users who download via the web are also strongly encouraged to verify checksum before they try to use an extension. The name of this file is the base extension name with a suffix of .md5.txt. For your Zile example, it would be zile.dsl.md5.txt. To create this file, simply use the md5sum program in DSL. To create it for Zile, type the following:

```
# md5sum zile.dsl > zile.dsl.ms5.txt
```

Submitting Your Extension for Publication

The final step is to collect all three files and email them to extensions@ damnsmalllinux.org. For your Zile example, you would send an email with the subject line to contain (at least) the following words: DSL Zile Extension. Then, attach zile.dsl, zile.dsl.info, and zile.dsl.md5.txt.

Submitted extensions are usually processed once a week. Once the extension is processed, a "Thank You" email is sent to you, indicating that the submitted extension is published to the testing area of the MyDSL repository. An announcement is also posted in the DSL forums testing area.

A new topic is created each month for extensions submitted during that month. The announcement alerts the user community to begin testing the new extension. As an extension submitter, you should respond to questions and make corrections when necessary.

If, on the other hand, the submitted extension is missing one of the required files or fails the md5sum integrity check during processing, an email is sent describing what is needed before the extension can be accepted.

SUMMARY

Adding applications to DSL can be as easy as using Debian Apt system. Because using Apt with DSL is very RAM inefficient, you learned how to create the much more memory efficient MyDSL extensions. You saw that it can be as easy as running two scripts: deb2dsl and dsl2unc.

You saw that adding menus and icons can be done in easy-to-make text files. You have learned the structure that the MyDSL download tool expects, as well as the structure needed to use the mydsl-load command to handle MyDSL desktop icons.

You also saw the more challenging aspects of compiling from source code and creating self-contained applications and how to package the most powerful type of MyDSL extension: the uci.

Overall, MyDSL extensions are just repackaged files and directories together with some common elements to support the live CD-ROM single user environment of DSL.

## CHAPTER 11

Setting Up a Full Remastering Environment

With many live CD-ROM-based systems, adding extra software packages typically requires a remaster. In Chapter 5, "Extending Applications with MyDSL," you saw how easy it is to add dozens of extra applications called *MyDSL extensions*. Just copy them to boot media or place them on persistent storage (a hard drive partition, a pen drive, or compact flash); without even requiring any extra boot options, the whole system boots and appears much larger and customized to your particular needs.

However, there will always be the desire to make a single bootable CD-ROM work just like your Damn Small Linux (DSL) system does. You can't always take your persistent media with you. DSL offers two ways to accomplish this task.

By just the normal procedure of booting from the live DSL CD-ROM and having all your MyDSL extensions loaded at boot time, DSL can make an easy combined image called mydsl.iso; this process is called MakeMyDSL (mkmydsl). This process is additive. It is the combining of all your chosen MyDSL selections and other non-changing data into a new self-contained, bootable CD-ROM image.

This is an extremely easy procedure. In fact, it is addictive. You can customize DSL with extra MyDSL applications, change the default desktop and wallpaper, and then help spread the Linux Revolution to your friends and relatives. You can create custom appliances. Normally, I advise to only include nonmachine and nonlocal environment-specific items. After all, you still want your mydsl.iso to enjoy the same nomadic boot capabilities as the original DSL.

Yet, there are times when you want to include machine or network environment features. For example, a classroom might share a common printer, or possibly some other common hardware device. If you can configure it within DSL and/or MyDSL, you can easily create a custom mydsl.iso bootable CD-ROM.

After you see this `mkmydsl` process, you may not need to read further. Because DSL is so small, using an additive method is quite appealing. However, there are times when you want to actually remove core DSL applications or change system internals. When this occurs, you need to do a full KNOPPIX-style remastering. Many books and documents can be found on the subject of remastering KNOPPIX. It is not the intent of this single chapter to duplicate such efforts. The intent of this chapter is to discuss areas that are specific to DSL.

MAKING YOUR FRUGAL MYDSL INSTALLATION INTO A BOOTABLE CD-ROM

The `mkmydsl` procedure is done locally from a live, running, CD-ROM-booted DSL system. It is based on the MyDSL extension concept. This provides a quick and simple way to make a custom DSL version including all the additional applications and configurations that are known to work with the standard DSL system. This has several advantages over the full remastering process, as follows:

- **Try before you burn**—You can download extensions and try them out before committing to the whole time-consuming cycle of making an ISO, burning it, and testing it.

- **Construction set**—By downloading in parts, you truly have a construction set method. This makes it easier for slow modem users to be able to download and test in parts and over time.

- **Privacy**—This is where the `myconf.tar.gz` comes into play. This is your "personal" and "private" configuration including passwords (if desired), or closed source proprietary drivers, and so on.

- **Proven system**—You already have the base ISO and have proved that it works on your system. You already have your local "proven" collection of extensions. Creating a `mydsl.iso` is trivial when compared to full remastering.

- **The sky's the limit**—Some users use the `mkmydsl` script to create DVD-sized images. You are only limited by your creativity and hardware constraints.

 NOTE

The `myconf.tar.gz` is for your configurations that you will not be changing. Thus, filetool list remains for backup. A typical `myconf.tar.gz` could have Firefox's Flash plug-in, Sylpheed email settings, network printer settings, and even several PPP settings and providers.

By answering only two simple questions, you can have your `mydsl.iso` created and ready to burn. If you have a burner, you can continue the script to burn to a CD-R.

Getting Started

Let's say that you have downloaded a nice, proven collection of extensions on your hard drive (say `hda4`). You know that because your extension collection is stored in a level 1 `mydsl` directory; these extensions all load upon boot. You have verified this by putting it all together on your target hardware platform.

Figure 11-1 shows an example of a set of MyDSL extensions being held in the `mydsl` directory on a hard disk partition (`/mnt/hda4`).

FIGURE 11-1   Shows a typical mydsl directory containing your extensions.

Now, you want to create a bootable CD-ROM with your collection of extensions. The CD should boot with no additional boot options and should contain the following applications:

- **AbiWord**—Word processor
- **ALSA**—Advanced Linux Sound System
- **Gimp**—Image-processing application
- **GNU-Utils**—The Busybox replacements for basic shell utilities
- **GNU Cash**—Cash management program
- **Gnumeric**—Spreadsheet
- **GTK2**—The GTK2 library needed by GTK2 applications
- **Myplugins**—A personal private extension for proprietary Firefox plug-ins

Upon boot, you want to have the Secure Shell Daemon (ssh), as well as the Filesystem in User Space (fuse) service. Your desktop should be Joe's Window Manager (jwm) and the system clock set to the US Pacific time zone. Finally, you want the Flash plug-in for Firefox to be included. You want everything to work seamlessly and provide a *hands-free* boot.

Sound difficult? Well, it is not. After you become familiar with the basics of DSL, from the boot options to the use of MyDSL extensions and some understanding of creating MyDSL extensions, creating a bootable CD-ROM is simple. The features just mentioned are discussed in Chapter 2, "Booting DSL," Chapter 5, and Chapter 10, "Adding Applications and Creating Shareable Extensions."

Here's how….

Booting from the DSL CD-ROM

To create a remastered DSL CD, you can work from a booted live DSL CD-ROM itself. Boot a Damn Small Linux CD, using any boot options that you would normally need to boot DSL. This process requires no specific boot options, so you would only add those required by your specific hardware. During the remastering process, you work from the booted live CD and use components on that CD to create your remastered CD.

One boot option you might want to add is the `toram` option. If you have enough RAM to run DSL entirely from RAM, entering `toram` here will let you eject the CD and insert a blank CD later in the process, so you can immediately burn your newly remastered live CD.

Mounting a Working Directory

You most likely need to mount a Linux partition (probably from your hard disk) to hold system files, extensions, and the new image. Within that partition, you should make a directory to keep things organized. I suggest you make a directory called `iso`. The partition should be a Linux partition because you need to maintain Linux ownership, file, and directory permissions as you create the remastered CD.

You should only use the ramdisk (for example, `/home/dsl/iso`) to store your extensions, data, and other items if you are only making small additions and have plenty of RAM available. That's because any remastering process will consume a lot of space. As was stated earlier, some users create DVD-sized images. So, assuming you have space available on a hard disk partition, use the mount tool (lower-right corner of the screen) to mount a disk partition (such as `hda4`) to hold your remastering software.

You do not need to mount the drive containing your extensions. However, you can use the same drive that stores your extensions. But, again, I suggest that you make a separate directory. So, for example, to create an iso directory on the hda4 partition, first mount that partition, then type the following from a terminal window (as root user):

```
# mkdir /mnt/hda4/iso
```

Adding MyDSL Extensions

Once you know which MyDSL extensions you want, you need to add those extensions to the remastering mydsl directory. For example, if the remaster directory is
/mnt/hda4/iso, type the following command from a terminal window to create the
mydsl directory:

```
# mkdir -p /mnt/hda4/iso/mydsl
```

Now you can download and save the MyDSL extensions you want using the
MyDSL Extension Tool, indicating /mnt/hda4/iso/mydsl (for example) as the directory to hold the saved extensions.

TIP

If you want to be able to run your live CD from RAM (using the toram feature) so you can eject the CD, do not use .unc or .uci MyDSL extensions.
While both of those types save space in RAM, they will prevent the CD from
being ejected, since they will be mounted directly from the CD.

So, for example, if you wanted to use an application such as mplayer, where
you need to eject the CD to play CD music or DVD movies from that drive,
only use extensions of .dsl or .tar.gz types.

Starting the MkMyDSL Script

Before running the MkMyDSL script, be sure that the remaster directory (for example, /mnt/hda4/iso) doesn't contain anything that you don't want to go on your
remastered CD. In particular, if you have run the script before, be sure to remove
the mydsl.iso file left behind by the previous MkMyDSL run.

To start the script from the menu, select Apps, Tools, Make MyDSL CD Remaster.
Figure 11-2 shows the Make myDSL CD window that appears.

FIGURE 11-2   Displays the
first of only two prompts
needed to make a custom,
bootable CD-ROM.

Enter Location of Target Directory

Enter a directory to hold all of the source files and final image. For example, if you had created an `iso` directory on the `/mnt/hda4` partition, you would enter the following: `/mnt/hda4/iso`. (If you type a directory name that doesn't exist, MkMyDSL exits and you have to start over.)

 NOTE

A common mistake is to use a Windows partition. You should always use a Linux partition so that filesystem permissions are preserved. Using Windows partitions does not provide this capability. Refer to the cfdisk procedure in Chapter 8, "Installing DSL in Alternate Ways," for information on partitioning your hard disk to create Linux partitions.

Additional Boot Time Options

You are then prompted to enter optional boot time options. Here is where you need to enter any options that you were required to use to successfully boot DSL. You can also enter any additional options. For your example project, enter the following:

```
ssh fuse tz=US/Pacific desktop=jwm
```

Figure 11-3 illustrates this example.

FIGURE 11-3   Displays the second prompt needed to create your custom CD-ROM.

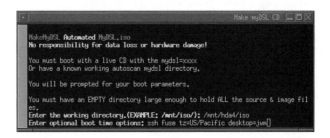

This example shows that the secure shell service (`ssh`) starts to allow remote login, file copy, and execution to the machine, file system in user space (`fuse`) support is loaded, and the timezone is set to United States Pacific (`US/Pacific`). Also, instead of the default Fluxbox window manager, JWM (`desktop=jwm`) is started as the window manager.

If you are sure that your live CD will only be used on computers with at least 128MB of RAM (or possibly more if you remaster a much larger ISO image), then consider adding `toram` as a boot option. That will load and run the entire CD from RAM, causing it to perform much faster. Other boot options are described in Chapter 2.

Creation of the Bootable Image

After entering the boot options, the creation of the ISO bootable image begins. Messages showing the progress as the ISO is created appear as shown in Figure 11-4.

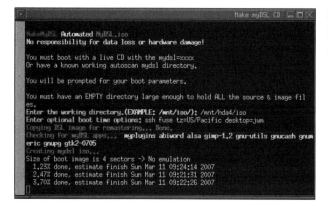

FIGURE 11-4   Shows the beginning of the automated CD-ROM ISO process.

Optional Burning of the Image

If you have a CD writer device, you have the option of recording the image now. You are prompted to continue selecting your cdwriter device.

NOTE

If you only have one CD-ROM device, which serves to boot from and record, you must have booted with the `toram` boot option. This is required so that you can remove the boot CD and place a blank CD-R to record.

If you did not boot with the `toram` option, or you cannot because of the heavy memory requirements to both boot `toram` and remaster, you can always answer this prompt with **n** and record later.

Should you have the requirements to record the image now, you have only two more easy questions to answer, as illustrated in Figure 11-5.

By answering **y** to record now, a scan is performed to find your CD writer. As seen in Figure 11-5, the recorder is a YAMAHA CRW2200E located at address 0,0,0. Enter the address for your CD writer at the prompt. For recording speed, I suggest a slow, safe speed of 4 (although newer CD writers can record as much higher speeds). Note that the CD writer appears as a SCSI device, even if it is an IDE CD drive, because the CD recording is done in SCSI emulation.

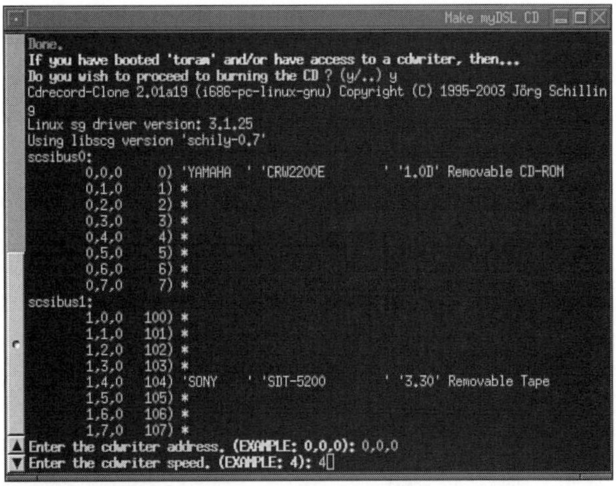

FIGURE 11-5 Displays the options to record the image to a CD-R.

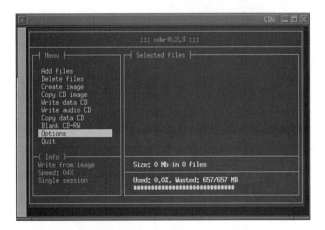

Recording Your ISO Later Using CDW

There will be times when you want to record the mydsl.iso later. After creating the image file, be sure that it is copied to a persistent storage area (such as a hard disk partition). You can always reboot DSL with the toram option, without adding any extra software, so you have enough resources to record the image.

DSL provides a general CD-ROM recording utility program called *CDW*. To access this program, select from the main menu Apps, Tools, CD Burn App. Figure 11-6 shows the CDW screen.

FIGURE 11-6 Burn your ISO image with the CDW CD-ROM burning application.

Using the arrow keys, select Options. The Options section is where you can specify the location and setting to record the image, as shown in Figure 11-7.

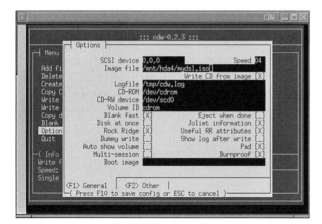

FIGURE 11-7   Displays the settings needed to record the CD image.

Be sure to enter the SCSI device address, the recording speed, and the location of the mydsl.iso file. Next, select Write Data CD to begin recording the image, as shown in Figure 11-8.

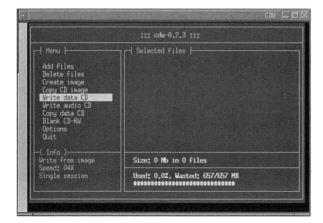

FIGURE 11-8   Displays the option needed to begin recording your new mydsl.iso image.

The application displays a progress bar as the image is being recorded, as shown in Figure 11-9.

After the image is recorded, select Quit to exit the application.

FIGURE 11-9 Shows the progress of writing your image file to the CD-R.

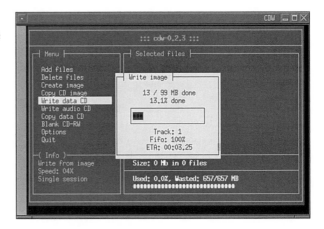

Booting Your New CD

After recording the image, either within the MkMyDSL process, with the application CDW, or even by using a Windows CD-ROM recording program, you can boot your new CD-ROM and view your new custom bootable remaster. Figure 11-10 shows the result of the procedure for building the MkMyDSL ISO image.

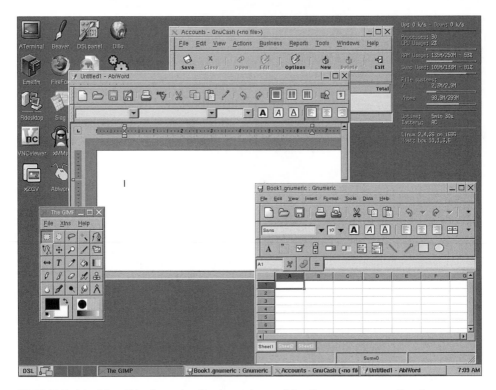

FIGURE 11-10 Displays the final product with all your new applications.

All the requirements of your project can be seen in Figure 11-10. Joe's Window Manager, Gnumeric, AbiWord, GnuCash, and daemons are all there.

FULL REMASTERING

There are many KNOPPIX remastering HOWTOs available on the Internet and in various publications. Because DSL is a derivative of KNOPPIX, all of these methods also should work with DSL. However, in this chapter, the remastering techniques actually used in the production of DSL are documented: from the initial setup from a DSL CD-ROM to the ISO creation of DSL Isolinux version, Syslinux version, Qemu version, and VMware version. The process is automated via scripts that are discussed here.

Setting Up from Published DSL CD-ROM

Boot from the DSL CD-ROM with a Linux partition available. That partition is used to hold the source, master, and iso directories during the remastering process. I call my method the *working directory* method. All the scripts are run from the relative directory that you initially set up.

> **NOTE**
>
> If you don't have an available Linux partition on your computer's hard disk, you can create one using the cfdisk procedure shown in Chapter 8. If you don't want to change the partitions on your hard disk, you could create a Linux partition on some other writeable medium (such as a 1GB USB flash drive).

To begin, I boot DSL with these boot options:

```
boot: dsl 2 base norestore legacy
```

I use 2 to signal runlevel 2 (shell interface with no desktop) to maximize available resources. I include base and norestore to start from a known pristine state. I use legacy to not have any unionfs influence while creating the image. After DSL boots up, do the following:

1. Mount a Linux partition and then change the directory to it.
   ```
   # mount /mnt/hda4
   # cd /mnt/hda4
   ```

2. Create a working directory to contain all of your files and directories and change to it:

```
# mkdir remaster
# cd remaster
```

3. Copy over the scripts from the /chapter11 directory on the enclosed CD-ROM.

```
# cp -a /cdrom/chapter11/remaster/* .
# cp /cdrom/chapter11/remaster/.bash_profile .
```

4. Create directories:

```
# mkdir source master iso
# mkdir source/KNOPPIX/
```

5. Copy the contents of the CD-ROM to the proper directories:

```
# cp -Rp /KNOPPIX/* source/KNOPPIX
# cp -Rp /cdrom/index.html master/
# cp -Rp /cdrom/boot/ master/
```

6. Perform a final cleanup by removing the existing KNOPPIX image, and then sync all files:

```
# rm master/KNOPPIX/KNOPPIX
# sync
```

As a result of the preceding steps, you now have your remastering working directory environment properly set up. After the setup scripts are copied to the working directory, you can automate the setup of the image remastering process by running the setupFromCD script contained in the working directory.

The setupFromCD script is shown here:

```
#!/bin/sh
rm -rf source master iso
mkdir source master iso
mkdir source/KNOPPIX
cp -Rp /KNOPPIX/* source/KNOPPIX/
cp -Rp /cdrom/* master/
rm master/KNOPPIX/KNOPPIX
sync
```

At this point, all files have been copied from the DSL CD-ROM to the source and master directories. I also use one other text file called release.txt. This is where I place the version number for the release I am working on, for example:

```
dsl-3.3
```

As you can see, release.txt is a simple, one-line text file. However, this makes it easy to change release numbers without having to remember where inside the main image file to update.

At this point, your working directory should contain the following files and directories:

```
.bash_profile
bootfloppy.img
dsl.vmx.txt
gnu/
iso/
makecd
makeimage
makeqemu
makesys
makevmx
master/
qemu/
release.txt
setupFromCD
source/
vmware/
```

Making Modifications, Additions, and Removals

Two methods are available to access the DSL system for modifications, additions, or removals. The first method is *direct*; the second is called *chrooting*.

Changing Content with the Direct Method

Use a full path to identify the location of your KNOPPIX source or change to that directory as your current working directory. For example, if your remaster directory were on the /mnt/hda4 partition, you could type:

```
# cd /mnt/hda4/remaster/source/KNOPPIX
```

Typically, I change to the working directory on my mounted disk partition (for example, cd /mnt/hda4/remaster), then I prefix the commands to access the new source image files with source/KNOPPIX. From this point, my discussion will always be using the path relative to the working directory—that is, the directory containing the scripts, master, source, and iso directories.

I mainly use the direct method. DSL is not pure Debian. Many packages, binaries, and scripts are not from the Debian repositories. Because of this and also the fact that often times using Debian implies the addition of many other unwanted packages, the direct method is usually used.

Most of the time, new applications, scripts, and modifications are first applied to a live DSL CD-ROM or frugal system. Often, these additions can be made into MyDSL extensions, and, when fully tested, they simply can be extracted directly with the use of the tar -C source/KNOPPIX option. Another option that I frequently use is to copy the new tar file to source/KNOPPIX and then later chroot in and do a tar extract as normal. Just be sure not to forget to delete the tar file sitting at the root (/) of the chrooted environment.

Using this style keeps very tight control of what is added, changed, or deleted from the 50MB core DSL system.

Changing Content with the chroot Method

You are now ready to issue the chroot command. The chroot method changes the root (/) directory to the directory containing the source files:

```
# chroot source/KNOPPIX
```

At this point, the new root directory is now pointing at the "root" of the DSL image. All file operations to copy, move, or remove files are relative to this directory. Be sure to exit from this chrooted environment before you continue the remastering process!

Most often, when KNOPPIX remastering is discussed, it is usually the chroot method. Using this method gives you access to the source directory as though it is actually the root filesystem. This means you will see /mnt/hda4/remaster/source/ KNOPPIX as though it were /. You now have full root shell access to what will become the root directory of the new image.

To install certain packages, you need to mount the proc filesystem:

```
# mount -t proc /proc proc
```

Most likely, you want to install software from the Debian Woody repositories. For this, you need Internet access. Test your Internet connection by pinging a well-known server:

```
# ping www.yahoo.com
```

If you do not get a response, you need to set up your nameserver. This is accomplished by editing the /etc/resolv.conf file. For each nameserver, as provided by your ISP, add a line:

```
nameserver 0.0.0.0
```

where nameserver is the literal string and 0.0.0.0 is the actual IP number of a nameserver. After this is accomplished, test by pinging a well-known Internet site.

To get Debian apt-get, you need to grab the standard utilities that are required:

```
# mydsl-load gnu-utils.dsl system
# mydsl-load dsl-dpkg.dsl system
# apt-get update
```

Now, you are ready to install Woody packages. If you know you want packages from other Debian repositories, edit the file at /etc/apt/sources.list. Here's an example of the contents of the sources.list file:

```
deb http://archive.debian.org/debian-archive/ woody main contrib non-free
#deb http://mirror.aarnet.edu.au/debian oldstable main contrib non-free
#deb http://mirror.linux.org.au/debian oldstable main contrib non-free
#deb http://mirrors.usc.edu/pub/linux/distributions/debian oldstable
main contrib non-free
```

The package Zile was used as an example in Chapter 10, of how to install a package in Damn Small Linux using the MyDSL facility. MyDSL is the normal approach for installing software in DSL. Another way to install Zile software in DSL is by using the following command:

```
# apt-get install zile
```

The preceding procedure is most common with KNOPPIX-style live CD-ROM systems. It is not normally used with DSL. The reasons are the same as given in Chapters 5 and 10. Using a package manager can quickly overrun "the small is beautiful" mantra of DSL.

As was shown in Chapter 10, many Debian packages are first pared down into MyDSL extensions and then loaded into the DSL core image via the direct method.

NOTE

If you have mounted the proc filesystem, be certain to unmount it before you exit the chroot environment.

Adding Common Elements: Menu and Icon

Because DSL does not normally use Debian packages, the menu item and icon have to be manually created. This area was discussed at length in Chapter 10. This time, instead of being based off of /tmp and /home/dsl/.xtdesktop, you must edit the following files:

```
/etc/skel/.fluxbox/menu
/etc/skel/.jwmrc
/etc/skel/.xtdesktop/
```

Here are suggestions for creating a menu item and adding a desktop icon:

- To create the menu item, edit `/etc/skel/.fluxbox/menu` and `/etc/skel/.jwmrc`. Because Zile is a console-based program and its path is `/usr/bin/zile`, our menu line item to be added looks like this:

    ```
    [exec] (Zile) {aterm -e /usr/bin/zile}
    ```

- The icon for Zile in `/etc/skel/.xdesktop/zile.lnk` looks like this:

    ```
    table Icon
    Type: Program
    Caption: Zile
    Command: aterm -e /usr/bin/zile
    Icon:  /home/dsl/.xtdesktop/program.png
    X: 420
    Y: 384
    end
    ```

NOTE

I am using one of the generic icons available in DSL. Other generic icons are `binary.png`, `gear.png`, and `shellscript.png`. You may change the icon later by right-clicking the displayed icon. See Chapter 4, "Configuring and Saving DSL Settings," for details.

Removing Applications

Because DSL is extremely small in size and is not pure Debian, core applications are usually removed by force. This usually implies using the `find` command to locate all related files. Often, the command `ldd` is used to display all the dependent libraries used by an application.

Still, the process of removing an application can be quite daunting. DSL's compact and denseness is the result of much hacking code. For example, one of the common applications that many want to remove is Firefox. Using the standard approach, `find / -name firefox` does not reveal all that was used for Firefox in DSL. There are Firefox references in configuration files. The system configuration for unionfs contains references to Firefox. The file at `/etc/init.d/mkunion` needs to be cleaned of the Firefox references. From this example, you can see that to unravel DSL, dense and compact size can be a challenge.

Other Customizations

Other features you may want to customize include passwords, themes and backgrounds, default time zones, DSL-specific features, and the default desktop.

Setting Passwords

You should always use the chroot method if you want to change passwords. Then, issue the standard command to perform this action.

```
# passwd
Changing password for user root
Enter the new password (minimum of 5, maximum of 8 characters)
Please use a combination of upper and lower case letters and numbers.
Enter new password: (Password entered will not be displayed)
Re-enter new password: (Password entered will not be displayed)
Password changed.
```

Themes and Backgrounds

The standard theme for DSL's Fluxbox desktop is /usr/share/fluxbox/styles/default. This is actually a link to the current default theme, envane. The background image is actually specified in the theme. In DSL, you typically use the Fluxbox rootCommand tag to specify the image. The default images available for Fluxbox are located at /usr/share/fluxbox/backgrounds.

> **NOTE**
>
> When using the direct method, always prefix the actual paths with source/KNOPPIX.

Language

The default language, currently us, can be supplied as a boot option (lang=it) or by editing line 95 of the standard KNOPPIX script at /etc/init.d/knoppix-autoconfig.

```
95 [ -n "$LANGUAGE" ] || LANGUAGE=us
```

Default Timezone

The default timezone is related to the language selection inside the knoppix-autoconfig script. Between lines 97 and 340, you can find one very large case statement. This case statement assigns basic time and language settings, based on the language that is currently set. Depending on language selection, you can also change the default timezone. For example, language en specifies a time-zone of US/Eastern. This is where you can change it, for example, to US/Pacific.

DSL Specific

Just as KNOPPIX uses a bash script from most of the boot time configurations, so does DSL. The script is located at /etc/init.d/dsl-config. Many boot options can be found here. This is where the processing of boot time MyDSL extensions occurs. It is where many of the daemon requests are processed. Most options unique to DSL are in the master boot time configuration file.

Default Desktop

The default desktop can be supplied as a boot option (for example, desktop=jwm) or by editing the script at /etc/init.d/dsl-config line 240. This line, as it is set by default, sets the default desktop to fluxbox, if jwn isn't specifically identified (prob-ably from a boot option):

```
240 case "$DESKTOP" in fluxbox|jwm) ;; *) DESKTOP="fluxbox"; ;; esac
```

Advanced Customizations

More advanced DSL customizations can be used to directly modify the DSL boot process itself. This can include changing Isolinux boot loader files (such as boot screens and options), as well as modifying the initial ramdisk used when DSL first boots.

Boot Screen and Initial Boot Options

Using the preceding remastering setup, the initial boot files for image, message, and default boot options are located at master/isolinux relative to your mount point and working remaster directory. The following three files are of interest:

- **isolinux.cfg**: This is the configuration file for the Isolinux boot loader. It specifies the image to be displayed, the boot message, and all of the default boot options, as well as several boot images to load. This is a simple text file and may be edited with any text editor.
- **boot.msg**: This is the initial displayed text that appears before the boot prompt. Again, it is a simple text file and any text editor can alter its contents.
- **logo.16**: This is the image shown on the initial boot screen. This image file must be of the LSS16 image format. This is a 16-color, 640×480 image.

Other sizes or resolutions will not work. You can use the Gimp MyDSL extension to edit and/or create a boot image file.

- **f2 and f3**: These are the help files displayed when the F2 and F3 function keys are pressed at the initial boot prompt. These are text files and can be edited with any text editor.

- **minirt24.gz**: This is the initial ramdisk used to bootstrap DSL.

NOTE

The Syslinux version has these files packed into a floppy-sized image. This is called boot.img. The unpacking and packing of this image file will be discussed later, in the "Creating the Syslinux ISO Image" section.

Default Boot Options

The default boot time options are stored in either isolinux.cfg or syslinux.cfg depending on the CD-ROM remaster type you are choosing. For your Isolinux-based remaster, the file to edit is located at master/boot/isolinux/isolinux.cfg. This is a simple text file and can be easily edited. It is the APPEND line where the boot options are specified.

The Boot Splash Screen

The boot splash screen contains an image that is shown at boot time. This is the image shown above the boot: prompt. This image is quite difficult to create as it is in the LSS16 format. I have provided utilities in the chapter11/remaster/gnu directory on the CD-ROM.

The usual procedure is to copy the image file logo.16 to a working directory on a machine running the X Windows System. To convert the LSS16 to a format that Gimp can display, use the following:

```
# lss16toppm < logo.16 > logo.ppm
# gimp logo.ppm
```

After editing or creating a new image file, use one of the utilities provided in the chapter11/remaster/gnu directory: giftoppm, pngtoppm, or bmptoppm. Then, convert back to LSS16 format. For example, if in Gimp you saved the image as .bmp, use

```
# bmptoppm < logo.bmp > logo.ppm
# ppmtolss16 < logo.ppm > logo.16
```

Much care needs to be taken to stay within the LSS16 specifications: a 640×480, 16-color image. It may take some trial and error to create or edit a useable LSS16 format `logo.16` file.

Initial Ramdisk

Also in the `master/boot/isolinux` directory is the initial ramdisk: `minirt24.gz`. Here's how you can modify the initial ramdisk:

1. To unpack the `minirt24.gz`, do the following:

```
# cd master/boot/isolinux
# mkdir mroot
# gunzip minirt24.gz
```

2. Mount the uncompressed `ext2` ramdisk by the following:

```
# mount minirt24 mroot -t ext2 -o loop=/dev/loop1
```

3. At this point, by changing directory to `mroot/`, you have access to the initial boot script and modules. (Both of these are discussed shortly.)

4. After any changes to the modules or the initial boot script, you need to repack the initial ramdisk. Use the following steps:

```
# cd ..
# umount mroot/
# gzip -9 minirt24
# rmdir mroot/
```

Initial Boot Modules

After the initial ramdisk is unpacked, change directory into `mroot/`. Any boot time modules need to be available in the `modules/` directory. Currently, you can see that the `cloop.o` file and `scsi/` directory of modules exist.

Initial Boot Script

While in the `mroot/` mounted initial ramdisk, you can see the `linuxrc` script. This script is where the boot process begins. You can change the ascii art DSL logo. You can change the order of searching for the KNOPPIX image. You can effectively change much of how DSL boots. If you do add modules, it is here that you must reference them.

Creating the Isolinux Standard ISO Image

The standard image used in DSL is the Isolinux version. This step is comprised of two stages. The first stage is creating the KNOPPIX image in the master directory. The second step is combining the boot files, the Linux kernel, and initial ramdisk to create the actual ISO.

After you have completed all the changes to the base system, you are ready to create a new compressed KNOPPIX/KNOPPIX file.

The makeimage Script

The makeimage script is on the enclosed CD-ROM in the chapter11/ remaster directory. The script is to be run from within your working directory. The following shows the script's contents, with line numbers added:

```
1.  #!/bin/sh
2.  #
3.  # Clean up .bash_history
4.  if [ -f source/KNOPPIX/.bash_history ]; then
5.      rm source/KNOPPIX/.bash_history
6.  fi
7.  if [ -f source/KNOPPIX/home/dsl/.bash_history ]; then
8.      rm source/KNOPPIX/home/dsl/.bash_history
9.  fi
10. #
11. # Clean up any ssh hosts
12. if [ -d source/KNOPPIX/root/.ssh ]; then
13.    rm -rf source/KNOPPIX/root/.ssh
14. fi
15. #
16. # Check to see if need .bash_profile
17. if [ ! -f source/KNOPPIX/.bash_profile ]; then
18.    cp .bash_profile source/KNOPPIX/.bash_profile
19. fi
20. # Copy over the release info.
21. cp -f release.txt source/KNOPPIX/usr/share/doc/dsl/.
22. #
23. mkisofs -R -U -hide-rr-moved -cache-inodes -no-bak -pad
       source/KNOPPIX | nice -5 create_compressed_fs -best - 65536 >
       master/KNOPPIX/KNOPPIX
24. #
25. sync
26. sync
```

The makeimage script does the following:

- Lines 4-9 remove all references from what was recorded while chrooted in.
- Lines 12-14 remove any references to ssh connections that you may have used.
- Lines 17-19 check to see if you need a .bash_profile.
- Line 21 writes the release information using the direct method.
- Line 23 creates the new compressed KNOPPIX/KNOPPIX image from your source/ directory and writes it into the master/ directory.

Depending on your machine's resources, running the makeimage script could take a long time. After a successful build of the new compressed image, you must next combine the boot files, the kernel, initial ramdisk, and the compressed runtime image. This process creates the actual ISO image file in your iso/ directory. The ISO file is ready to be burned onto a CD-R CD-ROM. If you add an optional parameter of cd, the script records the image.

The makeiso Script

After cleaning up the chrooted environment, the next stage actually creates the ISO image. This stage combines the newly created KNOPPIX image file with the boot image files into a single bootable CD or DVD image.

```
1.   #!/bin/sh
2.   RELEASE=`cat release.txt`
3.   #
4.   if [ -f master/KNOPPIX/boot.img ]; then
5.       rm master/KNOPPIX/boot.img
6.       tar -zxvf boot.isolinux.tgz
7.   fi
8.   #
9. mkisofs -pad -l -r -J -v -V KNOPPIX -no-emul-boot -boot-load-size
     4 -boot-info-table -b boot/isolinux/isolinux.bin -c
     boot/isolinux/boot.cat -hide-rr-moved -o iso/"$RELEASE".iso master
10. #
11. sync
12. sync
13. if [ -n "$1" ]; then
14.     if [ "$1" == "cd" ]; then
15.       cdrecord -v speed=4 dev=0,0,0 -data iso/"$RELEASE".iso
16.     fi
17. fi
18. cd iso
19. md5sum "$RELEASE".iso > "$RELEASE".iso.md5.txt
20. sync
21. md5sum -c "$RELEASE".iso.md5.txt
22. cd ../.
```

The makeiso script can be found on the enclosed CD-ROM in the chapter11/ remaster directory. The script is to be run from within your working directory. Note the following:

- Line 2 provides the name of your ISO image file and checksum file.

- Lines 4 through 7 allow for handling both Isolinux and Syslinux versions of DSL. Syslinux uses a boot.img for the boot files, whereas Isolinux uses a directory. These lines provide a mechanism to back up/restore your Isolinux directory. The Syslinux `boot.img` is the standard DSL floppy image and therefore does not need to be included in the backup/restore process.

- Line 9 is the actual ISO creation. This combines the files in the `master/` directory into an ISO image file in the `iso/` directory.
- Lines 13 through 17 check if the script was started with `cd` as an option. The script defaults with the CD-ROM burner at device location 0,0,0. Using this option writes the new ISO image to a CD-R.
- Line 19 creates an `md5sum` checksum file for network transport and verification.
- Line 21 verifies the consistency of the checksum.

Creating the Syslinux ISO Image

Many older computers cannot boot Isolinux-based CD-ROMS. These older computers are limited to an initial boot image that is the actual size of a floppy disk. The older Syslinux boot loader uses just such a mechanism.

The makesys Script

The `makesys` script can be found on the enclosed CD-ROM in the `chapter11/` remaster directory. The script is to be run from within your working directory to create a Syslinux bootable ISO image. The following shows the contents of that script:

```
1.  #!/bin/sh
2.  RELEASE=`cat release.txt`
3.  #
4.  if [ -d master/boot ]; then
5.    tar -czvf boot.isolinux.tgz master/boot/
6.    rm -rf master/boot
7.  fi
8.  cp boot.img master/KNOPPIX/.
9.  mkisofs -pad -l -r -J -b KNOPPIX/boot.img -c KNOPPIX/boot.cat -hide-
    rr-moved -o iso/"$RELEASE"-syslinux.iso master
10. sync
11. sync
12. if [ -n "$1" ]; then
13.  if [ "$1" == "cd" ]; then
14.    cdrecord -v speed=4 dev=0,0,0 -data iso/"$RELEASE"-syslinux.iso
15.  fi
16. fi
17. cd iso
18. md5sum "$RELEASE"-syslinux.iso > "$RELEASE"-syslinux.iso.md5.txt
19. sync
20. md5sum -c "$RELEASE"-syslinux.iso.md5.txt
21. cd ../.
```

Note the following about the makesys script:

- Line 2 provides the name of your ISO image file and checksum file.
- Lines 4 through 7 allow for handling both Isolinux and Syslinux versions of DSL. Syslinux uses a boot.img for the boot files, whereas Isolinux uses a directory. These lines provide a mechanism to back up/restore your Isolinux directory. The Syslinux boot.img is the standard DSL floppy image and therefore does not need to be included in the backup/restore process.
- Line 8 copies the DSL standard boot floppy to replace the isolinux/ directory of boot files.
- Line 9 is the actual ISO creation. This combines the file in the master/ directory and the boot.img into an ISO image file in the iso/ directory.
- Lines 12 through 16 check if the script was started with cd as an option. The script defaults with the CD-ROM burner at device location 0,0,0. Using this option writes the new ISO image to a CD-R.
- Line 18 creates an md5sum checksum file for network transport and verification.
- Line 20 verifies the consistency of the checksum.

Syslinux Initial Ramdisk

To change the Syslinux version of the initial ramdisk, use the following procedure:

1. Change directory to master/KNOPPIX. There, you can find a file called boot.img. This file is really the same as the bootfloppy.img used for boot DSL from an actual floppy diskette.

2. Make a mount point and mount the floppy image:
   ```
   # mkdir boot
   # mount boot.img boot/ -t msdos -o loop
   ```

3. Copy and unpack the minirt24.gz initial ramdisk:
   ```
   # cp boot/minirt24.gz .
   # gunzip minirt24.gz
   ```

4. Make a mount point and mount the initial ramdisk:
   ```
   # mkdir mroot
   # mount minirt24 mroot/ -t ext2 -o loop
   ```

5. As before with the Isolinux version, change directory into mroot and perform necessary edits as previously described for boot modules or changes to the boot script linuxrc. Just be aware that the Syslinux version's initial ramdisk must be within the size of a physical floppy disk.

To reverse the process and repack the initial ramdisk and related files back into the boot.img file, perform the following:

1. Change directory out of mroot, unmount, and compress the initial ramdisk:

```
# cd ..
# umount mroot/
# gzip -9 minirt24
```

2. Move the compressed ramdisk back into the boot mount point:

```
# mv minirt24.gz boot/
mv: Overwrite 'boot/minirt24.gz'? y
```

3. Unmount the boot mount point and remove the work directories:

```
# umount boot
# rmdir boot/ mroot/
```

Building the DSL Qemu Embedded Version

Virtualization is currently very popular. DSL has incorporated many features to make running DSL in a sandbox standalone virtual environment very easy. The creation of the zip image is also very easy, using your mkqemu automated script from within your working directory.

The makeqemu Script

The makeqemu script is on the CD-ROM in the chapter11/ remaster directory. This script, as the others, is to be run from within the base of your working directory. The following shows the contents of the makeqemu script:

```
1.   #!/bin/bash
2.   RELEASE=`cat release.txt`
3.   rm iso/"$RELEASE"-embedded.zip
4.   cd qemu
5.   pwd
6.   cp ../master/KNOPPIX/KNOPPIX knoppix/.
7.   ../gnu/zip -r ../iso/"$RELEASE"-embedded.zip .
8.   cd ../iso
9.   md5sum "$RELEASE"-embedded.zip > "$RELEASE"-embedded.zip.md5.txt
10.  sync
11.  md5sum -c "$RELEASE"-embedded.zip.md5.txt
12.  cd ../.
```

Note the following about the makeqemu script:

- Line 2 names your distribution file.
- Line 3 removes any preexisting copy of your distribution file.
- Line 6 copies the compressed runtime image file into the qemu/ directory.

- Line 7 uses the GNU version of zip to make a compatible zip file of this release.
- Line 9 generates the checksum file.
- Line 11 verifies the checksum integrity.

Building the DSL VMware Edition

Another popular virtualization system is VMware. DSL also supports this by publishing a VMX edition. Running the mkvmx script from within your working directory automates this process.

The makevmx Script

The makvemx script is also on the CD-ROM in the chapter11/ remaster directory. This script, as the others, is to be run from within the base of your working directory. The following shows the contents of the makevmx script.

```
1.   #!/bin/bash
2.   RELEASE=`cat release.txt`
3.   rm iso/"$RELEASE"-vmx.zip
4.   cd vmware
5.   pwd
6.   sed "s/XXXXX/$RELEASE/" ../dsl.vmx.txt > dsl.vmx
7.   cp ../iso/"$RELEASE".iso .
8.   ../gnu/zip -r ../iso/"$RELEASE"-vmx.zip .
9.   rm "$RELEASE".iso
10.  cd ../iso
11.  md5sum "$RELEASE"-vmx.zip > "$RELEASE"-vmx.zip.md5.txt
12.  sync
13.  md5sum -c "$RELEASE"-vmx.zip.md5.txt
14.  cd ../.
```

Note the following about the makevmx script:

- Line 2 names your distribution file.
- Line 3 removes any preexisting copy of your distribution file.
- Line 6 updates the VmWare configuration file for this release.
- Line 7 copies the complete ISO image file into the vmware/ directory.
- Line 8 uses the GNU version of zip to make a compatible zip file of this release.
- Line 11 generates the checksum file.
- Line 13 verifies the checksum integrity.

Using a New Kernel for DSL

So far in this chapter, you have seen how you can easily create a custom bootable MyDSL CD-ROM from a normal boot of your DSL/Frugal system. You have seen how you can remaster all four DSL images from the live DSL CD-ROM booted to runlevel 2. So how do you change the kernel in DSL? As always, there are many ways to accomplish this task. However, I find that it is best to perform this task from a traditional hard drive install of DSL.

With a traditional hard drive install, you can be sure of correct permissions. You can use the standard make procedures. You can easily test your new kernel and modules in a traditional environment. Then, finally, after thorough testing, you can copy the new kernel and modules to the proper layout required by the DSL live CD-ROM system.

Compiling a New Kernel

In keeping with my usual recommendation of always starting from a known state, let's do so for this task as well.

1. Boot from the live DSL CD-ROM using the install menu:
   ```
   boot: install
   ```

2. Install to a Linux hard disk partition. I recommend you do a full install and use the Grub boot loader. I also recommend you edit the grub menu to boot to runlevel 2.

3. Make and change to a typical source directory:
   ```
   # mkdir /usr/src
   # cd /usr/src
   ```

4. Load utilities and compiler (these may be found on the enclosed CD-ROM):
   ```
   # mydsl-load /cdrom/chapter11/kernel/gnu-utils.dsl
   # mydsl-load /cdrom/chapter11/kernel/gcc1-with-libs.dsl
   # mydsl-load /cdrom/chapter11/kernel/gcc-2.95.dsl
   ```

5. Load the Linux kernel and cloop sources:
   ```
   # tar -zxvf /cdrom/chapter11/kernel/linux-2.4.31.tar.gz
   # tar -zxvf /cdrom/chapter11/kernel/cloop-2.01.tar.gz
   ```

6. Configure the kernel for DSL:
   ```
   # cd linux-2.4.31
   # make menuconfig
   Load Alternate Configuration file: dsl.configure
   # patch -p1 < knoppix-kernel.patch
   ```

7. Compile the kernel:
   ```
   # make dep
   # make clean
   # make bzImage
   ```

8. Compile the modules:

```
# make modules
```

9. Install kernel and modules:

```
# make install
# make modules_install
```

10. Update modules dependencies:

```
# depmod -a
```

After successful build of new kernel and modules, reboot using those components and fully test them.

DSL also uses a modified `cloop` module. DSL supports 64 `cloop`s. So we need to modify the source for `cloop` and build this module.

1. Change to main source directory.

```
# cd /usr/src
```

2. Extract the `cloop` source files and change to its directory:

```
# tar -zxvf /cdrom/chapter11/kernel/cloop-2.01.tar.gz
# ln -s /usr/bin/gcc-2.95 cc
# ln -s linux-2.4.31 linux
# cd cloop-2.01/
```

3. Modify a source file to up the `cloop` count to 64:

```
# vi compressed_loop.c
Change #define CLOOP_MAX 64
```

4. Modify the `Makefile` for DSL:

```
# vi Makefile
  Comment out the following line (line 9)
    # include $(KERNEL_DIR)/conf.vars
  Edit the following line (line 12)
    CKERNOPS:+ -O2 -D__KERNEL__ …
```

5. Finally, make the modified module:

```
# make all
```

6. Manually install this modified module and update the module dependencies:

```
# cp cloop.o /lib/modules/2.4.31/kernel/drivers/block/.
# depmod -a
```

If you need to make additional `cloop` devices, the procedure is:

```
# cd /dev
# mknod /dev/cloop4 b 240 4
# mknod /dev/cloop5 b 240 5
  …
# mknod /dev/cloopN b 240 N
```

This should be the minimum you need to have DSL running in the new environment. Of course, you may want or need to compile special modules for your particular hardware.

After installing the cloop module, you should reboot your hard drive installation. This ensures a good test of the new kernel and modules, especially the new cloop module. Figure 11-11 shows the new 2.4.31 kernel and cloop module being used to successfully load xchat.uci.

FIGURE 11-11   Load a MyDSL extension (xchat.uci) to check that the cloop driver is working.

The final process is to copy the new kernel and modules over to a live CD-ROM environment. Compiling most new(er) kernels usually results in a kernel too large to fit on a single floppy disk. This is one reason why DSL has stayed with the current kernel. Being too large for a single floppy disk means no Syslinux version of the DSL CD-ROM. That means many older computers will not be able to boot the Isolinux CD-ROM. Therefore, the following discussion only addresses the setup of DSL using the Isolinux version.

Let's boot again from the standard DSL CD-ROM and set up your remaster working directory on the same partition that you installed DSL and have your new kernel and modules. Let's assume it is hard drive partition hda4. To briefly review, follow these steps:

1. Boot DSL with minimal options:

   boot: **dsl 2 base norestore legacy**

2. Mount the hard drive installation partition and change the directory to /tmp:

   # **mount /mnt/hda4**
   # **cd /mnt/hda4**

3. Create the remaster directory and move there:

   # **mkdir remaster**
   # **cd remaster**

4. Copy the remaster scripts from the enclosed CD-ROM:

   # **cp -a /cdrom/chapter11/remaster/* .**
   # **cp /cdrom/chapter11/remaster/.bash_profile .**

5. Set up the working directory environment:

   # **./setupFromCD**

As was previously discussed in the working directory remaster method, the initial ramdisk contains the boot time modules and kernel. The first step to install your new kernel and modules for the live CD-ROM is to unpack the `minirt24.gz`. Recall that this file resides in your remastering working directory of `master/boot/isolinux`. Recall the procedure to unpack this file to gain access to the modules directory:

1. Change the directory to the initial ramdisk file, unpack, and mount it:

```
# cd master/boot/isolinux
# gunzip minirt24.gz
# mkdir mroot
# mount minirt24 mroot/ -o loop
```

2. Change directory to the boot time modules:

```
# cd mroot/modules
```

3. Copy over the new cloop module and selectively copy required SCSI modules:

```
# cp /mnt/hda4/lib/modules/2.4.31.kernel/drivers/block/cloop.o .
# cd scsi
# cp /mnt/hda4/lib/modules/2.4.31/kernel/drivers/scsi/* .
```

4. Unmount, repack, and clean up this process:

```
# cd ../../..
# umount mroot
# gzip -9 minit24
# rmdir mroot
```

5. Copy over the new kernel:

```
# cp /mnt/hda4/boot/vmlinuz-2.4.31 linux24
# cd ../../..
```

6. Copy over the remaining modules into the runtime image:

```
# cp -a /mnt/hda4/lib/modules/2.4.31 source/KNOPPIX/lib/modules/.
```

7. Update the runtime system map:

```
# cp /mnt/hda4/boot/System.map-2.4.31 source/KNOPPIX/boot/.
# chroot source/KNOPPIX
# cd /boot
# rm System.map-2.4.26
# ln -sf System.map-2.4.31 System.map
```

8. Remove references to 2.4.26 modules:

```
# cd /lib/modules
# rm -rf 2.4.26/
```

9. Optionally remove unneeded modules for the runtime image:

```
# cd 2.4.31/
# rm -rf kernel/drivers/atm
# rm -rf kernel/drivers/isdn
# rm -rf kernel/drivers/telephony
```

```
# rm -rf kernel/net/atm
# rm -rf kernel/net/ipv6
# rm -rf kernel/fs/affs
# rm -rf kernel/fs/coda
# rm -rf kernel/fs/cramfs
# rm -rf kernel/fs/freexfs
# rm -rf kernel/fs/hpfs
# rm -rf kernel/fs/ncpfs
# rm -rf kernel/qnx4
# rm -rf kernel/romfs
```

10. Exit the chrooted environment:

```
# exit
```

NOTE

You should remove existing SCSI modules from the initial ramdisk before you begin to copy any new modules you want to add. You only need to copy the ones that you will actually need to boot your system. This area can be greatly reduced if your systems do not use SCSI. The minimum needed to boot DSL is `ide-scsi.o`.

The preceding module deletion was based on the actual DSL v2.x system. Your choice of module deletion is entirely up to you. If you do not need a firewall, the netfilter modules can be removed. If you do not need SCSI, much space can be saved by removing SCSI modules. The challenge for DSL is to provide enough modules for the public. You cannot go with the saying, "Well it works for me!" The modules in DSL have endured the test of time with many users and over several years.

This completes the process of upgrading the kernel and modules. Continue on with the normal full remastering process as was previously discussed. To make the ISO from your working directory, simply run the `./makeimage` script followed by the `./makeiso` script.

SUMMARY

This chapter has covered the spectrum with regard to remastering DSL. You have seen how simple it can be—from booting your typical and well-tested frugal system resulting in a complete bootable MyDSL CD-ROM to the full remastering using the working directory method.

With full remastering, you saw how to have much more control over setting defaults and adding applications. You should also have gained an understanding of the challenges of application removals. You also learned the process of creating all four of the DSL published images.

Finally, you learned the most difficult part of remastering: compiling a new kernel and modules, then installing them all into the working directory of the DSL live CD-ROM remastering environment. Armed with this knowledge, you should now be able to create your own distribution, be it small or large, a live CD-ROM, or a virtual embedded system; it will be your own.

Part IV

Making Damn Small Linux Projects

## CHAPTER 12

Running DSL on Alternative Hardware

Most of the alternative hardware people are using to run Linux has some type of performance or physical limitation. Often, such hardware has limited space or significantly reduced performance when compared to a conventional PC. For the sake of discourse in this chapter, I will divide such appliances into two groups: alternative media devices and alternative devices with CPUs.

The *alternative media devices* group consists of mountable devices such as cameras, mp3 players, wrist watches, portable video players, and PDAs. The *alternative devices* group includes thin clients, Internet appliances, embedded computers, diskless PCs, industrial computers, PC100 motherboard computers, homemade mini-ITX systems, AMD Geode computers, and other people's trash (more on this later).

AN ARGUMENT FOR USING DSL IN EMBEDDED SYSTEMS

Why use Damn Small Linux (DSL) instead of another distribution for your alternative hardware system? DSL is small (only 50MB), it requires little RAM or CPU processing power, and it may be run via USB, CD, or disk on image mode (known as the Frugal install method).

The Frugal and USB boot methods make use of a ramdisk that keeps the docwrites such as log files and cache files in memory. This is critical for keeping CompactFlash drives alive. The unique combination makes DSL the best choice for the job. Although there are other light desktop-oriented operating systems available, they require much more disk space and/or RAM and do not use a ramdisk to protect drives with limited write use. Most manufacturers claim that CompactFlash is good for many tens of thousands of docwrites, which may sound like a lot, but in normal Linux kernel function, those docwrites will add upvery quickly.

Additionally, we invested a significant amount of research and selected the best combination of functionality, small footprint, and RAM efficiency when we chose which programs to include in DSL. There are years of investigation and community feedback that helped us derive our current native program list.

Finally, we have our extension system that can greatly increase the functionality of DSL while not requiring a conventional installation. Because our UNC and UCI extensions are highly efficient in their RAM use, they are particularly suited for alternative hardware.

USB MOUNTABLE APPLIANCES

Many devices that are USB mountable can boot DSL, but some have operational problems if you write over their Master Boot Record, MBR. Hence, you should be careful if you decide to experiment with making the device bootable (as though it were a pen drive with Syslinux applied). A much safer choice is to limit usage of such a device to instead run DSL embedded, which does not need any modifications to the MBR to run.

Other than the novelty of doing so, there is not much value in making your device usable as a bootable USB storage device. In comparison to the cost of a conventional pen drive, the actual cost of the device (such as a PDA, digital camera, or media player) is significantly higher. I suggest waiting until the device is absolutely disposable before attempting to complete such an experiment.

At this point, if you are still undeterred by my warnings and are going to proceed anyway with modifying the MBR of the appliance, you want to at least back up the original MBR just in case you need to restore it later.

To save the original MBR, you use the **dd** command in a Terminal window as root type:

```
# dd if=/dev/sda of=mbr.backup bs=512 count=1
```

This command assumes that your USB device is at address /dev/sda. Please verify for yourself and refer to Chapter 6, "Running a Native Pen Drive Install," for details. Make sure you save your backup to another drive for safe keeping.

If you need to restore the MBR later, you can type this command:

```
# dd if=mbr.backup of=/dev/sda bs=512 count=1
```

The rest of the process is similar to either creating a bootable pen drive or an embedded system on any other portable media. It is unusual and novel to have a fully functional USB bootable media device contained in your appliance. However, what you essentially have at the end of the process is something that has dual function: its original intended purpose and the capacity to double as a $15 pen drive (which would actually fit into your pocket much easier than most cameras, PDAs, or media players). For most users, this is really not the most practical thing to do.

With the possibility of damaging the device and the impracticality of using it as a portable bootable device, why would anybody do this? Most people try it just to see if it can be done or for the "geek" pride in accomplishing such a project. Or, perhaps it is finding a new purpose for an otherwise obsolete product?

ALTERNATIVE CPU-BASED HARDWARE

Alternative hardware usually means limited resources. Typically, the hardware has one or more of the following restrictions:

- Limited RAM
- Limited processor power
- Unusual storage device
- Boots from a flash drive
- Limited storage space
- No swap partition

Each limitation in the preceding list has its own challenge. I will outline the difficulty of each and review some practical steps to alleviate these limitations when operating DSL in such environments.

Embedded Systems and Thin Clients

There are a whole host of computer systems that were never intended to run a complete desktop operating system. These include SBCs (single board computers), industrial computers, systems designed to be thin clients, and systems intended to be net appliances (such as the classic two hundred dollar ThinkNic from the beginning of the twenty-first century).

The proliferation of Via chip and AMD Geode-based *embedded* systems has lowered the price of SBC-based units rapidly in the past few years. Currently, there are modestly powered systems selling for just over $100; for that price, you can expect to get something with a very modest CPU (say 200MHz) and limited RAM (one example has 128MB).

Slightly higher in the price scale, there are units with plenty of power to run DSL. For instance, there is the eBox III, which we sell at the DSL store as the *Damn Small Machine*; this model has a 700MHz Via processor and 256MB of embedded RAM. Such a system can run DSL with little consideration.

The range in capabilities for computers that fall into this category is vast, but computers frequently have a few limitations in common:

- Most have limited storage space.
- Most have CPUs that are less powerful than what you would expect in a typical normal-use computer.
- Most are not designed to run a native operating system.
- Many have a flash module in place of a hard drive.
- Many have embedded RAM, which means the size is fixed.

On the other hand, many of these computers also have some very positive features:

- They are very small.
- They are silent.
- They are exceptionally energy efficient.
- They have no moving parts (meaning their failure rate is fairly low).

Mini-ITX Systems

Mini-ITX systems are based on the Mini-ITX motherboard form factor of 17cm square. There are several manufacturers of this form factor, but the company most often associated with Mini-ITX motherboards is Via.

Even within the standard motherboard size, there are many variations in configurations. Some motherboards are designed with special cool running processors that do not require a CPU fan; in contrast, some motherboards are set up to accept a Pentium 4 processor. Other units have built in PCMCIA slots and compact flash readers. In addition, other motherboards are designed to be modular and accept various *daughterboards* that can be configured to have multiple LAN lines, extra SUB plugs, serial ports, or a CompactFlash cardbus and PCMCIA reader.

Mini-ITX systems can vary greatly in performance and configuration. Some Mini-ITX systems have common PC functions including normal size hard drive, a CD/DVD drive, plenty of RAM, and conventional CPU cooling. These Mini-ITX systems (particularly those with the newer and more powerful CPUs) are capable of running any operating system that a typical PC can run.

However, one restriction is that many of the Via Mini-ITX boards are limited to a gigabyte of RAM. Although this is not exactly a small amount, for those who are avidly into gaming, video processing, or other memory intensive usages, this might be something to keep in mind. If you buy or build such a system, there is no real special consideration needed while installing or running Damn Small Linux.

In contrast, a Mini-ITX computer can be set up without a hard drive, CD/DVD drive, or any type of media storage device. Every Mini-IT board I have tested has been capable of booting via a USB drive (the early Via boards require a USB Zip configuration; see Chapter 6). At the most minimal configuration, a Mini-ITX system can even be diskless, without any form of a drive and boot via network using a PXE server.

An especially nice trait about Mini-ITX systems is that you can build a unit according to your preferences. If you have the desire to build a compact yet high performing machine, you can select the latest top-of-the-line motherboard, and a pre-manufactured case that includes the necessary power and bracketing to install a hard drive and an optical drive. Or, if you want to build your own case, you could buy components (such as the power supply) separately.

Every Mini-ITX motherboard I have tested was powerful enough to run Damn Small Linux and had normal functionality, including sound and Ethernet, with no difficulty. If you obtain an old board, odds are that it will run DSL just fine.

John's Cheap Little Mini (an Example of Minimalist Computing)

I wanted to build a system that was 100% silent, looked cool, and had no moving parts. I used parts that were affordable: the Via Epia 5000 motherboard, the PW-60 power supply, and an IDE Compact Flash adapter. The system was built inexpensively.

Although the project is a few years old now, even at the time of its creation, the Epia 5000 was not the top-of-the-line motherboard from Via. However, the Epia 5000's CPU is much cooler than the later fanless models from Via. This was good because I used plexiglass and wanted to keep the operating temperature low enough that I did not have to worry about melting the plexiglass. The mesh on the side was a gutter guard available at any hardware or home improvement store. Figure 12-1 shows a picture of this machine.

The Epia 5000 is only 533MHz; in comparison, today there are fanless Mini-ITX motherboards that are 1.5Ghz. The power supplies have also become much smaller since this project, but I think this set up is still a viable option.

FIGURE 12-1 A snapshot of the Mini.

Although underpowered next to the latest Mini-ITX boards, the Epia 5000 is a high-quality board, and this particular set up will last for years without any problem. I built this machine with only 256MB of RAM and this suited my needs more than adequately. I used the Mini as my daily computer for about a year without any problem. If I built it again, I would use a more powerful motherboard and at least 512MB of RAM simply so I could forget about RAM usage and just enjoy my silent computer.

When the DSL store started selling the Damn Small Machines, I finally retired the Mini in favor of the smaller yet more powerful thin client. I miss the look of the homemade case though, and I may build something similar again in the future.

If you want to read more about my Mini project or see more pictures, go to:

```
http://www.damnsmalllinux.org/mini.html
```

Special Considerations for Running Alternative Hardware

In this section, we will examine a few alternative hardware limitations, and look at some real-world examples.

Limited Processing Power

Damn Small Linux is usable on some fairly outdated hardware. I have been able to accomplish a day's work on a 233Mhz Pentium. Thus, it would appear that most thin clients should have powerful enough CPUs to run DSL without any difficulty. However, not all processors perform equally.

For example, currently there is a very affordable single board computer that is based on the SiS550 200Mhz processor. These units look great and can be bought for just over $100. However, you will find them painfully slow to use with DSL in graphical mode. If you are working on one of these units, you may consider using it only in text mode.

We provide a lot of text applications that can turn this machine into a useful application (see Chapter 3, "Using DSL Applications"). If you do venture into the GUI desktop, you will want to avoid any program that requires a lot of CPU cycles. Firefox should be avoided on such a thin client, as well as any of the GTK2 extensions. In addition, do not even try to use OpenOffice.org office applications.

In graphic mode, try to use our lighter-weight program options. For instance, use Ogg123 or Mpg321 to listen to your music. Use Dillo, Netrik, or Links for browsing the web. Additionally, use Naim instead of the Gaim extension for instant messaging. You may want to download the gLinks.uci extension and use that as your default browser. It is substantially lighter than Firefox, but it does good table rendering and also manages resources well.

Limited RAM and No Hard Drive

Limited RAM can pose a challenge. Many thin client type systems do not have a real hard drive, so there is no capability to use a swap partition. In this case, the question is becomes, "How much RAM do you have to work with?"

You can have fairly normal PC operation using DSL without a swap file in a system with 256MB. I use the Damn Small Machine daily at this amount of RAM. If you are careful, you can have normal functionality with 128MB of RAM and no swap drive, but you should monitor your RAM use closely, particularly when surfing the web. Figure 12-2 is a picture of the Damn Small Linux machine.

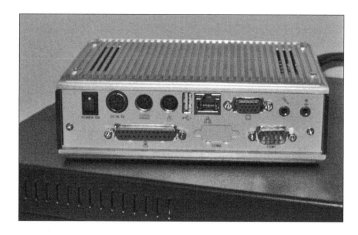

FIGURE 12-2 The Damn Small Machine has 256MB of RAM.

In this scenario, you want to limit RAM usage by not having too many memory-draining applications open simultaneously. You will be surprised at how much you can run on 128MB of RAM. All the native applications in DSL launch and run fine, from the XMMS media player to Ted, the word processor.

Dillo, the web browser, also runs adequately, but you need to be careful with Dillo because it caches every page and image displayed until it closes down the program. If you are using Dillo, restrict its page views.

We have already limited the cache size in Firefox, so it does a reasonable job of memory management on its own. However, it does not clear the cache for pages that are currently open, so if you like to surf with a lot of tabs open or if you view a page with a lot of images, you can use up all of your available RAM.

As an alternative to using Dillo, consider using the `gLinks.uci` extension and manually lowering the cache use. GLinks does a good job of handling memory and is substantially lighter than Firefox.

If you want to use a driveless and limited RAM machine with OpenOffice.org, get the `OpenOffice.uci` extension. It operates fine with 128MB of RAM without a swap as long as it is not sharing memory space with another large application such as Firefox.

Please keep in mind that if you use up all of your RAM and you do not have a swap file, your computer will lock up and any document that you have unsaved will be lost.

Other People's Garbage (Resurrecting Old Laptops)

To most people, a five-year-old laptop is hardly worth anything. These laptops seem to be gathering dust in the corners of many offices. If you cruise eBay or Craigslist, you see many old notebooks for under $100. Add a broken optical drive or hard drive and you are likely to see the unit in the recycle bin or given away. However, with a little work, many of these computers are still usable.

Recently, I was given a Sony VAIO laptop (model PCG-Z505SX). Figure 12-3 shows a picture of the laptop.

This laptop is a sexy, little lightweight notebook. It has a very thin profile and good resolution. The person who owned it was trying to give it away, and the first three people he offered it to declined it. After talking to a two people across the room, the owner walked over to my work area and started asking questions about the VAIO again.

The conversation went something like this:

Owner: How much do you think my laptop is worth?

Person One: How much RAM does it have?

Owner: I think 64MB.

Person One: Wow, so it's running Windows 98?

Owner: Yeah. So, you want it?

Person One: No thanks, I have enough unusable junk.

Owner: John, you want it?

Me: Yeah, I'll take it.

And that was that.

FIGURE 12-3   Old VAIO notebook running DSL.

In addition, it turns out that this computer did not have an optical drive or a floppy drive! It still booted Windows 98 just fine, but that is not really for me. The PCMCIA slot contained an old Linksys WPC11 802.11B wireless card.

The VAIO did have a USB plug, but it was not capable of booting via USB. My only choice was to disassemble it. I was lucky to find a disassembly HOWTO on the Internet. This discovery was a fortunate thing because these old VAIOs are constructed very compactly and I had a fair chance of damaging it without a photo guide. It is worth noting that there are a lot of such tutorials on the web for various laptop models.

After I disassembled the computer, I considered replacing the hard drive with a laptop IDE compact flash adapter from the DSL store. But the computer only had

64MB of RAM, so I kept the hard drive to run a swap space. IDE compact flash would have been great; then I would have had a very compact silent portable computer to lug around. I could have purchased a RAM upgrade for the VAIO, but that contradicts my frugal nature.

After carefully taking out the hard drive, I needed to format and install Damn Small Linux on it. For my primary desktop computer at home, I use a Damn Small Machine that boots from a USB drive. Despite their compact size, these units have room for a laptop hard drive. I disassembled the Damn Small Machine, hooked up the laptop from the VAIO, put the unit back together, and booted DSL from the pen drive as I usually do.

Next, I performed a Frugal Grub installation (see Chapter 8, "Installing DSL in Alternate Ways"). The nice thing about having a Damn Small Machine for such tasks is that it is a lot less surgically invasive to hook up a hard drive to it than to disassemble another laptop. However, you can use another laptop with a working optical drive (i.e., CD drive) to accomplish the same goal.

After I had reassembled the VAIO, I booted up DSL right away and everything worked immediately: sound, the old Linksys WPC11 802.11B wireless card, and so on. The Sony has a beautiful screen that does the default 1024×768 resolution perfectly. From using it, I could tell that the VAIO was a high-quality notebook when it was new. It is unfortunate that a short span of five years could cause it to become perceived as useless junk.

If I had a floppy drive, I could have attempted to install DSL via the modified Toms Root Boot that Robert Shingledecker put together. This scenario could have been used to pull the latest ISO from the Internet and install it to hard drive. Such a method works if you have a recognized NIC card and your notebook has enough RAM (see Chapter 8).

If you come into possession of a laptop with an optical drive but a defunct hard drive, you can always use DSL from a CD and back up your work to a USB pen drive or a floppy. Alternatively, you may want to consider an IDE compact flash conversion, which makes the laptop very energy efficient and silent.

From Thin Client to Work Station Paradise

I am not fond of computer noise. I dislike the clickety-click-click of processors, the whirling sound of CPU fans, the spinning up and down of optical drives, the constant buzz of a desktop power supply, and even the quiet hum of a hard drive. This complaint may sound extreme, but I spend a great deal of time in front of a computer and after so many years, I have become really particular about my work environment.

If you have never tried working on a silent computer, you really do not know what a joy it can be. The only noise you hear is what you want to hear (e.g., some music or a radio stream). I have heard many computer users say that after they go silent, they could never ever again use a noisy computer.

There are silent computers on the market, and some high-end units cost several thousand dollars. There are also Mini-ITX-based small form factor PCs specially built to be silent, but these also tend to be very expensive (frequently on the plus side of $800 for a basic unit). These computers are often priced expensively because they are produced in limited quantity as a special order. To have an affordable silent PC, the units need to be made in mass amounts, but this is too much of a niche market to occur.

The Thin Client as a Silent PC

Thin clients are plentiful and many are affordable. Often, they are silent with no moving parts, and instead, relying on passive cooling to lower the temperature of the CPU.

Computers designed to be thin clients can also be very small and attractive. Many of the more modern thin clients have some provision for on-board storage, such as an IDE flash, a built-in compact flash reader, or provisions for a laptop-size hard drive. Many of the newer thin clients can also boot via USB.

Thin clients are often priced under $300. Used ones can be bought for next to nothing at sites like eBay, although they are usually the older models that tend to be underpowered.

Two of the most popular models we sell in the DSL store are the eBox III, a.k.a. the Damn Small Machine (DSM), and a Mini-ITX-based thin client from Taiwan, which we call the Bargain BareBones. Both are intended for the thin client market, so they are affordable, but they are also well suited to running DSL. Figure 12-4 shows an example of the eBox III.

The DSM has embedded RAM, which means that it is fixed at 256MB. This amount is really not enough to run one of the name-brand operating systems well, but it is plenty to run DSL. As it comes, the DSM can boot right off of a USB pen drive, so there is no need to use an IDE drive at all if you choose.

You do have a few options for IDE booting if you prefer this option. You could opt for an IDE DOM (disk on module) specifically made for the DSM. In addition, the DSM has provisions for a laptop-size hard drive. Thus, you can use a conventional hard drive, but you can also opt for a conventional CF card mounted to a IDE CF adapter. The motherboard is powered by a Via 700MHz Nano processor, again, plenty of power for DSL. Figure 12-5 shows our BareBones machine next to a more typically sized Mini-ITX case.

FIGURE 12-4   The eBox III, a very compact machine with room for a hard drive.

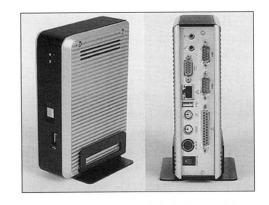

FIGURE 12-5   Compare the size of the BareBones to a typical Mini-ITX case.

The Bargain BareBones is an example of a Mini-ITX-based thin client. Again, the design is very small, much more compact than a typical Mini-ITX computer. The BareBones was never intended to be a standalone work station, and it has no provision for a hard drive or a media drive. Although the unit comes without RAM, it accepts 184-pin DIMM socket DDR RAM up to 1GB.

Unlike the DSM, the BareBones cannot take a hard drive, but there is room for an IDE DOM; at the DSL store, we have 1GB units available. The DOM is not needed if you are content with booting via USB.

Personally, I use one of each of these thin client computers. I have the DSM in my home office and the BareBones at work. Each of them has an IDE DOM, but I do not use them for booting. Instead, I only use them for occasional backup when I have important documents I want to save in more than one place.

I go back and forth between the two units using a single bootable pen drive that I use as my portable office. This way, regardless of where I am, I have my desktop the way I like it and I can continue working from the point at which I last stopped. DSL's auto configuration automatically sets the ramdisk according to the available RAM.

Other than this adjustment, I have the same system, same files, same every-thing on both thin clients. It is a nice way to work. Unlike the traditional use of these computers as thin clients, I am not dependent on any network for my files or applications, and I have all my work with me on the pen drive.

If you are not the mobile type, you may want to consider running DSL from an IDE drive, whether it is a hard drive (DSM), IDE CF conversion (DSM), or disk on module (DSM or Bargain BareBones). The units are self-contained with this approach. The fact that most of the newer thin clients can boot from USB makes installing to an IDE drive easy. Simply boot up DSL via USB and perform a Frugal install (see Chapter 8).

Green Machines

In general, alternative hardware is often environmentally friendly, whether it is a driveless homemade PC, a Mini-ITX system, a discarded laptop, or a thin client converted to run as a desktop PC. You can feel good about using less energy than with a conventional computer. In addition, when working with used equipment, you are keeping usable systems out of landfills. By using Damn Small Linux, you are contributing to a healthier planet. Now about that SUV....

SUMMARY

Alternative hardware is often cheap, silent, and very energy efficient. With the alternative installation methods available for DSL, such as the USB and Frugal installations, you have an operating system that is perfect for such systems.

Making an Edna Music Server in DSL

Damn Small Linux is a very good base for creating an Edna Music Server. It is compact, yet it has everything needed to run a basic server and the tools in place to do remote streaming, while accessing files locally and over a network. This means that one may have access to one's music shared over a local network even if the music files are stored elsewhere on the Internet. With DSL plus Edna, you have the power to get your music where you want without having to worry about storing local copies, which is a problem that occurs in many office situations. Let's explore how this is done.

ABOUT THE EDNA MUSIC SERVER

The Edna Music Server was written in the Python scripting language by Greg Stein. He calls it a *quick hack*, which is not a term that does it justice. Edna is an HTTP server that allows users to stream audio files, including MP3, Ogg Vorbis (.ogg), and other audio files. It is compatible with XMMS (included in DSL) and other popular MP3 players such as Winamp, Sonique, and FreeAmp.

Edna is constructed so that you can browse a music selection remotely. It uses a URL construct that allows you to link to a specific song. Edna also automatically makes a playlist for directory structures that can be played in sequence or a random shuffle.

Edna also dynamically builds pages according to the underlying directory structure of your music collection. Thus, categorizing is very simple and logical. You can organize your music by using the names of your directories and subdirectories as the categories and subcategories. Similarly, Edna servers offer .m3u playlists of recursive directory structures that media players use to stream the MP3s. Person-ally, I like this method of sorting because it is a way of having classification without the need for a database. This makes the code simple and reduces the overhead of the music server. This clever practice helps keep the server down to just a thousand lines of code.

Edna is licensed under the GPL. In addition, it is an interpretive script written in Python, which is a scripting language that has a strong fan base because of its neatness and code rigidity.

INSTALLING THE EDNA SERVER ON DSL

Taking advantage of your extensions is the simplest way to install the Edna Music Server on the Damn Small Linux OS. You need a Python extension to get a working Python interpreter. We have a couple of builds available in the repository; both `python.uci` and `python2.3.tar.gz` are based on Python 2.3.4. If you are running from a live CD, a USB installation, or a frugal installation, you will benefit from using the UCI extension. If you are running from a conventional hard drive installa-tion, use the `tar.gz` build. You also need to grab the Edna extension (`edna.dsl`), which is found in the Net section of the repository. In our example, you will install Edna as if it were being run from a frugal or a USB installation.

First, you need to install the Python scripting language. You are going to install the `python.uci` extension. Open the MyDSL panel and click UCI. Then, click the `python.uci` extension—it is a 12MB download. No configuration of Python is necessary.

Next, you need to download the Edna extension. It is found under Net. `Edna.dsl` is a smaller download (less than 1MB) so the download time should be much faster than the Python extension. After DSL has loaded, the extension Edna is ready to run.

The Edna files can be found at:

```
/usr/bin/ednastart
/usr/share/edna/MP3Info.py
/usr/share/edna/MP3Info.pyc
/usr/share/edna/daemon
/usr/share/edna/daemon/edna
/usr/share/edna/daemon/ednad
/usr/share/edna/edna.conf
/usr/share/edna/edna.py
/usr/share/edna/ezt.py
/usr/share/edna/ezt.pyc
/usr/share/edna/ntsvc/
```

```
/usr/share/edna/ntsvc/TCPServerService.py
/usr/share/edna/ntsvc/ednaNTSvc.py
/usr/share/edna/ntsvc/regsetup.py
/usr/share/edna/templates/
/usr/share/edna/templates/default.ezt
/usr/share/edna/templates/default_complex.ezt
/usr/share/edna/templates/stats.ezt
/usr/share/edna/templates/style-xml.ezt
/usr/share/edna/www/
/usr/share/edna/www/anoncvs.html
/usr/share/edna/www/client.html
/usr/share/edna/www/images/
/usr/share/edna/www/images/browser.jpg
/usr/share/edna/www/images/chalk.jpg
/usr/share/edna/www/images/client.jpg
/usr/share/edna/www/images/redpix.gif
/usr/share/edna/www/images/taskbar.jpg
/usr/share/edna/www/images/term.jpg
/usr/share/edna/www/index.html
/usr/share/edna/www/new-index.html
/usr/share/edna/www/taskbar.html
/opt/mp3s
```

You can start the Edna server by selecting Edna MP3 Server in your MyDSL submenu, or alternatively, you may open up a term window and type **sudo python edna.py**. At this point, you are launching Edna with a default configuration that looks for files in /opt/mp3s/. If you look in /opt/mp3s/, you find a sample MP3 provided with the Edna extension.

At this point, you should be able to point your browser to the server and see if it is working. From DSL, you can launch Firefox and point it to http://127.0.0.1:8080. Figure 13-1 shows the default layout of the Edna Music Server.

As you can see, there are two subdirectories listed in the default configuration. MP3 CDROM points to /mnt/cdrom where Edna searches for music files on your optical device. It is important to note that Edna cannot read music CD formats that are not mountable in the normal sense, but instead looks for media files the same way it would probe a normal file directory. So, if you store your Ogg Vorbis or MP3 files on CDs, Edna can access them and share them with a network. It is worth noting that there are lots of options for ripping and encoding music CDs from Damn Small Linux in the Media section of the DSL Extension repository. Even without any extensions, you could rip CDs with XMMS by switching the audio preference to "Disk Writer Plugin," which will save the audio as a wav file, and then you could encode the wave file into an Ogg Vorbis file by using the command line utility 'oggenc'.

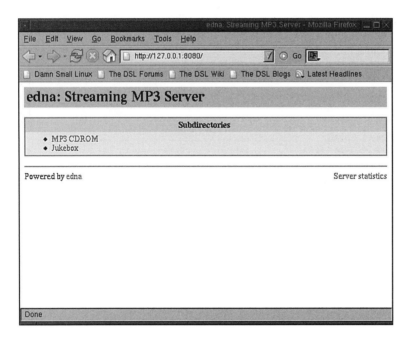

FIGURE 13-1 The default configuration for Edna as seen via the Firefox browser in DSL.

The other directory listed is Jukebox. It points to /opt/mp3s, which lives within the ramdisk that DSL creates at boot time. This means that the size /opt/mp3s is limited by the amount of RAM space DSL has allocated. Obviously, this is not a location where you would store a massive amount of music. Most of the time, users want to access music on a hard drive. Fortunately, there is a configuration file that makes it easy to edit the path to your music.

EDITING THE PATH TO YOUR MUSIC

To point Edna to the right directory, you need to edit the edna.conf file. This file can be found at /usr/share/edna/edna.conf.

You will want to open it in your editor of choice. In this example, you use Beaver for your editor. You need to have super user (root) privileges to edit this document, as shown in Figure 13-2.

Open a term window and enter this command:

```
sudo beaver /usr/share/edna/edna.conf
```

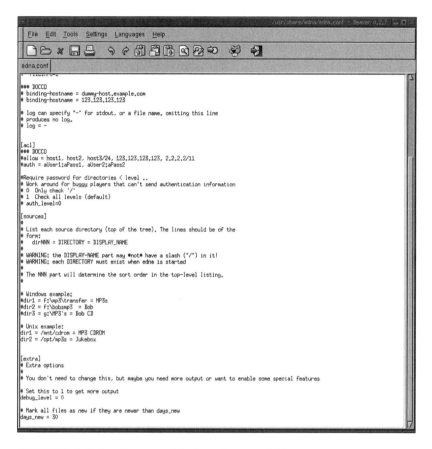

FIGURE 13-2   Beaver with the *edna.conf* file open.

The defaults for the config file are fine for most people. The lines you want to edit are lines 56 and 57.

This is what the section should look like:

```
# Unix example:
dir1 = /mnt/cdrom = MP3 CDROM
dir2 = /opt/mp3s = Jukebox
```

If you are not planning on running MP3s from CDs, you can comment out `dir1` with a pound symbol (#) at the beginning of the line. You are free to add and delete directories within the server path to files, and Edna automatically adjusts to include or exclude them. However, after Edna is running, you have to restart the server for it to reread the config file, if you alter file paths. The simplest way to do this is to give a command-line command that restarts the server. This process also restarts any other Python script you have running. Note: Damn Small Linux does not have any native Python scripts, so it should be safe unless you are a Python hacker; and if you are, why are you reading this How To?

To restart Edna, type:

```
sudo killall -HUP python
```

If you keep your music on a particular drive, you want to configure Edna to seek the directory on that drive. Please note that the drive needs to be mounted first.

Here is an example entry in the config file for accessing music on a hard drive:

```
dir3 = /mnt/hda1/music/ = Hard Drive Tunes
```

Here is an example for music stored on a pen drive:

```
dir4 = /mnt/sda1/mp3s_and_oggs/ = My Portable Music
```

If you are using DSL from a computer that pulls double duty as a MS Windows machine and you store your music on the Windows side, you should be able to mount your Windows partition and point Edna to the correct path for your music. Just be sure to remember that the path should be /mnt *plus* the path to the drive and partition where the Windows OS sits *plus* the physical path to your music (not the virtual path given by MS Explorer). If you have any doubts as to the true path to your music on the Windows partition, you can mount the drive and then navigate to the directory in the file manager Emelfm. You will notice that Emelfm displays the full directory path as you navigate—you can use this as a reference. Be sure to mount the drive before you try to navigate, or you won't be able to see anything!

SET UP WALK-THROUGH

For this walk-through, I am going to use public domain music grabbed from archive.org. By the way, archive.org has a very nice collection of freely available music that can be added to your music collection legally and without cost. It is also a neat way to discover new music. Okay, back on topic.

For this demonstration, I am making a directory tree on the first partition of a hard drive. I will be original and call it music.

Thus, the initial path for the directory is:

```
/mnt/hda1/music
```

Next, I make a few directories inside the music directory: Live_Music, Grateful_Dead, and Jazz. We are keeping it simple for this demonstration.

The complete path to these directories would look like this:

```
/mnt/hda1/music/Live_Music
/mnt/hda1/music/Grateful_Dead
/mnt/hda1/music/Jazz
```

So, in the Edna configuration file, my file path entries look like this:

```
dir1 = /mnt/hda1/music/Live_Music = Live Music
dir2 = /mnt/hda1/music/Grateful_Dead = The Grateful Dead
dir3 = /mnt/hda1/music/Jazz = Jazz
```

After commenting out the original directory paths and adding my entry, I restart the server with the `sudo killall -HUP python` command. To confirm that it all went well, I recheck the display in the server. Refer to Figure 13-3 for an example of how Edna looks after adding the file paths.

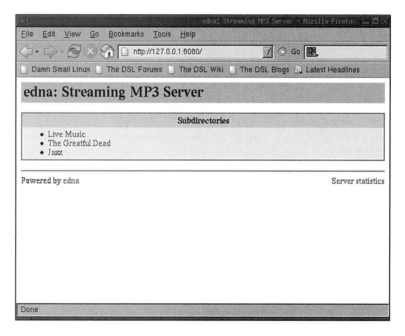

FIGURE 13-3   Edna with the new categories displayed.

After you have the initial directory path, you can fill it up any way you like. You can organize your music several levels deep or have your music directory shallow and broad. You can also mix it up by having some music files at a top-level directory and an extensive tree of subdirectories for your more organized music. After just a few minutes of downloading some live concerts from Archive.org, you can see the unorganized collection I put together in Figure 13-4. Edna automatically updates its music tree when you place new music or folders in its path.

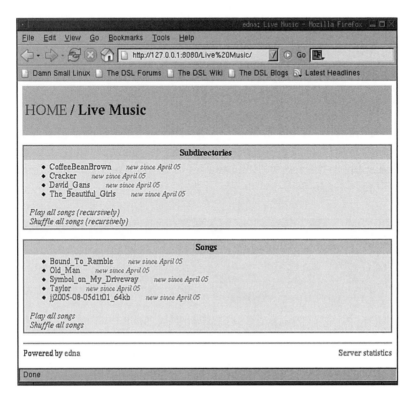

FIGURE 13-4   Edna shows directories in the top table and music files in the lower.

As you can see in Figure 13-4, Edna splits the directories and the music files for easy visual sorting. Any text that appears in purple is clickable for easy navigation. The links in the lower left of each table provide m3u files, which are a playlist for your media player. Play All Songs plays all songs within the domain of the table recursively, whereas Shuffle All Songs gives a random order to the same list.

Edna also gives usage statistics. Notice the link in the lower-right corner of the page in Figure 13-4. The data available includes a table that shows the user IP, time of access per song, what songs were accessed, and a list of unique IPs and initial visitation in another table (see Figure 13-5). This could be very valuable information, particularly if your music server is supposed to be private and you see a foreign IP poking around.

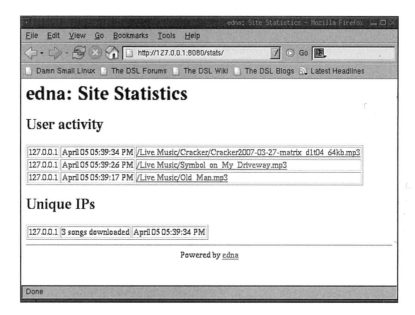

FIGURE 13-5   View a snapshot of local use and remote access to your Edna Server.

CONFIGURATION OPTIONS, CUSTOMIZATION, AND SAVING SETTING

There are a few options in the config file that you may find interesting. You can change the default port from 8080 to any free port you desire. This may help in getting around some firewalls. There is also the option of binding Edna to a host name so that the server headings will comply with remote domain access. Also available are user and password authentication and restricting access to only specific resolved domains or remote Ips (be sure to reference /etc/services to avoid conflicts with other applications while choosing a port)—both are handy if you want to restrict access to your remote music.

You can also customize the look of your Edna server by editing the HTML or images. The files to edit are located in the following directories:

```
/usr/share/edna/www/
/usr/share/edna/www/images/
```

If you edit the defaults, be sure to back up your work and to include the Edna directory in your .filetool.lst.

The entry in ~/.filetool.lst should look like this:

```
usr/share/edna/
```

This entry makes sure your configuration file and any alterations are automatically saved and restored at shutdown and startup time. If you are running Edna with only a modified config file, all you need to back up and restore is the file itself.

To back up just the config file, add this line to ~/.filetool.lst:

```
usr/share/edna/edna.conf
```

To have Edna boot and run automatically upon startup, you need to enter the Edna launching script into the boot local file, which can be found at /opt/bootlocal.sh. If you have your music on a particular drive, you also have to mount that drive first.

For the example in this chapter, the bootlocal.sh entries look like this:

```
mount /dev/hda1
cd /usr/share/edna
exec python edna.py &
```

EDNA AND ACCESSING REMOTE MUSIC

Okay, let's pretend that you have a job at a repressive company that does not allow you to bring in your music, and also deploys a restrictive firewall that forbids you access to a remote music server where you can access your music. What to do? Many work environments monitor and restrict access via HTTP, but do nothing about Secure Shell (SSH) access to remote hosts. How does that help you if the music is on your private server but you can't bring it into work? You may remember in Chapter 3, "Using DSL Applications," when I went on about the FUSE file system (SSHFS) and how cool it is because it allows mounting remote drives via SSH. Well, you could use that in combination with the Edna server to access your remote music as if it were locally hosted! Yes, I know it's geeky, but it is also pretty damn cool!

Here is what you do: The first step is to mount your remote file system via SSHFS. You need to have root privileges, so open up a root term window. Before you use SSHFS, you need to load the *fuse* module. To do this, type **modprobe fuse**. Now, you can use SSHFS to access your remote drive. You have to decide on a place for your mount point; we conveniently have /mnt/test/ available in DSL, so you may just want to use it. The syntax for the sshfs command is similar to that of the ssh and scp commands—it works with an IP address or domain name.

Here is the syntax to use:

```
# sshfs user@remote_address:/path/to/music/ /mnt/test/
```

Next, you press Enter and then type in your password just like using SSH or SCP. After this is done, your remote music (MP3s, Ogg files, etc.) is accessible at `/mnt/test/path/to/music/`. All you need to do is add this path to your Edna config file and (re)start Edna. Bam! Done. Now, you have access to your tunes despite the man trying to keep you down :-). Perhaps the greatest benefit of using SSHFS and Edna is that you can share your remote music with others on your network as well.

Here is the entry, keeping consistent with the previous example entries:

```
dir4 = /mnt/test/path/to/music/ = Remote Tunes
```

If Edna is already running, you need to restart it for it to pick up the remote file.

Let's send a HUP signal to the python process to accomplish the restart:

```
sudo killall -HUP python
```

Now, you should be able to access your remote files on the computer running DSL via localhost access at `http://127.0.0.1:8080/Remote%20Tunes/`. Other people on your local network should also be able to access your tunes via your local IP. If you don't know what it is, you can look at the Torsmo display at the upper right of your desktop or open a Terminal window and type **/sbin/ifconfig** and look for the four part number that comes after `inet addr:` on the device that is not the "local loopback" or "lo" listing.

For example, if your address turns out to be 192.168.1.200, people in your local area network could access your remote tunes by pointing their browser to `http://192.168.1.200:8080/Remote%20Tunes/`.

SUMMARY

This should be enough to get you going with a basic Edna setup. As you can see, there are many ways to use Edna to enjoy your music or any other type of audio files. One last tip: If you include an image in a directory with your music, Edna displays that image while you access it. This could be a way to add some personality to your music server.

## CHAPTER 14

Using Skype VoIP Service in DSL

By adding Skype software to Damn Small Linux (DSL), you can make calls from your computer to a person at another computer (for free) or to any telephone in the world (for a bit of money). You can also use text chat to communicate with other Skype users.

Besides being offered for Linux, Skype software is available for Windows, Mac OS X, and Pocket PCs. So, if you can get a group of family, friends, or associates to sign up for Skype accounts, you can make calls, send files, and participate in chats among those people, even if they are not all using the same type of computer.

Because Skype software has been packaged for Damn Small Linux, you can easily install Skype using the MyDSL feature. You can then apply all the advantages of using DSL to your Skype application, so you can have your own calling tools that run on a low-end PC or from a custom, portable USB stick or CD.

This chapter describes how to use the Skype software package that is available for DSL to place calls to people over the Internet. It also describes how to extend your use of Skype to include other free and inexpensive services. Although this chapter describes how to set up Skype from any recent version of DSL you might have, refer to Appendix A for information on the DSL software included on the CD that comes with this book.

NOTE

Although this chapter describes some of the free Skype services available using software created for Linux, it also touches on some of the for-pay services available from Skype. The authors of this book have no affiliation with Skype and our coverage of their products doesn't represent an endorsement of Skype. If you are interested in those services, you should research their suitability for yourself.

INTRODUCTION TO SKYPE AND VoIP

To encourage people to purchase its voice over Internet protocol (VoIP) Internet telephone products, Skype Limited (www.skype.com) offers a variety of free Internet communications services to people who sign up for a free user account. By downloading and installing Skype software, setting up a user account, and doing some simple configuration, you can be making calls to others over the Internet within just a few minutes.

Skype describes its Internet-based telephony service as a *decentralized peer-to-peer network*. The concept of peer-to-peer (P2P) networked applications was popularized by file-sharing applications, such as KaZaA (www.kazaa.com), where clients can offer and share files (containing documents, music, video, or other content) directly to other clients. In its P2P VoIP offering, Skype emphasizes the decentralized aspect of how it implements its communications services.

By decentralizing the processing and networking power needed to run the Skype service, the Skype network can grow without adding more centralized servers. In other words, each client using Skype shares its processing power and network bandwidth to increase the general pool of resources available to all Skype users. So, in theory, adding more Skype users shouldn't require more servers, bandwidth, and other computing resources to maintain the same performance level for all users.

Traditionally, standard telephone service has been far superior to VoIP in quality and reliability. The following is a list of common shortcomings of VoIP services and how Skype is designed to deal with them:

- **Poor call completion**—Firewalls (which often block most incoming service requests) and network address translation (which can hide many private IP addresses behind a single public IP address) prevented many VoIP calls from getting through. To more effectively route calls, Skype uses Skype clients with public IP addresses to act as proxies to route calls to clients that are behind firewalls.

- **Poor call quality**—Inefficient routing of calls often resulted in poor quality of transmission on VoIP networks. Skype uses multiple connection paths so that the best possible route for data can be chosen as it is needed.

- **Difficult configuration**—Instead of just contacting a phone company and plugging in a phone, many VoIP services require complex firewall configuration and manual identification of servers. A simplified user interface that requires no special incoming firewall configuration makes Skype easy to set up for most users. (See Skype and Firewalls: www.skype.com/help/guides/firewall.html.)

- **Expensive centralized servers**—Many VoIP services rely on central directory servers to maintain information about users, such as their identities, IP addresses, and whether they are currently connected. As more people joined the service, the VoIP provider either had to add more servers or allow the overall service to degrade. Skype uses a decentralized, global user directory. This *Global Index* technology consists of a hierarchy of nodes that allow every node in the network to identify all users and resources in the network with little latency.

- **Insecure transmissions**—Because the Internet is a public network, it's possible for calls to be intercepted. To keep potential intruders from listening in on Skype calls, Skype encrypts all file transfers, instant messages, and calls at both ends of the transmission.

There are some aspects of VoIP that are inherently different from standard plain old telephone system (POTS) phones. You should keep these in mind before you consider replacing your current phone system with Skype or other VoIP service:

- **No emergency service**—Unlike land line telephones that are hard wired into a particular location, your VoIP service is tied to an IP address that can easily change. Skype documentation makes it clear that its service should not be used to replace your current telephony system because it cannot support emergency 911 (or other local emergency service) dialing.

- **Restrictive firewalls**—Although Skype doesn't require special firewall configuration to allow incoming calls, some very restrictive corporate firewalls may prevent some outgoing services as well. From a computer that is behind such a firewall, Skype may work poorly or not at all.

- **Single phone**—The VoIP protocol doesn't handle multiple telephones on the same line very well. With Skype, you are restricted to having to answer the phone from a single location (your computer or wireless handheld device).

- **Other telephone services**—You should do a service-by-service comparison of your current phone service before switching to Skype, to be sure you're not going to lose something you rely on. For example, outgoing caller ID is not yet supported by Skype (although it is being considered) so a lot of people who don't answer anonymous calls may not pick up when you call.

- **Unreliable Internet connection**—Poor call quality can also result from having a slow or unreliable Internet connection.

Although the number of people who use Skype to replace their standard telephony service is growing (despite Skype's warnings against it), most Skype users still maintain their old service along with Skype. For more talk on the pros and cons of using Skype as your only phone service, as well as more general discussions about using Skype, refer to the Skype forums (`http://forum.skype.com`). Refer to the Skype for Linux forum (`http://forum.skype.com/index.php?showforum=18`) for more specific information on using Skype in Linux.

SETTING UP VoIP HARDWARE

The entry point of the hardware you need for using Skype VoIP service in Damn Small Linux is quite low. Almost any computer that runs Damn Small Linux and has working sound hardware (input and output) can be used for Skype. (For example, most PCs with Pentium processors and at least 64MB of RAM should work fine.)

Using your computer that is running Damn Small Linux, here is the list of minimum hardware requirements you need to get started:

- **Network hardware**—You need to have hardware to connect you to the Internet. A relatively fast Internet connection is needed to get the best performance.
- **Microphone**—Any microphone you can plug into the microphone jack (usually pink or red) on your sound card should work.
- **Headphones**—Although you could use your PC speakers, headphones are recommended to prevent the feedback that can occur from picking up output on your microphone.

There are a variety of headsets you can purchase for hands-free operation. Some of the headsets offered directly from Skype contain call minutes for SkypeOut calling. You can look into headsets and other Skype gear at the Skype shot (`http://us.accessories.skype.com`).

Before setting up Skype software, you should plug in your headphones (Line Out, green port) and microphone (Microphone, pink or red port). Then, with DSL booted and running, check that your sound system is working.

 NOTE

Although other versions of Skype support video calls, the Linux version (as of this writing) does not. Video support is one of the most requested new features on the Linux Skype forums, so you can expect later versions of Skype for Linux to include video support.

Setting Up ALSA Sound in DSL

To make sure that your sound system is working in DSL and to set sound levels, you can use several applications that come with DSL or can be easily added using MyDSL. In particular, the Advanced Linux Sound Architecture (ALSA) sound system is required to use Skype in DSL, along with the gnu-utils package (which is required by ALSA).

To begin this procedure, boot up DSL. You can boot directly from a DSL live CD or from any medium you prefer (pen drive, hard disk, etc.).

Because I'm assuming that you want to set up Skype to work persistently in DSL (and not just go away after you reboot), the following procedure describes how to get the extensions you need for sound in Skype and reload them upon reboot. Here's how to do that:

1. Before you begin downloading DSL extensions, determine where you want to save them for future use. For example, mount a hard disk partition or inserted USB flash drive (pen drive) so it is ready to save your extensions. Then, create a mydsl directory at the root of that device. With a pen drive, for example, you might type the following from a Terminal window with root permissions:

   ```
   # mkdir /mnt/sda1/mydsl
   ```

 NOTE

If your computer is a Windows system, it's quite likely that your hard disk partition is formatted for the NTFS file system. If this is the case with your computer, you need to use a USB pen drive, create a hard disk partition of some other type (such as FAT32 or ext3), or remaster a CD (as described in Chapter 4, "Configuring and Saving DSL Settings") to save the needed packages. DSL does not support writing to NTFS file systems.

2. From the DSL desktop, select the MyDSL icon.
3. Select UNC and select the ALSA package.
4. Read the description of the ALSA package. Note that the ALSA package requires the gnu-utils package to be installed (which we'll get next) and an ALSA boot option to work.
5. Select Download. A pop-up window asks where to install the package.
6. When prompted, indicate where you want the ALSA package to be downloaded. The /tmp directory is used by default. To save it to a pen drive,

however, you might type /mnt/sda1/mydsl instead. Select Download and you can watch the progress as the package is downloaded and installed.

7. Select UNC and select the gnu-utils package.

8. Read the description of the gnu-utils package.

9. Select Download. A pop-up window asks where to install the package.

10. When prompted, indicate where you want the gnu-utils package to be downloaded. The /tmp directory is used by default. Instead, you should type /mnt/sda1/mydsl to save the extension to a pen drive. Select Download and you can watch the progress as the package is downloaded and installed.

11. Open a Terminal window (right-click the desktop and select XShells, Root Access, Dark) and type the following commands to start the ALSA sound system:

```
# alsa_snddevices
# alsa_init
```

The alsa_snddevices command creates the audio group and sound devices (in /dev) that you need for ALSA to work. The alsa_init command starts the ALSA service. Your ALSA sound system should now be running.

Next, you can try to adjust your audio in DSL:

1. **Start audio mixer**—Start DMix to adjust sound levels by right-clicking the desktop and selecting Apps→ Sound/MPEG/VoIP→ Dmix Sound Mixer.

2. **Adjust audio output**—In the DMix window, select Master Volume. Then, move the sliders to adjust the audio levels for the right and left channels.

3. **Adjust audio input**—In the DMix window, select the name of your input device (it may be Microphone, Phone Input, or Line In). Click the Rec button (so the button turns on) to have the microphone be selected as your recording device. Move the sliders up to adjust the audio input levels.

4. **Play sound**—You can check your Internet connection at the same time you test sound output by starting XMMS to play a streaming radio station. Right-click the desktop and select Apps→ Sound/MPEG/VoIP→ XMMS→ Xmms News Feeds→ Xmms "KCPW NPR NEWS." Streaming audio should play in your headphones.

At this point, you can close the DMix and XMMS windows. If your sound system is still not working, refer to the Troubleshooting Skype section near the end of this chapter for suggestions on debugging the problem.

STARTING WITH SKYPE IN DSL

Before you can start using Skype in DSL, you need to get and install the Skype software, then create a user account. The following sections describe how to do that.

Installing Skype

To get and install Skype, you can use the MyDSL feature. Here's how:

1. From the DSL desktop, select the MyDSL icon.
2. Select UNC and choose the latest version of Skype that is available and select it. For this procedure, I chose `skype-1.2.0.18`.
3. Read the description of the Skype package and select Download.
4. When prompted, indicate where you want the Skype package to be downloaded. The `/tmp` directory is used by default. Instead, you should type **/mnt/sda1/mydsl** to save the extension to a pen drive. Select Download and you can watch the progress as Skype is downloaded and installed.

After Skype is installed, a Skype icon appears on the desktop, as shown in Figure 14-1.

FIGURE 14-1   A Skype icon appears on the DSL desktop when Skype is installed.

 NOTE

If you want to look for later versions of the Skype software for Linux as they become available, check out the Skype software download page for Linux (`http://skype.com/download/skype/linux`). Later, from the Skype window, you can select Help→ Check for Update to find if any software updates are available.

At this point, everything should be ready to begin using Skype.

Getting a Skype User Account

When you first launch Skype software from the icon on the DSL desktop, you are asked to sign in with your Skype user account, if you don't have one yet, here's how you can go about getting one:

1. **Start Skype**—Select the Skype icon on the DSL desktop. A Log in to Skype window appears.

2. **User account**—If you already have a Skype user account, type the username and password as prompted (then skip to the upcoming "Using Skype" section). Otherwise, select the New Users tab, click Next, and continue on with this procedure.

3. **Add new account**—Enter the following information into the Create a New Skype Account screen:

    - **Choose Skype Name**—Type a username between 6 and 32 characters. The first character must be a letter, but numbers can be included after the first character. No spaces are allowed in the username.

    - **Password**—Type a 4- to 20-character password. Then, type that password again in the Repeat Password field.

    - **Store my Contacts...**—Click this box if you want your contacts, call history, and instant messaging history stored on the local computer.

    - **Your e-mail address**—Enter your email address.

    - **Yes, I have read...**—Click the link to the Skype End User License Agreement and read the license. See the Agreeing to Use Skype sidebar for some highlights of the license you should be aware of.

    - **Please contact...**—Click this box to agree to let Skype contact you about Skype features and services.

    Select Next to add your user account.

    At this point, the Skype main window appears.

AGREEING TO USE SKYPE

Before you can have a Skype user account, you must agree to the Skype End User License Agreement (EULA). Besides helping you understand the terms of use set down by Skype Software Inc. for using the Skype software, this agreement also helps you see some of the limitations of the software itself.

I urge you to read the entire agreement yourself. Here are a few of the highlights:

- **Covers your use**—By agreeing to use the version of Skype you install, you agree to adhere to the terms of the agreement, whether you use Skype from this install or any other installation of the software.

- **Use of processor/bandwidth**—Skype helps keep the cost of providing services down by utilizing resources from Skype clients. To that end, the license requires you to agree to let Skype software use your processor and network bandwidth to facilitate communications among Skype users.

- **No emergency calls**—As mentioned earlier, Skype doesn't recommend that you use Skype software to provide your only phone service. One reason is that Skype software doesn't support or carry emergency calls.

- **Personal and noncommercial**—You can't grant your rights to use the software to anyone else. So, you can't legally make a Skype system to resell to others.

As with most freely distributed software, Skype software is provided without warranty. The EULA also reminds you that using Skype software doesn't grant you ownership to any of Skype's intellectual property contained in that software.

---

4. **Add account information**—If you want other Skype users to be able to find you, you may want to add information about yourself to your user account. An Edit Profile window may open automatically the first time you log in. If it doesn't, from the Skype window, select File→ Your Personal Profile. Figure 14-2 shows an example of the My Profile screen that appears.

As you can see from Figure 14-2, you can add name, city, state, phone number, and other personal information about yourself. This information makes it easier for people to search for you through the Skype search feature.

Now you are ready to start using Skype to communicate with others.

FIGURE 14-2 Add information to your Skype profile to help others find you.

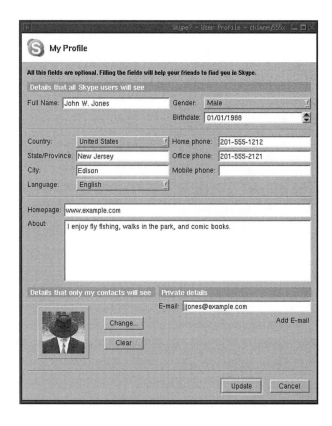

USING SKYPE

After you have a user account, you can start using Skype. If the Skype window is not already open, open it by clicking the Skype icon on the DSL desktop. When prompted, log in using the Skype login and password you created. The Skype window appears, as shown in Figure 14-3.

Here are a few things you should learn about the Skype window:

- **Toolbar**—The default toolbar lets you add a contact (plus icon), search for Skype users (magnifying glass icon), start a conference call (people icon), send an instant message (A in a bubble icon), send a file (page with up-arrow icon), or view profile (i in a circle icon). Select Configure (tools icon to the right) to change which icons appear on the toolbar.

- **Contacts**—Shows the contacts you have added to your list. Contacts can be added to groups or kept as ungrouped. An icon next to each contact name shows whether the contact is currently connected to the Skype service. Right-click any contact name to see a list of actions to take on that contact (telephone call, instant message, view profile, and so on).

FIGURE 14-3

Start your session from the Skype window.

- **Dial**—If you are using the for-pay SkypeOut service to call traditional telephones, you can use the keypad on the Dial tab to key in a telephone number to call.

- **Call List**—The Call List tab keeps a record of your missed calls, incoming calls, and outgoing calls. It also has a button for retrieving voice mails, if you have signed up for that service with Skype.

- **Events**—The events area of the window lets you see contact events that have occurred. For example, it shows missed chats and calls that have occurred. You can select an event to respond to it (for example, to call the person back).

- **Services**—Skype for-pay services are available from this area of the Skype window. Select SkypeOut, VoiceMail, or SkypeIn to connect to the Skype website to enable any of those services.

- **Phone call**—Type in a Skype username or phone number you want to call and click the green phone icon to place the call. Click the red phone icon to hang up.

- **Status list**—Click the icon in the lower-left corner of the screen to see the status list. The grayed item in the status list (in this case, Online) shows the current status of your Skype session. Select Do Not Disturb to have incoming calls queued to respond to later, without showing you alerts at the moment each call arrives. Selecting Skype Me opens your session so that any Skype user can try to contact you.

When Skype is running (/opt/skype/skype command in DSL), your computer is accessible to the Skype service, even if you are just signed in but not currently making a call. Those contacts you have allowed will be able to see that you are online. The Skype services itself will have access to your computer's processor and bandwidth.

The following sections describe how to use Skype to find and communicate with Skype users in various ways. Later, you can find information on how to use the Skype for-pay services, such as making calls to traditional telephones.

If you find that you need more information on using Skype, you can refer to the online guides available from the Skype website (www.skype.com/help/guides). In particular, you can find out how to get software and instructions for setting up Skype on other computer systems (such as Windows and Mac OS X).

Trying a Test Call

Before proceeding, you should check that your microphone and speakers/headset are working with Skype by trying a test call. In the text box near the bottom of the Skype screen, type the account name:

echo123

and click the green call icon. Skype makes a call to the Skype Test Call account. A voice tells you to record a message at the tone. After you speak for a few seconds into the microphone, the Skype Test Call plays the message back for you that you just recorded. If you hear it, your Skype service is working well enough to proceed to using Skype. (If not, refer to the "Troubleshooting Skype" section later.)

Finding People to Connect To

Skype keeps a public record of every Skype user account, which can optionally include a lot of personal information. You can search that database of information to find people to call. Then, after you find a person you are looking for, you can view his profile, add him to your contact list, or send him an instant message. Here's how:

1. **Start search**—Select the Find icon (a magnifying glass) from the Skype toolbar. The Search for Skype Users screen appears.

2. **Choose search terms**—Type a word to search for into the Look For box and select Find. The Skype Name field in the Skype user account database is searched for that word. By selecting Advanced, you can instead search for a

user by full name, birth date, email address, sex, language, address, or phone number. Continue to refine your search until the person you are looking for appears on the list.

3. **Select a user**—Right-click the user account you are interested in contacting. Figure 14-4 shows an example of the menu that appears in the search box when you right-click a user account.

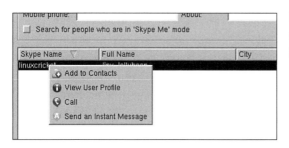

FIGURE 14-4   Choose how to contact someone after searching for Skype users.

4. **View user profile**—Select View User Profile to make sure that the user account you selected represents the person you want to contact.

5. **Add to contacts**—Select Add to Contacts from the menu. A Request Authorization window appears that asks if you want to send a message to that user requesting to "Please allow me to see when you are online." You can type a different message, if you like, as well as make one of the following requests:

- **Request authorization to see his/her/status and allow this user to see when I am online**
- **Request authorization to see his/her/online status but do not allow this user to see when I am online**

Choose the option you want and select OK. If the person you want to add to your list is currently connected to Skype, that person will see a message asking if she wants to:

- **Allow this person to see when you are online and contact you**
- **Do not allow this person to see when you are online**
- **Block this person from contacting you in the future**
- **Add** *Full Name* (*Skype Name*) **to my contacts**

If the person allows you to see when she is online and adds you to her contacts list (the default behavior), the person's full name appears in your contacts list under ungrouped buddies. You can now contact that person in different ways from your contacts list or add that person to a contacts group.

Working with Groups of Contacts

To create a group of contacts, right-click a username in the Skype window and select Groups→ Create New. Enter a new group name when prompted. Add others to that group by right-clicking their names, selecting Groups, and choosing the new group name from the menu.

Sending Contacts Lists

After you have put together a good list of contacts, you might want to share that list with your friends or coworkers. To do that, select Tools→ Send Contacts. In the Send Contacts window that appears, type the Skype Name you want to send the contacts to in the top box. Next, choose the contacts you want to send from the All Contacts box and select Add to add each one to the Contacts to Send box. Select Send to send the list.

If the person you are sending the list is currently connected to Skype, an Incoming contacts list should appear on that person's desktop. Figure 14-5 shows an example of a contacts list that appears on a desktop for a Skype user from a Mac OS X desktop.

FIGURE 14-5 Choose contacts sent from a Skype user's contacts list.

The person receiving the list can select Add Selected to add all the contacts sent to him on that list. Otherwise, he can remove the checkmarks from those users that he doesn't want to have on his own contacts list.

Making Free Calls

After you have gotten your Skype session all set up, making calls is the easy part. Here are some of the ways you can go about making free calls to other Skype users on a computer:

- **Contact List**—Select a user from your contacts list, then click the green phone icon on the bottom of the screen to make the call. Or, you could right-click the contact name and select Call This Contact from the menu that appears.

- **Search List**—Search for the contact you are looking for, as described in the "Finding People to Connect To" section. Select the contact from the list and click the green call icon from the lower-left corner of the screen to call that person.

After the call is placed, a pop-up window appears on the recipient's desktop. Figure 14-6 shows an example of such a pop-up appearing on the Mac OS X desktop of a Skype user.

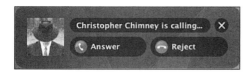

FIGURE 14-6   A Skype client is alerted that a Skype call is coming in.

The recipient can simply select the Answer button to begin conversing. Either party can end the call by selecting the red hang up button.

Participating in Chats

Although there are a lot of applications that let you carry on typed chats with one or more other people, Skype lets you leverage the same Skype contacts database to carry on typed chats with the same people you are set up to call. You can start a typed chat in much the same way you begin an audio call:

- **Contact list**—Right-click a user from your contacts list, and then select Send an Instant Message from the menu that appears.

- **Search list**—Search for the contact you are looking for, as described in the "Finding People to Connect To" section. Right-click the contact from the list, and then select Send an Instant Message.

The chat window opens, ready for you to type a message to the chosen recipient. Type a message and press Enter. A chat window opens on the recipient's desktop.

Both sides can begin typing messages, with the results looking like the window shown in Figure 14-7.

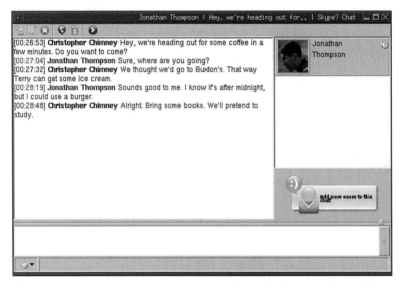

FIGURE 14-7   Open an instant message window to chat with another Skype contact.

You can add other contacts to the chat by selecting the Add More Users to This Chat button. Then, you can choose people from your contacts list to add as chat participants. The result is that the users you choose are asked to participate.

During the chat, you have many of the features available that you would expect to see during a chat session. For example, you can change the chat topic or select to bookmark the chat.

USING SKYPE FOR-PAY SERVICES AND PRODUCTS

Before you can start making local, national, or international calls from Skype to phones on the standard telephone system, you need to pay for one of the Skype programs that let you do that. Other purchases you can make from Skype include wireless phones and other telephone hardware. Check the Skype website (http://skype.com/products) to learn about the different products available from Skype.

Purchasing Calling Time

Because these programs change often, you need to check the Skype website for the latest programs and pricing. However, at the time of this writing, here are some of the available telephone calling programs:

- **SkypeOut**—This program lets you make calls from your computer to phones and mobile devices on the traditional phone system. There are yearly rates for unlimited calls within the United States and Canada (currently $29.95 per year). For international calls, there are per minute rates offered (currently starting at $.021 cents per minute).

    Calls to a group of countries where Skype is most popular are available at a single SkypeOut Global Rate. Calls to countries covered under that rate include countries in North America, Europe, Australia, some countries in the Far East, and a few in South and Central America. Check the Skype website for exactly which countries are covered (www.skype.com/products/ skypeout/rates).

- **SkypeIn**—To allow other people to call your Skype account on your computer, you can sign up for SkypeIn service. That service assigns a phone number to your Skype service so it can be reached from a traditional telephone.

    One advantage to this service is that you can have a phone number assigned from an area that is in a particular area from which you expect a lot of calls. In that way, people that call you from that same area can pay local charges, instead of long-distance charges. You, on the other hand, can be logged in from anywhere in the world that you can fire up your Skype account.

Some traditional extra telephone services are also available from Skype. For example, you can get Skype Voicemail (to answer your calls when you aren't around) or Call Forwarding (to have your Skype calls forwarded to your traditional landline phone or mobile phone).

Purchasing Accessories

Skype sells accessories that you can use with your Skype free and for-pay call services. The Skype Accessories Shop has the latest available products (http://accessories.skype.com). The following are some Skype products that might be useful to use with DSL.

- **Headsets**—Although you can purchase similar headsets to the ones that Skype offers at most stores that sell computer accessories, Skype offers some modestly priced headsets that include free SkypeOut minutes. Skype also sells a speaker/headset switch, to make it easier to change back to speakers when you are not making phone calls.

- **Starter kit**—If you are setting up several people at once to use Skype, a starter kit including a headset and software (usually Windows and/or Mac OS X) can help get everyone started. Some of the kits also include SkypeOut calling minutes.

If you get hooked on using Skype, but you prefer to use a hand set to make and receive calls, Skype offers several different models of VoIP phones. Some of these phones connect to the computer via USB cables, whereas others connect wirelessly via a broadband Internet connection.

RESTARTING DSL TO USE SKYPE

If you followed the procedure for installing Skype and the ALSA sound system, the extensions you need should already be set up to be loaded the next time you reboot DSL. If, when you boot DSL, you indicate that you want to use the ALSA sound system, you don't even need to run any setup commands to start ALSA. It should just work.

Here's an example of what you should enter at the boot prompt when you restart DSL to start the ALSA sound system (so you can use Skype):

```
boot: dsl alsa
```

If ALSA doesn't start for some reason, try running the alsa_snddevices and alsa_init commands, as described in the "Setting Up ALSA Sound in DSL" section earlier in this chapter. You might also need to use other boot options if, for example, you had saved your MyDSL extension to some directory other than a top-level mydsl directory on a local hard disk or pen drive.

TROUBLESHOOTING SKYPE

Skype requires an active Internet connection, working sound card, microphone, and speakers/headphones to be able to make audio calls. If any of those items isn't working properly, you won't be able to make audio calls with Skype.

Because Skype supports Linux, there are some Skype resources you can turn to if something goes wrong. You can begin at the Skype Help site (`http://support.skype.com`). Next, try the Skype for Linux forums (`http://forum.skype.com/bb/viewforum.php?f=18`). Here are a few tips for overcoming potential problems with Skype:

- **Calls not going through**—Check that you have an active Internet connection. In many cases, wired Ethernet connections start automatically if a DHCP server is present. If you cannot browse the web or ping a remote computer (`sudo ping example.com`), you may have to configure your network manually. For a wired Ethernet connection, right-click the desktop and select System→ Net Setup→ Netcardconfig and fill in the appropriate information for your Ethernet connection.

- **Unable to log in**—You cannot log in multiple times under the same username. There are times when the Skype process doesn't get killed if the Skype window isn't shut down properly, which might prevent you from logging in again. If you think this might be the case, close the Skype window, open a Terminal window, and type **killall skype** at the prompt. Restart Skype and try logging in again.

- **Microphone not working**—If your microphone is not working at all, use the dMix audio mixer to check that you have selected the correct input device and that the sliders are up (indicating the volume level at which you are recording).

  If you think that Damn Small Linux doesn't include support for your sound card, try installing the ALSA Drivers package from MyDSL. Determine the type of sound card you have (type `dmesg | less` or `lspci -vv | less`). Determine the name of the driver the card needs by searching the web for the name of the audio device and the word Linux. Then, use the `modprobe` command (as root user from a Terminal window) to load the driver.

Some additional configuration of Skype can be done from the Options window. Select Tools→ Options from the Skype window to see the Skype Options window. Besides being able to set options from this window that establish the behavior of Skype (such as what to do when your Skype session is inactive and which browser to use), you can also set some more advanced options.

For example, the Hand/Headset settings let you choose the device name (`/dev/dsp1`, by default) representing the sound card to make calls on. The Advanced tab lets you choose a port to use for incoming connections and lets you select to display technical call information.

SUMMARY

The Skype VoIP service provides a way of making free calls over the Internet from Linux, Windows, Mac OS X, or handheld PC devices. A Linux port of Skype software is available for Damn Small Linux, which you can easily install using the MyDSL feature.

Besides being able to make free Internet calls using Skype, Skype offers a database of Skype users that you can search to find people to call. Another free service that Skype offers is the ability to send instant messages to other Skype users to carry on Internet chats.

If you want to expand your use of Skype, you can sign up to be able to call people on regular telephone lines from your computer using the for-pay SkypeOut service. If you want others to be able to call you from your Skype session on your computer, you can sign up for the SkypeIn service (which is also a for-pay service).

Although Skype is not recommended to be used as your only telephone service (partly because it doesn't offer emergency service), it can be a low-cost and convenient way to make telephone calls to others around the world.

## CHAPTER 15

Running a Digital Media Frame with DSL

Ever since people began retiring used laptop computers, converting some of those old machines into digital picture frames has been a popular do-it-yourself project. Because it would be frivolous to spend even a few hundred dollars on such a project, laptops used to make digital picture frames are usually cheap (under $100), have little memory, and feature weak processors. With its low RAM and CPU requirements, Damn Small Linux (DSL) is an excellent operating system platform for such a project.

Of course, with lots of multimedia tools available in free and open source software today, there's no reason to limit a digital picture frame to images alone. Why not use such a frame to play music, movies, or other content as well? For that reason, this project is called a *digital media frame* and includes features for substituting music and video players for the slideshow software. (Although with the least powerful computers that run Damn Small Linux, you might not be able to do much more than a slideshow.)

From a hardware standpoint, the hard part of building a digital media frame is to get all the parts you need out of the laptop and into a thick, shadowbox-type frame. Along the way, you try to separate out the parts you don't need (like the case and the keyboard) and try not to break the parts you do need. Besides the requisite frame, other hardware items you might want to add include wired or wireless LAN cards.

On the software side, you want the digital picture frame to play the content you choose as automatically and without intervention as possible. However, you also want to at least provide mechanisms for adding and removing content. After all, how often can you watch nothing but your cousin Harvey's wedding pictures before you want to change to a new slideshow?

Making a digital media frame can be a fun project. But before diving into it, I strongly recommend you read the following warnings regarding both the hardware and software aspects of this project:

- **Hardware Warning!**—In making a digital media frame, you need to take apart a laptop computer in such a way that it will probably not go back together again. So, if you want the laptop to be a laptop again, don't use it for this project. Also, it is quite possible that you might do irreparable damage to the laptop in the process of adapting it into a digital media frame. So, please don't use a laptop that you can't afford to be without. Finally, the resulting media frame will not be UL approved (www.ul.com), so you run some risk of burning your house down.
- **Software Warning!**—This is not a click-and-go project on the software side either. In this project, you repartition disks, modify bootloaders, and work with initialization scripts. If you find the command line to be challenging, you will probably find this project difficult to do.

The bottom line is that this project is for more advanced Linux do-it-yourselfers who have an old laptop to spare. If that's not you, you might want to limit yourself to playing with some of the multimedia software described in this chapter.

SETTING PROJECT GOALS

In its most basic form, a digital picture frame simply plays a bunch of digital images it is given, without needing any intervention, after it is booted up. The images are usually played as a slideshow, with the images changing automatically every few seconds.

To make this project different from basic digital picture frames, I want to expand the features in the following basic ways to make it more as a digital media frame:

- **Play different media types**—Allow the unit to play music, presentations, or videos, along with digital image slideshows. So, for example, the frame could be set up to loop a video at a trade show or a real estate open house.
- **Make it easy to add content**—Set up ways to add any of the supported content types easily, using different types of network connections (wired or wireless), as well as removable media (such as a USB pen drive).

Shopping for the software for the project is easy (it's all on the CD that comes with this book). For me, getting the frame meant sending my wife Sheree on a trip to find a picture frame that is more than two-inches deep and large enough to display the laptop's screen. After that, a few extra pieces for mounting the laptop in that frame are needed. But the big chore is finding the right laptop at the right price.

Choosing a Laptop

When you go to search for a laptop to use for your media frame, you need to decide if time or money is more important. The cheaper the laptop, the more probable that it will require extra work to do the things you want it to do. Also, be aware that replacement parts can sometimes cost more than the value of the laptop itself (especially if you need to add RAM or replace a broken screen). So, in general, the cheapest laptop may not be the best choice.

Asking About a Used Laptop

Old laptops are available everywhere from garage sales to online sites. If you are heading to a used computer store or online auction to get a used laptop, here are some things you should check for:

- **Working?**—Many older laptops are being sold for parts only. If you are purchasing a laptop online, be sure to get a guarantee that if it is not working, you can return it. If you have access to the laptop before you buy, take your handy Damn Small Linux CD and a boot floppy with you to see if the laptop can boot DSL. (While the laptop is booted, use DSL to check out what's available—disk space, RAM, etc.—as described in the "Evaluating a Used Laptop" section in this chapter.)

  Keep in mind that our definition of *working* is not the same as other people's definition of working. For example, a missing hard drive and a few broken keyboard keys might get you a good price, but still work fine for your digital frame. Without a hard drive, you can run the project from CD and get images over your LAN or from a USB flash drive.

- **Boot media**—Some older laptops don't have CD drives. That poses problems not only for booting, but also for accessing the 50MB image you need to run Damn Small Linux.

  A 3.5-inch floppy disk was the standard removable boot medium before CD drives became popular, but it can only hold up to about 1.7MB of data at a time (although it is referred to as a 1.44MB floppy). Using floppy disk installation procedures and a stack of 35 floppies (see Chapter 8, "Installing DSL in Alternate Ways"), you can get DSL on to a hard disk and boot from there.

Some older machines may have ZIP drives (internal or external). DSL offers procedures for booting and installing Damn Small Linux from a Zip drive. A Zip drive is easier to use than a stack of floppies, because the Zip media is larger. (100MB was an early standard size; however, later, 250MB and 750MB Zip drives became more popular.)

After DSL is installed on one of these older machines, however, you may find that it lacks other hardware needed to make it a useful machine. For example, an old laptop with no CD drive probably also has a small hard disk, no LAN interface, and little RAM.

- **Hard disk**—Speaking of hard disks, you don't need one at all to run DSL. However, consider that if you want to install DSL to hard disk, you need at least 64MB of disk space for DSL and at least that much space in a swap partition. You also need to consider whether you want to keep the content you play with the digital media frame on the hard disk (or get it from over the network or from some other removable medium, if available).

- **RAM**—There is no special RAM requirements, beyond what you already need to run DSL. Of course, having more than the minimum 32MB (CD boot) or 16MB (hard drive boot) doesn't hurt. Honestly, I found that about 32MB was about as low as I wanted to go, even with just a slideshow media frame.

- **Network interface**—Having a wired or wireless Ethernet network interface makes everything easier with a digital media frame. From another computer on your LAN, you can use a variety of network services to get the images you want to display to your digital frame. You can also log in remotely to do any other maintenance on the machine. Remote login is a real plus because you probably won't have a keyboard attached to the computer.

Although most recent laptops have wired and/or wireless networking built-in, many older laptops include built-in modems (usually cheap WinModems). To add a LAN interface, you typically add a PCMCIA card (provided a slot is available). USB Ethernet adapters are another option, if you have a USB port (but again, some older machines don't).

A final option for networking your no-Ethernet, no-PCMCIA, no-USB laptop is to use the parallel port (which many older laptops have) to create a connection using Parallel Line Internet Protocol (PLIP). DSL includes the PLIP driver (`plip.o`). So, with the right cable (`www.tldp.org/HOWTO/ NET3-4-HOWTO-9.html#ss9.2`) and PLIP HOWTO (`www.linux.com/howtos/ PLIP.shtml`), you should theoretically be able to get this to work. Personally, I haven't tried PLIP for several years, and when I did, I had some trouble getting the cable right.

- **Accessories**—Make sure that you get a power supply and battery with the laptop. Without those items, even if the machine works otherwise, you really don't have a usable machine. If you can find a power cord, you might end up paying an extra $10 or $20 (or more if it's hard to find) to get a replacement.

Sometimes, you can find a business or school selling multiple, similar laptops. If some aren't working, and you are so inclined, you can try to piece together a good, working laptop. Also, with older machines, having some spare parts isn't a bad idea.

Evaluating a Used Laptop

If you are in a position to test out a laptop (whether you are buying it or just digging it out of your closet), Damn Small Linux itself is a great tool for evaluating whether a laptop will work for this digital media frame. For a really low-end machine, however, you might want to grab a floppy Linux distribution. I suggest having these media handy:

- **Damn Small Linux CD**—Use the CD that comes with this book or obtain one from Damnsmalllinux.org.
- **Damn Small Linux Boot Image**—Copy the bootfloppy.img to floppy disk, as described in Chapter 8. Use this in case you find a laptop that has a CD drive and floppy drive, but the CD drive is not bootable.
- **Tom's Root Boot**—Download Tom's Root Boot floppy disk installer from http://toms.net/rb/download.html (tomsrtbt-*-tar.gz). Extract the archive on a computer that has a floppy drive you can write to. Then, copy the floppy image to a blank floppy disk using the install.s script, as described in the tomsrtbt.FAQ file. Use this floppy disk in case you encounter a laptop that has a floppy drive but no CD drive.

The two laptops I had available as candidates for the digital media frame serve as good ways to illustrate how to evaluate laptops with and without CD drives.

Evaluating a Laptop with Damn Small Linux

With the Damn Small Linux CD in hand, I tried out the first of two laptops I had in my closet: a Compaq Pressario 1620 laptop. After having the screen appearance make it unusable by the default boot, I booted DSL by typing **fb800x600** as the boot command (frame buffer). That came up fine, so I selected Xfbdev xserver when prompted to configure X Setup.

With DSL running on my Compaq Presario, I could determine a lot of stuff about the machine. The first, and most important, thing it told me was that the laptop will run Damn Small Linux! Next, I opened a terminal window as root (right-click the ATerminal icon and choose Aterm as Super User). Then, I ran the dmesg command to see boot messages from the kernel. Here's an example:

```
# dmesg | less
<5>0MB HIGHMEM available.
<5>32MB LOWMEM available.
<4>Detected 167.049 MHz processor.
<6>Memory: 28652k/32768k available (1371k kernel code, 3728k reserved,
561k data, 140k init, 0k highmem)
<6>Floppy drive(s): fd0 is 1.44M
<4>hdc: TOSHIBA CD-ROM XM-1602B, ATAPI CD/DVD-ROM drive
<4>hda: attached ide-disk driver.
<6>hda: 4233600 sectors (2168 MB) w/96KiB Cache, CHS=525/128/63
<6>PCI: Found IRQ 11 for device 00:01.2
<6>usb-uhci.c: USB UHCI at I/O 0xfce0, IRQ 11
<4>usb-uhci.c: Detected 2 ports
<6>Yenta ISA IRQ mask 0x0498, PCI irq 5
<6>ttyS00 at 0x03f8 (irq = 4) is a 16550A
<6>parport0: PC-style at 0x378 [PCSPP,TRISTATE,EPP]
<6>parport0: irq 7 detected
```

The output just shown, which has been edited, tells you some things you can see on the laptop and some you can't. This laptop has 32MB of RAM and a 167.049MHz processor (both of which are low, but workable, for our purposes).

The machine has a floppy drive and CD-ROM drive (which you can already see if you are looking at the machine), and a hard disk. The hard disk has about 2GB of space (2168MB). Other available ports on the laptop include two USB ports, a CardBus slot (Yenta), a COM1 port (ttyS00), and a parallel port (parport00). Next, I did a quick check of the processor type:

```
# cat /proc/cpuinfo
vendor_id        : GenuineIntel
cpu family       : 5
model name       : Pentium MMX
cpu HMz          : 167.049
```

So far, it looks like this laptop would work for the project.

Evaluating a Laptop with Tom's Root Boot

The second laptop I had to try out was a Texas Instruments TravelMate 4000E 486 WinDX2/50 MHz laptop. Because it has no CD-ROM drive, I booted up the Tom's Root Boot floppy and logged in as root user (xxxx is the password). Because there is only a shell interface, I could immediately type **dmesg** to check out the hardware:

```
# dmesg | less
Memory: 5836k/8192k available (1560k kernel code, 416k reserved, 288k
data, 92k init)
CPU: 486
parport0: PC-style at 0x378, irq 7 [SPP]
ttyS00 at 0x03f8 (irq = 4) is a 16450
ttyS01 at 0x02f8 (irq = 3) is a 16550A
hda: ST9235AG, 200MB w/32kB Cache, CHS=985/13/32
Floppy drive(s): fd0 is 1.44M
Partition check:
  hda: hda1
```

From the output, you can see that there are 8MB of RAM on this 486DX machine. It has a floppy drive (fd0) parallel port (parport0) and two serial ports (ttyS00 and ttyS01). It has a 200MB hard disk, which was probably pretty big at the time the laptop was made. There is a single partition on the IDE hard disk (hda1).

The low amount of RAM immediately put this machine out of the running (only 8MB). However, if it had at least 16MB of RAM, you could give it a try. Some of the hardships you would face include: installing DSL from a stack of floppies, configuring PLIP for a network interface, and having limited disk space for content. If you are up for the challenge, however, others have run DSL on similar systems (see www.damnsmalllinux.org/486.html).

The rest of this chapter reuses the Compaq Presario 1620 I just described to create a digital media picture frame.

GETTING THE PARTS YOU NEED

After you have sized up your laptop, you need to consider what else you need to add to it. The first set of parts consists of those you need to make the laptop do what you want. The second consists of the frame and the parts you need to mount the laptop into it.

Adding Parts to the Laptop

Which parts you need to add to your laptop depends on what parts your laptop is missing and how you want to add content to the laptop. In my case, and others where you have a sub-$100 laptop, you may be missing the hardware needed for your network interface.

Because the laptop I was using had both USB ports and a CardBus slot, I had a choice of how I added a network interface. Digging around in my stuff again, I came up with a Linksys USB200M Compact USB 2.0 10/100 Network adapter (for wired Ethernet connection). I also found an old Lucent Orinoco Gold PC Card (for wireless Ethernet).

Both network adapters had drivers in Damn Small Linux. When I plugged the Linksys into my network switch, it was automatically configured from DHCP and I was up on my LAN immediately. I decided to go with a wired Ethernet, figuring that two cords coming out of the frame was no worse than one. I added a small cable extension to the USB adapter, so I had more flexibility in how it was attached to the frame. (See Chapter 4, "Configuring and Saving DSL Settings," for more information on configuring your network interfaces.)

One other hardware addition you should consider is a USB flash drive (or pen drive). You can conceivably store your multimedia content, backed up DSL settings, MyDSL extensions, and even DSL itself on one of these removable drives. Using the drive in this way, you could create the whole project on the USB flash drive and update the project without a network connection, by modifying the device on another machine and then plugging it into the frame again and rebooting to get updated software and content.

Getting Parts for the Frame

For the frame, I ended up with something a bit different than I expected. The visible area of the laptop screen is 7.25×9.5 inches. So, I asked my wife to buy a picture frame that was at least 8.5 inches high×11 inches wide×2 inches deep. What she came back with was a square wall shelf with a front like a picture frame. The opening was 12×12 inches and the frame itself was 5 inches deep. Figure 15-1 shows this frame and the laptop I had to adapt to it.

On the back of the frame was hardware for mounting the frame directly to your wall studs. So, the weight of the frame wasn't going to be a problem. For mounting the laptop into the frame, I cut a 12×12-inch square pine board and cut out the 7.25×9.5-inch opening needed to display the screen. To connect the plywood to the frame, I got some strips of wood that could be attached around the side that faced into the frame and attached that to the frame as well.

I purchased some clamps for connecting the laptop screen to the plywood board. Then, I needed some screws for connecting the other laptop components to the frame. The final pieces I needed were an antistatic mat (to put the laptop on as I worked on it) and a good set of small screwdrivers and pliers.

Before starting to take apart the laptop, however, the next step was to get all the software installed on it.

FIGURE 15-1   The frame front and wide opening made this square
shelf a good frame for an old Compaq Presario.

INSTALLING AND CONFIGURING THE SOFTWARE

Before starting to modify the laptop, it's a good idea to make sure all the software for
the project works. One main reason for doing this first is that you won't have a keyboard to work from after a while, so it's easiest to get all the software working before
dismantling the laptop.

At this point, you should already have an idea that DSL will boot. So, the next
task is to get the laptop ready to install the software, get all the software needed,
make sure it runs, and then store it so it can be available on the next reboot.

NOTE

If your laptop doesn't have a hard disk, you can still do this project. Instead of installing the software to hard disk, you can create a remastered Damn Small Linux, as described in Chapter 11, "Setting Up a Full Remastering Environment," using the components described here. Then, you can add the digital media content from over the network (using Samba) or from any available removable medium (such as a USB flash drive or a Zip drive).

Partitioning the Disk

Because I have enough room on the hard disk (and so I can disconnect the CD drive), I decided to install Damn Small Linux directly to the hard disk on the laptop. Before I could do that, however, I decided to partition the hard disk.

In Chapter 9, "Performing a Traditional Hard Drive Install," there is a procedure for partitioning your hard disk to prepare it for a Damn Small Linux installation (type **install** from the boot prompt to start it, then type **12**). You can repartition during the installation instead, but doing partitioning separately gives you a bit more flexibility.

In my case, I created a 200MB swap partition (hda2) and assigned the rest (just under 2GB) to a Linux partition (hda1). Although the swap size is more than the general rule of double the amount of RAM, because the laptop has a small amount of RAM (under 128MB), it's good to assign extra swap space.

Choosing an Install Type

The installation type you choose depends somewhat on the amount of disk space and RAM you have. With a smaller amount of disk space, you can choose a Frugal install (which saves space by copying the compressed image to hard drive). I chose to do a regular hard drive installation because my computer had a low amount of RAM.

The traditional hard drive installation procedure (described in Chapter 9) uncompresses the operating system files and copies them from the CD to the Linux hard disk partition. Then, the procedure lets you choose to install a bootloader (I chose Grub) to actually boot the installed DSL from hard disk.

Another advantage of the hard drive installation procedure is that it steps you through additional configuration for your installed DSL system. Type **no** when you are asked if you want to add multiple user accounts (saying **yes** would force you to enter a password, which you don't want to do). You can also select to use an ext3 file system, which might run a bit slower, but will recover better if your digital media frame is not shut down properly. I always use ext3, but that's your choice.

After the installation is complete, pop out the CD and reboot the laptop, as suggested. In fact, turn it off and turn it back on again. When the machine boots up, you will see the Grub boot screen. In my case, the default boot command wouldn't work, so I used the arrow keys to move to the fb800x600 entry to use the framebuffer X driver with 800×600 screen resolution.

When asked to enter a password for the root and ds1 users, I just pressed Enter. Having a blank password allows the laptop to boot directly to DSL (as the ds1 user) without entering a password. You are also asked to select your X driver. Because you installed DSL to hard disk, all these settings are restored automatically, without having to back them up (as you would if you ran DSL from read-only media, such as a CD).

With DSL installed, I only used about 160MB of disk space. I still had 1.8GB of space remaining for software and digital media content (images, video, and music).

Before proceeding, be sure to assign your swap area and turn it on. In my case, the swap partition was hda2 (yours may be different). Open a terminal window as root and type the following:

```
# mkswap /dev/hda2
# swapon /dev/hda2
```

Next, shutdown your laptop and remove the CD. Then restart the laptop from hard disk.

Adding Multimedia Player and Networking Software

If everything went well to this point, you should have a version of Damn Small Linux running from your laptop's hard disk. Now, you need to add some software to be able to play your digital media from the frame.

With a traditional hard disk install, you don't need to save your MyDSL extensions for the next reboot. Provided you use .dsl extensions, you can simply install the software extensions you want and they will be on your hard disk the next time you reboot.

Next, from the DSL desktop, select the MyDSL icon and add the following software using the MyDSL Extension Tool:

- **GQview**—From the Apps menu, select the gqview package. This package can be used to play slideshows of digital images.

- **Mplayer**—From the Multimedia menu, you can add the mplayer extension. You can use mplayer to play video. You also need to add software extensions that contains the codecs needed by the video content you want to play (such as ones that you get by selecting System, then `codecpak`). (I recommend you have at least 128MB of RAM to use mplayer.)

To play PowerPoint presentations, you could install the openoffice extension from the apps menu in the MyDSL Extension tool. You should also consider adding software to your media frame that can help you get content over the network. In particular, consider adding Samba software from the Net menu. With Samba, you can share your directories so other Linux and Windows machines can access them (using Windows file sharing).

Configuring the Digital Media Frame

Most of the configuration you do to set up the digital media frame is to be able to start the digital media frame without manual intervention. I'll begin by focusing on how to get the digital media frame to boot up directly to a slideshow.

Configuring the Player

To get an idea of how to boot up directly to a media player, the first example shows how to start up the GQview image viewer. The general approach is to set up the default values for GQview, then configure GQview to start up automatically from the boot prompt. With GQview installed, as described earlier, do the following:

1. Select the GQview icon from the desktop. The GQview image player starts.
2. From the GQview window, select Edit and then Options. The GQview Configuration window appears, as shown in Figure 15-2.
3. Set defaults for GQview to play images continuously. In particular, I selected Random and Repeat in the Slide Show box. I also unselected the box next to Cache Thumbnails, so I wouldn't fill up the disk with thumbnails. The default is to change images every 15 seconds, but you may want to change that to suit your taste. Select other tabs to change different settings. For example, selecting Fit Image to Window (on the Image tab) is a good idea. Choosing Preload New Image may help load the images faster.
4. Save the settings by clicking Apply and then OK.

Try different options. With the image player ready to go, you are ready to configure the bootloader to tell DSL to boot up to GQview.

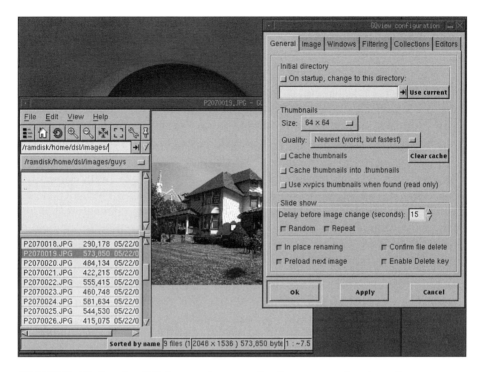

FIGURE 15-2   Set GQview options to play images randomly and continuously.

Changing the Bootloader

The bootloader defines the kernel to boot and any options you want to pass to the kernel. For this example, I used the Grub boot loader. You can change the Grub boot loader by editing the /boot/grub/menu.1st file. Changes to that file are automatically picked up when you reboot.

The following shows how I edited the existing menu.1st file (I removed comment lines for clarity):

```
default 2
timeout 15

title DSL
kernel /boot/linux24 root=/dev/hda1 quiet vga=normal noacpi noapm nodma
noscsi frugal

title DSL fb800x600
kernel /boot/linux24 root=/dev/hda1 quiet vga=788 noacpi noapm nodma
noscsi frugal
```

```
title DSL fb800x600-F
kernel /boot/linux24 root=/dev/hda1 quiet vga=788 noacpi noapm nodma
noscsi frugal desktop=frame
```

The changes to the menu.1st file are shown in bold. For the default value, I changed 0 to 2 so that the third entry (DSL fb800x600-F) is booted by default. I then copied the DSL fb800x600 entry and created a new third entry (calling it DSL fb800x600-F). After that, I added the desktop=frame option. The desktop=frame option tells DSL that instead of running fluxbox or jwm as the window manager, it should start a window manager definition called frame (which we will define in the next section).

There are other options you can set as well. If you set up a static IP address for your media frame (which is a good idea), add the nodhcp option to the boot prompt. For example, if your laptop supports higher resolution, you could set fb1024x768 or fb1280x1024 as the default boot entries.

Keep in mind that at this point, your laptop will try to boot directly to the slideshow viewer. Therefore, if you need the DSL desktop to make further changes, be sure to select one of the other entries on the boot screen.

Modifying .xinitrc to Start Player

The way that Damn Small Linux is configured, with no password set for the DSL user, DSL logs in the dsl user automatically and starts the desktop. How the desktop starts is directed by the contents of the /home/dsl/.xinitrc file. By adding a new desktop entry for your frame desktop, you can set the GQview application (gqview command) to start immediately when the desktop starts.

Open the /home/dsl/.xinitrc file using any text editor. Then, add an entry for the frame desktop as shown:

```
# put X windows programs that you want started here.
# Be sure to add at the end of each command the &
      .
      .
      .
case $DESKTOP in
  frame )
    /usr/bin/gqview -s -f /var/mediaframe/pics
  ;;
  fluxbox )
    fluxter &>/dev/null &
    wmswallow -geometry 70x80 docked   docked.lua &
    exec fluxbox 2>/dev/null
  ;;
  jwm )
    ./.background
```

```
    sleep 2
    exec jwm 2>/dev/null
 ;;
 * )
    exec fluxbox 2>/dev/null
 ;;
esac
```

The text shown in bold illustrates the entry added to the $DESKTOP case state-
ment when the boot option desktop=frame is used. With the X display already
started at this point, instead of starting a window manager, the frame entry starts the
gqview command with the -s option (slideshow), -f option (full screen), and the
name of the directory containing the images to play (/var/mediaframe/pics).

Adding Digital Content

At this point, the laptop is all set up to start playing digital images. You need to find
a way to add them to your digital media frame on an ongoing basis. There are two
basic ways for adding images to your digital media frame:

■ **Removable media**—If you don't have a network interface to the digital
  media frame, you can add content via a CD, USB flash drive, or other removable medium. This is not a good long-term solution, because after the keyboard is removed, you don't have a way to copy files from those media to your
  hard disk. It might also be hard to access removable drives after everything
  is tucked inside the frame.

  In the meantime, however, you could copy a bunch of images onto a USB
  flash drive and then plug that drive into your laptop, mount the partition
  (probably /dev/sda1), and copy files to the /var/mediaframe/pics directory.
  You could also configure DSL to automatically mount the USB flash drive at
  boot time and have gqview use a directory on the drive for images (such as
  /mnt/sda1/images). That way, you wouldn't need a network connection at all
  to change content. You could just change images on the drive, plug it back
  in, and reboot.

■ **Network interface**—Having a network connection to your media frame is
  important for being able to add images easily and make any ongoing changes
  to DSL and your media content. As I noted earlier, I connected a USB
  Ethernet adapter to my laptop and plugged a standard RJ-45 Ethernet cable
  into that and my network switch.

Configure your network interface with a static IP address. For a wired Ethernet
interface, run the netcardconfig command (or select System, followed by Net Setup

and netcardconfig from the DSL menu). Say No to using DHCP broadcast, and enter a static IP address for your DSL system. You can use that address to log in to your digital media frame later from other computers on your LAN.

Using the ssh Service to Get Content

After you get your network interface running, I suggest you have DSL start up the ssh interface automatically. That service lets you do remote login and remote copy from other computers on your LAN. For example, you could add the following line to the /etc/rc5.d/S99bootlocal init script:

```
/etc/init.d/ssh start
```

With your network interface and secure shell service running in DSL, there are several ways you could access your digital media frame from another computer on your LAN. First, I suggest you add a password for the root user in DSL. (Don't add a password for dsl or you won't be able to boot DSL without being prompted for a password.)

Assuming your IP address is 10.0.10.1, here are some ways you could access the media frame from another computer on your LAN from another Linux system:

```
# ssh root@10.0.10.1
# scp *.jpg root@10.0.10.1:/var/mediaframe/pics/
```

For both the command lines, you are prompted for the root password. The ssh command shown lets you log in as root to a shell interface. The scp command shown copies all files ending in .jpg from the current directory on the local system to the /var/mediaframe/pics directory on the media frame.

If you have a Mac OSX system, you already have ssh on your computer (just open a Terminal window to use the command). For Windows systems, there is a set of open source tools called PuTTY that you could look into for accessing ssh, scp, and other secure shell services from Windows systems. See www.chiark.greenend.org/uk/~sgtatham/putty. There is also SSHDOS to use those tools from DOS (http://sshdos.sourceforge.net). Of course, you could also just boot DSL from any PC on your LAN as well.

Using Samba to Get Content

DSL also supports Samba, which can be used to share files and folders with Windows systems. With Samba installed using MyDSL (as described earlier), here is an example of how you could create a shared directory from DSL so that people from Windows clients could add and remove images from your /var/mediaframe/pics directory:

1. Edit the /etc/samba/smb.conf file to add a section to the Share Definitions section that appears as follows:

```
[mediaframe]
        comment = Images for Digital Media Frame
        path = /var/mediaframe/pics
        writable = yes
        read only = no
        public = yes
```

The permissions shown here are wide open. After you determine that Samba is working, you should look into providing password protection for securing your Samba service. The system name appears as the name box (you might want to change that in /etc/samba/smb.conf while you are at it).

2. Start the nmbd and smbd services. As root user, type the following:

```
# /usr/sbin/nmbd -D
# /usr/sbin/smbd -D
```

The commands just shown start the NetBIOS (nmbd) and Samba (smbd) services is daemon (background) mode (-D). The mediaframe share should now be available on your LAN.

3. Try accessing the mediaframe share from another computer on your LAN. Open the Network or Network Neighborhood windows to see if your DSL system appears. From a Linux system, you could access the share by mounting it on your local file system. For example:

```
# mkdir /mnt/box
# mount -t smbfs //box/mediaframe /mnt/box
```

You should then be able to copy files to and remove them from the /mnt/box directory and have them appear on your digital media frame. You may need to restart GQview for the new images to be picked up.

 NOTE

Copying files over Samba on my 167MHz Pentium with 64MB of RAM does slow the performance of the media frame. Some image effects don't complete before GQview goes on to the next image. After the copy is over, however, performance goes back to normal.

Adding Other Media Players and Content

Now that the basic structure of the digital media is set up, you can add other kinds of players and media content. By adding the ogg123 music player and some music content to your media frame, you could create a combination music and slideshow player as follows:

- **Changing the bootloader**—Add another entry to the boot loader, but have it set `desktop=music` instead of `desktop=frame`. Add it after the default entry (so not to mess up the default). Here's an example:

```
title DSL fb800x600-V
kernel /boot/linux24 root=/dev/hda1 quiet vga=788 noacpi
noapm nodma noscsi frugal desktop=music
```

- **Modifying .xinitrc to start the player**—Add another case entry to have the `ogg123` player start up when `desktop=music` is used at the boot prompt and play music from the `/var/mediaframe/music` directory along with a slideshow:

```
case $DESKTOP in
  music )
    /usr/bin/gqview -s -f /var/mediaframe/pics &
    ogg123 -z /var/mediaframe/music
  ;;
    ...
```

If you want the default to change from `frame` to `music`, you can simply change the default from 2 to 3 (or whatever the number is in your boot order) in the `/boot/grub/menu.1st` file. If the software is installed the way you want it now, you can get ready to start dismantling the laptop to create the digital media frame.

You can hook up some speakers to your laptop if the ones on the laptop do not play well from inside the frame. You will have three cords coming out of the frame (power, network, and audio). If your sound isn't working, try opening the xMMs icon on the desktop. Select the play button on the X Multimedia System player to configure the OSS sound. Then, play a test sound.

MODIFYING THE LAPTOP HARDWARE

For several reasons, you won't spend a lot of time on the hardware aspects of this project. For one thing, the focus of this book is Damn Small Linux, so the software is our primary interest. For another, it's hard to know the exact hardware you are starting with, since we suggest beginning with some laptop you can pick up for under $100.

As a result, in this section, I tell you the specific pieces I put together to build the project. Then, I present a bunch of tips that might help you with problems you might encounter taking apart a laptop to fit into a digital picture frame.

> **WARNING**
>
> When you take apart a laptop and remount it in a frame, besides clearly voiding any warranty, you are also risking injury and damage. LCD displays run at high voltages that can provide quite a jolt if you are shocked. Even in their original cases, laptop batteries have been known to catch on fire. In a picture frame, it is not possible to get the same cooling system to work. So be warned that while many people have created digital picture frames like the one described here, you assume responsibility yourself for the safety of the unit you put together.

Before Dismantling the Laptop

Check the laptop's BIOS before dismantling it. Make sure that the screen doesn't go blank after a few minutes to save power. Also, disable hardware in the BIOS that you don't need. For example, if you want to disconnect the floppy drive, you can also turn that off in the BIOS.

Also, while the laptop is still running, check the viewing area and mark the corners of that area with a bit of tape. You want to use those markings to choose where to cut the opening in the matting, so that only the viewing area shows through.

Tips for Dismantling and Mounting the Laptop

Laptops fit a lot of components in a small space. As you try to dismantle your laptop to get the component you want into a frame, you have to be very careful to not break delicate connections or lose tiny screws and springs that are needed. Here are some tips for taking apart your laptop in a way that does the least damage:

- **Get tools ready**—Set up an antistatic mat to put the laptop on. Make it large enough that you can place parts outside of the laptop case and be on the mat if they still need to be attached. Get a range of small screwdrivers and wire cutters to work with.
- **Manufacturer's instructions**—Even for old laptops, there are usually instructions from the manufacturers available on the web for dismantling laptops to replace critical components. Check the support areas for the company that made your laptop before you begin taking it apart.
- **Be gentle**—Don't force components when you go to remove them. If something seems stuck, look for screws you might have missed. Components are often screwed in from multiple sides and screws can be hidden under little

plastic pieces. Connecting cables are often fragile. Very gently disconnect those cables when necessary. The LCD ribbon cables tend to be particularly prone to tearing.

- **Reboot occasionally**—As you try to extract the components from the case, you may find yourself removing and reattaching cables. Try rebooting the laptop every once in a while to make sure that it will still boot. If it doesn't, at least you have fewer things to check.

- **Remove components**—If you are booting from hard disk, you can probably remove the CD drive and floppy drive. The trackpad can go too, along with various mounting pieces. Before you remove the keyboard, do a final reboot to make sure everything is okay. If there is a port for an external keyboard, try to keep that accessible. You may find that you need to connect a keyboard if at some point you can't access the laptop from its network interface.

- **Attach the screen to the matting**—With thick cardboard matting, some people glue the LCD directly to that matting. For a thin wooden board, some people clip the LCD to the frame, using clips that are similar to those used to hold up mirrors. Some use Styrofoam to hold the screen snuggly in place. A piece of Plexiglas that is cut to fit the frame is another possibility.

- **Mount the motherboard**—The motherboard is usually attached next. Usually the motherboard is raised off of the screen using small blocks of wood or using risers or spacers. The hard drive is probably the next component to be attached. I've heard suggestions that attaching the hard drive with rubber grommets can reduce vibration.

- **Make connectors accessible**—Attach the components in such a way that cords you need to connect to the laptop can be accessed. For example, you might need to access a USB port for an Ethernet adapter or USB flash drive. I recommend you get a USB small extender so you have more choice of where you connect any USB devices.

- **Open access to the frame**—Whether you are adding an extended frame to a regular picture frame or using a shadowbox type of frame, you need to cut access points open to the frame. At the very least, you need an opening for your power cord. With wired Ethernet network interfaces, you need an Ethernet cable to be able to get in. Consider cutting a hole in the top of the frame to allow heat to escape.

You may want to drill openings to be able to expose ports and switches outside of the frame. A USB extender might be useful to expose, if you want to be able to attach a USB flash drive or other type of USB device. Likewise, an on/off switch might be nicer than just unplugging the unit. (It may take some extra soldering to extend those kinds of switches.)

When you are finished mounting all the components, check that everything is securely attached. Boot up the laptop to make sure that it is still working and try to log in to it over the network.

EXPANDING YOUR DIGITAL MEDIA FRAME

There are lots of great ideas around for expanding what a digital media frame can do. Here are a few:

- **Remote control**—It would be nice to work with the digital media frame from a remote control. The Linux Infra-red Remote Control (LIRC) project is a popular way to use a remote control with multimedia applications. There are inexpensive receivers described at the LIRC site (`http://lirc.org/receivers.html`). By coupling that technology with a menu system, you could select different content or players, without needing a keyboard.

- **Adding applets**—You could stick small applications to the desktop while playing slideshows or other content. For example, you might want a constant clock, weather report, or stock ticker to play along with the multimedia content.

- **Timers**—To keep from running the digital media frame day and night, it is a good idea to add timers that shut down the media frame at a certain time every night. For example, you could use the cron facility to run the `sudo shutdown -h now` command every night at midnight.

SUMMARY

A digital media frame is a fun way to reuse an old laptop. Using the descriptions in this chapter, you can evaluate an old laptop, add software needed to play different multimedia content, and adapt the laptop to fit in a picture frame.

The digital media frame described is made to run without any intervention. The laptop components inside the frame are configured to just boot it up to a slideshow. By adapting the procedure for making a digital image slideshow, you could have the device play video, music, or other content as well.

## CHAPTER 16

Setting Up an XAMPP Web Server in DSL

Serving up content for most common web servers doesn't require a very powerful computer. With Damn Small Linux's (DSL's) small size and some prepackaged web server software, it's possible to configure a powerful web server on a machine with as little as 64MB of RAM and about 120MB of disk space.

XAMPP is a neat little project that combines a powerful selection of open source software that can be used to create a professional-quality web service on most popular operating systems. The popular combination of Web server software often referred to as LAMPP (Linux, Apache, MySQL, PHP, and Perl) has the "L" here replaced by an "X" to indicate that instead of just Linux, the project can run on OS X, Solaris, and all 32-bit Windows systems.

XAMPP for Linux (www.apachefriends.org/en/xamp-linux.html) can be dropped into most Linux systems, including Damn Small Linux, and quickly configured to serve up your web content. XAMPP includes the following software:

- **Apache**—Serves the web content
- **MySQL**—Database software for organizing and storing data
- **PHP and PEAR**—Scripting language support
- **Perl**—Scripting language support
- **ProFTPD**—FTP service for uploading content to the server
- **OpenSSL**—To support encrypted communications with the server
- **Webalizer**—Software for reporting activity (hits, pages viewed, and so on) of the server

XAMPP also includes many smaller components, such as fonts, server modules, and libraries. All-in-all, there is a lot of software packed into a 50MB tarball.

The project described in this chapter starts with a basic DSL installation, then adds XAMPP and firewall software to create an easy-to-use web server that, because of its size and efficient resource uses, can work on PCs with even very limited resources. Because XAMPP is delivered in a state that's basically ready to run, it's possible to have the server up and running (and permanently saved) in less than an hour, using the instructions in this chapter.

After you have gathered all the pieces for your web server, you can save them permanently in many different ways (to hard disk, a remastered CD, and so on). This procedure should work well on almost any old PC you have lying around. When the procedure is finished, you will have saved a working web server, web content, and DSL operating system so that it is ready to run from your hard disk or a USB pen drive you can carry with you.

INSTALLING XAMPP

Although there is no special MyDSL package for XAMPP, here is a case where you can download the software directly from the open source project and drop it into Damn Small Linux. XAMPP works particularly well for DSL in this way because it can be unpacked and used entirely from the /opt directory. Here's how to get and install XAMPP:

1. **Visit XAMPP for Linux**—From the XAMPP for Linux page, you can download the entire XAMPP software tarball. The page is located here:

   ```
   http://www.apachefriends.org/en/xampp-linux.html
   ```

2. **Select to download XAMPP**—In most cases, select the first package listed for download: XAMPP Linux. For this example, the version was 1.6. If you already have XAMPP installed, you can select the Upgrade package. There is also a development package, in case you want to compile the software yourself. Next, you are asked what to do with the following package name:

   ```
   xampp-linux-1.6.tar.gz
   ```

 NOTE

Depending on the type of storage medium you want to use (hard disk USB pendrive, etc.), available RAM, and other factors, you may want to choose different ways of storing and restoring your XAMPP software. The "Saving Your XAMPP Server" section later in this chapter describes different ways you can save and restore your XAMPP server with DSL.

3. **Save XAMPP package**—Select to save the XAMPP package to disk. The tarball is downloaded to the /home/dsl directory. (If you don't have enough space available in /home/dsl, you might have to save the XAMPP package to your hard disk or pendrive.)

4. **Extract the XAMPP software**—Open a Terminal window (right-click the desktop and select XShells, Root Access, Transparent). Then, to extract the files to the /opt directory, type:

```
# tar xvfz /home/dsl/xampp-linux-1.6.tar.gz -C /opt
```

The exact version of the xampp-linux package you use may be different by the time you read this. This command copies all the XAMPP files you need to the /opt directory.

Before continuing, check to see if an upgrade of your XAMPP package is also available from the XAMPP site. If so, you should be sure to install the upgrade as well, because it might well include some important security patch you need to secure your XAMPP server.

WARNING

It's important to run the tar command just shown below as the root user and not simply run the sudo command to untar the files. If you use sudo, the DSL user will own all XAMPP files and the server will not work.

CHECK THAT XAMPP IS WORKING

Because XAMPP is configured, by default, for ease-of-use, you can start up all the XAMPP components immediately with a single command. Then, there are several steps you can take to make sure that it is working:

1. **Start XAMPP**—While still logged in as the root user from a Terminal window, type the following:

```
# /opt/lampp/lampp start
Starting XAMPP for Linux 1.6...
XAMPP: Starting Apache with SSL (and PHP5)...
XAMPP: Starting MySQL...
XAMPP: Starting ProFTPD...
XAMPP for Linux started.
```

After displaying the XAMPP version (1.6), each of the major XAMPP components is started. The Apache web server starts, with SSL and PHP5 enabled. The MySQL database server and the ProFTPD file transfer protocol server is started. At this point, the features are running to serve web pages, store data, and access the server (via FTP) to upload and download content over the network.

2. **View web page**—To check that the XAMPP web server is working, open a web browser and request a web page from the local host. For example, open Firefox from the DSL desktop and type in the address `http://localhost`. If you see an XAMPP splash page, select your language (in this example, English) and you should see the page shown in Figure 16-1.

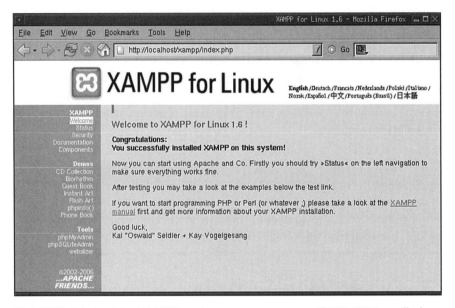

FIGURE 16-1   The XAMPP welcome page appears if XAMPP installed properly.

As the message says, you have successfully installed XAMPP on your system.

3. **Check status**—Using selections in your left column, you can now check out how your server is running. Select Status. You can see the status of services on your XAMPP server as shown in Figure 16-2.

As you can see, all the major features are running in Figure 16-2. Click the FAQ link for information on turning on certain PHP extensions.

If any of the major components aren't running, try restarting the XAMPP server as root (`/opt/lampp/lampp restart`). If you find that you are still not able to start your XAMPP server, refer to the XAMPP forum for help in troubleshooting the problem (`www.apachefriends.org/f/?language=english`).

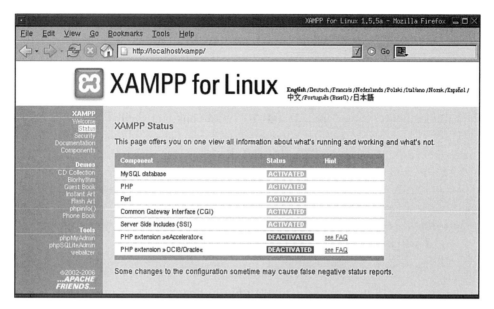

FIGURE 16-2   Check that MySQL, PHP, Perl, CGI, and SSI are running.

4. **Play demos**—Select from the following demos in the left column:

- **CD Collection**—Add CD names, titles, and years. Then, display those titles on a list or as a PDF document.

- **Biorhythm**—Display your biorhythms based on your birthday.

- **Guest Book**—Enter name, email, and text for this simple guestbook.

- **Instant Art**—Type a phrase and click OK to have the words appear as calligraphy on the page.

- **Flash Art**—Same as the Instant Art, except that the calligraphy lines spin around. (A Flash plug-in is required by your browser to view the Flash Art text. Click the download link that appears to download the plug-in.)

- **phpinfo**—Show the phpinfo.php page, which displays information about how PHP is configured for your XAMPP server.

- **Phone Book**—A simple phone book application, where you enter a last name, first name, and phone number for people you want to appear in the phone listing.

5. **Check over network**—Although XAMPP is not really ready yet to be shared over the Internet, you might want to check that you can access your XAMPP server from another computer on your local area network. The easiest way to do that is to determine your computer's IP address and try to

access the XAMPP server at that address from another computer on your LAN. To do that, type the following from your XAMPP server system:

```
# /sbin/ifconfig |grep inet
    inet addr:10.0.0.100 Bcast:10.0.0.255 Mask:255.255.255.0
    inet addr:127.0.0.1 Mask:255.0.0.0
```

In this example, the address 10.0.0.100 is the one you want. The other one (127.0.0.1) is your computer's loopback address. Going to another computer on your LAN, type in the IP address of the computer containing your XAMPP server into a web browser's location box. For example,

```
http://10.0.0.100
```

You should see the XAMPP splash page from the remote browser. You can then browse any content that interests you on the XAMPP server.

If the steps you just completed were successful, the components of your XAMPP server (Apache, MySQL, and PHP) are up and running and accessible to your LAN. The next step, before adding and sharing your content with the world, is to secure your server.

SECURING YOUR XAMPP SERVER

To make the default XAMPP server easy to start up, access to the server is wide open. Also, because Damn Small Linux itself is designed as a minimal desktop system, it doesn't include firewall software. These security issues might not be such a big deal if you use XAMPP as a temporary server behind a firewall—for example, in a classroom. If you plan to expose your server to the Internet, however, you will surely want to lock down the security a little tighter.

Luckily, XAMPP has some nice tools available for checking and tightening up the security of your system. As for a firewall, there is a MyDSL package you can install to lock down outside entry to your newly configured Damn Small Linux server.

Understanding General Security Issues

Before getting into some specifics for securing your XAMPP server in DSL, you should be aware of some general security issues.

Securing a public Internet server that is exposed to the Internet 24×7 is not something you should do without some forethought. A vulnerable web server is a valuable asset for an intruder who wants to host all kinds of evil content. The level of security described in this chapter may be enough for a server behind a firewall or used in temporary situations. However, to use this server in more permanent and public situations, you should do more study.

Documentation is available for securing each of the services included with your XAMPP server software. I recommend that, along with the suggestions in this chapter, you refer to some of the following security pages for further suggestions on securing your XAMPP server:

- **Apache Security** (`http://apache.org/docs/2.0/misc/security_tips.html`)—Contains warnings related to maintaining an Apache server, as well as the risks of enabling various services.

- **PHP Security** (`www.php.net/manual/en/security.php`)—Both coding and configuration information for securing the PHP content of your XAMPP server are contained in the Security section of the PHP manual.

- **MySQL Security** (`http://dev.mysql.com/doc/refman/4.1/en/security.html`)—Ways of securing your MySQL databases are described in the Security section of the MySQL manual.

There are also organizations that provide information for helping you secure your web server. The World Wide Web consortium Security FAQ (`www.w3.org/Security/Faq/`) contains facts about web security and different types of attacks. The Linux Security HOWTO (`http://tldp.org/HOWTO/Security-HOWTO/`) contains both general information on securing Linux and information specific to securing network services.

Checking Basic XAMPP Security

Some nice tools for checking and correcting potential security weaknesses in XAMPP are included with the XAMPP software. Again, start by pointing your web browser to the XAMPP server, then select Security (`http://localhost/xampp/security.php`). The XAMPP security page appears, as shown in Figure 16-3.

The first issues related to your XAMPP server's security are the services available to the network. As Figure 16-3 shows, the demo XAMPP web pages can be viewed from the network and the MySQL service itself can be accessed from the network. Also, the phpMyAdmin user (pma) and the MySQL user (root) have no passwords assigned, so anyone can access those services. Likewise, the FTP user nobody has a well-known password assigned (lampp).

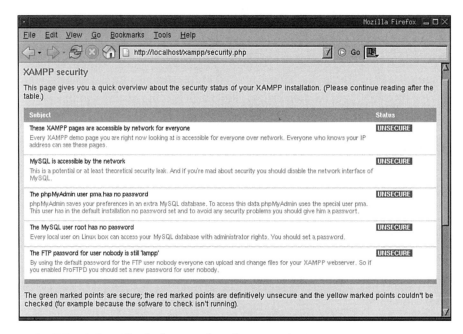

FIGURE 16-3   Check the security of your XAMPP server.

Before you begin more refined configuration of your XAMPP server, you can deal with these issues using tools provided with XAMPP. Start by running the following command (as root user from a Terminal window):

```
# /opt/lampp/lampp security
XAMPP: Quick security check...
XAMPP: Your XAMPP pages are NOT secured by a password.
XAMPP: Do you want to set a password? [yes] yes
XAMPP: Password: *******
XAMPP: Password (again): *******
XAMPP: Password protection active. Please use 'lampp' as user name!
XAMPP: MySQL is accessable via network.
XAMPP: Normally that's not recommended. Do you want me to turn it off?
       [yes] yes
XAMPP: Turned off.
XAMPP: Stopping MySQL...
XAMPP: Starting MySQL...
XAMPP: The MySQL/phpMyAdmin user pma has no password set!!!
XAMPP: Do you want to set a password? [yes] yes
XAMPP: Password: ********
XAMPP: Password (again): ********
XAMPP: Setting new MySQL pma password.
```

```
XAMPP: Setting phpMyAdmin's pma password to the new one.
XAMPP: MySQL has no root password set!!!
XAMPP: Do you want to set a password? [yes] yes
XAMPP: Write the password somewhere to make sure you won't forget it!!!
XAMPP: Password: *********
XAMPP: Password (again): *********
XAMPP: Setting new MySQL root password.
XAMPP: Change phpMyAdmin's authentication method.
XAMPP: The FTP password is still set to 'lampp'.
XAMPP: Do you want to change the password? [yes] yes
XAMPP: Password: ******
XAMPP: Password (again): ******
XAMPP: Reload ProFTPD...
XAMPP: Done.
```

By stepping through the xampp security command, you had an opportunity to add a password to the following:

- The lampp user (allowing you to access XAMPP web pages from the network). For a public server, you may not want to require a password to simply view web content from the server.
- The pma user of the MySQL/phpMyAdmin service.
- The root user for the MySQL service.
- The nobody user for the ProFTPD service (that password had been set to lampp).

You were also able to make MySQL administration inaccessible from the network. So, to configure MySQL, you would have to access that service from the DSL machine instead of from the network.

With password protection and access to services set as you would like, the next thing you should do is set up a firewall.

Setting Up a Firewall

The rcfirewall package that is available from the MyDSL Extension tool provides a mechanism for configuring a firewall on your DSL system. All of the configuration you need to do can be done in the rc.firewall script (located in the /etc/init.d directory). The RC.firewall Linux Firewall project (http://lfw.sourceforge.net) is built on the iptables facility, which is built into the kernel and used for most Linux firewalls.

> ## NOTE
>
> The `rc.firewall` script basically adds iptables rules to your DSL system. Because the rcfirewall package also includes the iptables facility itself, you can instead configure your firewall using the `iptables` command directly or by grabbing other scripts that set up iptables rules. A great place to find such scripts, particularly for more complex firewalls, is the LinuxGuruz site (`www.linuxguruz.com/iptables`).

Installing Firewall Software

To use the rcfirewall package in DSL, you must install both the rcfirewall package and gnu-utils package from the MyDSL facility. First, select the MyDSL icon from the desktop. After that, select the following:

- **Firewall Package**—Select UNC→ rcfirewall.unc.info. When the `rcfirewall.unc.info` page appears, select Download and download the package to the `/tmp` directory.
- **GNU Utils Package**—Select UNC→ gnu-utils.unc.info. When the `gnu-utils.unc.info` page appears, select Download and download the package to the `/tmp` directory.

Both the rcfirewall and gnu-utils packages are installed automatically after the download. Although iptables is immediately enabled, the `rc.firewall` script is not run at installation and no incoming connections are blocked. The next step is to configure and run the `rc.firewall` script.

Configuring the rc.firewall Script

As delivered, the `rc.firewall` script is configured to block all incoming connections to your computer. It's your job to open access to those ports associated with the services you want to allow outside people to use: namely Web and FTP services.

Because `rc.firewall` is a shell script, you can edit it using any text editor. I'm going to start by making a copy of `rc.firewall` to the /opt directory, so you can run it from there. (Also, if you screw up, you can just make a fresh copy of the file.) For example, open a root Terminal window and run this copy command, then use the `vi` command or the Beaver editor and open the file as follows:

```
# cp /etc/init.d/rc.firewall /opt/
# beaver /opt/rc.firewall
```

There are many ways you can change your firewall configuration in the rc.firewall file. For our purposes, we are only going to open a few ports to allow outside access to the web server (port 80) and the FTP server (port 21).

With the rc.firewall script open, you can open access to the web server and FTP server ports by adding those port numbers to the PERMIT="" line. So, for the easiest case, edit the permit line so it appears as follows:

```
PERMIT="80 21"
```

The preceding PERMIT line opens access to the standard web service port (80) and FTP service port (21). Notice that a space is needed to separate the entries. With this line, all network interfaces allow anyone accessing those interfaces to request Web and FTP service. Of course, if you protected those services with passwords, users also need that username/password information to ultimately view the content associated with those services.

Here are a few different ways that you could configure your PERMIT line to open access to your Web and FTP services:

```
PERMIT="80/tcp 21/tcp"
PERMIT="192.168.0.0/24:80 192.168.0.0/24:21"
PERMIT="192.168.0.0/24 10.0.0.150"
```

You can use the examples in any of the preceding PERMIT lines to allow access to your server. In the first example, tcp is added to each port number, to indicate that only TCP protocols can access those services (by default, both TCP and UDP are allowed). The next example only allows access to ports 80 and 21 from computers on the 192.168.0 network (a good approach if you want to limit access to computers on your LAN). The final example allows access to any available port on the 192.168.0 network, as well as specifically permits access from the host at IP address 10.0.0.50.

There are many, many other ways to configure firewall services in your rc.firewall script. For example, if your web server is also being used as a router between your LAN and the Internet (not a terribly secure arrangement, but one that many people do), the script lets you set up your firewall for that. Assuming you want to allow routing to the Internet (eth0 interface) from computers on your LAN (eth1 interface), the following line would tell your firewall to allow that:

```
INTERNAL_INTERFACES="eth0"
```

A more secure approach to having your servers and the workstations on your LAN exist behind the same Internet connection is to configure what is called a Demilitarized Zone (DMZ). With a DMZ configuration, servers are behind one firewall, whereas your private LAN (generally your user workstations) is behind another, separate firewall. For more on using `rc.firewall` to configure a DMZ or other more complex arrangements, refer to the Linux Firewall Configuration page for this project (`http://lfw.sourceforge.net/config.html`).

Start Up Your Firewall

With your `rc.firewall` file edited, you can try out your new firewall configuration by running the `rc.firewall` script manually as follows:

```
# /opt/rc.firewall
-> Projectfiles.com Linux Firewall version 2.0rc9 running.
-> Performing sanity checks..... [ PASSED ]
-> Building firewall.... [ DONE] ]
-> Successfully secured the following addresses: 10.0.0.100
```

There is no indication of errors in the example just shown. Make sure that the information is formatted correctly in the `rc.firewall` file. To view the rules that are now set on your firewall, use the `iptables` command as follows:

```
# /sbin/iptables -L
Chain INPUT (policy DROP)
target  prot opt source      destination
ACCEPT  all  -   anywhere    anywhere            state RELATED,ESTABLISHED
ACCEPT  tcp  -   anywhere    anywhere            state NEW tcp dpt:www
ACCEPT  udp  -   anywhere    anywhere            state NEW udp dpt:www
ACCEPT  tcp  -   anywhere    anywhere            state NEW tcp dpt:ftp
ACCEPT  udp  -   anywhere    anywhere            state NEW udp dpt:fsp
...
```

The partial output of `iptables` shows what happens for your firewall's INPUT chain. The policy is to drop any incoming connection requests, except in those cases where the connection is related to an established connection (presumably started by a client behind the firewall). The last four entries, however, show that new incoming connections will be established for requests coming in from anywhere for `tcp` and `udp` www (port 80) connections, as well as `tcp` and `udp` `ftp` and `fsp` (port 21) connections. (The FSP protocol is similar to anonymous FTP and also accepts connections on port 21.)

At this point, you can make sure that you can connect to your XAMPP server by logging into a different computer (on your LAN or on the Internet) and trying to connect to the server. To check the web service, point your web browser at the server's IP address (such as `http://10.0.0.100`, as described earlier). Or, you can connect to the FTP service (for example, `ftp://nobody@10.0.0.100` and enter the password you created earlier). Presumably, you will use FTP to add content to your web server or offer file download service to users.

CONFIGURING YOUR XAMPP SERVER

Tools for managing your XAMPP server are also included with the XAMPP package. As with many Linux services, most services in the XAMPP package can be configured using plain text files. However, there are also several graphical tools for managing XAMPP from a browser. Another part of setting up a server is to give it a static IP address, so those who are looking for your web server can find it.

Setting Up Your Network Interface

For a desktop system, getting an arbitrary IP addressed assigned to you at boot time (usually by a DHCP service) generally works just fine. However, with a web server that you want people to find, you typically want to assign a permanent IP address that doesn't potentially change with each reboot.

If you are creating a web server to use in temporary situations (such as in a classroom setting), you can simply have a DHCP server assign your server's IP address. Then, you can tell your customers (or students) what that IP address is to let them connect to your server. However, for a more permanent web server, you need to assign a static IP address.

To run a permanent web server out of your home or small business, you might want to contact your Internet service provider and request a static IP address and purchase a domain name for your server. The ISP (or other domain registrar) will charge a yearly fee for securing the Internet domain name and probably charge a fee for the static IP address.

Whether you get a static IP address and DNS name from your ISP or simply want a private static IP address behind your home or business firewall (which costs you nothing), you can use the DSL Netconfig tool to try out your static IP address.

From the DSL desktop, select System→ Net Setup→ netcardconfig (assuming you are configuring your server for a wired Ethernet connection). Then, do the following to configure your static IP address:

1. When asked whether to use DHCP broadcast, select No. You are asked to enter an IP address for your Ethernet interface (probably eth0).

2. Enter the IP address assigned by your ISP or a private IP address and select OK. (If you are using your web server only on your LAN, choose a private IP address from the pool of IP addresses that is not already in use and not being handed out by a local DHCP server. For example, the addresses 192.168.0.1 through 192.168.0.254 are often used for private LANs.)

3. Enter the network Mask for your IP address and select OK. Again, you should get this number from your ISP. For private IP addresses, a netmask of 255.255.255.0 leaves you with 254 potential IP addresses on your LAN.

4. Enter the broadcast address for your Ethernet interface and select OK. For the example just shown, your broadcast address will be assigned to 192.168.0.255 by default.

5. Enter the default gateway IP address and press Enter. This is the IP address of the router attached to your computer or to your LAN that gets you to the Internet.

6. Enter the IP addresses of the DNS servers your system will use to resolve DNS host names into IP address. You can also get this information from your ISP.

7. To check that your addresses were set properly, type `/sbin/ifconfig` from a Terminal window. You should see the IP address, broadcast, and netmask that you just configured for your Ethernet interface (eth0).

The procedure shown here sets your IP address information for the current session, so you can make sure it is working. To set your IP address permanently, refer to the "Saving Your XAMPP Server" section later in this chapter.

Editing XAMPP Configuration Files

Because XAMPP keeps everything contained within one directory structure, you can find configuration files there as well. The following sections describe files in the `/opt/lampp/etc` directory for configuring XAMPP services.

Editing httpd.conf (Apache Web Services)

Configure your Apache web server settings in this file. If you plan to make this a public web server, you can change the ServerName entry from localhost to a full DNS name (such as www.example.com) or to an IP address.

If want to host web content for multiple domain names from the same physical server, you can do that by setting up virtual hosts. First, have your domain name registrar (or other DNS service provider) configure your domain names to point to the IP address of your server. Then, you need to add a `NameVirtualHost` line to `httpd.conf`, as well as a `VirtualHost` container for each host name you want to be handled by the server. Here is an example:

```
NameVirtualHost *
<VirtualHost *>
ServerName www.example.com
```

```
DocumentRoot /opt/lampp/htdocs/example-com
</VirtualHost>

<VirtualHost *>
ServerName www.example.net
DocumentRoot /opt/lampp/htdocs/example-net
</VirtualHost>
```

In the virtual host examples just shown, all network interfaces on the computer listen for incoming HTTP requests for servers named www.example.com and www.example.net. You would place Web content for example.com in the /opt/lampp/htdocs/example-com directory, with content for example.net going in the /opt/lampp/htdocs/example-net directory.

Check through the httpd.conf file to see if you want to change other features. For example, you should check that all the modules you need are loaded. Notice that the httpd daemon is run as the nobody user and group. See which files are presented when a directory name is requested (index.html, index.html.var. index. php, and so on).

As set in httpd.conf, log files are stored in the /opt/lampp/logs directory. The log level and format of those logs are defined in httpd.conf as well. The last line in the httpd.conf file sources in the httpd-xampp.conf file, which you can check for special settings that are added by the XAMPP project.

For more information on configuring httpd.conf and other features in Apache 2.2, refer to the Apache online documentation: http://httpd.apache.org/docs/2.2.

Editing php.ini (PHP Configuration)

Depending on the type of PHP content you are hosting, you may need to change some of the settings in the php.ini file. For example, ASP-style tags (<% %>) are off by default as is Year 2000 compliance.

You may not need to change any of the settings in this file. However, you might want to just step through this file to make sure that the settings don't conflict with the type of PHP code included on your website.

Editing proftpd.conf (FTP Server Configuration)

The proftpd.conf file is configured to allow content to be added and removed from your FTP site. By default, the nobody username is configured so it can be used to log in through the FTP service (using lampp as the password) and upload files to populate the content of your web server. You were instructed to change the nobody user's password earlier in this chapter.

The DefaultRoot, which is the home directory when the user logs into the FTP server, is set to /opt/lampp/htdocs. After the user logs in, that user has the right to overwrite any content in the home directory and its subdirectories.

You can use any FTP client (in Linux, commands such as ftp, ncftp, or gftp are often available) to log in to the FTP server and upload content.

Configuring XAMPP from Your Browser

There are a couple of administrative interfaces available from XAMPP for checking and changing settings for your XAMPP server. You can open the interfaces from a browser on the local system or over the network (if you configure XAMPP to allow that):

- **MySQL Administration (phpMyAdmin)**—The phpMyAdmin tool is available with XAMPP to administer your MySQL database. From the local system, type **http://localhost/phpmyadmin/** and enter the **lampp** username and password. (Use the **root** account later for the Web site login.) Figure 16-4 shows an example of the phpMyAdmin page running from an XAMPP server in DSL.

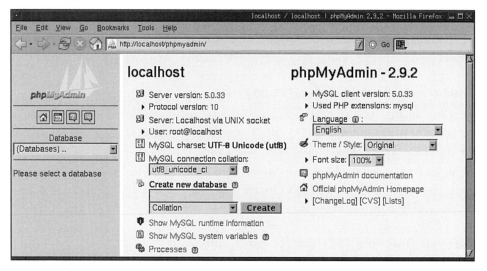

FIGURE 16-4   With phpMyAdmin, access information about your XAMPP MySQL Server.

From the phpMyAdmin screen, you can immediately see information about the server (version information, host name, character set, and so on). From links on this page, you can see MySQL system variables and runtime statistics. You can also view and change user privileges and new databases of various types. For more information on using phpMyAdmin, select the link to the phpMyAdmin documentation.

- **MySQL Databases (phpSQLiteAdmin)**—The phpSQLiteAdmin tool provides another option you can use to manage the MySQL databases on your XAMPP server. Select phpSQLiteAdmin from the left column on the main XAMPP for Linux screen or type `http://localhost/phpsqliteadmin/index.php` to see the screen shown in Figure 16-5.

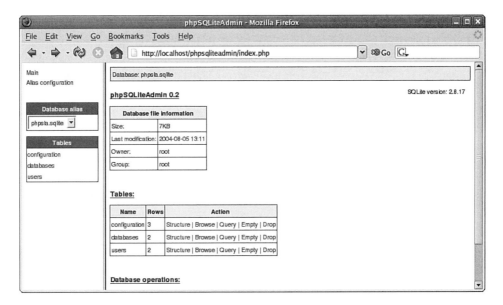

FIGURE 16-5   Work with your MySQL databases from the phpSQLiteAdmin screen.

From phpSQLiteAdmin, you can select the database that interests you from the Database Alias box. Then, view information about that database, such as viewing its structure, browsing through the data it contains, and querying the database.

- **Web Usage Statistics (Webalizer)**—By selecting Webalizer from the main XAMPP page, you can see daily and monthly statistics for the activities on your website. You can configure how those statistics are displayed and gathered using settings in the `/opt/lampp/etc/webalizer.conf` file. Figure 16-6 shows an example of the data on an XAMPP server that has only been installed a few days.

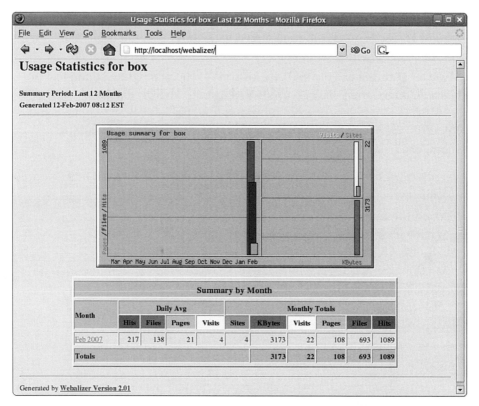

FIGURE 16-6 View Webalizer statistics for activity on your XAMPP server.

Now that you have a handle on your XAMPP server configuration, it's time to add some content.

ADDING CONTENT TO YOUR XAMPP SERVER

As your XAMPP server is configured by default, it expects the web content (HTTP) you add to the server to be located in the /opt/lampp/htdocs directory. You can start by adding an index page to that directory. When the home page for your website is requested (for example, http://localhost or www.example.com), the first page encountered in the htdocs directory that carries one of the following names is displayed (in the order shown):

index.html   index.html.var   index.php   index.php3   index.php4

As noted earlier, the ProFTPd FTP server should be available for you to log in and upload content. If you are adding multiple virtual hosts, you may want to create additional logins to upload content to multiple directories, so that each website can separate its contents from the other. Besides that, just get a good book on web development and have at it.

Saving Your XAMPP Server

Now that you have gone to all the trouble to configure a web server and build in all your content, you certainly don't want to lose it all on your next reboot. To save all the good software and settings you just created, we're going to use some of the information you've already learned about MyDSL and backups to save the bootable web server permanently.

Because I think it is cool to carry around a whole web server in my pocket, I'm going to put together this whole system on a USB flash drive (also called a pen drive or thumb drive). Although most of the components in this DSL web server should fit in less than 256MB, I'm using a 1GB pen drive to leave room for future expansion.

The following procedure steps you through the process of creating the DSL system on the USB flash drive, then saving your XAMPP software, web server content, extra software packages, and desktop settings. With the final result, you should be able to insert your USB drive into a port on your PC, reboot, and begin serving up web content.

Just because I am a cautious person, I backed up all the key components of my DSL XAMPP server before starting the procedure. I did this by opening a partition on my hard disk, creating a directory called `xamppstuff` on it, and copying my `rc.firewall` script, `/opt/lampp` directory, and MyDSL packages (`rcfirewall` and `gnu-utils`) to that directory.

NOTE

Because the USB flash drives are not the best medium for applications that require a lot of writing to the drive, it's probably more effective to place some or all of your XAMPP server on a hard drive. See the sidebar, "Other Ways of Storing Your Web Server," after this procedure, for some other ways of storing your XAMPP server than putting it all on a USB flash drive.

1. **Add startup scripts**—So far, we've run both the XAMPP server and the firewall script manually. To have those features run when your saved DSL system boots, you can add their start-up scripts to the `/opt/bootlocal.sh` file. Open the `bootlocal.sh` file using any text editor, and then add the last two lines so the file appears as follows:

```
#!/bin/bash
# put other system startup commands here
/opt/lampp/lampp start
/opt/rc.firewall
```

If you installed the XAMPP tarball and copied the `rc.firewall` script as described earlier, both those services are now set up to start automatically the next time DSL boots.

If you also want to add a static IP address for your server, instead of getting addresses assigned from a DHCP server, you can add commands for that to your `bootlocal.sh` script. For example, you could add the following lines to set your IP address for the eth0 interface to 192.168.0.10, set the default router (gateway) to 192.168.0.1, and identify your DNS servers as **192.168.0.5** and **192.168.0.6**.

```
ifconfig eth0 192.168.0.10
route add default gw 192.168.0.1
echo nameserver 192.168.0.5 > /etc/resolv.conf
echo nameserver 192.168.0.6 >> /etc/resolv.conf
```

Note that the addresses used here are all private IP addresses. If you are configuring a public server, you either need to have public IP addresses assigned or use some sort of port forwarding from a public IP address to a machine behind a firewall/router.

2. **Create DSL on USB flash drive**—Insert your USB flash drive, that you are prepared to erase and use for your Web server, into your computer's USB port (don't mount it). Next, from the DSL menu on the desktop, select Apps, Tools, Install to USB Pendrive. Then, select either For USB-ZIP Pendrive (if you expect to run the server on an older PC) or For USB-HDD Pendrive (to run the server on newer PCs).

This procedure erases everything on your USB drive! So make sure you've removed everything you need from the drive. Answer the questions as prompted. (See Chapter 6, "Running a Native Pen Drive Install," for details on installing DSL to a pen drive.)

3. **Select files/directories to back up**—The files and directories that DSL backs up for you need to be listed in the `/home/dsl/.filetool.lst` file. Several entries are already in that file. Open that file using any text editor and add the last lines shown here in bold:

```
opt/ppp
opt/bootlocal.sh
opt/powerdown.sh
opt/.dslrc
opt/.mydsl_dir
opt/lampp/
opt/rc.firewall
```

4. **Back up files and directories**—To back up the files that you just added in your `.filetool.list` file to your USB flash drive, from the desktop select DSLpanel, Backup/Restore. You are prompted to enter the device on which you want to back up your files. It's important to get this right.

   For a system that has no other SCSI or SATA drives on it, the USB flash drive device will probably be `sda1` (for a USB-HDD drive) or `sda2` (for a USB-ZIP drive). After typing in the device name, select Backup.

   The result is a `backup.tar.gz` file in the root of the USB drive device you entered.

5. **Save MyDSL packages**—Any MyDSL packages that you want restored can also be copied on to the USB flash drive. If you just downloaded them, they should still be in the `/tmp` directory.

   You will have the opportunity to copy your MyDSL packages when you reboot DSL. Or you can copy them manually. For example, you could mount the USB flash device, using the mounting tool in the lower-right corner of the screen. Then, for example, to copy the files needed for this project to a `mydsl` directory on `sda1`, you could type the following from a Terminal window:

```
# cd /tmp
# mkdir /mnt/sda1/mydsl/
# cp gnu-utils* rcfirewall* /mnt/sda1/mydsl/
```

At this point, everything you need should be installed on your USB flash drive. Before adding web content, my XAMPP installation required 50MB of space for DSL and 61MB of space for XAMPP and the other packages I added. On a 256MB USB flash drive, that would leave me more than 140MB for web content or other packages I want to add.

When you reboot your computer (select Power Down→ Reboot from the DSL menu), DSL backs up your settings again and asks if you want to save your MyDSL packages.

OTHER WAYS OF STORING YOUR WEB SERVER

Although having a complete DSL web server on a USB flash drive is fun, a more practical, permanent solution is to put some, or all, of the project on hard disk. Using the procedure just shown as your guide, here are ideas for changing that procedure to store your server in different ways:

- **Save MyDSL packages to hard disk**—Instead of downloading the MyDSL packages to /tmp, then copying them to storage, you can directly download the pages to the permanent storage. For example, use the desktop mount tool to mount a hard disk partition (such as hda1 for your first IDE hard disk partition). Then, create a mydsl directory on the device (mkdir /mnt/hda1/mydsl). When asked where to download the package, type /mnt/hda1/mydsl.

  Later, when you reboot, DSL should automatically find and restore the packages in the /mnt/hda1/mydsl directory. To specifically identify that directory from the boot prompt (in case you have MyDSL packages in multiple places), use the mydsl=/mnt/hda1/mydsl option at the boot prompt.

- **Save your backup archive to hard disk**—Instead of using sda1 or sda2 (presuming they represent your USB flash drive), when you choose where to back up your files, select a hard disk partition (such as hda1, hda2, etc.). The backup.tar.gz archive is placed in the root of that partition, so it can be restored later.

- **Create a persistent /opt**—By dedicating a disk partition to your /opt directory, you can save yourself the trouble of restoring the files when you reboot. Instead, you just tell DSL to mount the dedicated partition to /opt and it's ready to roll.

  To set up your persistent /opt partition to work with your XAMPP server, you need to modify several steps from the setup procedure. First, create an empty hard disk partition (for example, /dev/hda2) and boot DSL as follows:

  boot: **dsl opt=hda2**

  Next, install the XAMPP software to the /opt directory and copy your MyDSL packages to a /opt/mydsl directory. Edit the .filetool.1st file and remove references to backing up files from the /opt directory. When you go to reboot your system later, start DSL and the XAMPP server with the following boot options:

> boot: **dsl nodhcp opt=hda2 mydsl=hda2/mydsl**
> Using the persistent /opt directory in this way saves you the time used to
> back up your XAMPP files.
>
> Refer to Chapters 6 through 9 for information on other ways of installing and
> configuring DSL that may best suit your XAMPP configuration and the type of
> equipment you are using.

RESTARTING YOUR XAMPP SERVER

Depending on where you put your XAMPP software, you need to enter different options to the boot prompt to have DSL find, restore, and boot up the proper software. The following sections describe how to restart your XAMPP server, depending on whether you stored the software on a USB flash drive or hard disk, as described earlier.

Restarting from a USB Flash Drive

To restart the XAMPP server you just installed on your USB flash drive, simply insert the USB flash drive into a USB port on your PC and reboot. If your PC skips the USB drive and tries to boot from hard disk or another device, you may need to change the BIOS settings to boot from USB devices.

When you see the boot prompt, identify the location of your backup archive and MyDSL packages as follows:

```
boot: dsl mydsl=sda1/mydsl restore=sda1 secure
```

The first option to dsl (mydsl=) restores your saved MyDSL applications, whereas the second option (restore=) restores your backed up files to the DSL file system. The next time you reboot DSL, just remember that any subsequent changes you make to the backed up files (such as those in /home/dsl and /opt/1ampp) will be backed up again.

I threw in the secure option, so that you can be prompted for passwords to protect your server from breakins. If you are using a static IP address, you can tell DSL not to start a network connection using DHCP by adding nodhcp to the boot prompt.

Restarting from the Hard Drive

If you had installed your backup archive and MyDSL packages to hard disk (as described in the "Other Ways of Storing Your Web Server" sidebar), with a static IP address, you could simply boot a DSL live CD and type this at the boot prompt:

```
boot: dsl nodhcp mydsl=hda1/mydsl restore=hda1 secure
```

Another way of rebooting DSL to include software stored on your hard disk (also from descriptions in the sidebar) is if you create a persistent /opt directory on a hard disk partition. For example, if your persistent /opt directory is on the second partition of your first IDE hard drive, you could boot DSL as follows:

```
boot: dsl nodhcp mydsl=hda1/mydsl opt=hda2 secure
```

If you have a large amount of RAM on your computer, you might also consider adding the toram option to the boot prompt. This helps make your slick XAMPP server blazing fast.

Backing Up Your XAMPP Server

The XAMPP service offers a feature that lets you securely back up you XAMPP databases, configuration files, log files, and content (htdocs) files. To do this, you run the lampp command with the backup option as follows:

```
# /opt/lampp/lampp backup mysecretpwd
Backing up databases...
Backing up configuration, log, and htdocs files...
Calculating checksums...
Building final backup file...
Backup finished.
Take care of /opt/lampp/backup/xampp-backup-12-02-07.sh
```

The resulting backup file (xampp-backup-??-??-??.sh) is copied to the /opt/lampp/backup directory, from which you can copy it to a backup medium. The password (shown here as mysecretpwd) is the root password for your MySQL server.

If at any point your data becomes corrupted or destroyed, you can restore the backup archive by running it as a shell script. For example, with the preceding example, you could type the following:

```
# sh /opt/lampp/backup/xampp-backup-22-01-04.sh mysecretpwd
Checking integrity of files...
Restoring configuration, log and htdocs files...
Checking versions...
Installed:   XAMPP 1.6
Backup from: XAMPP 1.6
Restoring MySQL databases...
Restoring MySQL user databases...
Backup complete. Have fun!
You may need to restart XAMPP to complete the restore.
```

Again, you need to enter the MySQL root password to be able to restore files to the MySQL database. After the files are restored, as the message indicates, you may need to restart the MySQL server for the restore to be completed (type `/opt/lampp/lampp restart`).

SUMMARY

XAMPP is a powerful web server solution that combines the components needed to serve content that includes scripting languages (PHP, PEAR, and Perl), database tables (MySQL), FTP service (ProFTPD), and of course web HTTP service (Apache). All the pieces of XAMPP are contained in one directory structure and, because there is a Linux version, can run almost out-of-the box in Damn Small Linux.

This chapter describes how to get and install XAMPP in Damn Small Linux. It also tells how to configure XAMPP, add web content, and save all the settings so the server can work across reboots. In particular, descriptions in this chapter can help you store a DSL XAMPP server and all your content on a USB flash drive that is less than 256MB.

Part V

Appendixes

On the CD

The CD that comes with this book represents a consolidation of different versions of Damn Small Linux that are produced by the Damn Small Linux project. It contains some extra tools you can use for remastering Damn Small Linux, as well as some MyDSL extensions that are particularly useful for building the projects described in the book.

The CD is part bootable Damn Small Linux and part Damn Small Linux software repository. It is made to not only boot directly, as you would a regular Damn Small Linux image, but also boot up to display enhanced versions of Damn Small Linux used to create the different projects that come with the book.

NOTE

If you are unable to boot Damn Small Linux from the CD included with this book, try to disable hardware items that appear to be stopping the boot process. Do this by adding boot options shown on the boot help screen (press F2) or other options such as `acpi=off` or `nodma`. If that fails, try searching www.damnsmalllinux.org for the model of your computer to see if others have had trouble using DSL on that type of computer.

The CD also includes software that you can use to run DSL in a virtual environment from a Windows desktop (just insert the CD and select the correct `.bat` file to run). There are also tools that can help you with remastering DSL.

The following list describes the software contained on the CD:

- **Official Damn Small Linux (dsl-3.3.iso)**—Simply press Enter or type dsl at the boot prompt, and the standard Damn Small Linux starts up. This is the Isolinux version of Damn Small Linux, meaning that it should boot from most PCs with a BIOS that was created in the past few years.

  Press the F2 or F3 function keys to see options you can add to the dsl boot command to run Damn Small Linux in different ways. Unless otherwise noted, this is the version of Damn Small Linux you should use with the examples described in this book.

- **Official Damn Small Linux, syslinux (dsl-3.3-syslinux.iso)**—The Syslinux version of DSL is included on this CD. Because you can't boot Syslinux and Isolinux from the same CD, we included the ISO image of the DSL Syslinux version that you can burn to a CD yourself. That image is located in the /images directory of the CD and is named dsl-3.3-syslinux.iso.

- **DSL Boot Images**—Also contained in the /images directory are several different boot images you can use with DSL. These boot images allow you to create boot media on floppy disks, PCMCIA floppies, or USB drives. It also contains the frugal_lite.sh script.

- **Virtual DSL with QEMU (dsl-3.3-embedded.zip)**—In the /dsl-qemu directory on the CD, there are components needed to run Damn Small Linux from a Windows desktop using open source PC emulation software called Qemu. The dsl-base.bat command in that directory starts a basic DSL when run from Windows. The dsl-vhd.bat command can be run to take advantage of a virtual hard drive. (The contents of the /dsl-qemu directory are the result of unzipping the dsl-3.3-embedded.zip file. You can get the zipped file itself from the /images directory on the CD.)

- **Virtual DSL with VMware (dsl-3.3-vmx.zip)**—The /dsl-vm directory on the CD contains components needed to run DSL virtually from a Windows desktop using VMware. Those components include a VMware configuration file and the DSL image needed to run in Windows. You need to download a copy of VMware Player to use with these files (as described in Chapter 7, "Running DSL Embedded in Windows"). The contents of the /dsl-vm directory are the result of unzipping the dsl-3.3-vmx.zip file. (You can get the zipped file itself from the /images directory on the CD.)

- **DSL Projects**—Projects described in Part IV, "Making Damn Small Linux Projects," all require that some software to be added to the basic DSL system. The /extras directory contains subdirectories containing software for each of the projects in those chapters. That software is automatically loaded when you boot the selected project from the CD.

- **DSL Remastering Tools**—The tools needed to do the remastering procedures in Chapter 11, "Setting Up a Full Remastering Environment," are contained in the /chapter11 directory on the CD. Tools for building your own MyDSL extensions, described in Chapter 10, "Adding Applications and Creating Sharable Extensions," are contained in the /chapter10 directory.

All the software contained on the CD is also available from Damn Small Linux mirror sites (www.damnsmalllinux.org/download.html) or purchased on CD or pen drive from DamnSmallLinux.org. You can also go to the DamnSmallLinux.org website to get software updates as they become available.

MyDSL Extensions

To extend beyond the applications available in the base Damn Small Linux system, the Damn Small Linux project offers hundreds of downloadable and installable software packages referred to as *MyDSL extensions*. This appendix contains a listing of available MyDSL extensions that you can download and install from online software repositories by opening the MyDSL icon on the DSL desktop.

Most of the descriptions in this appendix come directly from info files included with each package extension. In many cases, you can find longer descriptions of each extension when you select to download and install it. Because extensions come from the Damn Small Linux community, you may find that the quality of both the descriptions and the extensions themselves can vary quite a bit.

You may notice that there are multiple versions of some extensions. That is because there are times when you may want an extension that copies its files directly to your file system (for example, with `.dsl` extensions), whereas other times it's more useful to have the extensions mounted (as is done with `.uci` extensions). See Chapter 5, "Extending Applications with MyDSL," for further information on different MyDSL extension types.

Besides providing the name and descriptions of each MyDSL extension, the table lists the version number, website containing more information, and size of the extension. You can also get more information on each extension by selecting that extension from the MyDSL Extension Tool (which displays the extension's info file). Extension headings in the table align with buttons on the MyDSL Extension Tool window (Apps, Games, UNC, Multimedia, and so on).

Title	Description / Version / Site / Size	Comments
Apps Extensions		
abiword.dsl	AbiWord word processor / 2.0.1 / http://www.abisource.com / 8.4MB	A free word processing program. Similar to Microsoft Word.
antiword.dsl	Word document converter / 0.32-2 / http://www.winfield.demon.nl/index.html / 86KB	Converts Word 6, 7, 97, and 2000 docs to text or PostScript for viewing. There is no menu item for this package as it is invoked from the command line.
bc.dsl	Arbitrary precision calculator language / 1.06-8 / http://www.gnu.org/software/bc/bc.html / 112KB	An arbitrary precision calculator language. It allows you to write and execute simple or complex programs to do calculations using arbitrary precision real numbers.
chameleon.dsl	X Display Control app / 1.1-3 / http://packages.qa.debian.org/c/chameleon.html / 151KB	Using GTK and Imlib, Chameleon allows the user to place a picture in any format or color chosen from a color wheel in the root window of X (the background).
cinepaint.dsl	CinePaint photo retouch app / 1.3.0-7 / http://www.cinepaint.org / 4.4MB	A free open source painting and image retouching program designed to work best with 35mm film and other high resolution high dynamic range images.
dia-0.88.1.dsl	Dia / 0.88.1 / http://www.gnome.org/projects/dia / 1.3MB	A diagram and blueprint creation program much like Microsoft Visio. It can be used to create detailed layout of buildings, network layouts, and so on.
dosbox.dsl	DOSbox DOS emulator / 0.63 / http://dosbox.sf.net / 1.6MB	DOS emulator used to run old DOS apps and games.
dsl-aterm.tar.gz	Terminal shell for Linux similar to rxvt / 0.4.2 / http://aterm.sourceforge.net / 51KB	Transparent aterm extension for DSL.

Title	Description / Version / Site / Size	Comments
Apps Extensions		
`endeavour2.dsl`	UNIX file management suite / 2.5.2 / http://wolfpack.twu.net/ Endeavour2 / 4.7MB	Endeavour Mark II is a UNIX file management suite that comes with a file browser, image viewer, archiver, and a recycle bin.
`figurine.dsl`	Figurine graphics editor / 1.0.5-6 / http://figurine.sourceforge.net/ 359KB	An X11 editor for xfig FIG3.2-format vector graphics. It is simpler to use than xfig while providing a mostly similar feature set. It includes transfig, so it can export to several other formats.
`gambas.dsl`	GUI compiler / 1.0 / http://gambas.sourceforge.net / 9.5MB	A BASIC language with object extensions.
`gimp-1.2.dsl`	The GNU image manipulation program / 1.2 / http://www.gimp.org / 8.9MB	The premier open source software for composing images, retouching photographs, and authoring images.
`gmoo.dsl`	gmoo mud client / 2.0.1 / ftp://nowmoo.demon.nl/pub/gmoo / 1.4MB	A mud client, GTK+, nice GUI.
`gnuplot.tar.gz`	2D and 3D plotting / 4.0.0 / http://www.gnuplot.info / 1.0MB	A plotting program that handles 2D and 3D plots. Gnuplot can output data directly to printers, pen plotters, interactive screen terminal, and many types of files.
`gpsk31.dsl`	PSK31 for Linux with GTK+ / 0.2.3 / http://sunsite.unc.edu/pub/Linux/ apps/ham / 290KB	PSK31 for Linux with a GTK+ interface. Uses DL9RDZ's new PSK31 Implementation (0.75).
`gqview.dsl`	GQview image viewer / 1.0.2 / http://gqview.sourceforge.net / 258KB	An image viewer for UNIX operating systems (developed on Linux). Its key features include single-click file viewing, external editor support, thumbnail preview, and zoom features.
`gtkedit.tar.gz`	A Notepad clone based on GTK+ / 0.2 / http://gtkedit1.sourceforge.net	A feature-for-feature clone of Notepad from Microsoft Windows. It is a good text editor for users who have migrated from that platform.

Title	Description / Version / Site / Size	Comments
Apps Extensions		
`gtkfind.dsl`	Tool for searching the file system / 25KB	Search for files based on name, atime, ctime, mtime, mode, type, owner, and contents.
`gtksee.dsl`	Image Viewer / 0.5.6 / http://gtksee.berlios.de / 153KB	A simple image viewer based on GTK1.2. Supported file formats include JPG, GIF, BMP, PCX, PNG, XWD, and others.
`gv.dsl`	PostScript and PDF viewer for X / 1:3.5.8-26.1 / http://www.thep.physik.uni-mainz.de/~plass/gv / 341KB	Simple viewer of PostScript and PDF files.
`imagemagick.tar.gz`	Image toolbox / 6.2.2-0 / http://www.imagemagick.org / 2.8MB	A collection of useful tools with which to create and edit images of many formats.
`impress1.1_beta9.dsl`	PowerPoint Clone for X / 1.1_beta9 / http://www.ntlug.org/~ccox/impress/Main.html / 1.1MB	A WYSIWYG layout program designed especially for Linux. It allows you to create presentations and PostScript documents using fully scalable graphics.
`jpilot.dsl`	Palm PDA interface / 0.99.2-2 / http://jpilot.org / 719KB	A GTK application that is used to support Palm OS PDAs. This extension also includes jpilot dependencies.
`kjvbible.dsl`	HTML KJV HTML Bible / 1.0.0 / http://www.latedecember.com / 1.4MB	HTML frameset based on Gutenberg Project ebook.
`latex2rtf.dsl`	Converts text from `.te`x file to `.rtf` / 1.9.13-2 / http://latex2rtf.sourceforge.net / 64KB	When used without a LaTex installation, this has only limited capabilities; but it is sufficient to extract text from documents and convert to `.rtf`.
`lifelines.dsl`	Text-based genealogy software / 3.0.10-3 / http://lifelines.sourceforge.net / 215KB	A genealogical software system for UNIX and related systems. It allows you to store any kind and any amount of genealogy data in a LifeLines database, and you can process and generate output based on that data in any way and in any format.

Title	Description / Version / Site / Size	Comments
Apps Extensions		
`linpsk.dsl`	LinPSK Psk31/RTTY Terminal / 0.6.2 / http://linpsk.sourceforge.net / 2.2MB	LinPSK is a Psk31 and RTTY program for Linux. Uses soundcard for mod/demod of audio from receiver. Offers Spectrum, Waterfall, and Input views.
`lout.dsl`	Lout typesetting system/ 3.25-1 / http://snark.ptc.spbu.ru/~uwe/lout / 1.2MB	A high-level typesetting system, like LaTeX, groff, and others. Although LaTeX is large and sometimes overkill for DSL, Lout is small, yet has many of the same features.
`maxima.dsl`	Symbolic math package / 5.9.1 / http://maxima.sourceforge.net / 17MB	A full symbolic computation program. It is full featured doing symbolic manipulation of polynomials, matrices, rational functions,integration, Todd-coxeter, graphing, and bigfloats.
`nedit.tar.gz`	Nirvana Editor / 5.5 / http://www.nedit.org / 905KB	A multipurpose text editor for the X Window system.
`octave.tar.gz`	MatLab clone / 2.0.16.92 / http://www.octave.org / 1.3MB	A MatLab clone for matrix math and numerical processing.
`openoffice-1.1.4.tar.gz`	OpenOffice Office Suite / 1.1.4 / http://www.openoffice.org / 384MB RAM	A free productivity suite that is compatible with all major office suites. It is set up to use the Java enhancements.
`openoffice.tar.gz`	OpenOffice Office Suite / 1.1 / (Requires 384MB RAM) / http://www.openoffice.org / 66MB	A free productivity suite compatible with all major office suites.
`parted.dsl`	Partition management app / 1.6.21 / http://www.gnu.org/software/parted/parted.html / 196KB	A program for creating, destroying, resizing, checking, and copying partitions (and the file systems on them).

Title	Description / Version / Site / Size	Comments
	Apps Extensions	
predict-gsat-2.2.2.dsl	Predict Element Server /GSat / 2.2.2 / http://www.qsl.net/kd2bd/predict.html / 1.7MB	An open source, multiuser satellite tracking and orbital prediction program written under the Linux operating system.
pspp.dsl	Statistical analysis tool / 0.3.0-7 / http://savannah.gnu.org/projects/pspp / 651KB	A program for statistical analysis of sampled data. It interprets commands in the SPSS language and produces tabular output in ASCII or PostScript format.
qcad.tar.gz	QCad Linux Autocad app / 2.0.3.1 / http://www.ribbonsoft.com/qcad.html / 39MB	QCad is an application for computer-aided drafting in two dimensions. With QCad, you can create technical drawings such as plans for buildings, interiors, or mechanical parts.
qsstv-5.2.dsl	Ham Radio software for Linux / 05.2d / http://users.telenet.be/on4qz/ 3.9MB	Slow scan ham radio program for Linux. Uses QT 3.3.3 and supports WeFax Reception.
R.tar.gz	R (statistical computing and graphics) / 2.0.1 / http://directory.fsf.org/science/math/stats/R.html / 15MB	Provides a variety of statistical (linear and nonlinear modelling, classical statistical tests, time-series analysis, classification, clustering, and so on) and graphical techniques. R provides an open source route to participation in S language statistical methodology.
rkhunter.dsl	Root Kit Hunter / 1.1.7 / http://www.rootkit.nl / 86KB	Root Kit detector.
rox.dsl	Graphical file manager and viewer / 1.2.0-1 / http://rox.sourceforge.net/phpwiki/index.php/ROX-Filer / 914KB	Graphical file manager, thumbnail viewer, and desktop icon generator packaged for DSL.
sc.dsl	Text-based spreadsheet / 7.13-2 / http://freshmeat.net/projects/sc / 134KB	A curses-based spreadsheet program that uses key bindings similar to vi and less. It does not have all the features of gnumeric and similar, but it is still useful.

Title	Description / Version / Site / Size	Comments
Apps Extensions		
`scite.dsl`	Scite GTK-based editor / 1.44-1 / http://scintilla.sourceforge.net/ SciTE.html / 381KB	Lightweight GTK-based programming with syntax highlighting and support for many languages. Also supports folding sections, exporting highlighted text into colored HTML, and RTF.
`sketch-0.6.15.dsl`	Vector drawing program / 0.6.15.1 / http://www.nongnu.org/skencil/ index.html / 7.3MB	An interactive vector drawing program, comparable to CorelDraw.
`soundmodem.dsl`	Software mod/demod for amateur use / 0.7-1 / http://www.baycom.org/ ~tom/ham/soundmodem / 372KB	Allows a standard PC soundcard to be used as a packet radio *modem*.
`ted.dsl`	Ted RTF word processor / 2.14 / http://www.nllgg.nl/Ted / 4.0MB	A rich text format word processor. Includes English spell check and help file.
`tlf.dsl`	TLF contest logger / 0.9.20 / http://home.iae.nl/users/reinc/ TLF-0.2.html / 918KB	A console (ncurses) mode general purpose CW/VOICE keyer, logging, and contest program for ham radio.
`tuxpaint.dsl`	A simple drawing program for children / 0.9.13 / http://www. newbreedsoftware.com/tuxpaint / 15MB	Create a variety of shapes and colors using this simple drawing program.
`tuxtype.dsl`	The Tuxtype typing game / 1.5.3 / http://tuxtype.sourceforge.net / 4.5MB	A game extension for DSL. It is designed for kids by Tux4Kids as a typing tutor and touch type skill builder.
`twisted-1.3.0. tar.gz`	Twisted / 1.3.0 / http://twistedmatrix.com / 1.0MB	A framework, written in Python, for writing networked applications. It includes implementations of a number of commonly used network services such as a web server, an IRC chat server, a mail server, a relational database interface, and an object broker.

TITLE	DESCRIPTION / VERSION / SITE / SIZE	COMMENTS
APPS EXTENSIONS		
`twlog.dsl`	The TWLog ham radio logger for X / 1.72 / http:// wa0eir.home.mchsi.com / 507KB	Ham radio logging program for X. Simple light logger for logging contacts.
`vim_full.tar.gz`	Vi IMproved + extras / 6.3 / http://www.vim.org / 3.1MB	Vim in its entirety. This package includes help files, scripts, and other features missing from the DSL version, including syntax highlighting and folding, as well as a GUI version, which uses GTK.
`worker.tar.gz`	File manager for X / 2.10.0 / http://www.boomerangsworld.de/ worker / 591KB	A small, fast, and highly config-urable file manager that combines features of EmelFM and Midnight Commander.
`wvdial.dsl`	WVDial/ISP Dialer / 1.53.0.1 / http://open.nit.ca / 68KB	Modem dialer for establishing connections to Internet service providers.
`wv.dsl`	Convert/preview MS word docs / 0.7.1+rvt-2 stripped / http:// download.sourceforge.net/wvware / 509KB	Stripped-down versions of wv tools to convert MS Word documents to a previewable form (Dillo and Ted, for example). wvHtml and wvLatex are available. wvLatex can be used with latex2rtf (if available).
`xastir-1.4.0.dsl`	APRS HamRadio Terminal / 1.4.0 / http://www.xastir.org / 11MB	A ham radio program for receiving and plotting APRS position packets.
`xcalc.dsl`	Xcalc calculator from Xfree86 / 4.2.1 / http://www.xfree86.org	Contains xcalc from the Xfree86 base package.
`xastir.dsl`	Xastir APRS tracking program / 1.0.0 / http://www.xastir.org / 800KB	Tracking/logging program for X offers Net, IGate, and VHF connections.
`xdesktopwaves. tar.gz`	Waves on your background / 1.3 / http://xdesktopwaves.sourceforge. net / 29KB	A cellular automata that sets the background of your X Windows desktop under water. Windows and mouse are like ships on the sea. Each movement ends up in moving water waves.

Title	Description / Version / Site / Size	Comments
Apps Extensions		
xephem.dsl	An Ephemeris for X / 3.5.2 / http://www.xephem.com / 2.9MB	An interactive astronomical ephemeris program for X planets, stars, weather, and constellations. Connects to the Internet for fresh updates.
xeyes.tar.gz	Classic Xeyes toy from XFree86 / 4.3.0 / http://www.xfree86.org / 6.4KB	This package contains the Xeyes toy from the Xfree86 base package.
xfireworks.dsl	Onscreen fireworks / 1.3-2 / http://wwwmiya.ee.kagu.sut.ac.jp/~sakai/myfreesoft / 18KB	Displays fireworks on your screen.
xfishtank.tar.gz	Onscreen fish tank / 2.2-20 /ftp://ftp.x.org/R5contrib / 69KB	Displays a fish tank on your screen. (Debian format by Joey Hess.)
xfoil.dsl	xfoil subsonic airfoil development system / 6.94 / http://raphael.mit.edu/xfoil/	An interactive program used to design and analyze subsonic iso-lated airfoils.
xlog-0.9.9.dsl	XLog ham radio logging app / 0.9.9 / http://www.qsl.net/pg4i/linux/xlog.html / 13MB	An easy-to-use program for log-ging your ham radio contacts. Contacts are saved in a browsable list that can be edited.
xmgr.dsl	An XY plotting tool / 4.1.2-10 / ftp://plasma-gate.weizmann.ac.il/pub/xmgr4/src/xmgr-4.0.1.tar.gz / 924KB	Point-and-click tool for drawing XY plots.
xplanet.dsl	XPlanet Planetview Simulator / 1.1.0 / http://xplanet.sourceforge.net / 8.5MB	Xplanet was inspired by Xearth, which renders an image of the earth into the X root window. All of the major planets and most satellites can be drawn, similar to the Solar System Simulator.
xscreensaverGTK.dsl	Xscreensaver GTK version / 3.34 / http://www.jwz.org/xscreensaver / 1.9MB	A collection of free screensaver.
xv.dsl	The XV picture file viewer / 3.10 / http://www.trilon.com/xv / 2.5MB	Picture file viewer for .jpg, .ps, .gif, and other formats.

Title	Description / Version / Site / Size	Comments
Apps Extensions		
`xvkbd.tar.gz`	Virtual keyboard / 2.6 / http://homepage3.nifty.com/tsato/xvkbd / 99KB	A virtual keyboard program for X Windows.
`yacas.tar.gz`	Yet Another Computer Algebra System / 1.0.57 / http://www.xs4all.nl/~apinkus/yatas.html / 3.8MB	A lighter-weight package that handles integration, differentiation, and ODEs symbolically and numerically. Also handles large number math.
`zgv.tar.gz`	Zgv svgalib picture viewer / 5.9 / http://www.svgalib.org/rus/zgv / 257KB	A console-based picture viewer with a thumbnail-based file selector.
`zile.dsl`	Zile Is Lossy Emacs / 1.6.2 / http://zile.sourceforge.net / 72KB	An Emacs clone.
Games Extensions		
`abe-sdl.dsl`	Abe's Amazing Adventure / 1.1-1 / http://abe.sourceforge.net	An ancient pyramid exploring game.
`abuse.dsl`	Abuse - Kill Everything shooter / 0.6.1-1 / http://www.labyrinth.net.au/~trandor/abuse	First-person shooter game.
`ace.dsl`	Ace of Penguins card games collection / 1.1 / http://www.delorie.com/store/ace / 163KB	A set of UNIX/X solitaire games similar to the ones available for Windows, plus enhancements.
`acm.dsl`	ACM, Flying Simulator / 5.0-3 / http://www.websimulations.com / 394KB	Flying simulation (converted to Debian format by Phil Brooke).
`armagetron.dsl`	A 3D Tron-like high speed game / http://armgetron.sourceforge.net / 13MB	Tron-like high speed game that requires 3D acceleration to run (`nvidia.dsl`).
`armagetron.dsl`	A 3D Tron-like high speed game / http://armagetron.sourceforge.net / 13MB	A multiplayer, 3D game that emulates the lightcycle sequence from the movie Tron. Requires `xfree.dsl` and 3D acceleration (`nvidia.dsl`).

Title	Description / Version / Site / Size	Comments
	Games Extensions	
a_steroid.dsl	XFree Asteroids Clone / 5.0 / http://vcg.iei.pi.cnr.it/~cignoni/a_steroid / 735KB	Shoot down asteroids in this Atari arcade Asteroids clone. Game play is 2D, while objects are rendered in 3D using OpenGL.
billard-gl.dsl	3D billiards game / 1.75-6 / www.tobias-nopper.de/BillardGL/index-en.html / 668KB	3D billiards game you play against the computer. You need a fast machine and good 3D graphics card for this one.
blast.tar.gz	Blast holes in applications / 1.1-12 / http://lune.csc.liv.ac.uk/hpux/X11/Demos / 3.1KB	Blast holes in applications that are currently displayed on your desktop.
briquolo.tar.gz	3D breakout game / 0.5 / http://briquolo.free.fr / 1.6MB	Offers 3D breakout fun, including a level editor.
bugsquish.dsl	Bugsquish / 0.0.4 / http://www.newbreedsoftware.com/bugsquish / 716KB	Defend your arm from an onslaught of blood-sucking insects. Use your fly swatter to squish them before they suck you dry. Based on the shareware game Blood Suckers.
buzz.tar.gz	Buzz Aldrin's Race into Space / 1 / 9.1MB	One of my favorite games from back in the day. Game tips are in /opt/BARIS/buzztips.txt. Copy protection answers are in /opt/BARIS/copyprotect.txt. Requires dosbox.dsl.
cgoban.dsl	Encircle your opponant / 1.9.11-3 / http://www.igoweb.org/~wms/comp/cgoban / 177KB	Worth playing if you like strategy board games (converted to Debian format by Richard Braakman).
chromium.dsl	2D space shooter / 0.9.12 / http://www.reptilelabour.com/software/chromium / 2.6MB	Chromium B.S.U. is a fast paced, arcade-style, top-scrolling space shooter. Requirements - OpenGL (XFree86.dsl). Requirements - Hardware Accel (nvidia.dsl). Requirements - Linux Utils (gnu-utils.dsl).

Title	Description / Version / Site / Size	Comments
GAMES EXTENSIONS		
circuslinux.dsl	Circus Linux balloon popping / 1.0.3 / http://www. newbreedsoftware.com/ circus-linux / 1.7MB	Clowns popping balloons game!
doom.dsl	LXDoom game engine for Doom / 1.4.4-7 / http://prboom. sourceforge.net / 1.9MB	LXDoom game engine extension (with original map) for the Doom first-person shooter game. (Runs in X.)
dossizola.dsl	Block your opponent from moving / 1.0-6 / http://lune.csc.liv.ac.uk/ hpux/X11/Demos/blast-1.0.html / 1.1MB	Great graphics and a fun game (converted to Debian format by Yann Dirson).
dsl-cube.tar.gz	3D first-person shooter / 2004_05_22 / http://www.cubeengine.com / 7.0MB	An open source 3D shooter game that features in-game editing and an uncomplicated approach to gaming. Due to bandwidth limits, package is missing several maps, textures, models, and music files, although the game is otherwise unchanged.
eboard.dsl	Chessboard for different engines / 0.43 / http://eboard.sourceforge. net / 2.6MB	Nice graphical chess board. You can play via the Internet by FICS-Server remote.
enrapture.tar.gz	Role playing space game / 0.53 / http://enrapture.janq.org / 27MB	An OpenGL-based role playing game in space. It is influenced by the old masterpiece ELITE.
falling_tower. tar.gz	Falling Tower Jump Up a Tower / 2.7.5-1 / http://packages.debian. org/stable/games / 10KB	Jump up a tower (surprisingly diffi-cult and addictive) (converted to Debian format by Masato Taruishi).
freeciv.dsl	Civilization II Clone / 1.12.0 / http://www.freeciv.org / 3.8MB	A turn-based multiplayer strategy game, playable online. Inspired by Sid Meier's classic Civilization 2 game. Contains both server and client applications.

Title	Description / Version / Site / Size	Comments
Games Extensions		
`frozen-bubble.dsl`	Bubble shooter game / 1.0.0 / http://www.frozen-bubble.org / 17MB	Colorful, animated penguin eyecandy with 100 levels of one-person game, hours and hours of two-person game, a level editor, three professional quality 20-channel music tracks, 15 stereo sound effects, and seven unique graphical transition effects.
`gcompris-1.2.1-2.dsl`	GCompris educational software / 1.2.1-2 / http://www.ofset.org/gcompris / 15MB	Educational software that provides different activities for kids from 2 to 10.
`gcompris2.dsl`	GCompris educational software / 6.4 / http://gcompris.net / 39MB	Educational software that provides different activities to kids from 2 to 10.
`glest.dsl`	Glest 3D adventure/strategy game / 1.0.10 / http://www.glest.org/eng/index.htm / 46MB	A project for making a free 3D real-time customizable strategy game. Requires Xfree86/NVidia acceleration.
`gtetrinet.dsl`	TeTRiNeT 1.13 client for gnome / 0.4.1-9woody1.1 / http://gtetrinet.sourceforge.net / 1.0MB	Based on the classic TeTRiNeT game for Windows by StormCat, this client is compatible with the 1.13 TeTRiNeT protocol. Up to six players. I urge all interested to meet up in IRC to play.
`hexxagon.tar.gz`	Hexxagon's Conquer the Board / 0.3.1-2 / http://nesqi.homeip.net/hexxagon / 90KB	Conquer the board.
`intellivision_gamepak.dsl`	Intellivision clone / http://sarrazip.com/dev/cosmosmash.html / 1.1MB	Clone of the Intellivision game Midnight Stalker and Clone of the Intellivision game Astrosmash.
`invaders.tar.gz`	Invaders for DosBox / v02 / http://www.dosgames.com / 51KB	Space Invaders for DosBox Classic 1980's DOS game. Shoot and defeat the aliens.

Title	Description / Version / Site / Size	Comments
Games Extensions		
`koth.dsl`	A two-player tank strategy game / 0.7.6a-3 / http://www-unix.oit.um ass.edu/~tetron/koth / 313KB	Multisystem tank strategy game (converted to Debian format by Gustavo Noronha Silva).
`koules.dsl`	Koules' Competitive Pushing Game / 1.4-9 / http://www.paru. cas.cz/~hubicka/koules/English/ koules.html / 187KB	Try not to get pushed out of the arena (converted to Debian format by Klee Dienes).
`lgames.dsl`	Linux classic games / 1.0.* / http://lgames.sourceforge.net / 2.5MB	Classic Linux games, including LBreakout (Arkanoid clone), LTris (tetris clone), LPairs (a classic memory game), and LMarbles (Atomix clone).
`lincity.dsl`	LinCity's Strategy Game / 1.11-6 / http://www.floot.demon.co.uk/ lincity.html / 354KB	A really cool strategy game (converted to Debian format by John Goerzen).
`liquidwar.dsl`	LiquidWar's World Domination / 5.4.5-2 / http://www.ufoot.org/ liquidwar / 1.6MB	A great game with less-than-stellar graphics.
`mathwar.dsl`	MathWar's math card game / 0.1.1 / stufflehead@bigfoot.com / 1.7MB	A simple, but fun, math game for grade-school-aged kids. Based loosely on the popular War card game.
`mmgolf.tar.gz`	Miniature golf for DosBox / 1.0 / http://www.dosgames.com / 58KB	Miniature golf for DosBox.
`nethack.tar.gz`	The popular NetHack RPG X11 version / 3.4.3 / http://www.nethack.org / 1.4MB	The ever-popular NetHack role playing game.
`pacpc.tar.gz`	Pac Man for DosBox / v2 / http://jrok.com / 201KB	Classic 1980's Pac Man DosBox arcade game clone. PacPC is a free clone that brings the hungry yellow dot and even hungrier ghosts to your PC's desktop.
`penguin-command.dsl`	Missile Command game clone / 1.6.6 / http://www.linux-games. com / 1.3MB	This Missle Command clone has better graphics and sounds than the original!

Title	Description / Version / Site / Size	Comments
Games Extensions		
`pente.tar.gz`	A five-in-a-row game / 2.2.5 / http://www.igoweb.org/~wms/comp/pente / 125KB	A 5-in-a-row game of strategy. It offers network play, one- or two-player, computer versus human, and game saves.
`pipenightdreams.dsl`	Redirect the Sewage / 0.9.0-2 / http://packages.debian.org/stable/games/pipenightdreams / 1.5MB	Puzzle game where you direct sewage to an exit using different types of pipes.
`quake2.dsl`	Quake II 3D gaming engine for X / 3.20 / http://www.idsoftware.com / 2.2MB	First-person shooter game engine extension for DSL. Lets you add your own maps.
`scummvm-0.8.0.dsl`	Virtual machine for your old click-and-point adventures / 0.8.0 / http://www.scummvm.org /	Great tool to enjoy the LucasArts games under DSL!
`sdlroids.dsl`	Asteroids Clone + / 1.3.4 / http://sourceforge.net/projects/sdlroids / 497KB	Essentially an Asteroids clone, but with a few extra features and some nice game physics.
`smc-0.97.dsl`	Secret Maryo Chronicles v0.97 / 0.97 / http://www.secretmaryo.org /	A very good clone of Super Mario Brothers.
`smc-0.97-music.dsl`	Secret Maryo Chronicles v0.97 music files / 0.97 / http://www.secretmaryo.org /	The music to go along with the smc-0.97.dsl MyDSL extension.
`snake.dsl`	A snake game / 1.0.12-1 / http://shh.thathost.com/pub-unix /	A snake game where you capture bonuses and stay alive.
`spearofdestiny.tar.gz`	Spear of Destiny wolfgl series / 0.93 / leo@gerf.org / 1.2MB	Old IDSoftware title. First-person 3D shooter *requires* `XFree86.dsl` and `nvidia.dsl` or you own MesaGL.
`stella-2600.dsl`	Stella Atari 2600 VCS emulator / 1.3 / http://stella.sourceforge.net / 498KB	A multiplatform Atari 2600 VCS emulator released under the GNU General Public License (GPL). No ROMs are available, except the Paul Slocum's console test cartridge (http://www.mindspring.com/~paul-slocum/testcart.html).

Title	Description / Version / Site / Size	Comments
Games Extensions		
`supermario.tar.gz`	Super Mario Bros. DosBox Clone / 1.0 / http://www.zone.ee/bloodl/ smario.html / 123KB	Dosbox implementation of Super Mario Brothers arcade game.
`supertux.dsl`	SuperTux SuperMario clone / 0.1.2 / http://super-tux.sourceforge.net / 7.1MB	Based on the classic 2D jump-and-run SuperMario arcade game.
`toppler.dsl`	Linux implementation of Tower Toppler game / 1.0.6 / http:// toppler.sourceforge.net / 1.1MB	A fully playable Tower Toppler game. Everything is in place.
`torcs.dsl`	Linux racing simulator / 1.2.2 / http://torcs.sourceforge.net / 28MB	A 3D racing cars simulator using OpenGL. The goal is to have programmed robot drivers racing against each other. You can also drive yourself with either a wheel, keyboard, or mouse.
`tuxnes.tar.gz`	TuxNES + gTuxNES frontend / 0.75 / http://tuxnes.sourceforge.net / http://www.scottweber.com/ projects/gtuxnes / 128KB	An emulator for the 8-bit Nintendo Entertainment System. gTuxNES provides an easy-to-use GTK frontend.
`tuxracer.dsl`	TuxRacer for DSL / 0.61 / http://www.sunspirestudios.com / 8.8MB	3D racing game (for NVidia video card owners).
`Ultima-AOD.tar.gz`	Ultima 1-2-3 for DosBox / 1.0 / http://www.uo.com / 367KB	Classic Ultima Age of Darkness role playing games for DosBox. Includes U1 (1st Age of Darkness), U2 (Revenge of the Enchantress), and U3 (Exodus).
`Ultima-AOE.tar.gz`	Ultima 4-5-6 for DosBox / 1.0 / http://www.uo.com / 3.0MB	Classic Ultima Age of Enlightment role-playing games for DosBox. Includes U4 (Quest of the Avatar), U5 (Warriors of Destiny), and U6 (The False Prophet).

Title	Description / Version / Site / Size	Comments
Games Extensions		
`vba.dsl`	Visual Boy Advance emulator for X / 1.72 / http://vba.ngemu.com / 428KB	Visual Boy Advance extension for DSL Gameboy emulator. (Add your own ROMs from shell by typing vba *name-of-rom*.)
`wesnoth.dsl`	The Battle for Wesnoth / 0.8.8 / http://www.wesnoth.org / 27MB	A turn-based strategy game with a fantasy theme.
`wof.tar.gz`	Wings of Fury for DosBox / 1.0 / http://www.abandonia.com / 358KB	Classic 1980's DOS game. Launch from aircraft carrier and drop bombs, torpedoes, and missles.
`wolfgl.tar.gz`	Wolfenstein 3D / 0.93 / leo@gerf.org / 648KB	Old IDSoftware first-person 3D shooter.
`xasteroids.tar.gz`	Asteroids clone / 0.6.1-1 / http://packages.debian.org/testing/games/xasteroids / 10KB	Clone of the arcade game by Atari.
`xboing.dsl`	XBoing Breakout style game / 2.4-26 / http://www.techrescue.org/xboing / 471KB	Breakout style game.
`xbubble.tar.gz`	A Frozen Bubble clone / 0.5.8 / http://savannah.nongnu.org/projects/xbubble / 1.8MB	XBubble Game extension for DSL. Bubble shooting game for X. Offers one or two player, challenge mode, and demo.
`xgalaga.dsl`	Shooting game / 2.0.34 / http://sourceforge.net/projects/xgalaga / 176KB	Xgalaga space shooting game (stripped from KNOPPIX 3.3).
`xgammon.dsl`	XGammon backgammon game / 0.98 / http://fawn.unibw-hamburg.de/steuer/xgammon/xgammon.html / 858KB	Game extension for DSL. Offers one or two player games, saves, and doubling.
`xmahjongg.tar.gz`	The Xmahjongg tile game for X / 3.6.1 / http://www.lcdf.org/~eddietwo/xmahjongg / 408KB	Game extension for DSL. Traditional tiles and Undo, Clean, and Hint options.

Title	Description / Version / Site / Size	Comments
Games Extensions		
xmame.dsl	The XMame arcade emulator for X / 0.74 / http://x.mame.net / 8.7MB	Emulates classic arcade consoles to play console games from the 1980s and 1990s.
xpat2.dsl	XPat2 card game collection / 1.07 / http:sunsite.unc.edu / 276KB	Card game collection that includes Spyder, Klondike, Canfield, and FreeCell.
xpuyopuyo.dsl	Puzzle game similar to Tetris / GTK - 0.95 / http://chaos2.org/ xpuyopuyo / 653KB	Tetri-type game for X. One- or two-player games, network play, and AI play.
xskat.dsl	XSkat card game / 3.41 / http://www.xskat.de / 223KB	German card game for three players.
zsnes-1.42.dsl	ZSNES /1.42/ http://www.zsnes.com / 497K	Emulator for Super Nintendo games (snes).
GTK2 Extensions		
abiword-gtk2-2.2.7.dsl	AbiWord W/P / 2.2.7 / http://www.abisource.com / 8.2MB	A free word processing program similar to Microsoft Word. It is suitable for typing papers, letters, reports, memos, and so forth.
airsnort-gtk2-0.2.7.dsl	AirSnort Key Retrieval / 0.2.7 / http://airsnort.shmoo.com / 103KB	A wireless LAN (WLAN) tool that recovers encryption keys. AirSnort passively monitors transmissions, computing the encryption key when enough packets have been gathered.
amule-gtk2-2.1.3.dsl	aMule peer-to-peer (P2P) filesharing program, Edonkey emule clone./ 2.1.3 / http://www.amule.org / 8.78MB	A multiplatform ed2k client, fork of the eMule client, using the wxWidgets class library.
cbb-gtk2-0.79.dsl	Check Book Balancer / 1.0 / http://prdownloads.sourceforge.net/cbb / 1.2MB	A checkbook balancing application.
emelfm2-gtk2-1.12.dsl	GTK2 version of Emelfm File Manager / 1.12 / http://emelfm2.org / 419KB	A factored GTK2 version of the popular file manager Emelfm.

Title	Description / Version / Site / Size	Comments
GTK2 Extensions		
firefox-gtk2-1.0.4.tar.gz	Mozilla Firefox 1.0.4 / 1.0.4	Patched version of Mozilla Firefox (requires GTK2).
gaim-gtk2-1.3.1.dsl	Gaim AOL IM / 1.3.1 / gaim.sourceforge.net / 5.6MB	Gaim AOL Instant Messenger (GTK2 version).
gftp-gtk2-2.0.17.dsl	gFTP FTP client / 2.0.17 / http://gftp.seul.org / 873KB	*Use this with the GTK2-0705.DSL only - it is missing GTK2.* gFTP is a free multithreaded FTP client for *NIX-based machines.
gimp-gtk2-2.2.8.dsl	The Gimp 2.2.8 / 2.2.8 / http://www.gimp.org / 13MB	The GNU Image Manipulation Program. It is suitable for photo retouching, image composition, and image authoring.
gkrellm-gtk2-2.2.2.dsl	System monitor + / 2.2.2 http://web.wt.net/~billw/gkrellm/gkrellm.html / 629KB	A single process stack of system monitors that supports applying themes to match its appearance to your window manager, GTK, or any other theme.
gnucash.dsl	GnuCash finance program / 1.8.10 / http://www.gnucash.org / 16MB	Lets you track bank accounts, stocks, income, and expenses. Easy as a checkbook register, it is based on professional accounting principles to ensure balanced books and accurate reports.
gnumeric.dsl	Gnumeric spreadsheet program / 1.5.2 / http://www.gnome.org/projects/gnumeric / 7.9MB	Rough build of the Gnumeric spreadsheet application. It can read files saved with other spreadsheets.
gscore-gtk2-0.79.dsl	Music notation application / 0.79 / http://www.gscore.org / 473KB	Music notation software.
gtk2-0705.dsl	GTK/Perl/Defoma/Pango / 1.1 / www.debian.org / 14MB	The GTK2-0705 version to use with factored applications.
gtkpod-gtk2-0.93.dsl	iPod sync/mgr app / 0.93 http://gtkpod.sourceforge.net / 488KB	A platform independent GUI for Apple's iPod using GTK2. It allows you to upload songs and playlists to your iPod. It supports ID3 tag editing, multiple charsets for ID3 tags, and more.

Title	Description / Version / Site / Size	Comments
GTK2 Extensions		
inkscape-gtk2-0.39.dsl	Inkscape SVG editor / 0.39 / www.inkscape.org / 3.8MB	An open source SVG editor with capabilities similar to Illustrator, CorelDraw, Visio, and so on. Supported SVG features include basic shapes, paths, text, alpha blending, transforms, and more.
mozilla-tbird-gtk2-1.0.2.dsl	Mozilla T-Bird email / 1.0.2 / www.mozilla.org / 11MB	Thunderbird email client includes intelligent spam filters, spell checking, security, customization, and newsgroups support.
nvu-gtk2-0.50.dsl	A WYSIWYG HTML editor / 0.50 / http://www.nvu.com / 11MB	Web authoring system. Nvu (pronounced N-view, for a *new view*). For people with no technical expertise or knowledge of HTML who want to create their own Web pages.
pan-gtk2-0.14.2.dsl	Pan news reader / 0.14.2 / http://pan.rebelbase.com / 2.5MB	Pan newsgroup reader.
pure-ftpd-gtk2-1.0.19.dsl	A secure FTP server / 1.0.19 / http://www.pureftpd.org / 89KB	A free (BSD), secure, production-quality, and standard-conformant FTP server.
qtparted-gtk2-0.4.4.dsl	QTParted partition resizing tool / 0.4.4 / http://qtparted.sourceforge.net / 3.3MB	An attempt to create a Linux-based clone of Partition Magic.
tuxcmd-gtk2-0.5.39.dsl	Tux Commander file manager / 0.5.39 / http://tuxcmd.sourceforge.net/download.php / 347KB	An open source file manager with two panels side by side (or GTK2).
xchat-gtk2-2.4.3.dsl	XChat GTK2 IRC client / 2.4.3 / http://www.xchat.org / 4.0MB	A GTK2 version of XChat. IRC client for UNIX operating systems.
Multimedia Extensions		
audacity-1.2.2.tar.gz	Audio editor / 1.2.2 / http://audacity.sourceforge.net / 5.2MB	A nice editor for digital audio files, with support for multiple channels, mp3, Ogg Vorbis, and LADSPA plug-ins.

Title	Description / Version / Site / Size	Comments
Multimedia Extensions		
`aumix.dsl`	Text-based mixer control / 2.7-18 / http://jpj.net/~trevor/aumix.html / 36KB	Used to change the volume (or other audio features) from the command line.
`blender223.dsl`	3D modeling and animation / 2.23 / http://www.blender3d.com / 2.4MB	Open source 3D modeling and animation program.
`camserv.dsl`	Webcam server for X / 0.5.1 / http://cserv.sourceforge.net / 131KB	Small webcam server works with Video4Linux. Can be used with Firefox.
`cdparanoia-9.8.` `tar.gz`	CDDA extraction tool / 9.8 and 1.0.2 / www.xiph.org/paranoia / 74KB	A CDDA extraction tool or *ripper*. This package includes dekagen, which is an interactive script that works as a GUI frontend. It can also be used from the command line.
`easytag-1.0.dsl`	A GTK+ version of EasyTag / 1.0-1 / http://easytag.sourceforge.net / 780KB	A utility for viewing and editing tags for MP3, MP2, FLAC, Ogg Vorbis, MusePack, and Monkey's audio files.
`etree-scripts_` `3.1-2.dsl`	Various audio scripts for etree users / 3.1-2 / http://etree-scripts. sourceforge.net	Set of audio scripts that include burn-shns, cdfill, flacify, make-toc, makehbx, md5check, parseinfo, shn2mp3, and shn2ogg.
`festival.dsl`	Festival speech synthesizer/server / 1.4.3 / http://www.cstr.ed.ac.uk/ projects/festival / 14MB	Offers a general framework for building speech synthesis systems as well as including examples of various modules.
`flac.dsl`	FLAC lossless audio encoder/decoder / 1.1.0-3 / http://flac.sourceforge.net	FLAC is a lossless audio encoder/decoder. Use it when you want to maintain high-quality audio while gaining some space savings through compression.

TITLE	DESCRIPTION / VERSION / SITE / SIZE	COMMENTS
MULTIMEDIA EXTENSIONS		
freebirth.dsl	Freebirth synth/bass sequencer / 0.3.2 / http://www.bitmechanic. com/projects/freebirth / 2.3MB	Sequencer/synthesizer, pitch shifter, bassline, tracker. Includes desktop icon and MyDSL menu selection.
gnupod.dsl	GNU iPod utilities / 0.94 / http://www.gnu.org/software/ gnupod / 7.5MB	A collection of Perl scripts that allow you to use your iPod under GNU/Linux.
grip-3.0.0.dsl	GRip CD player and ripper / 3.0.0.0-1 / http://www.nostatic. org/grip / 1.3MB	A CD player and CD ripper for the Gnome desktop. It has the ripping capabilities of cdparanoia built in, but can also use external rippers (such as cdda2wav).
gtkam.dsl	GTK+ application for digital cameras / 0.1.2-2 /http://www. gphoto.org/proj/gtkam / 1.9MB	The official GTK2 GUI for libg-photo2. Its purpose is to provide a standard client for libgphoto2 aimed at Gnome users.
gtkgep.dsl	Guitar effects processor / 0.2.3 /http://gtkgep.prv.pl	Turns your computer into a real-time effects processor. For example, you can plug your guitar into the computer and play with cool distortion effects. It has a modular plug-in structure, with standard plug-ins including distortion, over-drive, delay, reverb, equalizers, and a flanger. It works in 16-bit resolution, in mono mode, and with frequencies from 11KHz to 44KHz
gtkguitune.dsl	GUI tuner for X / 0.7 / http://www.geocities.com/harpin_ floh/kguitune_page.html / 418KB	Small GUI tuner for X. Can be used to tune guitars and other instruments.
gtoaster_1.0beta6. dsl	Gnome Toaster / 1.0beta6 / http://gnometoaster.rulez.org / 2.7MB	A CD recording frontend for X/GTK. (A drag-and-drop CD burner for X.)
hydrogen.dsl	Advanced drum machine / 0.9.1 / http://www.hydrogen-music.org / 11MB	An advanced drum machine for GNU/Linux. It allows professional, intuitive, pattern-based drum programming.

Title	Description / Version / Site / Size	Comments
Multimedia Extensions		
`k3b.dsl`	CD burning suite / 0.11.17 / http://www.k3b.org / 47MB	A CD and DVD burning application for Linux systems optimized for KDE. It provides a comfortable user interface to perform most CD/DVD burning tasks like creating an audio CD from a set of audio files or copying a CD.
`lame.dsl`	MP3 encoder/decoder / 3.97 / http://www.mp3dev.org	An MP3 encoder/decoder. Used by various audio and video players to play audio files that are stored in mp3 format.
`monkeys-audio.dsl`	Monkey's lossless audio encoder/decoder / 3.99 / http://sourceforge.net/projects/mac-port	Another lossless audio encoder/decoder. Maintains a high quality of audio output.
`motion.tar.gz`	Motion detection video capture software / 3.1.19 / http://www.larvsen.dk/twiki/bin/view/Motion/WebHome / 144KB	Does timed video captures or motion video captures.
`mp3blaster.tar.gz`	Interactive text-based audio player / 3.2.2 / http://mp3blaster.source-forge.net	A program that plays MP3, Ogg Vorbis, WAV, and SID audio files.
`mp3gain.dsl`	Lossless MP3 normalizer / 1.4.5-1 / http://www.mp3gain.sourceforge.net / 47KB	Command-line MP3 normalizer with statistical analysis. Modifies gain field in MP3 file to preset value without prior conversion to wav and reconversion.
`mpc.tar.gz`	An MPD command-line client / 0.11.2 / http://www.musicpd.org / 21KB	Command-line client for the MPD music playing daemon. Without an MPD server on your network to point it toward, this extension is nearly useless.
`mplayer.dsl`	MPlayer multimedia player / 0.92 / http://www.uhulinux.hu / 4.5MB	MPlayer multimedia player extension for DSL player for audio/video files. Added several skins to package.

Title	Description / Version / Site / Size	Comments
Multimedia Extensions		
`mplayerplug-in.dsl`	MPlayer plug-in for Firefox web browser / 2.66 / http://mplayerplug-in.sourceforge.net / 1.0MB	Gives Mozilla the capability to play media from a website on the Internet without reading the source HTML and getting the URL manually. Media is played embedded in the page or in a separate window depending on how the author of the web page intended the media to be seen.
`mplayer-xfree86.tar.gz`	MPlayer media player / 1.0pre6 http://www.mplayerhq.hu / 3.0MB	This version of MPlayer was specifically compiled for use with the `Xfree86.dsl` extension, which allows full-screen viewing.
`qiv.dsl`	Tiny picture viewer / 1.7 / http://www.klografx.net/qiv / 70.17KB	A very small and fairly fast GDK/Imlib image viewer. It has working incremental zoom and frameless full screen in Fluxbox (unlike xzgv), as well as brightness, contrast, and gamma controls (unlike gqview).
`sdl-libs.dsl`	Simple DirectMedia Layer / 1.2 / http://www.libsdl.org/index.php	A cross-platform multimedia library designed to provide low-level access to audio, keyboard, mouse, joystick, 3D hardware via OpenGL, and 2D video framebuffer.
`shntool.dsl`	Tool for working with the .shn lossless audio format / 2.0.3 / http://shnutils.freeshell.org	A multi-purpose waveform data processing and reporting utility.
`shorten.dsl`	Tool for working with the .shn lossless audio format / 3.60 / http://shnutils.freeshell.org	A fast, low complexity waveform coder (i.e., audio compressor). It can operate in both lossy and lossless modes.
`soundtracker.dsl`	Mod and XM player / 0.6.4 / http://www.soundtracker.org / 1.1MB	Sound module, editor, player for X, supporting .mod, .xm, and .xi extensions.

Title	Description / Version / Site / Size	Comments
Multimedia Extensions		
`sox-12.17.6.tar.gz`	Sound eXchange sound processing / 12.17.6 / http://sox.sourceforge.net / 477KB	The swiss army knife of sound processing programs. SoX is a command-line utility that can convert various formats of computer audio files to other formats.
`stellarium.dsl`	Real-time photorealistic sky generator / 0.6.2-2 / http://www.stellarium.org / 9.13 MB	Renders 3D photorealistic skies in real time. With Stellarium, you really see what you can see with your eyes, binoculars, or a small telescope.
`streamripper.dsl`	Command-line streaming radio ripper / 1.61.4 / http://streamripper.sourceforge.net / 85KB	Shoutcast and Icecast streaming radio ripper. Comes with an updated libmad.
`sweep.dsl`	Audio file editor / 0.8.2 / http://www.metadecks.org/software/sweep/index.html / 725KB	An audio editor and live playback tool that supports many audio formats, including WAV, AIFF, Ogg Vorbis, Speex, and MP3.
`tkdvd.dsl`	TclTk app for burning DVD 5 and 9 / 3.4 / http://regis.damongeot.free.fr/tkdvd / 2.0MB	Frontend for burning DVDs from files or `.isos` Uses the `growisofs` command and an updated `cdrecord` command.
`trommler-3.4.tar.gz`	GTK drum machine / 3.4 / http://muth.org/Robert/Trommler / 781KB	Contains 16-bit 44100KHz mono drum samples. Produces real-time audio output using the `/dev/dsp` device or audio output to file.
`wavbreaker_0.6.1-1-fixed.dsl`	Splits WAV files on sector boundaries (i.e., win32 cdwav) / 0.6.1-1 / http://huli.org/wavbreaker	A program that splits up WAV files where you place track markers and cuts the tracks on sector boundaries. This program looks and runs very similar to the Windows program cdwav.
`xawtvdebs.dsl`	TV and web cam application / 3.72 / http://linux.bytesex.org/xawtv / 1.1MB	TV and web cam app for X (for use with video4linux).
`xdrum.dsl`	Small drum machine for X / 1.7.2 / unknown / 1013KB	Drum machine works on small systems.

Title	Description / Version / Site / Size	Comments
Multimedia Extensions		
`xine.dsl`	Xine multimedia player for Linux / 0.99-1 / http://www.zinehq.de / 5.3MB	Xine multimedia player extension for DSL. Player for audio/video files and streams. Resizes nicely in X.
`xmms-alarm.dsl`	Alarm clock plug-in for XMMS / 0.3.6 / http://packages.debian.org/ stable/utils/xmms-alarm / 24.15KB	XMMS alarm clock includes many features for activating and setting alarms.
`xmms-cdread.dsl`	XMMS plug-in to play CDs digitally / 0.14a-12 177KB	XMMS input plug-in that can read an audio CD as data and play it in real time.
`xmms_chipmusic_ plugins.dsl`	Three XMMS plug-ins for chip-songs / http://modplug-xmms. sourceforge.net / 433KB	Plays computer music made with C64, Nintendo, Amiga/PC. If used together with `chiptunes.dsl`, you get 231 song files.
`xmms_chipmusic_song s.tar.gz`	231 chiptunefiles / 1.0 / http://www.modarchive.org / http://www.2a03.org / 2.9MB	Contains 231 files of music created in real time by video game or computer sound chips (also called chip music).
`xmms.dsl`	XMMS multimedia player for Linux / 1.2.8 / http:// www.xmms.org / 665KB	XMMS multimedia player extension for DSL player for audio/video files and streams.
`xmms-equ.dsl`	Equalizer for XMMS / 0.6 / http://equ.sourceforge.net / 336KB	An EQ for XMMS that works with OGG files.
`xmms-flac.dsl`	XMMS plugin to play flac audio files / 1.1.0-3 / http://pkgsrc.se/audio/xmms-flac	XMMS plug-in to play Flac audio files. Flac is an open source, loss-less audio format. Flac gives you better-quality audio than you get with OGG or MP3 music files, but the Flac files are much larger.
`xmms-musepack-1.1. dsl`	Allows XMMS to play MPC files / 1.1	Plays MPC files with XMMS.
`xmms-shn.dsl`	XMMS plug-in to play SHN audio files / 2.40 / http://shnutils. freeshell.org	XMMS input plug-in to play shorten (`.shn`) files.

TITLE	DESCRIPTION / VERSION / SITE / SIZE	COMMENTS
MULTIMEDIA EXTENSIONS		
`xmms_skins.tar.gz`	XMMS skins collection / 1.0 / http://www.xmms.org / 2.2MB	XMMS skins collection for DSL. With this collection, you have more than 30 different skins you can choose to change the look of the XMMS player.
`xvid4conf-gtk2.dsl`	XviD configuration tool / 1.12 / http://zebra.fh-weingarten.de/ ~transcode/xvid4conf / 45KB	Creates XviD configuration files. The generated configuration file can be read by transcode and XviD, which are included in the `mplayer-1.0pre8cvs.uci` package.
`xwave.dsl`	Wave recorder for X / 0.6 / http://www.funet.fi/~kouhia/waves/ xwave2.tar.gz / 82KB	Wave recorder for small machines.
`yasr.dsl`	Console screen reader voice/synth / 0.6.7 / http:// yasr.sourceforge.net / 7.8MB	A general purpose console screen reader for GNU/Linux and other UNIX-like operating systems.
NET EXTENSIONS		
`airsnort-0.1.1.dsl`	AirSnort Key Retrieval / 0.1.1 / http://airsnort.shmoo.com / 779KB	A wireless LAN (WLAN) tool that recovers encryption keys.
`amsn-0.94.tar.gz`	Alvaro's MSN messenger / 0.94 / http://amsn.sourceforge.net / 1.6MB	A full-featured messenger for one of the most popular chat clients around. This is version 0.94.
`amsn.tar.gz`	Alvaro's MSN messenger / .93 / http://amsn.sourceforge.net / 1.9MB	A full-featured messenger for one of the most popular chat clients. This is version 0.93.
`amsn-tcltk-0. 95-ver3.dsl`	Alvaro's MSN messenger / 0.95 / http://amsn.sourceforge.net / 2.25MB	A full-featured messenger for one of the most popular chat clients around. This is version 0.95.
`apache-2.0.54. tar.gz`	Apache Web Server with PHP / 2.0.54 / http://www.apache.org / 7.3MB	Apache 2.0.54 Web Server, including PHP-4.4.0. Compiled from sources at www.apache.org and www.php.net.

Title	Description / Version / Site / Size	Comments
Net Extensions		
`bittorrent-cli.dsl`	BitTorrent p2p client / 3.4.2 / http://www.bittorrent.com / 2.0MB	A protocol for distributing files over the Internet by swarming the file between all users downloading it.
`bittorrent-gui.dsl`	BitTorrent File Protocol / 3.4.2 / http://bitconjurer.org / 8.0MB	A protocol for distributing files. When multiple downloads of the same file happen concurrently, the downloaders upload to each other, making it possible for the file source to support very large numbers of downloaders.
`cheops.dsl`	Network Swiss army knife / 0.61-2 / http://www.marko.net/cheops / 797KB	A combination of a variety of network tools to provide system adminstrators and users with a simple interface to managing and accessing their networks.
`cicq.dsl`	CenterIcq multiprotocol IM / 4.11.0 / www.centericq.org / 2.9MB	CenterIcq multiprotocol Instant Messenger Console mode.
`ctorrent.tar.gz`	CTorrent's small BitTorrent client in C / 1.3.4 / http://ctorrent.sf.net / 168KB	A very popular file swarming application. This is a tiny client.
`d4x.dsl`	File downloader for X / http://www.krasu.ru/soft/chuchelo / 928KB	X-based tool that you can use to download files from the Internet. It supports FTP and HTTP download.
`eciadsl-usermode-0.11-ver2.dsl`	Globespan chipset-based driver for ADSL USB modems / 0.11 / http://eciadsl.flashtux.org / 200KB	A GNU/Linux driver for Globespan chipset-based ADSL USB modems. The driver works in many countries, for many ADSL USB modems, with different PPP encapsulation layers modes.
`edna.dsl`	An MP3 server / 0.5 / http://edna.sourceforge.net / 1.0MB	Allows you to access your MP3 collection from any networked computer.
`elmo.dsl`	Elmo mail client / 1.3.2 / http://elmo.sourceforge.net / 218KB	A feature-rich, highly configurable, and fast mail client. It's a mail user agent that offers much more than traditional MUAs.

Title	Description / Version / Site / Size	Comments
Net Extensions		
`epic4.dsl`	Enhanced programmable IRCII client / 1.1.2 / http://www.epicsol.org / 1.4MB	An IRC client, very similar to irssi, but not 100% compatible. EPIC offers a staggering number of features.
`firefox-gtk1.2-1.0.4.tar.gz`	Mozilla Firefox GTK1.2 version / 1.0.4 / www.mozilla.org / 7.1MB	Mozilla Firefox compiled against the GTK1.2 toolkit. The GTK2 libraries are *not* required.
`firefox.tar.gz`	Firefox web browser (Mozilla based) / 0.9 / http://www.mozilla.org / 8.1MB	Firefox 0.9 is the award-winning preview of Mozilla's next generation browser. Firefox empowers you to browse faster, more safely, and more efficiently than any other browser.
`gnomeicu.dsl`	Internet communications utility / http://gnomeicu.sourceforge.net / 2.1MB	Internet chat utility.
`inadyn.dsl`	A free dynDNS IP updater / 1.96 / http://inadyn.ina-tech.net	A free DynDNS client. It lets you have a hostname registered on the Internet, although your IP might be changing.
`iscribe.dsl`	i.scribe mail program / 1.87 / www.memecode.com/scribe.php / 1.4MB	A small and fast email client with an intergrated contact database and calendar. It supports all the major Internet mail protocols and uses international standards where possible.
`limewire4.8.0.dsl`	File-sharing app for X / 4.8.0 / http://www.limewire.com / 4.3MB	Offers an advanced peer-to-peer client software package compatible with the Gnutella file-sharing protocol.
`lynx.dsl`	Text web browser / 2.8.4.rel.1 / lynx.isc.org / 1.4MB	Very tiny but powerful web browser similar to `links`.
`micq.dsl`	Console mode ICQ IM / 0.4.11 / www.micq.org / 1.1MB	Instant Messenger ICQ protocol Console mode.

Title	Description / Version / Site / Size	Comments
	NET EXTENSIONS	
nessus.dsl	Nessus client / 1.0.10 / http://www.nessus.org / 303KB	A remote security scanner for Linux. This is the client program for Nessus.
nessusd.dsl	Nessus server daemon program / 1.0.10 / http://www.nessus.org / 314KB	A remote security scanner for Linux. This is the server daemon program for Nessus.
netcat.dsl	Netcat: The TCP/IP Swiss army knife / 1.10 http://netcat.sourceforge.net / 58.5K	A simple UNIX utility that reads and writes data across network connections using TCP or UDP protocol.
nmap.dsl	The nmap port scanner / 3.50 / http://www.insecure.org / 592KB	Nmap (Network Mapper) is a free open source utility for network exploration or security auditing.
no-ip.dsl	Dynamic IP updater / 2.1.1 - D1.0 / http://www.no-ip.com / 50KB	Client for updating your server's IP address with DNS service.
nxclient-1.4.0-75.dsl	A client for NoMachine/Freenx / 1.4.0-75 / http://www.nomachine.com / 3.4MB	NoMachine, and its GPLed version freenx, are remote desktop tools designed for low latency links such as dialup and wi-fi.
nxclient.tar.gz	NoMachine's NX client v1.5.0. / 1.5.0-135 / http://www.nomachine.com	Contains the nxclient from Nomachine.com.
opera852.dsl	Opera 8.52 web browser / 8.52 / http://www.opera.com	Now ad free! Opera is a fast, full-featured web browser that runs very well on older and newer computers. This is the free version that no longer contains a small banner.
ProzGUI.dsl	Download accelerator with GUI / ProzGUI v2.0.4beta3 ProZilla v1.3.6 / http://prozilla.genesys.ro / 620KB	Speeds file downloads for FTP and HTTP protocols.
ProZilla.dsl	CLI download accelerator / ProZilla v1.3.6 / http://prozilla.genesys.ro / 50KB	Small, command-line interface to ProZilla accelerated download tools.

Title	Description / Version / Site / Size	Comments
Net Extensions		
pureadmin-0.2.2-1.dsl	A GUI for pureftpd / 0.2.2-1 / http://purify.sourceforge.net	A GUI tool for pureftpd. You need to be running the pureftpd.dsl for this to work.
rcfirewall.dsl	rc.firewall for iptables / 2.0rc9 / http://projectfiles.com/firewall / 291KB	The Projectfiles.com Linux firewall is a powerful firewall based on netfilter/iptables designed for Linux workstations, routers, and servers.
samba.dsl	Samba/LinNeighborhood file/print services / 0.6.5 / http://www.bnro.de/~schmidjo	An open source/free software suite that provides seamless file and print services to SMB/CIFS clients.
skype-0.93.tar.gz	Skype Internet Telephone Messenger / 0.93.0.3 / http://www.skype.com / 6.7MB	Skype Telephone Messenger version 0.93.0.3.
skype-1.2.0.18.dsl	Skype Internet Telephone Messenger / 1.2.0.18 / http://www.skype.com / 11MB	Skype Telephone Messenger version 1.2.0.18. Works with ALSA.
skype.tar.gz	Skype Internet Telephone Messenger / 0.91 / http://www.skype.com / 6.1MB	An early version (0.91) of the incredible Skype Telephone Messenger.
snownews.dsl	Snownews RSS/RDF newsreader / 1.5.5.1 / http://kiza.kcore.de	A text mode RSS/RDF newsreader. It supports all versions of RSS natively and supports other formats via plug-ins.
sshfs.dsl	Fuse and SSHFS / fuse 2.5.3 / shhfs-fuse 1.6 / http://fuse.sourceforge.net / 612KB	Allows you to mount a remote SSH site so it appears to be a mounted directory. This has many uses. For example, you could easily copy files to and from the remote site.
sunbird_0.2a.tar.gz	Redesigned Mozilla calendar / 0.2a / http://www.mozilla.org/projects/calendar/sunbird.html / 8.3MB	The Sunbird Project is a redesign of the Mozilla Calendar component.

Title	Description / Version / Site / Size	Comments
Net Extensions		
`synaptic.dsl`	GUI for APT (install `dsl-dpkg.dsl` first) / 0.16-6 / http://www.nongnu.org/synaptic / 584KB	GUI frontend for Apt. Allows easy install and update programs.
`tf.tar.gz`	TinyFugue MUD client / 5.0 beta 7 / http://tf.tcp.com/~hawkeye/tf / 357.9KB	A MUD/MUSH client. It has many features such as macros and multiple connections.
`tinyfugue.tar.gz`	TinyFugue MUD client / 4.0 / http://www.tf.tcp.com/~hawkeye/tf / 208KB	A MUD client. It helps you connect to a MUD in a much more convenient manner than Telnet.
`tinyirc.tar.gz`	TinyIRC / 1 1.1-7 / http://linux.maruhn.com/sec/tinyirc.html / 10KB	The TinyIRC IRC client. Because sometimes even Naim (nirc) is too big.
`tor.dsl`	Tor and Privoxy / 0.1.1.20 http://tor.eff.org and http://privoxy.org / 1.1MB	Contains the Tor and Privoxy proxy applications.
`vnc4x-1.4.6.dsl`	Realvnc desktop sharing utility 1.4.6 / http://www.realvnc.com / 2.6MB	A free desktop sharing utility.
`wavemon.dsl`	Wavemon wireless network signal monitor / 0.4.0 / http://www.janmorgenstern.de/projects-software.html / 20KB	A wireless network signal monitor. It shows the signal properties of the network you are connected to.
`wvdial.dsl`	WVDial ISP Dialer / 1.53.0.1 / http://open.nit.ca / 68KB	Install and run the `/usr/bin/wvdialconf` modem dialer.
`xchat.tar.gz`	XChat IRC client / 1.8.9 / http://www.xchat.org / 1.7MB	An IRC client for UNIX operating systems. IRC stands for Internet Relay Chat.
System Extensions		
`aespipe.dsl`	Strong encryption in a pipe / 2.3b / 73KB	An encryption tool that reads from standard input and writes to standard output. It uses the AES (Rijndael) cipher.

Title	Description / Version / Site / Size	Comments
System Extensions		
aliendebs.dsl	.rpm to .deb converter / 2.0.1 / www.debian.org / 13MB	Copies the alien command to convert an RPM to a DEB package.
alsa4dslv2.dsl	ALSA for DSL v2.0 v2.1 only / 1.0.9 / http://www.alsa-project.org / 4.4MB	The Advanced Linux Sound Architecture (ALSA) provides audio and MIDI functionality to the Linux operating system.
alsadebs.dsl	ALSA packages from KNOPPIX 3.4 / 1.0.4 / http://www.alsa-project.org / 1.8MB	Installs the ALSA drivers and supporting packages that were included with KNOPPIX. ALSA is needed to provide sound support for some sound cards and integrated sound systems.
ALSA-Drivers-1.0.11.dsl	ALSA modules for Damn Small Linux / 1.0.11 / http://www.alsa-project.org	Includes all the cards that are currently supported by the ALSA project.
alsa.dsl	ALSA packages from KNOPPIX 3.4 /1.0.4 / http://www.alsa-project.org / 1.8MB	The ALSA drivers and supporting packages that were included with the KNOPPIX 3.4 5-17-2004 release from which DSL was built.
atmelusbdrivers.dsl	Atmel USB WLAN drivers / 0.11 / http://at76c503a.berlios.de / 191KB	Contains the BerliOS at76c503a Linux driver package version 0.11 for Atmel AT76C503/505A-based USB WLAN adaptors.
atmelwlandrivers.dsl	Atmel WLAN drivers / 3.4.1.0 http://atmelwlandriver.sourceforge.net / 830KB	Contains the atmelwlandriver package version 3.4.1.0 for Atmel AT76C5XXx-based wireless devices.
bcm5700.tar.gz	broadcom 57xx Ethernet drivers / 7.3.5 / http://www.broadcom.com/drivers/driver-sla.php?driver=570x-Linux / 117KB	Drivers for the new Ethernet cards. A menu item runs insmod, then the user needs to set up pppoe on his own.
checkinstall.dsl	Package builder / 1.6.0 / http://asic-linux.com.mx/~izto/checkinstall / 50KB	Builds a .deb, .rpm, or slackware package from most install processes.

Title	Description / Version / Site / Size	Comments
System Extensions		
`codecpak.dsl`	Collection of audio/video codecs / 1.0 / apt-get.org / 16MB	Collection of audio/video codecs for players.
`cron30.dsl`	Cron automating tasks / 3.0pl1.72 / 50KB	Cron facility for automating tasks.
`cups.dsl`	Common UNIX Printing System / 1.1.14 / ftp://ftp2.easysw.com/ pub/cups / 5.7MB	Provides a portable printing layer for UNIX-based operating systems. It has been developed by Easy Software Products to promote a standard printing solution for UNIX vendors and users.
`cups-client.dsl`	Client programs for Common UNIX Printing System (CUPS) / http://packages.debian.org/stable/ net/cupsys-bsd / 303KB	Provides various clients— command line and graphical— to the CUPS printing system.
`cvs.dsl`	CVS Version control system / 1.11.21 / http://directory.fsf.org/ cvs.html / 762KB	Controls the release and changes on new files. It also allows owners to maintain a clear audit trail on changes. This program lets you get the latest versions of some programs' source code.
`dfm.dsl`	File and desktop manager / 0.99.9	A file manager for Linux. The idea is to write a file manager like the OS/2 WPS. DFM does nearly the same as ROX, but it is much smaller and should work much faster on older machines. (This extension seems to be broken at the moment. I recommend you not try it until it is fixed.)
`dsl-dpkg.dsl`	The dpkg add-on to enable Apt for DSL / 1.10.10 / http://www. delorie.com/store/ace / 1.5MB	The Package maintenance system for Debian.
`flex-bison-libtool. dsl`	flex bison libtool and m4 / flex 2.5.33 bison 2.1 libtool 1.5.22 m4 1.4.4 / http://www.gnu.org / 1.4MB	The GNU version of lex (the lexical analyzer); bison is the GNU version of yacc. m4 is the GNU macro language; libtool is a collection of tools for dealing with libraries.

TITLE	DESCRIPTION / VERSION / SITE / SIZE	COMMENTS
SYSTEM EXTENSIONS		
`gcc1.dsl`	gcc g++ make for DSL 2.2+ / 3.3.4 / http://packages.debian.org / 19MB	The `gcc`, `g++`, `make`, and `patch` commands are the core utilities needed to compile applications from sources. Includes lots of header files to allow the use of libraries that already exist in DSL in those new programs.
`gcc1-with-libs.dsl`	gcc g++ make for DSL 2.2+/ 3.3.4 / http://packages.debian.org / 19MB	The `gcc`, `g++`, `make`, and `patch` commands are core utilities needed to compile applications from sources. Also included are a variety of header files to allow the use of libraries that already exist in DSL in those new programs.
`gnupg.dsl`	PGP replacement / 1.2.5-3 / www.gnupg.org / 2.6MB	A complete and free replacement for PGP encryption features.
`gnu-utils.dsl`	GNU core utilities - Busybox replacement / 5.2 / http://www.gnu.org/home / 9.0MB	The basic file, shell, and text manipulation utilities of the GNU operating system.
`gps.dsl`	gPS Task Manager / 0.9.4 / http://gps.seul.org / 108KB	Contains graphical process statistics tools.
`grub.dsl`	Grand Unified Bootloader / 0.95 / http://www.gnu.org/software/grub / 239KB	A very powerful bootloader.
`imlib-palette.dsl`	Library to allow 8bpp video / 0 / http://stuff.mit.edu/afs/athena/contrib/graphics/etc/	DSL is missing files that would allow relatively normal operation in 8bpp video mode, which some old hardware may require. Allows things like xtdesk to function in 8bpp.
`iptables.dsl`	IPTables for DSL security / 1.2.6a / 276KB	IPTables firewall facility for DSL.
`ipw2100-k2.4.31.dsl`	Intel PRO/wireless ipw2100 driver for the IPW2100 / 1.1.0 / http://ipw2100.sourceforge.net / 1130KB	Contains Intel PRO ipw2100 wireless drivers.

Title	Description / Version / Site / Size	Comments
System Extensions		
`ipw2200-k2.4.31.dsl`	Intel PRO/wireless ipw2200 driver for the IPW2200BG and IPW2915ABG / 1.0.1 / http://ipw2200.sourceforge.net / 1040KB	Contains Intel PRO ipw2200 wireless drivers.
`john-1.7.0.2.tar.gz`	John the Ripper Brute Force Password Cracker / 1.7.0.2 / http://www.openwall.com/john	Because optimization is important for a brute force cracker, three versions of john are included in this extension: john-linux-x86-any, john-linux-x86-mmx, and john-linux-x86-64.
`lfp_fixed_fonts.tar.gz`	Linux Font Project fixed-width fonts / 0.83 / http://dreamer.nitro.dk/linux/lfp	A collection of various fixed-width bitmap fonts for use in X.
`libc6-dev.dsl`	Standard C dev library / 2.3.2. ds1-22_i386.deb / http://packages.debian.org/stable/libdevel/libc6-dev / 2.4MB	Contains the symlinks, headers, and object files needed to compile and link programs that use the standard C library.
`libc6.dsl`	Standard C libraries / 6_2.3.2.ds1-22_i386.deb / http://packages.debian.org/stable/base/libc6 / 4.6MB	Contains the standard libraries that are used by nearly all programs on the system. This package includes shared versions of the standard C library and the standard math library, as well as many others. Timezone data is also included.
`libmysqlclient10.dsl`	Mysql client library 1.0 library. / 3.23.49-8.13 / http://www.mysql.com / 234KB	For applications using the libmysqlclient10. This library gives access to a Mysql Server 3.0 to 4.1.
`libncurses5-dev.dsl`	ncurses dev / libncurses5-dev_5.4-4_i386.deb / http://packages.debian.org/stable/libdevel/libncurses5-dev / 1005.6KB	This package contains the header files, static libraries, and symbolic links that developers using ncurses need. It also includes the libraries' man pages and other documentation.
`libncurses5.dsl`	Shared libraries needed to run ncurses programs / 5_5.4-4_i386.deb / http://packages.debian.org/stable/base/libncurses5 / 267.7KB	Contains ncurses libraries.

Title	Description / Version / Site / Size	Comments
System Extensions		
libssh-0.11.dsl	The SSH library / 0.11 / http://0xbadc0de.be	This is an SSH library in C. It is compiled for i386, and should work on any computer running DSL or DSL-N.
linux-kernel-headers.dsl	Kernel headers / 2.5.999-test7-bk-17_i386.deb / http://packages.debian.org/stable/devel/linux-kernel-headers / 1.3MB	Provides headers from the Linux kernel, glibc, and other system libraries. These installed headers for GNU uses these headers.
madwifi.dsl	Madwifi (Atheros) wi-fi drivers for DSL v2.x / r1325-20051111 / http://sourceforge.net/projects/madwi-fi / 260KB	Contains Madwifi (Atheros) wi-fi drivers.
ntpdate_4.1.0-8_i386.dsl	Ntpdate / 4.1.0-8 / http://www.eecis.udel.edu/~mills/ntp.html / 217KB	Contains the ntpdate utility for setting date and time via a Network Time Protocol (NTP) server.
nvidia_1.0.8762.dsl	NVidia accelerated drivers / 1.0.8762 / http://www.nvidia.com / 6.0MB	This package contains the NVidia driver for the 2.4.26 kernel build for DSL 3.0.1.
nvidia2.dsl	NVidia accelerated drivers / 1.0.8178 / http://www.nvidia.com / 6.7MB	This package contains the NVidia driver for the 2.4.31 kernel. Use with the XFree86.dsl to improve your graphic performance when using NVidia graphic cards.
nvidia.dsl	NVidia accelerated drivers / 1.0.6111 / http://www.nvidia.com / 4.2MB	Contains the NVidia driver for the 2.4.26 kernel in DSL 0.8.X and later.
opengl-libs.dsl	Libraries for supertux-0.1.3.uci /	Contains OpenGL libraries for SuperTux. (This extension seems to be broken at the moment. I recommend you not try it until it is fixed.)
openssl-0.9.7j-includes.dsl	OpenSSL Library Include header files / 0.9.7j / http://www.openssl.org	Include files necessary for compiling code against SSL libraries.

Title	Description / Version / Site / Size	Comments
System Extensions		
`p7zip-4.42.dsl`	7-zip for Linux / 4.42 / http://www.7-zip.org / 2.5MB	A powerful all-in-one archiver.
`p7zip.dsl`	7-zip for Linux / 4.14 / http://www.7-zip.org / 1.3MB	A powerful all-in-one archiver for all operating systems.
`php-4-monkey-0.9.1.tar.gz`	The PHP general scripting language / 4.3.7 / www.php.net / 1.9MB	PHP is a widely used general purpose scripting language that is especially suited for web development and can be embedded into HTML. This extension adds PHP support to the Monkey Web server.
`php.tar.gz`	The PHP general scripting language / 4.3.7 / www.php.net / 1.9MB	PHP is a widely used general purpose scripting language that is especially suited for web development and can be embedded into HTML.
`ptbr.dsl`	Brazilian language pack / 1.0 / http://dotproject.net / 37KB	Brazilian language pack locale files.
`python2.3.tar.gz`	The Python general scripting language / 2.3.4 / www.python.org / 12MB	An interpreted, interactive, object-oriented, extensible programming language.
`rar.dsl`	RAR utilities for Linux / 3.41 CLI / http://www.rarlabs.com or http://www.win-rar.com / 291KB	A popular set of compression utilities (zip, ace, 7z).
`reiserfsprogs.dsl`	Utilities to create, check, resize, and debug ReiserFS filesystems. / 3.6.17 / http://www.namesys.org	Contains ReiserFS file system command-line tools such as debugreiserfs, fsck.reiserfs, mkfs.reiserfs, mkreiserfs, and others.
`ruby.dsl`	Ruby general scripting language / 1.8 / http://www.ruby-lang.org / 308KB	The interpreted scripting language for quick and easy object-oriented programming. It has many features to process text files and do system management tasks (as in Perl).

Title	Description / Version / Site / Size	Comments
System Extensions		
`sgi-fonts.tar.gz`	SGI fonts / 1.0-709 / www.novell.com/products/ suselinux/downloads/ftp	A few extra fonts from SGI. These fonts were extracted directly from the SGI fonts RPM package for Suse Linux 9.3 i586.
`tcc.dsl`	Tiny C compiler / 0.9.20 / http://fabrice.bellard.free.fr/tcc	Tiny C compiler.
`tcl_lib-blt.tar.gz`	Tcl/Tk widget set / 2.4z / http://blt.sourceforge.net	Contains the Tcl/Tk widget set.
`tcl_lib-bwidget. tar.gz`	Tcl/Tk widget set / 1.7.0 / http://tcllib.sourceforge.net	A high-level TclTk widget set featuring a professional look and feel.
`tcl_lib-img.tar.gz`	Tk image support / 1.3 / http:// sourceforge.net/projects/tkimg	A Tk extension that adds support for many image formats not supported natively (formerly Img).
`tcl_lib-tablelist. tar.gz`	Tcl/Tk widget set / 4.2 / http://www.nemethi.de /	A multicolumn listbox supporting resizable columns, column headings, editable cells, and other features.
`tcl_lib-tix.tar.gz`	Tix Tcl/Tk widget set / 4.2 / http://tix.sourceforge.net /	Adds many new widgets, image types, and other commands that allow you to create compelling GUIs.
`tcl_lib- tkhtml.tar.gz`	Tcl/Tk HTML widget / 3-alpha-11 / http://tkhtml.tcl.tk /	A Tk widget to render HTML documents.
`tcl_lib-tkpng. tar.gz`	PNG support for Tcl/Tk / 0.7 / http://www.muonics.com/FreeStuff/ TkPNG /	Implements support for loading and using PNG images with Tcl/Tk without the dependency of libpng.
`tcl_lib-tktable. tar.gz`	Tcl/Tk table widget / 2.9 / http://tktable.sourceforge.net /	A table/matrix widget extension to TkTcl.
`tcltk8.3.dsl`	Tcl 8.3 + Tk GUI Toolkit / 8.3 / http://www.tcl.tk/software/tcltk / 1.3MB	A simple and programmable syntax and can be either used as a standalone application or embedded in application programs. Tk is a graphical user interface toolkit that makes it possible to create powerful GUIs quickly.

Title	Description / Version / Site / Size	Comments
System Extensions		
`terminus_font.tar.gz`	Terminus bitmap font / 4.16 / http://www.is-vn.bg/hamster/jimmy-en.html	A nice clean font for the Linux console and X11 Window System.
`tkdvd.dsl`	TclTk App for burning DVD 5 and 9 / 3.9 / http://regis.damongeot.free.fr/tkdvd / 2.0MB	Frontend for burning DVDs from files or ISOs.
`torsmo.tar.gz`	Tyopoyta ORvelo System MOnitor / 0.17 / http://torsmo.sourceforge.net / 50KB	A system monitor for Linux that sits in the corner of your desktop. Torsmo renders itself on the root window or to its own transparent window and shows lots of info about your system.
`unionfs.dsl`	A stackable unification file system / 1.0.14 / http://www.fsl.cs.sunysb.edu/project-unionfs.html / 1.5MB	Developed at Stony Brook University since 2004, Unionfs is a stackable unification file system that can merge the contents of several directories (so called branches) while keeping their physical content separate.
`USBview`	USB connection viewer / 196KB	Tool for viewing USB connections.
`vgui.dsl`	Vgui C++ Gui Library + IDE + Tools / D1.2 (Vgui-1.9 Vide-2.0) / http://www.objectcentral.com / 648KB	Contains the Vgui C++ GUI library. Includes a simple app generator Vgen and an icon editor (right-click the desktop icon).
`vgui_light.tar.gz`	Vgui C++ GUI library + IDE + tools / Vgui 1.9 Vide 2.0 (light, no X11 libs) / http://www.objectcentral.com / 1.88MB	Contains the Vgui C++ library, IDE, and other tools needed to create applications for the V graphical user interface framework.
`wine-0.9.22.dsl`	Wine Windows API on X and UNIX / 0.9.22 / http://www.winehq.com	An open source implementation of the Windows API on top of the X Window System and UNIX. You can then run Windows programs from the command prompt by using the `wine` command.

TITLE	DESCRIPTION / VERSION / SITE / SIZE	COMMENTS
SYSTEM EXTENSIONS		
`wipe.dsl`	Secure file-wiping utility / 0.16 / http://abaababa.ouvaton.org/wipe / 20KB	Contains the wipe command for erasing files and directories from various magnetic media.
`X11Basic.tar.gz`	X11-Basic: The BASIC interpreter for UNIX / 1.13-2 / http://x11basic.sourceforge.net / 182KB	Contains the BASIC interpreter.
`xbindkeys.tar.gz`	Key grabber for X / 1.7.2 / http://hocwp.free.fr/xbindkeys/xbindkeys.html / 12KB	Allows you to easily set hotkeys for any command in X windows, using them with any window manager.
`xf86config.dsl`	XFree86 configuration tool / 4.3.0.1 (XFree86 version) / http://www.xfree86.org / 328KB	An interactive text-based program for generating an XF86Config file for use with `XFree86.dsl`.
`XFree86.dsl`	XFree86 / 4.3.0 / http://www.xfree86.org / 9.9MB	Contains the XFree86 X-server, as well as many video and input drivers. This X server provides the foundation for the desktop graphical user interface (GUI) used in Damn Small Linux.
`XFree86-devel.dsl`	Xlib dev / 4.3.0 / ftp://ftp.xfree86.org/pub/XFree86/4.3.0/binaries/Linux-ix86-glibc23/Xprog.tgz / 3.7MB	Xlib development software.
THEMES EXTENSIONS		
`7color-theme.tar.gz`	No. 7 theme for Fluxbox / 1.0 / http://themes.freshmeat.net / 321K	Fluorescent 7 theme.
`7matrix-theme.tar.gz`	7Matrix theme for Fluxbox / 1.0 / http://themes.freshmeat.net / 542KB	7Matrix theme for Fluxbox.
`almostX-theme.tar.gz`	A blue theme for Fluxbox / 0.5 / http://themes.freshmeat.net/~elfelipe / 17KB	Blue theme for Fluxbox.

Title	Description / Version / Site / Size	Comments
THEMES EXTENSIONS		
`altitude-theme.tar.gz`	A serene theme for Fluxbox / 1.0.0 / http://fusionx.deviantart.com / 120KB	Calming theme based on Perfect Blue.
`amber-theme.tar.gz`	Amber theme for Fluxbox / 1.0 / http://themes.freshmeat.net / 416KB	Amber theme for Fluxbox backgrounds are from NV-91 style.
`clapton-theme.tar.gz`	Eric Clapton Fluxbox theme / 1.0.0 / http://themes.freshmeat.net/projects / 60KB	Eric Clapton theme.
`copperwine-theme.tar.gz`	Copperwine theme for Fluxbox / 1.0.0 / http://geekgirl.bz / 101KB	Copperwine theme for Fluxbox. Other worldly background with maroon items for Fluxbox.
`dreaming-theme.tar.gz`	Dreaming Fluxbox theme / 1.0.0 / http://themes.freshmeat.net/projects/dreaming / 46KB	A theme based on the Results theme with a cool eye background.
`dsl_logo-theme.tar.gz`	DSL logo theme for Fluxbox / 1.0 / 19KB	A theme featuring the DSL.
`fusion_dsl_xmms_skin.tar.gz`	Purple Fusion DSL XMMS Skin / 0 / http://www.xmms.org / 98KB	Based on the original Fusion AMP desk theme.
`linvwin-theme.tar.gz`	Bill versus Tux theme / 1.0 / 5.1KB	A theme featuring Tux and Bill Gates.
`liquidglass-theme.tar.gz`	3D dark Fluxbox theme / 1.0.0 / http://themes.freshmeat.net/projects / 263KB	A dark Fluxbox theme.
`naturered-theme.tar.gz`	Nature Red theme for Fluxbox / 1.0 / http://themes.freshmeat.net / 110KB	Nature Red theme for Fluxbox.
`nature-themes.tar.gz`	Nature themes for Fluxbox / 1.0.0 / http://themes.freshmeat.net/projects / 744KB	Various nature settings.
`perfect-blue.tar.gz`	Perfect Blue Fluxbox theme / 1.0.0 / http://themes.freshmeat.net/projects/perfectblue_flux / 126KB	A Fluxbox port of the Window Maker theme called Perfect Blue. It has a really fantastic CG background.

Title	Description / Version / Site / Size	Comments
Themes Extensions		
rogue_theme. tar.gz	Rogue theme for Fluxbox / 1.0 / 5.0KB	Blue and silver theme with blue desktop and Damn Small Penguin!
rox-theme.tar.gz	Rox theme for Fluxbox / 1.0 / http://themes.freshmeat.net / 283KB	Rox theme for Fluxbox.
sid1-theme.tar.gz	Sid combination theme / .01 / http://fluxbox.sourceforge.net/ themes.php / 389KB	Sid combination theme. If you like themes that are purple and kind of creepy, you might like it.
strawberry-theme. tar.gz	Strawberry theme for Fluxbox / 1.0 / http://themes.freshmeat.net / 663KB	Strawberry theme for Fluxbox.
striking-theme. tar.gz	Striking theme for Fluxbox / 1.0.0 /http://geekgirl.bz / 172KB	Theme is based on a sunset and lightning background.
switch.dsl	GTK 1.2 theme switcher / 1.0-2 / http://ftp.us.debian.net / 692KB	Easily switch GTK+ themes that can be run from the console. This has an optional GUI dock and theme preview.
trippy-theme.tar.gz	A theme for Fluxbox / 1.0.0 / 47KB	Theme that is not for the faint hearted!!
tuxvxp-theme.tar.gz	Fluxbox theme featuring Tux / 1.0 / 36KB	Tux-based Fluxbox theme.
wingmaker-theme. tar.gz	Very colorful theme for Fluxbox / 1.0 / http://themes.freshmeat.net / 113KB	Wingmaker theme for Fluxbox.
winspace-theme. tar.gz	WinSpace theme for Fluxbox / 1.0.0 / http://xlife.zuavra.net/ blackbox/ styles / 921KB	WinSpace theme for Fluxbox.
UCI Extensions		
abs-guide.uci	Advanced Bash Scripting Guide / 4.1.02 / http://personal.riverusers. com/~thegrendel	An in-depth exploration of the art of shell scripting. This guide explains *everything* about scripting for the Bash shell and can be used successfully by anyone, from a newbie to a script master.

Title	Description / Version / Site / Size	Comments
UCI Extensions		
`ace.uci`	Ace of Penguins card games collection / 1.1 / http://www.delorie.com/store/ace / 172KB	A set of UNIX/X solitaire games based on the ones available for Windows, but with a number of enhancements.
`amaya.uci`	GTK2 Amaya web page editor / 9.51 - D1.1 / http://www.w3.org/Amaya / 11.2MB	Useful HTML web page editor.
`amsn-0.94.uci`	Alvaro's MSN messenger / 0.94 / http://amsn.sourceforge.net / 1.6MB	A full-featured messenger for one of the most popular chat clients around.
`audacity.uci`	Audio editor / 1.2.4 / http://audacity.sourceforge.net	A nice editor for digital audio files with support for multiple channels, MP3, Ogg Vorbis, and LADSPA plug-ins.
`audacity-1.2.2.uci`	Audio editor / 1.2.2 / http://audacity.sourceforge.net / 5.2MB	A nice editor for digital audio files, with support for multiple channels, MP3, Ogg Vorbis, and LADSPA plug-ins.
`azbook.uci`	AZ Book, an address book / 2.0 / http://petepr.hopto.org/azbook/azbook.html / 79KB	Simple address book with 20 fields per record. Records can be tagged to one of 10 groups. Reads and writes to CSV files.
`azureus-2.3.0.6.uci`	BitTorrent client / 2.3.0.6 / http://azureus.sourceforge.net	File sharing peer to peer P2P client for the BitTorrent protocol. Requires Java and uses the `jre1_5_0.uci`.
`BitTornado.uci`	BitTornado (alternative BitTorrent GUI) / 0.3.17 D4.0 / http://www.bittornado.com / 203KB	Contains the BitTornado alternative BitTorrent GUI.
`blender.uci`	3D graphics package / 2.36 / http://www.blender.org / 4.3MB	This package was made from Blender static, which does not utilize hardware acceleration. As such, it should run on any machine with adequate RAM, but won't show much performance gain through the use of a state-of-the-art graphics processor.

Title	Description / Version / Site / Size	Comments
UCI Extensions		
`briquolo.uci`	3D breakout game / 0.5 / http://briquolo.free.fr / 1.6MB	3D breakout fun, including level editor.
`calc.uci`	Calc precision calculator / 2.11.10.1 / http://www.isthe.com/ chongo/tech/comp/calc/index.html / 4.1MB	Calc C-style arbitrary precision calculator. Calc is also known as Apcalc in the Debian packages.
`conky.uci`	System monitor / 1.3.3 / http://conky.sourceforge.net	Originally based on the Torsmo source code. It provides a way to display system information directly on the desktop.
`consolefonts.uci`	Console fonts + setfont / setfont from kbd-1.08 /	Fonts for your Linux console (tty) and the setfont program with which to apply your font to the console.
`coreutils.uci`	File shell and text manipulation utilities / 5.92 / http://www.gnu. org/software/coreutils	The GNU core utilities. Although many of these applications are already available in DSL with Busybox, the functionality of those tools is somewhat limited in favor of a much smaller file size.
`e16.uci`	Enlightenment window manager / 0.16.8.4 / http:// www.enlightenment.org / 3.7MB	Enlightenment window manager that can be used to replace Fluxbox or jwm in DSL.
`enigma.uci`	Puzzle game / 0.92 / http://www.nongnu.org/enigma	A tribute to and a reimplementation of one of the most original and intriguing computer games of the 1990s: Oxyd.
`evilwm.uci`	Minimalist window manager for X / 0.99.25 / http://www.6809. org.uk/evilwm	A minimalist window manager based on aewm, extended to feature keyboard controls and otherwise altered to be more friendly.
`findutils.uci`	GNU find locate xargs / 4.2.25 / http://www.gnu.org/software/ findutils	The Busybox versions of find and xargs are included in DSL, so you must use a full path or modify your PATH variable in order to use these GNU versions.

Title	Description / Version / Site / Size	Comments
UCI Extensions		
`firefox-1.5.0.6.uci`	Mozilla Firefox web browser / 1.5.0.6 / http://www.mozilla.com	Mozilla Firefox web browser binaries from mozilla.com, repackaged for DSL.
`firefox-1.5.uci`	Mozilla Firefox web browser / 1.5 / http://www.mozilla.com	Firefox web browser that includes the Flash plug-in and a symbolic link to Java if you use the `jre1_5_0.uci`.
`firefox-2.0-gtk1.uci`	Firefox web browser for DSL / 2.0 / http://www.mozilla.com	A version of Firefox compiled from Mozilla source code with various options. Includes different desktop logo and branding.
`firefox-gtk1.2-1.0.6.uci`	Mozilla Firefox GTK1.2 version / 1.0.6 / www.mozilla.org / 7.38MB	Mozilla Firefox compiled against the GTK1.2 toolkit.
`fltk.uci`	Fast Light Toolkit / 1.1.7 / http://www.fltk.org	Provides the headers needed for building FLTK applications, the Fluid interface designer, and John Murga's tool for converting FLTK `*.cxx` files to murgaLua scripts.
`fluxbox_0.9.14.uci`	Window manager for X / 0.9.14 / http://www.fluxbox.org	Contains a UCI version of the fluxbox window manager (0.9.14). Fluxbox is the default window manager used with DSL.
`frobtads.uci`	frob player for TADS ineractive fiction files / 0.6 / http://www.tads.org/frobtads.htm / 3MB	Plays TADS 2 and 3 files. It also includes t3make and tadsc for compiling your own text adventures.
`glinks.uci`	Links web browser (modified) / 030709 / http://xray.sai.msu.ru/~karpov/links-hacked / 2.3MB	Small quick graphical web browser. Originally part of DSL base.
`gqview-1.2.2.uci`	GQview image viewer / 1.2.2 / http://gqview.sourceforge.net / 275KB	An image viewer for UNIX operating systems (developed on Linux). Its key features include single-click file viewing, external editor support, thumbnail preview, and zoom features.

Title	Description / Version / Site / Size	Comments
UCI Extensions		
guile.uci	GUILE Scheme interpreter/ 1.6.7 / http://www.gnu.org/software/guile/guile.html / 2.5MB	GNU Extensibility Library (GUILE), an implementation of the Scheme programming language.
helixplayer.uci	Open source media player / 1.0.6.778 (gold) / https://player.helixcommunity.org	Multimedia Helixplayer application.
hydra-5.2.uci	THC-hydra parallelized login hacker / 5.2 / http://www.thc.org/thc-hydra	THC-hydra is a parallelized login cracker that can be used to test the security of passwords for different login services (FTP, telnet, SMB, POP3, HTTP, and others).
icewm.uci	Cool window manager / 1.2.26 / http://www.icewm.org	Provides a small, fast, and familiar window manager for the X11 Window System.
imagemagick.uci	Image toolbox / 6.2.4-1 / http://www.imagemagick.org / 1.9MB	A collection of useful tools with which to create and edit images of many formats.
inform.uci	Inform compiler xfrotz player / 6.30 / http://www.inform-fiction.org/inform6.html / 3MB	The inform compiler for compiling interactive text adventure games as well as the xfrotz package for playing the resulting Z code files.
irssi.uci	Textmode IRC client / 0.8.10a / http://irssi.org	This textmode IRC client was compiled without Perl support.
jhead.uci	Digicam JPEG Exif header manipulation tool / v2.6 / http://www.sentex.net/~mwandel/jhead / 50KB	Used to display and manipulate data contained in the Exif header of JPEG images from digital cameras. By default, jhead displays useful camera settings from the file in a user friendly way.
jre1_5_0.uci	The Java runtime plug-in for Firefox / 1.5.0 / java.sun.com / 30MB	The Java runtime plug-in for Firefox repackaged for DSL.
kismet-2006-04-R1.uci	802.11 layer 2 wireless traffic monitor / 2006-04-R1 / http://www.kismetwireless.net	Kismet is a wireless LAN detector, sniffer, and IDS.

TITLE	DESCRIPTION / VERSION / SITE / SIZE	COMMENTS
UCI EXTENSIONS		
`lighttpd.uci`	Lightweight web server / 1.4.12 / http://www.lighttpd.net	Small, secure, fast, compliant, and flexible web server that has been optimized for high-performance environments.
`madwifi-ng-2.4.26.uci`	Madwifi-NG (Atheros) wi-fi drivers for Damn Small Linux running Kernel 2.4.26 / r1453-20060220 / http://www.madwifi.org	Madwifi Atheros drivers.
`man.uci`	Linux manual pager / 1.6 / http://primates.ximian.com/ ~flucifredi/man / 5.1MB	Includes the man application, plus the standard collection of Linux man pages and man pages for many of the programs available in DSL 1.2.
`mc.uci`	GNU Midnight Commander / 4.6.1 / http://www.ibiblio.org/mc	The "full" version of the Midnight Commander. It includes features such as subshell support, virtual file systems, and built-in editor, not available in DSL.
`mozilla-1.7.uci`	Mozilla suite / 1.7 / http://www.mozilla.com	The complete Mozilla suite. Includes the flash plug-in and a symbolic link to the Java plug-in if you use the `jre1_5_0.uci`.
`mplayer-1.0pre8cvs.uci`	MPlayer-CVS mencoder and related tools / MPlayer + mencoder dev-CVS-060515 / http://www.mplayerhq.hu / 30MB	Recent CVS build of MPlayer with mencoder, the current stable transcode suite, ffmpeg (CVS), vobcopy, lame, oggvorbis, ogm-tools, and stuff. A powerful, up-to-date media toolkit.
`mrxvt.uci`	Tabbed VT102 terminal emulator / 0.5.2 / http://materm.sourceforge.net	Based on rxvt version 2.7.11 CVS and features most of the functionality of rxvt, with a few major enhancements (namely multiple tabs and transparency).
`naim_TOC2.uci`	nAIM nIRC nICQ / 0.11.7.4-jw4 / http://joshuawise.com/code/naim / 169KB	A console client for AOL Instant Messenger (AIM), AOL I Seek You (ICQ), Internet Relay Chat (IRC), and the lily CMC.

Title	Description / Version / Site / Size	Comments
UCI Extensions		
`nedit-5.5.uci`	Nirvana Editor / 5.5 / http://www.nedit.org / 905KB	A multi-purpose text editor for the X Window System, which combines a standard, easy-to-use, graphical user interface with the thorough functionality and stability required by users who edit text eight hours a day.
`nmap-4.03.uci`	nmap network mapper / 4.03 / http://www.insecure.org/nmap	Network exploration tool and security/port scanner.
`nvu-1.0.uci`	GTK2- WYSIWYG HTML editor GTK2- / 1.0 - D1.1 / http://www.nvu.com / 9.2MB	Very comprehensive and easy-to-use HTML editor.
`NX.uci`	NoMachine's NX Client v2.0 / 2.0.0-98 / http://www.nomachine.com	An up-to-date version of the nxclient command. It was made from the statically compiled version available on nomachine's site, specifically, the `.tar` version that does not require the `.xft` extensions.
`openoffice.org2.0.uci`	Openoffice Office Suite / 2.0.4 / http://www.openoffice.org	Both a multiplatform and multilingual office suite and an open source project. Compatible with all other major office suites, the product is free to download, use, and distribute.
`openoffice.uci`	Openoffice Office Suite / 1.1 / http://www.openoffice.org / 66MB	The compressed `.iso` + userfiles version of OpenOffice.org office suite.
`openoffice-2.0.uci`	Openoffice Office Suite / 2.0 beta / http://www.openoffice.org / 110MB	Both a multiplatform and multilingual office suite and an open source project. Compatible with all other major office suites, the product is free to download, use, and distribute.
`opera-8.01.uci`	Opera 8.01 web browser / 8.01 / http://www.opera.com / 6.1MB	A fast, full-featured web browser that runs very well on older and newer computers. This is the free version that contains a small banner.

Title	Description / Version / Site / Size	Comments
UCI Extensions		
opera850.uci	Opera 8.50 web browser / 8.50 / http://www.opera.com	A fast, full-featured web browser that runs very well on older and newer computers. This is the free version that no longer contains a small banner.
opera9.uci	Opera 9.0 web browser / 9.0 Build 334 / http://www.opera.com / 7.3MB	The newest version of the one of the best browsers around. This package only includes English. May require `opera9_prefs.dsl`.
outguess.uci	Outguess universal steganographic tool / 0.2 / http://www.outguess.org/download.php / 123KB	A universal steganographic tool that allows the insertion of hidden information into the redundant bits of data sources.
owfs.uci	One Wire filesystem / 2.2 / http://owfs.sourceforge.net / 181KB	Uses Dallas one-wire sensors from the command line.
procps.uci	Tools to view and control processes / 3.2.6 / http://procps.sourceforge.net	Although these applications are already included in DSL as part of Busybox, the functionality of those tools is somewhat limited in favor of a much smaller file size.
python.uci	The Python general scripting language / 2.3.4 / www.python.org / 12MB	An interpreted, interactive, object-oriented, extensible programming language.
python2.3-gtk2.uci	Archive containing modules that allow you to use GTK+ in Python programs / 2.3-gtk2	Package containing the bindings for the new version 2.0 of that toolkit.
qcad.uci	QCad Linux Autocad app / 2.0.3.1 / http://www.ribbonsoft.com/qcad.html / 41MB	QCad is an application for computer aided drafting in two dimensions. With QCad, you can create technical drawings such as plans for buildings, interiors, or mechanical parts.

Title	Description / Version / Site / Size	Comments
UCI Extensions		
realplayer.uci	Multimedia player from Real Networks / 10.0.6.776 (gold) / https://helixcommunity.org	Version of Real Player from Real Networks.
rexima.uci	Curses-based (command-line) mixer / 1.4 / http://rus.members.beeb.net/rexima.html	A curses-based interactive mixer that can also be used from the command line or script. It runs on any terminal with a screen size of 80×24 or greater. It's intended to be a simple, general, usable mixer without all the chrome usually present in other mixers.
scite.uci	SciTE, a programmer's text editor / 1.54 / http://www.scintilla.org / 481.54KB	The SciTE text editor for programmers.
scummvm-0.8.0.uci	Virtual machine for your old click-and-point adventures / 0.8.0 / http://www.scummvm.org	Great tool to enjoy the great LucasArts games under DSL!
seamonkey.uci	New Mozilla suite project /1.0 / http://www.mozilla.com	Mozilla web browser suite, recently renamed to SeaMonkey.
seamonkey-1.0.3-gtk1.uci	GTK1 build of the SeaMonkey Project / 1.0.3 / http://www.mozilla.org/projects/seamonkey	A community effort to deliver production-quality releases of code derived from the application formerly known as Mozilla Application Suite.
simutrans.uci	Economic and transport simulation game / 0.84.16.4 / http://www.simutrans.de / 1.9MB	A SimCity/transport tychoon type of simulation game, Simutrans is developed by Hansjorg Malthaner as a noncommercial project.
snes9x.uci	SNES emulator / 1.43 / http://www.my_program.org	The other great SNES emulator. Because it has no GUI like zsnes, it includes a simple user interface written in flua.
snownews.uci	A textmode RSS reader / 1.5.7 / http://kiza.kcore.de/software/snownews	A text mode RSS/RDF newsreader. It supports all versions of RSS natively and supports other formats via plug-ins.

TITLE	DESCRIPTION / VERSION / SITE / SIZE	COMMENTS
UCI EXTENSIONS		
sox.uci	Sound eXchange sound processing / 12.18.2 / http://sox.sourceforge.net	The Swiss army knife of sound processing programs. SoX is a command-line utility that can convert various audio files into other audio formats.
spice.uci	Berkeley SPICE3 general-purpose circuit simulator / 3F5 / http://bwrc.eecs.berkeley.edu/ Classes/IcBook/SPICE / 738KB	SPICE 3F5, compiled from source with X11 disabled.
steghide.uci	Steganography program / 0.5.1 / http://steghide.sourceforge.net / 888KB	A cli steganography program that can hide data in many kinds of image and audio files. Color-respective sample-frequencies aren't changed, making the embedding resistant to statistical attacks.
sunbird.uci	Redesigned Mozilla calendar / 0.2a / http://www.mozilla.org/ projects/calendar/sunbird.html / 8.6MB	A redesign of the Mozilla calendar component.
supertux-0.1.3.uci	SuperTux is a classic 2D jump and run sidescroller game / 0.1.3 / http://supertux.berlios.de	A classic 2D jump and run sidescroller game in a style similar to the original SuperMario games.
tcltk-8.4.uci	Tcl/Tk interpreter / 8.4.12 / http://www.tcl.tk/software/tcltk/ 8.4.html	Tcl (Tool Command Language) has a simple and programmable syntax and can be either used as a stand-alone application or embedded in application programs. Tk is a graphical user interface toolkit that makes it possible to create powerful GUIs quickly
TclTutor.uci	Tcl tutorial program / 2.0 beta4 / http://www.msen.com/~clif/ TclTutor.html / 130KB	Gives easy-to-follow instructions on using the Tcl scripting language, including examples.
thunderbird-1.5. uci	Mozilla Thunderbird email client / 1.5 / http://www.mozilla.com	Thunderbird email client.

Title	Description / Version / Site / Size	Comments
UCI Extensions		
`tuxrip.uci`	DVD ripper / v0.99beta6 / http://tuxrip.free.fr / 432KB	Used to rip DVD content. (You should only use this software to make copies of unencrypted DVD content that you have the proper authority to copy under applicable law.)
`tuxtype.uci`	The Tuxtype typing game / 1.5.3 / http://tuxtype.sourceforge.net / 4.5MB	Tuxtype game extension for DSL.
`vim.uci`	Vi IMproved full version / 6.4 / http://www.vim.org	Includes help files, scripts, and other features missing from the DSL version, including syntax highlighting and folding, as well as a GUI version that uses GTK.
`vtcl.uci`	Visual Tcl / 1.6.0 / http://vtcl.sourceforge.net	An application development environment using Tcl/Tk. It is written entirely in Tcl/Tk and generates pure Tcl/Tk code.
`wesnoth-0.9.7.uci`	The Battle for Wesnoth / 0.9.7 / http://www.wesnoth.org / 31MB	A turn-based strategy game with a fantasy theme.
`wine-20050524.uci`	An open source implementation of the Windows API for X and UNIX / 20050524 / http://www.winehq.com	Runs Windows applications in DSL.
`wmdrawer.uci`	An icon manager dock app / 0.10.4.1 / http://people.easter-eggs.org/~valos/wmdrawer 362KB.	A dock application (dockapp) that provides a drawer (retractable button bar) to launch applications. Select WMDrawer from the DSL menu to add the drawer to other docked apps on the desktop.
`wmii.uci`	Window Manager Improved 2 / wmii-3.1 / http://wmii.suckless.org	A dynamic window manager for X11. It supports classic and tiled window management with extended keyboard, mouse, and file system-based remote control.

Title	Description / Version / Site / Size	Comments
UCI Extensions		
`xbubble.uci`	A frozen bubble clone / 0.5.8 / http://savannah.nongnu.org/ projects/xbubble / 1.8MB	XBubble game extension for DSL.
`xchat.uci`	XChat IRC client / 1.8.9 / http://www.xchat.org / 1.7MB	An IRC client for UNIX operating systems. IRC stands for Internet Relay Chat.
`xjig.uci`	Xjig, the jigsaw puzzle / 2.4 / ftp.x.org/contrib/games/xjig-2.4.tgz	A puzzle that tries to replicate a jigsaw puzzle on the screen as close as possible. Gif images can be loaded and sliced into pieces. As with every jigsaw puzzle, the goal is to get the parts together again.
`xmahjongg.uci`	The Xmahjongg tile game for X / 3.6.1 / http://www.lcdf.org/ ~eddietwo/xmahjongg / 408KB	Xmahjongg tile matching game extension for DSL.
`xnview.uci`	Xnview multiformat graphics viewer/converter / 1.70 / http://www.xnview.com / 2.44MB	Multiformat graphics viewer and converter.
`xpdf-3.01p12.uci`	Xpdf, a PDF viewer for X / 3.01p12 / http://www.foolabs. com/xpdf	Linux binary of the xpdf PDF file reader, offered on the original website.
WM_Apps Extensions		
`evilwm.tar.gz`	Minimalist window manager / 0.99.17 / http://evilwm. sourceforge.net / 13KB	A tiny window manager for X. There is no menu, toolbar, or icons, just the root window and the keyboard. This makes it extremely slim and fast.
`fluxbox-0.9.11. tar.gz`	Window manager for X / 0.9.11 / http://fluxbox.sourceforge.net / 478KB	Fluxbox window manager (0.9.11).

Title	Description / Version / Site / Size	Comments
WM_Apps Extensions		
`ion2.dsl`	Ion2, an X Window manager / 2-20040407 / http://iki.fi/tuomov/ion / 344KB	A lightweight, keyboard-driven window manager that features window splitting and tabbing, as well as mouse support. Ion 2 requires Lua for its configs, which is already available in DSL.
`pclock.tar.gz`	Clock dock app / 0.13.1 / http://web.cs.mun.ca/~gstarkes/wmaker/dockapps/time.html#pclock / 57KB	A nice analog clock. It allows different XPMs as backgrounds as well as different configurations of hands and such to match with the XPM.
`ratpoison-1.3.0.dsl`	A mouseless window manager / 1.3.0 / http://www.nongnu.org/ratpoison / 281KB	A simple window manager with no fat library dependencies, no fancy graphics, no window decorations, and no rodent dependence. It is largely modeled after GNU Screen, which has done wonders in the virtual terminal market.
`screen.dsl`	Terminal multiplexor / 0.1 / http://www.gnu.org/software/screen / 354KB	A full-screen window manager that multiplexes a physical terminal between several processes, typically interactive shells.
`twm.tar.gz`	Tab/Tom's window manager / 4.3.0.dfsg.1-12.0.1 // 73.5KB	An extremely flexible, lightweight window manager.
`whitebox.dsl`	Fluxbox config editor / 5.0 PATCHED / http://whitebox.sourceforge.net / 243KB	Easy-to-use Fluxbox/Blackbox configuration editor. Edit user menus, add desktop wallpaper images, create your own themes, or modify existing ones.
`wmacpi_1.99r7.dsl`	ACPI battery monitor dock app / 1.99r7-1 / http://packages.debian.org/unstable/x11/wmacpi / 18KB	Bundled with libdockapp1 (1:0.4.0-8).
`wmapm.tar.gz`	APM battery monitor dock app / 3.1 / http://www.debian.org / 10KB	Monitors battery levels from dock.

Title	Description / Version / Site / Size	Comments
WM_Apps Extensions		
wmbubble.dsl	WMBubble dock app / 1.46-1 / http://packages.debian.org/unstable/ x11/wmbubble.html / 18KB	A system monitor with a duck and several bubbles depending on the load.
wmcalc.dsl	Dockable calculator app / 0.3-2 / http://members.access1.net/ ehflora / 12KB	Dockable calculator application.
wmclock.tar.gz	WMClock dock app / 1.0.12.2-2.1 / http://www.bensinclair.com/ dockapp / 8.1KB	Attractive, useful, dockable desktop clock.
wmcube.dsl	WM3D cube dock app / 0.98-6 / http://boombox.campus.luth.se / 23KB	A system monitor that shows different 3D objects and the speed depending on the workload.
wmdiskmon.tar.gz	WMDiskMon dock app / 0.0.1 / http://tnemeth.free.fr/projets/ dockapps.html / 11KB	This dock app monitors your disk usage. The program uses the POSIX command df -P. It is in the coreutils package.
wmdrawer.tar.gz	An icon manager dock app / 0.10.4.1 / http://people. easter-eggs.org/~valos/wmdrawer / 357KB	A dock application (dockapp) that provides a drawer (retractable button bar) to launch applications.
wmfrog.dsl	WMFrog weather dock app / 0.1.6-2 /http://www.colar.net/wmapps / 54KB	Dockable weather forecast application.
wmmatrix.dsl	A Matrix-style dock app / 0.2 / 155KB	An early beta version of a CPU monitor built around the display from the movie *The Matrix*.
wmmemmon.tar.gz	WMMemMon dock app / 1.0.1 / http://www.sh.rim.or.jp/~ssato/ dockapp/index.shtml / 30KB	A program to monitor memory/swap usages.
wmmoonclock.dsl	WMMoonclock dock app / 1.27-4 / 249KB	Displays moon phases from desktop dock. An essential download for the werewolf using Linux.

Title	Description / Version / Site / Size	Comments
WM_Apps Extensions		
`wmnetload.dsl`	WMNetLoad dock app / 1.3 /http://freshmeat.net/projects/ wmnetload / 16KB	A simple network interface monitoring tool.
`wmpinboard.dsl`	WMPinboard dock app / 1.0-10 / http://www.tu-ilmenau.de/ ~gomar/stuff/wmpinboard / 33KB	Dockable post-it notes for DSL.
`wmppp.dsl`	WMppp dial-up status dock app / 1.3.0-7 / 9.8KB	Dockable dial-up status application (works with wvdial).
`wmpuzzle.dsl`	WMPuzzle puzzle dock app / 0.1.1-2 / http://packages.debian. org/stable/games/wmpuzzle / 50KB	A cool dockable puzzle game.
`wmrack.tar.gz`	WMRack audio CD/mixer dock app / 1.2.1 / http://wmrack. sourceforge.net / 21KB	A combination sound mixer and CD player, designed for use with the WindowMaker dock.
`wmtictactoe.tar.gz`	WMtictactoe dock app game / 1.1-3 / http://atlas.ucpel.tche.br/ ~acamargo / 11KB	Dockable game for playing tic-tac-toe on the desktop.
`wmwave.tar.gz`	Wireless link quality monitor / 0.4 / http://www.schuermann.org/ ~dockapps / 8.8KB	Displays statistical information about a current wireless Ethernet connection.
`wmweather+2.9.dsl`	WmWeather + dock app / 2.9 / www.sourceforge.net/projects/ wmweatherplus / 769KB	Downloads the National Weather Serivce METAR bulletins; AVN, ETA, and MRF forecasts; and any weather map for display in a WindowMaker dock app. It is like wmweather with a smaller font, forecasts, a weather map, and a sky condition display.
`wmwifi.dsl`	WMWifi wireless monitor / 0.4 / http://wmwifi.digitalssg.net / 9.9KB	Displays signal strength and other important information for wireless users.
`wmwifi.tar.gz`	Wireless monitor dock app / 0.5 / http://wmwifi.digitalssg.net / 11KB	Displays the signal strength, link level, noise level, and bitrate of current access point, with the access point's name.

Title	Description / Version / Site / Size	Comments
UNC Extensions		
abiword.unc	AbiWord word processor / 2.0.1 / http://www.abisource.com / 8.4MB	A free word processing program similar to Microsoft Word. It is suitable for typing papers, letters, reports, and so forth.
abiword-gtk2-2.2.7.unc	AbiWord word processor / 2.2.7 / http://www.abisource.com / 8.2MB	A free word processing program similar to Microsoft Word. It is suitable for typing papers, letters, reports, memos, and so forth.
acpid.unc	Acpid daemon and event scripts / 1.0.4 / http://acpid.sourceforge.net / 15KB	Detects ACPI events on a compliant machine, but does not work with APM. AC, battery, button, and processor modules must be loaded.
alsa.unc	ALSA packages from KNOPPIX 3.4 / 1.0.4 / http://www.alsa-project.org / 1.8MB	Installs the ALSA drivers and supporting packages that were included with the KNOPPIX 3.4 5-17-2004 release (which DSL is built upon). ALSA is needed to provide sound support for some sound cards and integrated sound systems.
bluez-utils.unc	Bluetooth utilities and modules from KNOPPIX 3.4 / 1.1 / http://www.bluez.org / 13,576KB	Required to use a Bluetooth device under DSL.
cups.unc	Common UNIX Printing System (CUPS) / 1.1.14 / ftp://ftp2.easysw.com/pub/cups / 5.7MB	Provides a portable printing layer for UNIX-based operating systems. It has been developed by Easy Software Products to promote a standard printing solution for all UNIX vendors and users. It provides System V and Berkeley command-line interfaces.
dsl-dpkg.unc	The dpkg add-on to enable Apt for DSL / 1.10.10 / http://www.delorie.com/store/ace / 1.5MB	The dpkg package maintenance system for Debian.

Title	Description / Version / Site / Size	Comments
UNC Extensions		
`emacs-21.4.unc`	Emacs text editor and much more / 21.4 / http://www.gnu.org/ software/emacs / 16.2MB	The emacs text editor package, built from source obtained from gnu.org.
`feh.unc`	Feh image viewer / 1.1.1 / http://linuxbrit.co.uk/feh	Powerful image viewer that can display lists of files as slide shows and montages. Many display options are available.
`festival.unc`	Festival speech synthesizer/ server / 1.4.3 / http://www.cstr.ed. ac.uk/projects/festival / 14MB	Offers a general framework for building speech synthesis systems as well as including examples of various modules. As a whole, it offers full text to speech through a number of APIs.
`gaim-1.5.0.unc`	Text messaging application / 1.5.0 / http://gaim.sourceforge.net / 2.2MB	An IM client that is capable of doing text chat using MSN, Yahoo, AIM/IRQ, Jabber, and a number of others.
`gcc1-with-libs.unc`	gcc g++ make for DSL / 3.3.4 / http://packages.debian.org / 20MB	gcc, g++, make, and patch are the core utilities you need to compile applications from sources for DSL. Also included are a variety of header files to allow the use of libraries that already exist in DSL in those new programs.
`gcc-2.95.unc`	gcc-2.95 corresponding to kernel 2.4.26 / 2.95.4 / http://www.gnu. org/software / 1.76MB	gcc-2.95 is required to recompile the Linux version 2.4.26 kernel sources. gcc1-with-libs and gnu-utils are also required.
`gnumeric.unc`	Gnumeric spreadsheet program / 1.5.2 / http://www.gnome.org/ projects/gnumeric / 7.9MB	A spreadsheet application that can read files saved with other spreadsheets.
`gnupg.unc`	PGP replacement / 1.2.5-3 / www.gnupg.org / 2.6MB	A complete and free replacement for PGP. Because it does not use the patented IDEA algorithm, it can be used without any restrictions.

Title	Description / Version / Site / Size	Comments
UNC Extensions		
gnu-utils.unc	GNU Core Utilities, Busybox Replacement / 5.2 / http://www.gnu.org/home / 9.0MB	The basic file, shell, and text manipulation utilities of the GNU operating system.
gtk+-2.10.9.unc	A group of base libs used for GTK2 apps / 2.10.9 // 15.7MB	Contains GTK2 base libraries.
gtk2-0705.unc	GTK/Perl/Defoma/Pango / 1.1 / www.debian.org	Provides Damn Small Linux with the needed libraries to run GTK applications.
gtk-theme-switch.unc	GTK1.2 theme switcher / 1.0-2 / http://www.muhri.net/ nav.php3?node=gts / 1.05MB	An easy way to spruce up the appearance of GTK1.2 applications and includes several themes to choose from.
irda-utils.unc	IRDA utilites / 1.0 / http://irda.sourceforge.net / 71KB	Infrared device utilities. The irda-utils and irda modules (included in DSL) are required to use an IRDA device under DSL.
konsole.unc	Konsole terminal program / 3.5.5 / http://konsole.kde.org / 12.0MB	Terminal program included with KDE desktop environments.
mplayer.unc	MPlayer multimedia player / 0.92 / http://www.uhulinux.hu / 4.5MB	MPlayer multimedia player extension for audio/video files. Added several skins to package.
mplayerplug-in.unc	Mplayer plug-in Firefox / 2.66 / http://mplayerplug-in. sourceforge.net / 1.0MB	Gives Firefox the capability to play media from a website on the Internet without reading the source HTML and getting the URL manually.
nicotine-python-gtk2-1.0.8.unc	SoulSeek clone for P2P file sharing / 1.0.8 / http://nicotine. thegraveyard.org	A SoulSeek client written in Python, based on the PySoulSeek project. It features, among other things, a completely rewritten graphical user interface that uses the PyGTK-2 toolkit.
opera910.unc	Opera 9.10 web browser / 9.10 / http://www.opera.com / 7.3MB	The newest version of the one of the best browsers around.

Title	Description / Version / Site / Size	Comments
UNC Extensions		
python2.5.unc	Python 2.5 for DSL 3.1+ / 2.5 / http://www.python.org / 13MB	An interpreted, interactive, object-oriented, extensible programming language.
rcfirewall.unc	rc.firewall for iptables / 2.0rc9 / http://projectfiles.com/firewall / 291KB	The Projectfiles.com Linux firewall is a powerful firewall based on netfilter/iptables designed for Linux workstations, routers, and servers.
samba.unc	Samba/LinNeighborhood File / Print Services / 0.6.5 / http://www.bnro.de/~schmidjo	An open source/free software suite that provides seamless file and print services to SMB/CIFS clients.
scsi.unc	SCSI modules from KNOPPIX 3.4 / 3.4 / http://www.knoppix.org / 9.0MB	The SCSI modules from KNOPPIX 3.4.
skype-1.2.0.18.unc	Skype Internet Telephone Messenger / 1.2.0.18 / http://www.skype.com / 11MB	Skype Telephone Messenger. Works with ALSA.
sox.unc	Sound eXchange sound processing / 12.17.6 / http://sox.sourceforge.net / 477KB	The Swiss army knife of sound processing programs. SoX is a command-line utility that can convert various formats of computer audio files into other formats.
synaptic.unc	GUI for Apt / 0.16-6 / http://www.nongnu.org/synaptic / 584KB	GUI frontend for Apt.
synergy-1.3.1.unc	Synergy lets you share a single mouse and keyboard across monitors from different computers / 1.3.1 / http://synergy2.sourceforge.net	The monitors from all the computers on your desktop form a single virtual screen. You use the mouse and keyboard of only one of the computers while you use all of the monitors on all of the computers.
texinfo-4.8.unc	Produces manuals, ASCII text, and online documentation / 4.8 / http://www.gnu.org/software/texinfo / 859.5KB	Contains the texinfo online, text-based documentation system.

Title	Description / Version / Site / Size	Comments
UNC Extensions		
wine-0.9.17.unc	An open source implementation of the Windows API for X and UNIX / 0.9.17 / http://www.winehq.com	Runs Windows applications in DSL.
wine-0.9.22.unc	An open source implementation of the Windows API for X and UNIX / 0.9.22 / http://www.winehq.com	Runs Windows applications in DSL.
wine-0.9.28_ with_opengl.unc	An open source implementation of the Windows API for X and UNIX / 0.9.28 / http://www.winehq.com	Runs Windows applications in DSL.
xfe-0.88.unc	Xfe file manager / 0.88 / http://roland65.free.fr/xfe / 3.71MB	An MS Explorer like file manager for X. It is based on the popular, but discontinued, X Win Commander. Xfe aims to be the lightweight file manager of choice.
XFree86.unc	XFree86 server for Damn Small Linux / 4.3.0 / http://www.xfree.org	The XFree86 X Window System server and related software.
XFree86-devel.unc	Xlib dev / 4.3.0 / ftp://ftp. xfree86.org/pub/XFree86/4.3.0/ binaries/Linux-ix86-glibc23/ Xprog.tgz / 3.0MB	XFree86 X Windows System server development components.
xine-0.99.4.unc	Xine multimedia player for Linux / 0.99-4 / http://www.xinehq.de / 5.39MB	A free (GPL licensed) high-performance, portable, and reusable multimedia playback engine. Xine itself is a shared library with an easy, yet powerful, API for video playback processing.
xpdf-3.01p12.unc	Xpdf, a PDF viewer for X / 3.01pl2 / http://www.foolabs.com/ xpdf	The Linux binary of xpdf, offered on the original website.
Modules Extensions		
8211.o	adm8211 chipset-based wireless cards / adm8211-20041111 / http://www.latinsud.com/adm8211	Driver for wireless LAN cards that contain the adm8211 chipset (recommended only if the open source adm8211 driver doesn't work).

TITLE	DESCRIPTION / VERSION / SITE / SIZE	COMMENTS
MODULES EXTENSIONS		
855patch	Fix for Intel 855 graphics BIOS/memory bug / 1.00 / http://www.chzsoft.com.ar/ 855patch.html / 21KB	Some PCs with Intel 845/855/865GM embedded video chips don't allocate enough shared memory for XFree86 to run at high resolutions, resulting in a lime-green screen of nothing. 855patch and 855wrap address this problem. 855patch is for older BIOS; 855wrap is for newer BIOS.
855wrap	Fix for Intel 855 graphics BIOS/memory bug / 1.00 / http://www.chzsoft.com.ar/ 855patch.html / 14KB	Some PCs with Intel 845/855/865GM embedded video chips don't allocate enough shared memory for XFree86 to run at high resolutions resulting in a lime-green screen of nothing. 855patch and 855wrap address this problem. 855patch is for older BIOS; 855wrap is for newer BIOS.
adm8211.o	adm8211 chipset-based wireless cards / adm8211-20041111 / http://aluminum.sourmilk.net/ adm8211	Driver for wireless LAN cards that contain the adm8211 chipset.
drmP.h	Modified kernel sources file / 2.4.26 / http://lkml.org/lkml/ 2004/4/19/202 / 34KB	Modified file to fix a bug that causes the command make modules to fail when recompiling 2.4.26 kernel using the KNOPPIX .config file.
synaptics_drv.o	Driver for Synaptics and Alps touchpads with XFree86 / 0.14.6 / http://web.telia.com/~u89404340/ touchpad/files / 38.93KB	Driver needed to use Synaptics and Alps touchpads with the XFree86 X Windows System server.

Index

Also Available in the Negus Live Linux Series

Live Linux® CDs
Building and Customizing Bootables
Christopher Negus | 0132432749 | ©2007

Create Custom Versions of Linux That Run "Live," Without Installation!

"Live" Linux® CDs let users run Linux on any PC, without affecting the operating system and data already present there. Live Linux distributions, such as Knoppix, are now among the most popular versions of Linux. What's more, because Linux is open source, you can customize your own Live Linux distribution for virtually any purpose. *Live Linux® CDs* is the first start-to-finish guide to creating, building, and remastering your own Live Linux distributions.

Bestselling *Linux Bible* author, Christopher Negus, walks you step-by-step through building complete Linux systems that run from CDs, DVDs, flash drives, and other bootable media. First learn exactly how Live Linux works and then walk through creating Live Linux distributions based on five different systems: KNOPPIX (Debian), Fedora/Kadischi, Gentoo, Slax (Slackware), and Damn Small Linux. Working from complete examples on the accompanying DVD, customize all these specialized bootable Linuxes.

Ajax Construction Kit
Building Plug-and-Play Ajax Applications
Michael Morrison | 0132350084 | ©2008

Supercharge Your Sites with Ajax Right Now...No Scripting Expertise Needed!

You've heard how great Ajax is—how it can help make your Web sites more usable, more interactive, more responsive, more successful. *Ajax Construction Kit* lets you put Ajax to work right now, even if you've never written a script! Just learn a few essentials, check out a few examples, and then run the live CD and discover all the plug-and-play code you need to hit the ground running.

Ajax Construction Kit's built-in applications work right out of the box. The CD contains all software needed to run Ajax examples in Windows, Mac OS X, or directly from the Linux live CD. And with easy guidance from Michael Morrison, you'll gradually deepen your understanding—learn how to customize, extend, and reuse these applications—and even build skills for creating new ones. Walk away an expert.

The Official Damn Small® Linux® Book
The Tiny Adaptable Linux That Runs on Anything
Robert Shingledecker, John Andrews, Christopher Negus | 0132338696 | ©2008

Make the Most of Today's Smallest, Fastest Linux Distribution—Damn Small Linux!

Damn Small Linux (DSL) is a super-efficient platform for everything from custom desktops to professional servers. Now, DSL's creator and lead developer have written the first definitive, practical guide to this remarkable system. *The Official Damn Small® Linux® Book* brings together everything you need to put DSL to work in just minutes. Simply learn a few essentials, boot the live CD, and master the rest...one step at a time, hands-on.

If you're new to Linux, you can quickly discover how to use DSL to take your data on the road, safely running your programs and personal environment on nearly any computer. Easily adapt DSL to run on anything from an alternative device (Internet appliance, hand-held, diskless PC, or mini-ITX system) to an older PC that might otherwise be headed for a landfill.

Practical PHP and MySQL®
Building Eight Dynamic Web Applications
Jono Bacon | 0132239973 | ©2007

Build Dynamic Web Sites Fast, with PHP and MySQL...Learn from Eight Ready-to-Run Applications!

Suddenly, it's easy to build commercial-quality Web applications using free and open source software. With this book, you learn from eight ready-to-run, real-world applications—all backed by clear diagrams and screenshots, well-documented code, and simple, practical explanations.

Leading open source author Jono Bacon teaches the core skills you need to build virtually any application. You discover how to connect with databases, upload content, perform cascading deletes, edit records, validate registrations, specify user security, create reusable components, use PEAR extensions, and even build Ajax applications.

PRENTICE
HALL